BALANCE OF POWER

BALANCE
OF POWER

THEORY AND PRACTICE IN THE 21ST CENTURY

Edited by

T. V. Paul, James J. Wirtz, and Michel Fortmann

STANFORD UNIVERSITY PRESS, STANFORD, CALIFORNIA

2004

Stanford University Press
Stanford, California

Printed in the United States of America on acid-free,
archival-quality paper

Library of Congress Cataloging-in-Publication Data
Balance of power : theory and practice in the 21st century / edited by
T.V. Paul, James J. Wirtz, and Michel Fortmann.
   p.   cm.
   Includes bibliographical references and index.
   ISBN 0-8047-5016-5 (cloth : alk. paper)—ISBN 0-8047-5017-3 (pbk : alk.
paper)
   1. Balance of power.   2. International relations.   I. Paul, T.V.
II. Wirtz, James J., 1958–   III. Fortmann, Michel.
JZ1313.B35 2004
327.1'01—dc22   2004011433

Designed by Janet Wood
Typeset by BookMatters in 11/14 Garamond

Original Printing 2004

Last figure below indicates year of this printing:
13   12   11   10   09   08   07   06   05   04

Contents

Tables

Acknowledgments

The chapters in this volume were first presented in May 2002 at a conference at McGill University cosponsored by the Research Group in International Security and the Center for Contemporary Conflict, the Naval Postgraduate School, Monterey, California. We received generous financial assistance from the International Security Research Outreach Program of the Canadian Department of Foreign Affairs; the Security and Defence Forum of the Canadian Department of National Defence; the Dean of Arts and the Conference Grants Program, McGill University; and the Fonds pour la Formation de chercheurs, Quebec. We also benefited from the support provided by Thomas Skrobala at the Navy Treaty Implementation Program, Pat Kolbas of the Defense Threat Reduction Agency, and Jim Smith of the U.S. Air Force Institute of National Security Studies. We thank Brian Job, Pierre Martin, Alex McLeod, Baldev Nayar, Paul Noble, Phil Oxhorn, Julian Schoefield, and Marie-Joëlle Zahar, who made the exchanges lively and productive in their roles as discussants and participants at the May conference. Subsequent to the conference, the papers were revised and edited, and our contributors deserve praise not only for their dedicated and timely work, but also for their patience. We organized two special panels at the American Political Science Association Convention in Boston in September 2002 and the International Studies Association Convention in Portland, Oregon, in March 2003. The chairs and discussants—Douglas MacDonald, Dan Copeland, Richard Rosecrance, and Anne Clunan—as well as the other participants at these panels helped us to sharpen our arguments. We want to express our sincere thanks to Elizabeth Skinner and William Hogg for their dedicated and efficient work throughout the project, to Izumi Wakugawa for her research assistance, and to Stanford editor Amanda Moran and production editor Judith Hibbard for their enthusiastic support. We also acknowledge the extensive and useful comments by the two anonymous reviewers.

About the Editors and Contributors

EDITORS

T. V. Paul is James McGill Professor of International Relations at McGill University, Montreal, Canada, where he has been teaching in the political science department since 1991. His published works include *Asymmetric Conflicts: War Initiation by Weaker Powers* (Cambridge University Press, 1994); *Power Versus Prudence: Why Nations Forgo Nuclear Weapons* (McGill-Queen's University Press, 2000); *India in the World Order: Searching for Major Power Status,* with Baldev Nayar (Cambridge University Press, 2003); *The Absolute Weapon Revisited: Nuclear Arms and the Emerging International Order*, coedited with Richard Harknett and James Wirtz (University of Michigan Press, 1998 & 2000); *International Order and the Future of World Politics*, coedited with John Hall (Cambridge University Press, 1999, 2000 (twice), 2001, & 2002); and *The Nation-State in Question,* coedited with John Ikenberry and John Hall (Princeton University Press, 2003).

James J. Wirtz is professor and chairman of the Department of National Security Affairs at the Naval Postgraduate School, Monterey, California. He is author of *The Tet Offensive: Intelligence Failure in War* (Cornell University Press, 1991 & 1994), coeditor with Peter Lavoy and Scott Sagan of *Planning the Unthinkable: New Doctrines for Using Chemical, Biological and Nuclear Weapons* (Cornell University Press, 2000); coeditor with Jeffrey Larsen of *Rocket's Red Glare: National Missile Defense and the Future of World Politics* (Westview Press, 2001); coeditor with Roy Godson of *Strategic Denial and Deception* (Transaction Press, 2002); and coeditor with Eliot Cohen, Colin Gray, and John Baylis of *Strategy in the Contemporary World* (Oxford University Press, 2002).

Michel Fortmann is professor of political science at the University of Montreal where he has been chair of military and strategic studies since 1986. His research interests are regional security cooperation, the evolution of arms control, and the history of warfare. He has written three books and more than three dozen articles and book chapters, including *A Diplomacy of Hope: Canada and Disarmament,* coauthored with Albert Legault (McGill-Queen's University Press, 1992); *Multilateralism and Regional Security,* coedited with S. Neil McFarlane and Stéphane Roussel (Queen's Centre for International Relations/Lester B. Pearson Canadian International Peacekeeping Training Centre, 1997); and *Le système politique américain, mécanismes et décisions,* coauthored with Edmond Orban (Presses de l'Université de Montréal, 2001).

CONTRIBUTORS

Robert J. Art is Christian A. Herter Professor of International Relations at Brandeis University. He is also research associate at the Olin Institute for Strategic Studies at Harvard University and senior fellow of the Security Studies Program at the Massachusetts Institute of Technology. Among his publications are *International Politics: Enduring Concepts and Contemporary Issues,* with Robert Jervis (Longman, 2002); *The TFX Decision: McNamara and the Military* (Little, Brown, 1968); *The United States and Coercive Diplomacy,* with Patrick Cronin (United States Institute of Peace Press, 2003); and *A Grand Strategy for America* (Cornell University Press, 2003).

Michael Barletta is senior research associate at the Center for Nonproliferation Studies (CNS) of the Monterey Institute of International Studies and lecturer in national security affairs at the Naval Postgraduate School. His publications include *After 9/11: Preventing Mass-Destruction Terrorism and Weapons Proliferation,* Occasional Paper no. 8 (CNS, June 2002); and "Biosecurity Measures for Preventing Bioterrorism" (CNS, Nov. 2002).

Mark Brawley is professor of political science at McGill University, Montreal. His publications include *Liberal Leadership: Great Powers and Their Challengers in Peace and War* (Cornell University Press, 1993); *Afterglow or Adjustment* (Columbia University Press, 1999); *The Politics of Globalization* (Broadview, 2003); *Alliance Politics, Kosovo, and NATO's War: Allied Force or Forced Allies?* coedited with Pierre Martin (Palgrave, 2001).

Christopher Layne is visiting fellow in foreign policy studies at the Cato Institute. He has taught at the University of Miami, the Naval Postgraduate School, and the University of California, Los Angeles. He has written several influential scholarly articles in *International Security* and *Security*

Studies. He also has written widely about American grand strategy and foreign policy for journals such as *Foreign Policy, The National Interest,* and the *Atlantic Monthly.*

Douglas Lemke is associate professor of political science at Pennsylvania State University. He studies the causes of international conflict, with specific interest in how they vary across regions and across levels of development. He has published articles in various journals on this and other topics, and his most recent book is *Regions of War and Peace* (Cambridge University Press, 2002).

Jack S. Levy is Board of Governors' Professor of Political Science at Rutgers University. Among his publications are *War in the Modern Great Power System, 1495–1975* (Kentucky University Press, 1983); "Balances and Balancing: Concepts, Propositions, and Research Design," in John A. Vasquez and Colin Elman, *Realism and the Balancing of Power: A New Debate* (Prentice Hall, 2002); and articles in many leading international relations journals.

Benjamin Miller is professor of international relations at the University of Haifa. His publications include *When Opponents Cooperate: Great Power Conflict and Collaboration in World Politics* (University of Michigan Press, 2002). He has also published numerous articles on international relations theory and international security, and is currently completing a book manuscript entitled "Regional War and Peace: States, Nations and the Great Powers."

Edward Rhodes is dean for social and behavioral sciences at Rutgers University. He is author of *Power and MADness: The Logic of Nuclear Coercion* (Columbia University Press, 1989); coeditor of *The Politics of Strategic Adjustment: Ideas, Institutions, and Interest* (Columbia University Press, 1998); and coauthor of *Presence, Prevention, and Persuasion* (Lexington Books, 2004).

Robert S. Ross is professor of political science at Boston College; associate of the John King Fairbank Center for East Asian Research, Harvard University; and senior advisor of the security studies program at the Massachusetts Institute of Technology. His recent publications include *Reexamining the Cold-War: U.S.-China Diplomacy, 1954–1973,* coedited with Jiang Changbin (Asia Center, Harvard University, 2001); *The Great Wall and the Empty Fortress: China's Search for Security,* coauthored with Andrew J. Nathan (Norton, 1998); and *Engaging China: The Management of an Emerging Power,* coedited with Alastair Iain Johnston (Routledge, 1999).

Raju G. C. Thomas is Allis Chalmers Professor of International Affairs at Marquette University in Milwaukee, Wisconsin. His authored publications include *Indian Security Policy* (Princeton University Press, 1986) and *Democracy, Security and Development in India* (St. Martin's, 1996); his edited publications include *Nuclear India in the 21st Century* (Palgrave, 2002) and *Yugoslavia Unraveled: Sovereignty, Self Determination, Intervention* (Lexington Books, 2003).

Harold Trinkunas is assistant professor in the Department of National Security Affairs at the Naval Postgraduate School, Monterey, California. Recent publications include "Crafting Civilian Control in Emerging Democracies," in the *Journal of Interamerican Studies and World Affairs,* and "The Crisis in Venezuelan Civil-Military Relations: From Punto Fijo to the Fifth Republic," in *Latin American Research Review.*

William C. Wohlforth is associate professor of government at Dartmouth College. He is author of *Elusive Balance: Power and Perceptions in the Cold War* (Cornell University Press, 1993) and editor of *Witnesses to the End of the Cold War* (Johns Hopkins University Press, 1996) and *Cold War Endgame* (Penn State University Press, 2003).

BALANCE OF POWER

Introduction: The Enduring Axioms of Balance of Power Theory and Their Contemporary Relevance

T. V. PAUL

Everywhere one turns today, the behavior of states, non-state actors, and even individuals appears to challenge traditional conceptions of balance of power theory. Supporters of globalization, democratic peace theory, and several forms of institutionalism suggest that deep forces are transforming international relations, pushing traditional power politics away from national agendas. The dark side of globalization has produced violent non-state actors who seek millenarian objectives through terrorist means, challenging the international order built around the power of nation-states. Although they possess only a fraction of the military capability of most states, terrorist networks have produced a near-universal response within the international community. States that often find it difficult to cooperate even over mundane matters have shown their willingness to join hands against the terrorist threat. By contrast, U.S. conventional military prowess, nuclear superiority, economic dynamism, and cultural power have failed to generate much traditional balancing behavior on the part of potential great-power rivals, although these powers have increasingly relied on international institutions as arenas in which to influence and constrain the way American policymakers wield political, military, and economic power.

As measures of status or as instruments to guarantee security, chemical, biological, and even nuclear weapons no longer seem to play as much of a role in many parts of the world as they did in the past. For regional rivals or states at odds with the culture and norms of a growing community of democratic states, however, nuclear, chemical, and biological (NBC) weapons apparently are viewed as offering significant protection from attack. And although they initially voiced strong reservations about U.S. plans to construct missile defenses, Russia, India, and much of Europe now seem willing to tolerate the U.S. decision to alter the basis of its national security strategy. Fundamental questions are emerging about exactly where, when, and how traditional notions of balance of power might still apply in international relations and in relations between states and emerging non-state actors.

This volume arises from the need to reevaluate balance of power theories in view of recent changes in world politics. Skeptics and critics of realism believe that balance of power theory has become irrelevant in the face of growing global social forces,[1] while proponents—in particular, realists—contend that balance of power dynamics still operate in world politics in varying forms and intensities. Some realists forecast that intense balancing is bound to happen in the future as relative power capabilities change and U.S. power becomes too threatening for other major states to tolerate.[2] To these realists, it is only a matter of time because hegemony can never be permanent. The crucial question for social scientists is who is likely to be more accurate in this debate? By examining the axioms of balance of power theory in a broad range of settings—at both the global and regional levels—we attempt to gauge the robustness and validity of the theoretical propositions deeply held by many international relations scholars and practitioners.

To better frame the issues and questions raised by events since the end of the Cold War, this chapter lists several axioms of balance of power theory and their significance for contemporary world politics. First, it describes the way balance of power behavior tends to be reflected at both the systemic and subsystemic levels of international relations. Second, it explores the logic of balancing and bandwagoning. Third, it presents a liberal critique of balance of power theory. It then addresses the absence of a balancing coalition vis-à-vis the United States, the preponderant power in the contemporary international system.

In tune with the commonly understood meanings of the terms, *balancing* is viewed as a state strategy or foreign policy behavior while *balances of power* are regarded as outcomes at the systemic or subsystemic levels, that is, as conditions of power equilibrium among key states. The purpose of balancing is to prevent a rising power from assuming hegemony, and if and when that prevention effort succeeds, a balance of power is expected to be present.[3] This chapter presents three concepts—*hard balancing, soft balancing,* and *asymmetric balancing*—to describe various manifestations of balancing behavior. Although critics could raise eyebrows at this expansion of a traditionally understood military-security concept, our position is that as long as the ultimate purpose of any balancing strategy is to reduce or match the capabilities of a powerful state or a threatening actor, the various means that states adopt, besides increasing their military strength or forming alliances, should be a part of our analysis to better understand today's balancing strategies. Traditional balancing through alliance formation and military buildups is significant, but it seems able to capture only one, albeit the most significant, form of balance of power behavior.

Hard balancing is a strategy often exhibited by states engaged in intense interstate rivalry. States thus adopt strategies to build and update their military capabilities, as well as create and maintain formal alliances and counteralliances, to match the capabilities of their key opponents. The traditional realist and neorealist conceptions of balancing are mainly confined to hard balancing.

Soft balancing involves tacit balancing short of formal alliances. It occurs when states generally develop ententes or limited security understandings with one another to balance a potentially threatening state or a rising power. Soft balancing is often based on a limited arms buildup, ad hoc cooperative exercises, or collaboration in regional or international institutions; these policies may be converted to open, hard-balancing strategies if and when security competition becomes intense and the powerful state becomes threatening.

Asymmetric balancing refers to efforts by nation-states to balance and contain indirect threats posed by subnational actors such as terrorist groups that do not have the ability to challenge key states using conventional military capabilities or strategies. Asymmetric balancing also refers to the other side of the coin, that is, to efforts by subnational actors and their state sponsors to challenge and weaken established states using asymmetric means such as terrorism.

The empirical evidence of limited hard balancing in contemporary world politics attests powerfully to the need for broadening the concept of power balancing. This chapter argues that the international system is not experiencing the same level of hard balancing it did in the past, but international relations do exhibit several attempts at soft balancing in varying degrees. The near-unipolarity of today's international system makes it very costly for weaker actors to form balancing coalitions by striking military alliances or engaging in an intense arms buildup to counter the power of the hegemonic actor. The adverse reaction by the hegemon would considerably undermine the upstart's economic and military security and potentially leave it less secure than before. Further, economic globalization, the rise of the common enemy of transnational terrorism, and the general difficulty in translating economic power into military power have all made it difficult to engage in traditional hard balancing. Potential states also wish to free ride economically, and the United States, despite its unilateralist tendencies, remains a status-quo power of considerable value to such states. Above all, they no longer fear physical extinction, as they used to, mainly because of increasingly powerful norms against outright conquest and annexation. Under these circumstances, the next logical step for actors concerned about the power of the United States is to resort to low-cost soft balancing, which is not likely to invite intense retribution by the sole superpower. At the regional level, evidence exists that hard balancing continues, especially in regions experiencing high levels of conflict, enduring rivalries, or protracted conflicts, but varying amounts of soft balancing and asymmetric balancing seem to be occurring just about everywhere. Is it possible that the rigidity in the way balance of power is conceived is the reason analysts are unable to notice efforts at balancing at either the systemic or regional subsystemic levels? In the evolving international order, are states pursuing a mixture of realist and liberal approaches to balance one another's power and obtain security?

Traditional Understandings of Balance of Power

Balance of power theory is predicated on the notion that states seek to survive as independent entities. They also seek power in the anarchical global system; without power, states can become subservient to the will of others or lose their security and prosperity. Anarchy thus compels states to increase their power, because security and physical survival cannot be divorced from power maximization. As a result, the competition for power becomes a natural state of affairs in international politics. If and when a single state or coalition of states gains preponderance, however, it will eventually attempt to impose its will on others. Weaker states could lose their security and, in rare cases, cease to exist. Thus, faced with the prospect of domination and possibly elimination, weaker actors flock together to form balancing coalitions, "for it is the stronger side that threatens them."[4] States, especially small states, often cannot achieve security on their own. Furthermore, the internal dynamics of a rising or dominant state could force it to seek hegemony or even eliminate weaker actors. Threatened states could also adopt the internal balancing strategy of building up arms, that is, to obtain countervailing capabilities and thereby attempt to balance the rising power's military strength.

Balance of power dynamics are supposed to operate at different levels and in different areas of state interaction, including the economic and military realms, although the latter dimension has received the most attention. Analysts have used the concept in multiple ways: as a state of affairs, as a normative guide to policy and statecraft, and as shorthand for the relative strength of potential opponents in terms of military capability, diplomatic resources, and political motivation. Although scholars disagree on the precise meaning of the term, balance of power is deemed to operate most prominently in the military, political, and economic relations of states.[5] Balance of power also has global (systemic) and regional (subsystemic) dimensions. Our focus in this volume is on the politico-military dimension, the most visible and historically significant aspect of balance of power in both the systemic and the regional subsystemic domains.

BALANCE OF POWER AT THE SYSTEMIC LEVEL

Does parity in power among states, or preponderance of power of a status quo state, best preserve peace among states?[6] From the perspective of balance of power theorists, the power preponderance of a single state or of a coalition of states is highly undesirable because the preponderant actor is likely to engage in aggressive behavior. Hegemony of a single power would encourage that state to impose its will on others. By contrast, theorists suggest that peace is generally preserved when an equilibrium of power exists among great powers. In a state of equilibrium, no single state or coalition of states possesses overwhelming power and thereby the incentive to launch war against weaker states. Power parity among states prevents war because no actor can expect victory, because the defender, *ceteris paribus*, is assumed to have a three to one advantage over the attacker. Although risk-acceptant actors have been known to devise strategies to overcome the advantages inherent in defense, most potential attackers prudently desist from offensive action, realizing that the chances of military victory are limited and that war initiation is riddled with uncertainties.[7]

The key means by which states balance one another are by building up arms through internal production or by procurement from outside sources, and by forming military alliances. At times preventive war is also thought necessary to maintain the balance.[8] The most logical way to obtain an equilibrium of power, however, is for the smaller states to align among themselves and with the great-power opponents of the powerful threatening state.[9] Weaker actors flock together to form coalitions to achieve defensive as well as deterrent strength sufficient to dissuade potential or actual adversaries. Balancing against the domination of a preponderant power is viewed as necessary and beneficial, because if weaker states do not check the rise of a hegemon, they may eventually lose their sovereignty and independence. Weaker states tend to ally among themselves because the stronger states might not respect them as much as other weaker states would. To Kenneth Waltz, "balancing is a sensible behavior when the victory of one coalition over another leaves weaker members of the winning coalition at the mercy of the stronger one. . . . On the weaker side, they are both more appreciated and safer, provided of course, the coalition they join achieves enough defensive or deterrent strength to dissuade adversaries from attacking."[10] Structural realists view balancing as a law-like phenomenon in international politics. According to Waltz:

> From the theory, one predicts that states will engage in balancing behavior whether or not balanced power is the end of their acts. From the theory, one predicts a strong tendency toward balance in the system. The expectation is not that a balance once achieved will be maintained, but that a balance once disrupted will be restored in one way or another. Balances of power recurrently form.[11]

Stability is a key goal of power balancing as a policy instrument. International stability implies that when a balance of power prevails, all units survive, no single state becomes preponderant, and no large-scale (great power) war takes place. To some balance of power theorists, the true virtue of the system is that all states, be they small or big, survive and that a certain order is maintained. Because the status quo is continuously maintained or reproduced, "no actor experiences a loss of resources or power."[12] Classical realists couple legitimacy with balance of power as the two necessary conditions for maintaining international order. As Henry Kissinger stated: "A balance of power makes the overthrow of international order physically difficult, deterring a challenge before it occurs. A broadly based principle of legitimacy produces reluctance to assault the international order. A stable peace testifies to a combination of physical and moral restraints."[13] The balance of power system is characterized by rules of legitimacy that impel states to "act to oppose any coalition or single actor which tends to assume a position of predominance with respect to the rest of the system; act to constrain actors who subscribe to supranational organizing principles" and "treat all essential actors as acceptable role partners."[14] Thus, the balance of power system strongly attests to the norms of Westphalian sovereignty; that is, sovereign states have a legitimate right to exist, regardless of their size and power capabilities, and that the equilibrium in power is essential to prevent a "lawless situation" from emerging.[15]

BALANCE OF POWER AT THE SUBSYSTEMIC (REGIONAL) LEVEL

The balance of power dynamics that affect great powers and global politics are also relevant to regional subsystems. In the regions it is the rising power of a regional state or regional coalition that causes problems. When one actor or a coalition of actors gains too much military power within a region, that actor or coalition may undertake aggressive and predatory behavior toward neighboring states. To counteract such a danger, coalitions of regional states can form balances with or without the association of extra-regional great-power states. The other method for balancing a rising regional power is to acquire or modernize weapons that could balance the capabilities of a neighbor who has or is about to obtain a military advantage through its own innovation or through procurement of arms from abroad. The objective of regional balancing is to generate a stable distribution of power with the aim of preventing war. To achieve balance of power, according to Patrick Morgan, regional states tend to "put great emphasis on autonomy and manipulate their relationships primarily on the basis of relative power capabilities."[16] One must admit that regional powers are less autonomous than great powers, and often it is the latter that undertake policies that preserve or upset regional balances.

Balancing can also occur against regional states pursuing revisionist policies, even if they are not powerful in an aggregate sense. Here offensive intentions matter more than sheer military capabilities. Revisionist states are viewed by their neighbors and by great powers involved in the region as especially threatening when such states are pursuing or already are in possession of NBC weapons. Neighbors fear that NBC weapons would encourage revisionist states to engage in threatening behavior, thereby generating regional instability. As regional NBC arsenals become a threat, preventive war, preemption, or inadvertent war become real possibilities.[17] The United States, as the preponderant global power, has also engaged in balancing against regional powers armed with NBC weapons. U.S. policymakers apparently believe that revisionist states armed with NBC weapons would make it difficult for America and its allies to intervene in regional conflicts, thus undermining deterrent threats intended to bolster regional stability.

ALTERNATIVE PROPOSITIONS: THE LOGIC OF BALANCING AGAINST THREATS AND BANDWAGONING

Stephen Walt modifies balance of power theory by emphasizing the role played by threat perceptions in stimulating balancing behavior among states. Walt argues that states tend to balance against threats and not necessarily against power. Weaker actors could therefore perceive the power of an existing or rising state as benign and not to be balanced by countervailing power. In his work on alliance formation in the Middle East, Walt tests his theory and concludes that balancing against power is not common, but balancing against threat is more prevalent in the regional subsystems.[18] The factors that determine balancing or bandwagoning are aggregate power, proximity, offensive capability, and the offensive intentions of a powerful actor. According to Walt's theory, states sometimes bandwagon with a powerful state, especially if that state offers them security and economic advantages.[19] Bandwagoning logic claims that balancing is not a natural behavior of states, that it is indeed joining hands with the powerful that is the dominant pattern of state behavior. Walt has identified two motives for bandwagoning with a threatening state or coalition: to avoid an attack on oneself and to "share the spoils of victory." Walt argues, however, that balancing is more common than bandwagoning because "an alignment that preserves most of a state's freedom of action is preferable to accepting subordination under a potential hegemon. Because intentions can change and perceptions are unreliable, it is safer to balance against potential threats than to hope that strong states will remain benevolent."[20]

There is a second logic to the bandwagoning hypothesis, most often articulated by the proponents of power transition and hegemonic stability theories. According to power transition theory, peace is maintained when the satisfied great powers predominate, while war is more likely when the capabilities of dissatisfied challengers begin to approximate those of the preponderant power. A. F. K. Organski contends, "A preponderance of power on one side . . . increases the chances of peace, for the greatly stronger side need not fight at all to get what it wants, while the weaker side would be plainly foolish to attempt to battle for what it wants."[21] The rising but still weaker powers tend to initiate wars, especially in the global system. These states believe that victory is possible if they act using windows of opportunity, because the stronger side may not be able to deter or defend if the attacker shows sufficient resolve and uses better strategies and tactics, including a fait-accompli strategy.[22] To prevent the weaker side from initiating wars, the sta-tus-quo states should be in preponderance at all times. Thus relative power, not balance of power, acts as the pacifying condition.[23] For transition theo-rists, it is imperative that status-quo powers maintain an edge in military terms and that their power is not balanced through any means by smaller actors. Hegemonic stability theorists also believe that war results from equal-ity in power whereas the dominance of the hegemonic power works as a nec-essary condition for peace preservation.[24]

Criticism of balance of power theory has centered on the theory's methodological and empirical weaknesses and historical anomalies, and on the general failure of theorists to predict the timing in which balance of power occurs, if at all. Further, the difficulty of accurately measuring power without taking into account such intangible factors as strategy, tactics, resolve, and morale complicates the determination of whether an equilib-rium of power exists.

BALANCE OF POWER THEORY'S LIBERAL CRITIQUES

Some liberal criticisms of balance of power theory rest on historical examples in which balance of power failed and on the inability of the theory, when applied to foreign policy behavior, to offer a long-term solution to the secu-rity dilemma. To liberals, anarchy is malleable and the structural condition of conflict is not so determinative as realists would have us believe. The key factors necessary to obviate the negative aspects of anarchy and thereby obtain lasting security and order are democracy, economic interdependence, and international institutions. Since democracies rarely fight one another, when satisfied democratic states are in ascendance, they tend to treat other democracies less belligerently than they treat nondemocracies. Liberals also suggest that states that are economically interdependent are unlikely to engage in disruptive military balancing vis-à-vis one another. Liberals acknowledge the existence of global anarchy but maintain that its effect varies depending on a state's prevailing political system. Liberal states view international politics not as a zero-sum game among themselves but as a "positive- or negative-sum game. They can win or lose together."[25]

Economic liberals argue that it is economic interdependence—and in recent years, globalization—that constrains balance of power politics. States intertwined by trade, investment, and commercial flows are less likely than those least tied economically to engage in the kinds of intense competition associated with balance of power politics or in aggressive behavior that would make them all vulnerable to war's economic disruptions. From a broadened liberal interdependence perspective, it is possible to go beyond the liberal states themselves and extrapolate that both China and Russia are not vigorously pursuing a balancing coalition against U.S. power because they are intertwined economically with the liberal economic order, and that any disruption of this order through balancing could upset the economic well-being of these countries. Similarly, most developing states in Latin America and Asia have been bandwagoning with the United States because economic concerns override balance of power concerns. American economic power and democratic principles exert a greater attraction than the threat posed by overwhelming U.S. conventional military power and nuclear superiority.

Liberal institutionalists believe that balance of power cannot ameliorate the security dilemma but institutions can. Institutions help to alleviate collective action problems and help reduce transaction costs, making cooperation possible.[26] From the liberal institutionalist perspective, international organizations can reduce the chances of conflict by providing functions such as collective security, mediation, peacekeeping, and peace building. These institutions, according to Bruce Russett, could "directly coerce and restrain those who break the peace, serve as agents of mediation and arbitration, or reduce uncertainty in negotiations by conveying information. They may encourage states to expand their conception of their interests at stake, promoting more inclusive and longer-term thinking, shape general norms and principles of appropriate behavior or encourage empathy and mutual identification among peoples."[27] Liberal institutionalists believe that functioning security communities are the answer to the problem of insecurity and the best way to prevent any single nation from becoming too strong in the regional system.[28]

Liberal theorist John Owen presents another noteworthy argument for the absence of balancing against the United States. Owen suggests that the nature of domestic political systems explains this puzzle. If a country's elites are liberal, they could perceive less of a need to balance against another liberal state. Thus, it is the democratic characteristics of states, not their power position, that matter most. Owen suggests that the "degree to which a state counterbalances U.S. power is a function of how politically liberal that state is, measured by the degree to which its internal institutions and practices are liberal and the degree which liberals influence foreign policy." The United States is not counterbalanced because potential challengers, influenced by liberalism, perceive that their interests coincide to a great extent with those of the United States. Moreover, Washington treats liberal states differently than it treats non-liberal states.[29] John Ikenberry, by contrast, contends that the legal character of the U.S. power relationship with many of its allies, the ability of the allies to penetrate U.S. institutions, and the international institutions that the United States has helped to create offer increasing returns to all participants. For Ikenberry, international institutions underlie the endurance of American hegemony and the absence of balancing against it.[30]

State Behavior in the Post-Cold War Era

How accurate are the various theoretical explanations of power relations when compared with empirical reality? At the beginning of the 21st century, do states behave in the purely dichotomous fashion that realists and liberals postulate, or do they exhibit mixed patterns of behavior? At the systemic level, the United States continues its rise as a global power unchallenged by any single state or coalition of states. In fact, since the end of the Cold War, almost all potential challengers, especially Russia and China, have maintained some form of nonbelligerent relationship with the United States. Simultaneously, the United States and its liberal allies have been attempting to engage and integrate potential rivals into a global capitalist, liberal order through institutional mechanisms. Systemic-level hard balancing at best is a minor concern of many state officials.[31] But major powers occasionally do exhibit some form of balancing behavior. U.S. efforts to balance China with the help of India and Russia; North Atlantic Treaty Organization (NATO) initiatives to balance Russia through eastward expansion, economic interaction, and a security partnership with its eastern neighbors, including Russia; and efforts by France, Russia, and Germany to prevent the United States from initiating war against Iraq in 2002–2003 are examples of mixed patterns of behavior that are not captured by any single theory. The United States is also forging economic links with China and Russia in the hope of gaining increasing political returns through cooperation. At the subsystemic level, balancing behavior seems to be dominant in regions of high conflict (such as the Middle East), while in zones of low conflict (such as Latin America) obvious balancing behavior is absent. Barring the high-conflict regions of the Middle East, South Asia, and the Korean Peninsula, states seem to be following a mix of realist and liberal security strategies. The important question is whether such a behavioral pattern is permanent, or will traditional balance of power behavior reemerge in response to an increasingly powerful United States? And does the democratic nature of American hegemony prevent such a contingency? What if the United States, as it seeks to consolidate its hegemony, adopts less democratic—that is, imperial—policies vis-à-vis other states, including allies? The trump card for skeptics who believe in the inevitability of a return to balance of power politics is that, historically, great powers have at times engaged in high levels of cooperation, only to revert back to balance of power politics and intense military competition.[32] Nineteenth-century Europe manifested a mixed system of balancing and cooperation through the concert system. On occasion, great powers cooperated to destroy common enemies: the suppression of the Boxer Rebellion in 1904 by the European great powers that were competing to gain a foothold in China is a case in point. But great-power cooperation tends not to last forever. Nevertheless, it is not clear that balance of power theory can forecast even the approximate timing of the return of balance of power politics. Unlike in the past, states seem to be increasingly mixing realist and liberal strategies to obtain security. In addition, depending on their contexts and situations, states may favor either a liberal or a realist strategy without completely abandoning the other option.

Mixed patterns of cooperation and balancing also appear to have emerged in relationships between regional actors. In regions of high conflict, balancing occurs occasionally. But in other regions, such as Europe, Southeast Asia, and Latin America, where interstate conflict is low, institutional cooperation has reduced the need for intense efforts to maintain a balance of power. Many regional states have resorted to institutionalized cooperation, although some still cling to traditional balance of power strategies. Perhaps both realists and liberals are right, but their ability to account for events now varies across regions, states, and the specific issues under consideration.

TABLE I.1

Balancing Behavior

	Nature of Rivalry	*Key Strategies*
Hard Balancing	Intense, open, often zero sum. Relative gains matter most.	Open arms buildup, formal alliances, or both.
Soft Balancing	Submerged, non-zero sum. Relative gains of limited concern for now.	Limited arms buildup. Informal, tacit, or ad hoc security understandings among affected states, within or outside of international institutions. Preventive strategy.
Asymmetric Balancing	By state or non-state actors (e.g., terrorists). Rivalry intense, although latter are elusive actors.	Non-state actors and their state sponsors pursue asymmetric strategies; state actors follow mixture of traditional and nontraditional strategies to counter threat.

Broadening the Concept of Balance of Power

Traditional conceptions of balance of power may not be able to capture fully the security behavior of states. Part of the problem lies in the dichotomous arguments of realists and their critics: states either balance or they do not. There are no in-between categories of security behavior that can be derived from different approaches. As a result, these rigid theories cannot satisfactorily explain the empirical reality of contemporary world politics. States could pursue tacit and indirect means other than open arms buildup and alliance formation to balance a powerful state or one threatening their security. The exclusive focus of classical and neorealists on interstate military balancing has made balance of power theory, although useful, narrow and inflexible. What is needed, perhaps, is to broaden concepts of balancing behavior to explain the various strategies states use to limit the power of a hegemonic actor or a threatening state, at both the global and regional levels. Moreover, the balancing behaviors of non-state actors, their state sponsors, and threatened states need to be understood as well. Table I.1 captures the various ways in which states and non-state actors can balance against one another.

Do variations exist in the balancing behavior of different states? For instance, could states adopt two variants of balance of power—hard balancing and soft balancing—to deal with different kinds of potential or actual threats?

Hard balancing reflects the traditional realist (both classical and neorealist) approach of forming and maintaining open military alliances to balance a strong state or to forestall the rise of a power or a threatening state. A robust armament or re-armament program, which can rely on internal and external sources of material and weaponry, is another prevalent way to achieve a balance of power. Today, traditional hard balancing, albeit in a weakened form, seems to be present only in conflict-ridden regions of the world—the Middle East, South Asia, and East Asia—where enduring rivalries persist.

Soft balancing involves tacit non-offensive coalition building to neutralize a rising or potentially threatening power. At the moment, the rising state may not be a challenge, but in the future, without counterbalancing, it may emerge as a key source of insecurity for the states concerned. States can adopt different means to engage in soft balancing: tacit understandings or ententes (short of formal alliances), the use of international institutions to create ad hoc coalitions and limit the power of the threatening state, or both. Examples of these strategies include the cooperation of East European states with NATO to balance Russia, of the United States and India balancing vis-à-vis China, and of China and Russia balancing (for a short period in the 1990s) vis-à-vis the United States. In the same way, Russia, France, and Germany cooperated within the UN Security Council to prevent the United States from initiating war against Iraq in 2002–2003. These are limited security cooperation understandings short of formal open alliances and are preventive in nature.

In the future, if American military power increases dramatically and the unilateralist tendencies of Washington persist or even deepen, we may see increased soft balancing by other European states. In fact, some European states, most notably France, have increasingly used rhetoric akin to soft balancing when reacting to recent U.S. policies.[33] While pursuing soft balancing, states could nevertheless engage the targeted powers and develop institutional links with them. Soft balancing may be occurring at the systemic level because the power differential between the United States and potential balancers is too big for a more aggressive strategy. Hard balancing efforts not only may not succeed but will likely elicit immediate politico-economic retribution from the hegemon. Furthermore, the economic costs of breaking ties with the hegemon are too high, especially in an era of economic globalization. Although China, Russia, France, and Germany may have some inclination to balance U.S. power, they are not eliciting cooperation from regional states. Potential allies such as India are bandwagoning with the United States because Washington can offer them more by way of economic and politico-military support and ideological affinity. Similarly, the European Union (EU) has not transformed itself into a viable political entity that can wield military power, because participating states perceive neither any immediate military threat on the horizon nor a fundamental challenge to their existence by other major powers. Whatever pressure they perceive is simply the result of a need to increase their bargaining power vis-à-vis Washington and to constrain American unilateralism, especially its military initiatives. So far, economic, political, and diplomatic tools, not countervailing military force, are viewed as the best ways to influence Washington. In the post-September 11 global strategic environment, many countries share Washington's concerns about global terrorism, although they may differ on the appropriate means to defeat the common elusive enemy.

It is difficult to predict whether hard balancing will occur at a particular point in the future, because states are not constantly attempting to maximize their relative military power positions. States sometimes choose to devote their resources and energies to improving their domestic well-being rather than bolster their military standing on the world stage. For instance, the United States in the interwar period turned away from great-power politics, and Japan has preferred to play only a minor role in international politics since the end of World War II. Given the absence of major systemic pressures, domestic factors have influenced the direction these states have taken in foreign and defense policies.[34] Similarly, a number of technologically capable states have eschewed the acquisition of nuclear weapons to avoid arms races and counterbalancing efforts by others.[35]

Thus the conditions that have made it impossible for hard balancing to occur are encouraging concerned major powers to resort to low-cost soft-balancing strategies in dealing with the American power. These conditions are as follows:

1. The near-unipolarity since the end of the Cold War
2. The increasing economic globalization, the engine of which has largely been the U.S.-based multinational corporations
3. The common enemy of transnational terrorism, which challenges not only the United States but the other major players as well
4. The difficulty of rapidly translating economic wealth into military power
5. The value of free-riding and buck-passing, especially for the European and Asian allies in the general security and economic protection that Washington offers

In addition, weaker states no longer fear outright occupation and annexation unless they frontally challenge the hegemon, as Iraq has done since the late 1980s until 2003. Even in this case, occupation is not tantamount to colonization, because Iraq is not wiped off the map of the world as a sovereign entity. The norms against forceful territorial change seem to have played a role in this respect. In the past, hard balancing was pursued when states feared that a powerful actor would upset their physical security and existence as independent states unless countered with matching power.

Asymmetric balancing encompasses interstate-level interactions and state versus non-state interactions. It could include the use of insurgency or terrorism by a weaker state to mitigate the power of a relatively stronger adversary (for example, Pakistan versus India). An international effort is under way to defeat the increased threat to state security coming from weaker non-state actors such as terrorist groups that attempt to reduce the power of the hegemonic state through asymmetric means. Do attempts by the United States to create floating coalitions to confront terrorism reflect traditional balancing by nation-states against the common threat posed by non-state actors that use asymmetric, albeit suicidal, attacks? Or are these attempts a hostile response to an "alien" threat to the state system by unsanctioned groups or individuals intruding in the field of world politics? In the latter interpretation, this conflict behavior could be termed asymmetric balancing, that is, balancing against the elusive yet powerful non-state threat to the state system itself. In fact, balancing efforts since September 11, 2001, have been so intense that the resulting coalition comprises all forms of states, including potential adversaries. Those states with the potential to balance against the

United States have instead bandwagoned with it to face a common threat to the states' virtual monopoly on the use of force in world politics. This cooperation in turn raises many questions. Will it dampen regional rivalries? Will it slow or prevent the emergence of great-power competition? Will it strengthen international institutions? In the aftermath of the 2003 U.S. attack on Iraq and the unilateralist policies of the Bush administration, major power relations suffered some strains, although nothing akin to hard balancing has yet emerged.

Critics might charge that the theories of balancing and bandwagoning should be reserved only to describe state-level behavior so as not to dilute their meaning and purpose. If major powers do not use hard balancing anymore but pursue tacit, soft balancing instead, is a fundamental change in world politics heralded? If so, what accounts for this change? Or as realists warn, is hard balancing bound to return in some fashion as an ineluctable law of international politics? If so, under what conditions will this happen? Can a single theory capture state security behavior in the post-Cold War era, or do we need eclectic theorizing to capture variations across regions and across different categories of states (such as liberal versus non-liberal) and their balancing behavior?

Research Questions and the Contents of this Book

The contributors to this volume were asked to reflect on several questions about the role of balance of power theory in understanding today's international relations.

— How accurate are liberal and globalist arguments that democracy, economic interdependence through globalization, and international institutions account for the decline of balance of power politics in the contemporary world?
— In the post-Cold War era, are states—at both the systemic and subsystemic levels, especially great powers—most likely to balance against power, balance against threats, or bandwagon with threatening or powerful actors?
— What strategies other than balancing or bandwagoning can best capture the security behavior of states in a given region?
— Do states pursue mixed (such as both liberal and realist) strategies?

— Do states engage in soft balancing rather than hard balancing in a given region or in the broader international arena?

— What role do the terrorist attacks of September 11, 2001, play in the strategic calculations of states? Can the rise of a stateless enemy explain the increased security cooperation among various states that otherwise would be expected to balance each other?

— What explains the absence of balancing against the United States? (Or were the September 11 terrorist attacks a form of balancing?) Why did U.S. efforts to acquire national and theater missile defenses fail to provoke immediate countervailing efforts by the most affected great powers, such as Russia and China?

— Do the efforts by the EU (especially by countries such as France and Germany) and Russia to constrain U.S. unilateralism through international institutions such as the United Nations and NATO (especially as manifested prior to and after the U.S. offensives in Iraq in 2003) constitute a form of balancing?

— What is the role, if any, of NBC weapons in the balance of power calculations of regional states? Why are status-quo powers so worried about the proliferation of these weapons? Do the authoritarian characteristics of the regimes seeking NBC weapons and the revisionist goals they pursue matter in understanding the amount of balancing behavior vis-à-vis such states?

— Finally, under what conditions would intense balance of power politics reemerge, if at all, among eligible great powers interested in challenging the U.S.-dominated status quo?

In subsequent chapters, our contributors answer these questions in order to offer a better understanding of balance of power theory in the contemporary world. Additionally, balance of power theory's claims are examined simultaneously at both the global and regional levels, a task rarely undertaken in previous works on balance of power. The chapters address most of these questions in varying ways and do not reach any unified, single conclusion with respect to the utility, application, or relevance of balance of power in the post-Cold War era and beyond. Some chapters argue vehemently for a narrower military definition of balance of power while others are willing to broaden the concept. The rich array of explanations and empirical materials presented in each chapter, however, offers fertile ground for further work.

In Part I, three chapters take a close look at the balance of power behavior of major powers over time through a theoretical lens. Historically, great powers have been the most active players in balance of power politics due to their large capabilities, wide interests, and high sensitivity to fluctuations in global and regional power balances. Jack S. Levy offers in Chapter 1 a historical summary of balance of power theory, arguing that the theory is very much a European phenomenon relevant largely to land powers; this is the reason, he explains, that hegemonic naval powers such as the United Kingdom and the United States have not faced balancing coalitions. Levy thus suggests one solution to a major empirical puzzle that is addressed in several other chapters of this volume as well as in much of the recent literature on balance of power theory.

Douglas Lemke presents in Chapter 2 an analysis of great-power behavior that is inconsistent with balance of power theory, especially as represented in offensive realism. Lemke's power-transition perspective suggests that as long as U.S. preponderance of power continues and the international system does not seek to contain dissatisfied challengers reaching near-parity with the status-quo power, there is little likelihood of balancing behavior or of violent challenge to the international order. Thus, Lemke describes great-power behavior since the end of the Cold War as a function of each state's relative capabilities and evaluation of the status quo. Great powers with domestic institutions similar to U.S. institutions would benefit from the status quo while those with dissimilar institutions are likely to take antagonistic steps, but only when they enjoy parity vis-à-vis the United States.

In Chapter 3, Mark R. Brawley brings in the economic dimensions of balance of power while arguing that power and wealth are linked in much more intricate ways than realists and liberals believe. Potential balancers in Europe are bandwagoning with the United States because such a strategy makes it possible for them to add to their relative economic strength, so that they could steer an independent course at some point in the future if the need arose. This may be the calculation made by China's leaders as well. The United States has not made serious efforts to stymie the economic growth of potential challengers such as China, and this policy seems likely to persist as long as U.S. industries continue to develop cutting-edge technologies and register relatively better economic growth. The expectation that no threat will manifest until some time in the future is thus a crucial reason for U.S. disinterest in active economic containment of potential challengers.

In Part II, three chapters look at key dimensions of the security environment of the post-Cold War era, especially with regard to the advent of transnational terrorism and its influence on balance of power and balancing behavior. In Chapter 4, Christopher Layne analyzes the relevance of balance of power in the context of asymmetric conflicts, especially terrorism, while James J. Wirtz, in Chapter 5, gives examples of inconsistencies in the theory based on state behavior, especially that of weaker challengers. In Chapter 6, Edward Rhodes pinpoints the increasing irrelevance of concepts such as nuclear balance in the non-trinitarian environment of globalization that characterizes the contemporary international order. According to Layne, the terrorist attacks of September 11, 2001, have done little to change the big questions surrounding great-power balances and American hegemony. The attacks revealed, however, that the asymmetric activities of subnational groups contain elements of balancing by undermining the hegemon or raising the costs of maintaining hegemony. Asymmetric threats can thus reduce the endurance of U.S. hegemony, especially if they weaken the hegemon internally. Rhodes sees the logic of balancing in Carl von Clausewitz's trinitarian view of warfare: a state engages in war through its military, which is supported by the populace. The logic is also based on the notion that a hegemon would necessarily threaten the sovereign state system and the independence of states. Due to the spread of democracy, technological changes, and the development of weapons of mass destruction, these assumptions are now under serious challenge. Rhodes thus concludes that the logic of balance of power has lost relevance.

Part III is devoted to regional subsystems. Each of the six chapters analyzes the relevance or irrelevance of balance of power theory in a selected region of the world. In the European regional subsystem, notes Robert J. Art in Chapter 7, there appears to be little actual balancing, despite rhetoric from France, Germany, and some other EU members. In Chapter 8, William C. Wohlforth finds a lack of balancing by Russia and other states in the ex-Soviet sphere. He attributes this to the absence among states in the region of the material capabilities necessary to balance against the United States. Although Russia would like to see the United States balanced and often uses rhetoric akin to balancing, it has thus far followed pragmatic policies of hedging and bandwagoning. The same goes for Russia's neighbors, who are generally so weak that their collective ability to balance Moscow is limited. Hence they face strong temptation to pass the balancing buck to others or even to bandwagon actively with the [regional] hegemon to curry its favor and derive benefits from Moscow.

In Chapter 9, Benjamin Miller sees balancing or bandwagoning occurring in the Middle East largely as a function of the previously bipolar or now unipolar international systems, specifically through the activities of the great powers. Regions where great powers are actively involved are not sufficiently autonomous to create their own balances of power. In the Middle East during the Cold War, balancing was the norm as great powers and regional actors vied unsuccessfully to dominate the regional system. In the post-Cold War unipolar system, the United States has emerged as the sole great-power arbiter in the region; despite resentment among the Arab states over Washington's policies they are not able to form any countervailing coalition but they bandwagon with the United States for military protection or economic assistance. The U.S.-inspired order is threatened, however, by the internecine Israeli-Palestinian conflict and the attempts by several regional actors to acquire unconventional weapons.

While Robert S. Ross, in Chapter 10, sees considerable balancing in East Asia, this behavior is largely confined to the two great powers that matter the most in the region, the United States and China. China has been trying to balance U.S. power through internal arms production but has not yet bridged the huge technological and economic gap between the two states. China's economic activities are at least in part driven by an intention to balance U.S. power in the future. The region is likely to remain stable because China lacks the naval power to challenge the United States in the Pacific, while American land forces are not sufficient to challenge China in Asia. Although China may grow stronger in the years to come, it is unlikely that it will develop the military, technological, and economic wherewithal to challenge the regional order anytime soon.

South Asia offers another theater in which balance of power logic might be expected to hold sway due to the presence of two dominant rivalries: India-Pakistan and India-China. Contrary to conventional wisdom, Raju G. C. Thomas argues in Chapter 11 that in the land of Kautilya it was bandwagoning and not power balancing that characterized the behavior of political units in the precolonial period. Balancing strategies such as the creation of buffer states were introduced by the British to prevent other extra-regional powers, especially Russia, from winning control of the huge Asian land mass. During the Cold War, the superpowers balanced one another through the alliances they created with key states in the region. After the September 11, 2001, terrorist attacks, even limited efforts at soft balancing between Russia, China, and India lost momentum. India thus generally bandwagons with the United States, although it remains wary of American power and policies in the region. The India-Pakistan nuclear balance, asymmetric balancing by Pakistan, which uses terrorism and irregular forces to balance India's superior conventional military capability, and the continuing China-Pakistan alliance have served to constrain India's great-power ambitions as well.

Chapter 12, by Michael Barletta and Harold Trinkunas, discusses the absence of balance of power behavior in Latin America and attributes this absence to the fact that states in the region face far greater threats from "regime insecurity" than from external aggression. The authors develop an argument in favor of a "balance of identity" theory. This constructivist account suggests that balance of power is not as universal a phenomenon as realists claim.

In the concluding chapter, the editors present general findings on the extent to which balancing is practiced and how balances of power are shaping up in the world arena at both the systemic and the regional subsystemic levels. Our findings do not lend much support to claims that balancing and balances of power are the dominant patterns of state behavior or outcome either now or for the near term. States seem to pursue eclectic, often opportunistic strategies to maximize their security in an ever more globalized international arena characterized by near-unipolarity under U.S. hegemony. Realism, despite its value in explaining many aspects of state behavior, seems not to capture current international politics all that well.

Notes

1. See, for example, Richard Ned Lebow, "The Long Peace, the End of the Cold War, and the Failure of Realism," *International Organization* 48 (Spring 1994): 249–77; Bruce Russett, *Grasping the Democratic Peace* (Princeton: Princeton University Press, 1991); John A. Vasquez, "The Realist Paradigm and Degenerative Versus Progressive Research Programs: An Appraisal of Neotraditional Research in Waltz's Balancing Proposition," *American Political Science Review* 91 (December 1997): 899–912; James H. Mittelman, *The Globalization Syndrome: Transformation and Resistance* (Princeton: Princeton University Press, 2000), 6; Kenichi Ohmae, *The End of the Nation State* (New York: Free Press, 1995).

2. Kenneth N. Waltz, "Structural Realism After the Cold War," *International Security* 25 (Summer 2000): 5–41; Colin Gray, "Clausewitz Rules, OK? The Future Is the Past—with GPS," *Review of International Studies* 25 (December 1999): 169.

3. For a useful distinction between *balancing* and *balances of power,* see Colin

Elman, "Introduction: Appraising Balance of Power Theory," in John A. Vasquez and Colin Elman (eds.), *Realism and the Balancing of Power: A New Debate* (Upper Saddle River, N.J.: Prentice Hall, 2003), 8–9. Richard Rosecrance has created a stringent set of criteria for identifying balancing by a state: it must entertain defensive and not offensive motives, join the weaker coalition, and be willing to defend its allies and restore equilibrium in power whenever it is threatened. See Rosecrance, "Is There a Balance of Power?" in Vasquez and Elman, *Realism and the Balancing of Power,* 159.

4. Kenneth N. Waltz, *Theory of International Politics* (New York: Random House, 1979), 127. No balancing coalition is eternal because "no permanent set of allegiances can be allowed, for to admit them would be to rigidify the system, and so to cause disaster." John A. Hall, *International Orders* (Cambridge, United Kingdom: Polity, 1996), 10.

5. The ambiguity of the concept is well captured by Haas, who attaches eight meanings to balance of power. The most salient of these meanings are a "description of the distribution of power, as an exact equilibrium of power between two or more contending parties"; an equivalent to "stability" or "peace as a universal law of history"; and a "guide to policymaking," emphasizing "conscious and deliberate behavior and decision making." Ernst B. Haas, "The Balance of Power: Prescription, Concept or Propaganda?" *World Politics* 5 (July 1953): 442–77.

6. On this see Jacek Kugler and Douglas Lemke (eds.), *Parity and War* (Ann Arbor: University of Michigan Press, 1996); Randolph M. Siverson and Michael P. Sullivan, "The Distribution of Power and the Onset of War," *Journal of Conflict Resolution* 27 (September 1983): 473–94; Wayne H. Ferris, *The Power Capabilities of Nation States* (Lexington, Mass.: Lexington, 1973).

7. Inis L. Claude, *Power and International Relations* (New York: Random House, 1964), 56; Ferris, *Power Capabilities of Nation States,* 15.

8. On the preventive motivation for war, especially for declining powers, see Dale C. Copeland, *The Origins of Major War* (Ithaca: Cornell University Press, 2000).

9. George Liska, *International Equilibrium: A Theoretical Essay on the Politics and Organization of Security* (Cambridge, Mass.: Harvard University Press, 1957), 34–41; Stephen M. Walt, "Alliance Formation and the Balance of World Power," *International Security* 9 (Spring 1985): 3–43; Stanley Hoffmann, "Balance of Power," in David L. Sills (ed.), *International Encyclopedia of the Social Sciences,* vol. 1 (New York: Macmillan, 1968), 507.

10. Waltz, *Theory of International Politics,* 126–27.

11. Ibid., 128.

12. Michael W. Doyle, *Ways of War and Peace* (New York: Norton, 1997), 166–67; Emerson Niou and Peter Ordeshook, "A Theory of Balance of Power in International Systems," *Journal of Conflict Resolution* 3 (December 1986): 689–715.

13. Henry Kissinger, "War Roared into Vacuum Formed by a Sidestepping of Statesmanship," *Los Angeles Times,* August 27, 1989, 1.

14. Morton A. Kaplan, *System and Process in International Politics* (New York: Wiley, 1957), 23.

15. George Liska, *Resurrecting a Discipline: Enduring Scholarship for Evolving World Politics* (Lanham, Md.: Lexington, 1999), 17.

16. Patrick M. Morgan, "Regional Security Complexes and Regional Orders," in David A. Lake and Patrick M. Morgan (eds.), *Regional Orders* (University Park: Penn State University Press, 1997), 33.

17. On this see Peter R. Lavoy, Scott D. Sagan, and James J. Wirtz (eds.), *Planning the Unthinkable* (Ithaca: Cornell University Press, 2000).

18. Stephen M. Walt, *The Origins of Alliances* (Ithaca: Cornell University Press, 1987).

19. Walt, "Alliance Formation," 9. While Walt's theory makes good intuitive sense, it has not been tested sufficiently by other researchers. It is important to figure out whether military threat or military power or a combination of both elements motivates states to seek to balance against one another.

20. Ibid., 8, 15.

21. A. F. K. Organski, *World Politics,* 2nd ed. (New York: Knopf, 1968), 294–95.

22. For the strategies of weaker states, see T. V. Paul, *Asymmetric Conflicts: War Initiation by Weaker Powers* (Cambridge: Cambridge University Press, 1994). For recent applications of this logic, see Thomas J. Christensen, "Posing Problems Without Catching Up: China's Rise and Challenges for U.S. Security Policy," *International Security* 23 (Spring 2001): 5–40; Ivan Arreguin-Toft, "How the Weak Win Wars: A Theory of Asymmetric Conflict," *International Security* 26 (Summer 2001): 93–128.

23. Claude, *Power and International Relations,* 56. Klaus Knorr, *The Power of Nations: The Political Economy of International Relations* (New York: Basic, 1975), 10; Eric Weede, "Overwhelming Preponderance as a Pacifying Condition Among Contiguous Asian Dyads," *Journal of Conflict Resolution* 20 (September 1976): 395–411.

24. Robert Gilpin, *Global Political Economy* (Princeton: Princeton University Press, 2001), 93–95; Joseph Joffee, "Europe's American Pacifier," *Foreign Policy* 14 (Spring 1984): 64–82. For a discussion of different versions of the theory and their criticisms, see Duncan Snidal, "The Limits of Hegemonic Stability Theory," *International Organization* 39 (Autumn 1985): 579–614.

25. Doyle, *Ways of War and Peace,* 211.

26. For discussions of the role of institutions, see Lisa L. Martin, "An Institutionalist View: International Institutions and State Strategies," in T. V. Paul and John A. Hall (eds.), *International Order and the Future of World Politics* (Cambridge: Cambridge University Press, 1999): 78–98; and Lloyd Gruber, *Ruling the World: Power Politics and the Rise of Supranational Institutions* (Princeton: Princeton University Press, 2000). For a criticism of realist attempts to incorporate institutions, see Richard Rosecrance, "Has Realism Become Cost-Benefit Analysis? A Review Essay," *International Security* 26 (Fall 2001): 132–54.

27. Bruce Russett and John Oneal, *Triangulating Peace: Democracy, Interdependence, and International Organization* (New York: Norton, 2001).

28. On this, see Emanuel Adler and Michael Barnett, *Security Communities* (Cambridge: Cambridge University Press, 1998).

29. John M. Owen IV, "Transnational Liberalism and U.S. Primacy," *International Security* 26 (Winter 2001/2002): 117–52. For alternative views on this, see William C. Wohlforth, "The Stability of a Unipolar World," *International Security* 24 (Summer 1999): 5–41; Charles A Kupchan, "After Pax Americana: Benign Power, Regional Integration, and the Sources of Stable Multipolarity," *International Security* 23 (Fall 1998): 40–79; Michael Mastanduno, "A Realist View: Three Images of the Coming International Order," in Paul and Hall, *International Order,* 19–40. See also Norrin M. Ripsman, *Peacemaking by Democracies* (University Park: Penn State University Press, 2002), for an explanation for how different types of democracies behave in the foreign policy realm.

30. G. John Ikenberry, "Liberal Hegemony and the Future of American Postwar Order," in Paul and Hall, *International Order,* 123–45; Ikenberry, *After Victory* (Princeton: Princeton University Press, 2000); Ikenberry (ed.), *America Unrivaled: The Future of the Balance of Power* (Ithaca: Cornell University Press, 2002).

31. Similarly, major powers no longer worry about immediate nuclear deterrence as they used to during the Cold War era. On this, see Patrick M. Morgan, *Deterrence Now* (Cambridge: Cambridge University Press, 2003).

32. Great powers tend to overstretch themselves and intervene in different regional theaters for reasons of prestige, power, and domestic politics. On this, see Jeffrey W. Taliaferro, *Balancing Risks: Great Power Intervention in the Periphery* (Ithaca: Cornell University Press, forthcoming).

33. For the European dilemma on this, see William Pfaff, "A Precarious Balance Emerges Between America and Europe," *International Herald Tribune,* January 5–6, 2002, 6; Thomas L. Friedman, "Brussels, We Have a Problem," reprinted from *New York Times* in the *Gazette* (Montreal), February 5, 2002, B3.

34. Hedley Bull, *The Anarchical Society: A Study of Order in World Politics* (New York: Columbia University Press, 1977), 112. See also Fareed Zakaria, *From Wealth to Power: The Unusual Origins of America's World Role* (Princeton: Princeton University Press, 1998).

35. On this see T. V. Paul, *Power Versus Prudence: Why Nations Forgo Nuclear Weapons* (Montreal: McGill-Queen's University Press, 2000).

PART I

Theories of Balance of Power and Major Powers

CHAPTER 1

What Do Great Powers Balance Against and When?

JACK S. LEVY

The balance of power is one of the oldest and most fundamental concepts in the study of international relations. David Hume regarded the balance of power as a scientific law, and Glenn Snyder called the balance of power "the central theoretical concept in international relations." Historians talk about the "golden age" of the balance of power in the 18th or 19th centuries, but they have also applied the concept to the Renaissance and to ancient civilizations in China and Greece. Hans Morgenthau, echoing Hume, referred to the balance of power as an "iron law of politics," while others, such as Henry Kissinger, treated the balance of power as more of an art than a science, practiced more skillfully by some political leaders than by others.[1]

Although the idea of the balance of power lost favor with the rise of idealism after World War I, it regained a prominent position with the turn to realist international theory after World War II. The writings of Morgenthau, Edward Gulick, Inis Claude, and Ludwig Dehio were particularly important, as was Kenneth Waltz's development of structural realism, which was intended to put realist theory on a more sound social science footing.[2]

While the balance of power concept is one of the most prominent ideas in the theory and practice of international relations, it also is one of the most ambiguous and intractable ones. While some theorists use the concept to describe the actual distribution of power in the international system, others use it to refer to an ideal distribution of power or a particular kind of system, and still others see balance of power as a state strategy rather than as an international outcome. Many treat balance of power as a theory of international politics, yet theorists do not agree on the key assumptions or propositions of the theory or even what the theory purports to explain. Some say a balance of power helps maintain the peace; others say it contributes to the onset of war; still others claim that the theory makes no determinant predictions about war and peace at all. A scholar may use the balance of power concept to mean several different things, even in a single article or book, usually without being explicit about exactly what is meant in any particular context. The varied ways in which the term *balance of power* has been used led Richard Cobden to call it "a chimera—an undescribed, indescribable, incomprehensible nothing."[3]

One manifestation of the ambiguity of balance of power theory is its application to the contemporary world. Despite the historically unprecedented power of the United States at the opening of the 21st century, the other leading states in the international system have not "balanced" against the United States either through the formation of defensive alliances or through a massive buildup of their own military strength. For many theorists, this behavior is a puzzle. Fareed Zakaria asks, "Why is no one ganging up against the United States?" John Ikenberry asks why, despite the unprecedented concentration of American power, "other great powers have not yet responded in a way anticipated by balance-of-power theory."[4]

Characterizing the absence of balancing against the United States as a puzzle constitutes an erroneous interpretation of balance of power theory. Few balance of power theorists, at least in the tradition of Western international theory that includes Morgenthau, Claude, Gulick, and Dehio, would predict balancing against the United States, at least given current magnitudes of American strength and current U.S. behavior. To understand this view, we must take a long step back and outline the essential features of balance of power theory. In doing this, the chapter clarifies its key concepts, resolves many of its ambiguities, and specifies its primary propositions. It then returns to the puzzle of the absence of balancing against American primacy.

Summary of Balance of Power Theory

While some theorists use the balance of power concept to refer to the actual distribution of power in the system, that usage is confusing because it might reflect an equal balance, a favorable balance, an unfavorable balance, or any other distribution of power.[5] If the focus is on the relative distribution of power in the system, it is better to use the term distribution of power. The concept of a balance of power system is also problematic, particularly when theorists couple it with a discussion of the "goals" of the system, such as maintaining the peace or the independence of the states in the system. This formulation confuses systems as structures with the behavior of units within that structure, and it confounds state preferences with international outcomes that are the joint product of the behavior of two or more actors. Units have goals, but systems do not. In addition, the common tendency to treat the balance of power as a system implies that systems are real and have some objective existence. It is better to think of systems as analytical constructions that theorists develop and use to describe and explain reality. Such analytical constructions are what we mean by *theory*. I treat the balance of power as a theory—one that purports to explain both the foreign policy behaviors of states and the resulting patterns of international outcomes.[6]

There is no single balance of power theory, but instead a variety of balance of power theories. Most of these theories are really sets of discrete hypotheses that have yet to be integrated into a well-developed theory.[7] All versions of balance of power theory begin with the hard-core assumptions of realist theory: the system is anarchic, the key actors are territorial states, their goals are the maximization of power or security, and they act rationally to promote those goals.[8] Scholars then add additional assumptions and provide different nominal and operational definitions of key concepts, and this results in different and sometimes contradictory propositions. For example, while classical balance of power theorists such as Morgenthau argue that multipolar systems are more stable than bipolar systems, Waltz makes the opposite argument.

Some balance of power theorists have suggested that the purpose or function of a balance of power system is to maintain the peace.[9] The problem with this conception, besides attributing goals or purposes to a system, is that it contradicts the argument of most balance of power theorists that states systematically rank some goals higher than peace, including maintaining their independence, avoiding hegemony, or perhaps preserving the general status quo.[10] Given these higher-order goals, states conceive of war as an acceptable instrument to advance their interests, if only as a last resort. For this reason we cannot make the general statement that balance of power systems or balance of power strategies promote peace, though it is conceivable that a particular version of balance of power theory might specify the conditions (including particular distributions of power) under which war or peace is most likely to occur.[11]

Balance of power theorists disagree over the relative importance of various state goals, but states' primary goals are interrelated and can be conceived as a nested hierarchy of instrumental goals. The primary aim of all states is their own survival, defined in terms of some combination of territorial integrity and autonomy. States also have secondary security goals, and these are best seen as instrumental for the higher-order aim of survival. The most important goal is the avoidance of hegemony, a situation in which one state amasses so much power that it is able to dominate the rest of the states in the system, which would put an end to the multistate system. Thus Polybius wrote that "we should never contribute to the attainment by one state of a power so preponderant, that none dare dispute with it even for their acknowledged rights." Similarly, Vattel wrote, "The balance of power . . . [is] an arrangement of affairs so that no State shall be in a position to have absolute mastery and dominate over others."[12] This is the single most important theme in the balance of power literature.

Several further goals are seen as instrumental to preventing hegemony. One is to maintain the independence of other states in the system, or at least the independence of the other great powers; another is to maintain an approximately equal distribution of power in the system, defined in terms of some combination of individual state capabilities and the aggregation of state capabilities in coalitions.[13] Each of these instrumental goals facilitates the formation of balancing coalitions against potential hegemons. Peace may also be a goal, both to promote state autonomy and security and to attain nonsecurity goals, but in balance of power theory the goal of peace is conditional on the avoidance of hegemony and perhaps the achievement of other instrumental goals.

The argument that the highest goal of states, besides securing their own survival and autonomy, is to prevent hegemony does not imply that states intentionally limit their own power for the sake of the system. Rather, state strategies to maintain a balance or equilibrium of power are not ends in themselves but means to maximize their own security. While some realists— particularly "defensive realists"—argue that states often limit their pursuit of power to maximize their security, others argue that even if all states aimed to maximize their power, the result would still be a balance or equilibrium in the system as a whole. In other words, the maintenance of the "system" is the unintended consequence of the actions of many states as each attempts to maximize its own interests under existing constraints.

This view is reflected in Claude's notion of an "automatic" balance of power system, in Waltz's formalization of neorealist theory, and in other conceptions of balance of power as a "law" of behavior. It is modeled after the ideas of Adam Smith and classical economics. Thus Morton Kaplan writes that "like Adam Smith's 'unseen hand' of competition, the international system is policed informally by self-interest," and Arnold Wolfers notes that "though no state is interested in a mere balance of power, the efforts of all states to maximize power may lead to equilibrium." This leads A. J. P. Taylor to conclude that "only those who rejected laissez faire rejected the Balance of Power."[14]

Others disagree with this view of an automatically functioning balance of power system and offer different conceptions. Claude identifies a "manually operated" balance of power system, in which balancing is not automatic but instead the result of "constant vigilance" and conscious and deliberate strategic choices by individual states, and a "semiautomatic" system, in which a conscious and vigilant balancing strategy is pursued by one state in particular, often known as the "balancer" or "holder of the balance." Historically this role is associated with Britain in the European system, and there is much evidence to suggest that British policymakers have self-consciously defined their role in this manner. In his famous memorandum of 1907, Sir Eyre Crowe noted Britain's historic role of "throwing her weight now in this scale and now in that, but ever on the side opposed to the political dictatorship of the strongest single State or group at a given time." Churchill echoed those words: "For four hundred years the foreign policy of England has been to oppose the strongest, most aggressive, most dominating power on the Continent."[15]

Though scholars often refer to Claude's distinction among automatic, semiautomatic, and manual balancing systems, that distinction is in fact rather blurred. The idea of states operating automatically, without "constant vigilance" and deliberate policy choice is not really plausible. Claude himself notes that "most writers who indulge in the language of automatism would, in fact, agree that equilibrium within a balance of power system is 'a diplomatic contrivance.'"[16]

I would reconceptualize the distinction between these different balancing systems in the following way. In the *automatic* system, all states make choices, but those choices are basically determined by the distribution of power, so state foreign policy strategies carry little independent causal weight on international outcomes. In the semiautomatic conception, only the foreign policy strategies of the "balancer" have a causal impact on outcomes, while in the manual conception the strategies of all states, or at least of all of the great powers, determine the degree of equilibrium in the system.

Most of these conceptions of the balance of power fall within a realist theory that strictly defines balance of power in terms of power and interest. In some conceptions of the balance of power, even classical ones, one can find references to the importance of the necessary normative underpinnings of balance of power systems. Morgenthau, for example, emphasized the importance of a "moral consensus" as to the legitimacy of the system, even during the "golden age" of the balance of power. The central role of norms of restraint and of policymakers' conceptions of their own self-interest in terms of the interests of the broader community is even more explicit, more systematic, and more central in Paul Schroeder's work on the Concert of Europe and other international systems.[17]

Let me return to the basic assumption of balance of power theory—that states act rationally to maximize their security or power in anarchic systems without a higher authority to regulate disputes. Some interpreters of balance of power theory include a number of additional assumptions: the existence of four or five great powers, an equilibrium of military power in the system, a balancer, a "flexible" alliance system, the existence of an "open colonial frontier," a consensus regarding the legitimacy of the system, the limited aims of states, and other considerations.[18]

The problem with injecting additional assumptions into the theoretical mix is that it deprives balance of power theories of much of their explanatory power by restricting their applicability to a very narrow set of theoretical conditions and, therefore, to a small number of specific historical eras. Within such systems, several key propositions of the theory would become nearly tautological. If, for example, the system is characterized by states with limited aims and consensus regarding the legitimacy of the system, then it will not be particularly surprising if there are few major wars to overthrow the system and establish one state's hegemony. These "assumptions" are better conceptualized as variables that form the basis of hypotheses that can then be tested against the evidence. Those who introduce these additional assumptions are basically proposing a set of hypotheses about the optimal conditions for the effective functioning of the system.

Given the primacy of avoiding hegemony in the hierarchy of state goals, balance of power theorists suggest a number of strategies that states can adopt. One important distinction they make is between *external balancing* and *internal balancing*. External balancing is primarily the formation of alliances as blocking coalitions against a prospective aggressor, but it also includes territorial compensations or partitions for the purposes of redistributing the sources of power and, if necessary, threats of force, intervention, and even war. Internal balancing is an internal buildup of military capabilities and the economic and industrial foundations of military strength. Although there have been few attempts to specify the precise conditions under which each of these means is used and in what combination, it is clear that alliances play a central role in most versions of balance of power theory.[19]

Predictions of Balance of Power Theory

Balance of power theorists disagree about many things, but there are two things they almost all agree on, one involving international outcomes and the other involving state strategies: sustained hegemonies rarely if ever arise in multistate systems, and a balancing coalition will form against any state that threatens to gain a position of hegemony that would enable it to impose its will on other states.

These hypotheses focus on the threat of hegemony over the system, not other kinds of threats, and consequently are unaffected by debates among balance of power theorists as to whether states balance against the strongest power in the system (Waltz and Mearsheimer) or against the greatest threats to their interests (Walt), which are defined by intentions as well as capabilities.[20] When the issue is hegemony, the Waltz-Walt debate vanishes, because hegemony over the system almost always constitutes the greatest threat to the interests of other states, or at least to the other great powers, and only the strongest power in the system can threaten to impose hegemony. If the question is whether states balance against concentrations of power or threats other than hegemony, however, intentions take on a greater role in explaining balancing behavior.

It is also important to note that Waltz and a few other structuralists argue that neorealist theory predicts only outcomes, not state strategies or foreign policies, though admittedly Waltz is not always consistent on this point.

Waltz predicts that balances of power (defined as non-hegemonic outcomes) occur naturally, but he leaves open the question of *how* they occur. For Waltz, outcomes of balanced power do not necessarily require deliberate balancing behavior by states.

It is certainly true that balanced outcomes and balancing strategies are analytically distinct, and that it is possible in principle to have one without the other. States might balance, but such balancing might not be sufficient to maintain a balanced outcome and prevent hegemony. It is also possible that no state is interested in dominating the system and that no state feels threatened, which would lead to a balanced outcome without balancing behavior.

Waltz is free to be neutral on the question of balancing strategies, but it then becomes incumbent on him to specify the alternative causal mechanisms through which non-hegemonic outcomes repeatedly (or always) arise. A theory that successfully predicts balanced outcomes and specifies the mechanisms leading to such outcomes is, all things being equal, superior to a theory that does the former but not the latter, because a theory of both outcomes and mechanisms has greater empirical content and explains more variation in the empirical world. For these reasons, nearly all balance of power realists focus on both balanced outcomes and the balancing strategies designed to achieve them, and I do the same.

One can identify, in balance of power theory, several distinct causal paths that might lead to the absence of hegemony in the system, and thus explain why the balancing mechanism almost always works to avoid hegemony. Three are particularly salient: (1) potential hegemons anticipate that expansionist behavior would lead to the formation of a military coalition against them and refrain from aggression for that reason; (2) they begin to expand or aggressively build up their armaments but pull back after being confronted by a balancing coalition or unwinnable arms race; or (3) they pursue expansionist policies and are defeated in war by a blocking coalition.[21]

It is important to note that the first two paths result in peace but the third does not. This is why the outbreak of war, even major war, does not necessarily constitute evidence against balance of power theory or the balancing hypothesis. Balancing hypotheses predict either state strategies of balancing or balanced outcomes. They do not predict peace or war.[22]

Another important point is that although balancing is observed in the second and third paths but not in the first (because in the first path the potential hegemon does nothing to trigger balancing), balancing plays an important causal role in all three causal paths. That is, unobserved balancing is just as important as observed balancing in terms of its causal impact on the outcome of non-hegemony.

A problem in earlier studies of balancing is that scholars have tended to focus on observed balancing rather than on unobserved balancing. Consequently, they failed to recognize the causal importance of balancing in the first path to non-hegemonic outcomes. They analyzed the wars that have occurred and asked whether states balanced against the aggressor, and they neglected cases where wars did not occur, perhaps because potential hegemons anticipated balancing. The result is a *selection bias* in the empirical examination of balancing and an *underestimation* of the causal impact of balancing.[23]

Nearly all balance of power theorists, despite their many disagreements, would accept the idea that hegemonies do not form in multistate systems because perceived threats of hegemony over the system generate balancing behavior by other leading states in the system. States with expansionist ambitions either are deterred by the anticipation of balancing coalitions or, if deterrence fails, are defeated in war by the emergence of a blocking coalition. Yet the United States, which would seem to qualify as a hegemon or potential hegemon by almost any definition,[24] has not faced a balancing coalition, at least not in the form of a defensive (or offensive) alliance of other major states, and I have argued that this absence of balancing is not a violation of balance of power theory. Let me now try to explain this apparent contradiction in my argument and demonstrate that the common characterization of the absence of anti-American balancing as a puzzle for balance of power theory represents a misleading interpretation of that theory.

The Scope Conditions of the Theory

The basic problem with nearly all interpretations of balance of power theory is that the theory and its central propositions about balanced outcomes and balancing strategies are presented as universals, applicable in principle to any international system.[25] But few social science theories are universally valid, nearly all have scope conditions that specify the domain of the theory, and balance of power theory is no exception. No system-level theory of international politics is complete without a specification of the system under consideration, the basis of power in the system, and the key actors in the system.[26] The scope conditions for balance of power theory are generally implicit rather than explicit. Balance of power theory—at least as developed and modified in a long tradition of Western international theory and passed along by Morgenthau, Gulick, Claude, and others—contains implicit assumptions that serve as scope conditions for the theory: the system is Europe, the basis of power in that system is land-based military power, and the key actors are the European great powers.

Thus, the "best case" for balance of power theory is Europe, or at least Europe before 1945, at which point the European system ceased to be the dominant subsystem in world politics. Patterns of balancing against potential European hegemons, from Philip II to Napoleon to Hitler, cannot necessarily be generalized to the contemporary period defined by American dominance in military, commercial, and financial power in the global system. Balancing against the United States might occur, but any such predictions cannot be based on the European experience or on a straightforward extrapolation of a balance of power theory that is derived from that experience.[27]

THE GREAT POWER BIAS IN BALANCE OF POWER THEORY

While balance of power theorists speak very loosely about "states" balancing, nearly all treatments of balance of power theory strongly imply that the great powers do most of the balancing. Small and medium states as well as great powers prefer that the power of an aspiring hegemon be limited, but only the great powers have the military capacity to make a difference. Weaker states know that they can have only a marginal impact on outcomes, and given their vulnerability and short-term time horizons, they will sometimes balance and sometimes bandwagon, depending on the context.

The great-power bias in balance of power theory and in the balancing proposition in particular is pervasive in the literature, and one that most traditional realist theories and many diplomatic histories share. Claude argues that "balance of power theory is concerned mainly with the rivalries and clashes of great powers." Waltz explicitly states that any theory of international politics must be based on the great powers because the great powers define the context for others as well as for themselves, and Mearsheimer's great-power focus is clear in his recent book on *The Tragedy of Great Power Politics*. As for diplomatic history, the majority of Western diplomatic historians have followed Leopold Von Ranke in conceiving European history as the history of great-power relations. A. J. P. Taylor, for example, argues that "the relations of the great powers have determined the history of Europe." Finally, formal theorists create stylized balance of power models consisting of just a handful of actors, representing the great powers.[28]

There are other manifestations of the great-power bias in balance of power theory. The very notion of equilibrium in the system refers to an equilibrium among the great powers, not among states in general. While balance of power theorists emphasize the importance of maintaining "independent states" as an important purpose of a balance of power system, what they mean is that the great powers attempt to preserve the independence and integrity of other great powers (and not of weaker states) because those great powers might be needed in a balancing coalition against hegemonic threats. The number of great powers in the system is, after all, a key independent variable in many formulations of the theory. One of Kaplan's "rules" for a balance of power system is to "stop fighting rather than eliminate an essential national actor," which leaves little doubt about the identity of the "essential actors." The concern for the independence of the great powers but not others is also clear in the argument advanced by Gulick and others that another means of maintaining the balance of power is partitioning weak states.[29] Finally, in debates over the relative stability of bipolar and multipolar systems, theorists usually define stability as the absence of war between the great powers, not the absence of war in general.[30]

THE EUROCENTRIC BIAS IN BALANCE OF POWER THEORY

Some scholars explicitly acknowledge the European focus of the Western literature on the balance of power. Several book titles reflect this: Gulick's *Europe's Classical Balance of Power* and Dehio's *The Precarious Balance: Four Centuries of the European Power Struggle*. Sheehan also recognizes the Eurocentric nature of the theory:

> The balance of power concept for some 200 years after its confirmation
> as the basis of the European state system remained a purely European phe-
> nomenon. Its logic was not applied beyond the boundaries of the European
> continent. This may have been because the strongest proponent of the

theory, Britain, had the most to lose from such a development. It may also have been related to the fact that the European balance of power idea was, in terms of its origins, part of a peculiarly European solution to the problems afflicting the European imagination.[31]

The Eurocentric bias in balance of power theory is not surprising given that most of the literature is written by Europeans, especially by the British and subsequently by Americans (whose security outlook was primarily Eurocentric until the late 20th century). The illustrative evidence for theories of balance of power draws on the modern European great-power system beginning with the Treaty of Westphalia, with some applications to the Italian city-state system and early modern Europe, but with a disproportionate focus on the "golden age" of the European balance of power in the 18th and 19th centuries. This Eurocentric bias in balance of power theory relates closely to its great-power bias—from the origins of the modern great-power system in the late 15th century until the end of the 19th century, all of the great powers in the system were European.

The Eurocentric bias manifests itself in numerous other ways in balance of power theory. The concept of a "balancer," while generalizable in principle, is nearly always illustrated by Britain's role in maintaining an equilibrium of power on the European continent, especially by its willingness to shift its weight to the side of the weaker coalition. The hypothesis that the stability of a balance of power system is enhanced by an open colonial frontier, which provides a "safety valve" for the dominant actors in the system to expand their power and influence without directly threatening each others' vital interests in the core of the system, clearly reflects the experience of the European colonial powers (and provides a self-interested rationalization for European colonialism).[32]

Most scholarship on the balance of power conceives of hegemony not in abstract terms but rather in terms of dominance over the European system, and illustrations of the formation of balancing coalitions in responses to threats of hegemony all come from the last five centuries of the European experience. Thus, balance of power theorists talk about balancing coalitions against the Habsburgs under Charles V in the early 16th century, Philip II at the end of the 16th century, and the combined strength of Spain and the Holy Roman Empire in the Thirty Years War; against France under Louis XIV and then Napoleon; and against Germany under Wilhelm and then Hitler. It is revealing that even Waltz, who frames his neorealist balance of power theory in more universal terms, illustrates his arguments with examples of balancing against Charles I,[33] Louis XIV, Napoleon, Wilhelm II, and Hitler.[34]

True, it is common to refer to Pax Britannica in the 19th century and to treat Britain as a hegemon or leader during much of that period, but that argument is associated with hegemonic stability theory, power transition theory, or leadership long cycle theory, not balance of power theory.[35] For balance of power theorists, the leading threats to hegemony over the system for the last five centuries have been posed by the states identified above, which have all been European continental powers focused primarily on the politics of the continent. For balance of power theorists, it was Germany, not Britain, who was the leading power in the system by the end of the 19th century, and it was against Germany, not Britain, that most of the other great powers aligned in the early 20th century.

This European continental focus of balance of power theory is closely related to another unstated assumption of the theory: the basis of power in the system, and thus the basis for hegemony in the system, is land-based military power in the form of large armies. It was the strength of the armies of Charles V, Philip II, Louis XIV, Napoleon, Wilhelm, and Hitler that constituted hegemonic threats and that triggered balancing coalitions over the last five centuries.

This conception of power in terms of land-based military power in nearly all applications of balance of power theory should be contrasted with hegemonic stability theory's focus on financial and commercial strength, with power transition theory's measurement of power in terms of gross national product, and leadership long cycle theory's conception of power in terms of naval capability (at least until the 20th century) and dominance in leading economic sectors.

Consider the different treatments of the late 19th century. Hegemonic theories identify Britain as the leading power in the system based on its dominance in finance, trade, and naval power on a global scale, while balance of power theorists see Britain, even at the peak of its strength, as posing little direct threat to the continental great powers of Europe. Similarly, to the extent that the United States was hegemonic after World War II, it was because of American dominance in the world economy and its ability to project military power on a global scale. The strategic balance was one of parity with the Soviet Union by the mid-1960s.

From a balance of power perspective, it is not surprising that no blocking coalition formed against Britain at the peak of its global economic and naval strength in the 1870s, but one did form against Germany, the leading power on the continent, in the period leading up to World War I. Similar logic explains why no balancing coalition formed against the Netherlands in the 17th century despite its dominance in world trade, finance, and naval strength, but instead against Louis XIV and his massive armies. The same logic explains why no great-power balancing coalition formed against the United States, by far the leading power in the world in terms of economic strength and naval and air power in the late 1940s, but instead against the Soviet Union, the leading land power in Eurasia and primary military threat to the major states of Europe. From this perspective, it is not surprising that no balancing coalition has formed against the United States in the early 21st century, despite its unprecedented military strength.[36]

Given that most of the great powers in the system have been European, at least until recently, there are several reasons why the threat posed by global powers is less than that posed by other continental powers. Global powers have fewer capabilities for imposing their will on major continental states, fewer incentives for doing so, and a greater range of strategies for increasing their influence by other means. Effective military power diminishes significantly over distance, especially over water. Large armies massing on borders, threatening to mass on borders, or simply having the potential to mass on borders threatens the territorial integrity of other states in a way that strong naval power or financial strength does not. Whereas contiguous states with large armies threaten their neighbors by virtue of their very existence, global hegemons do not.

This argument is reinforced by evidence from the literature on territory and international conflict, which suggests that a disproportionately high number of wars involve territorially contiguous states, that unsettled territorial disputes are an important predictor of war, and that rivalries are significantly more likely to escalate to war if they involve territorial disputes. The absence of territorial contiguity removes both a direct path for conquest and a source of many of the disputes that escalate to war, and hence an important source of threat.[37]

Global powers differ from continental states in their interests as well as their capabilities, and those interests lead to different strategies. The goals of increasing commercial, financial, and naval power on a global scale do not require military or political control on the continent, which means they are less threatening to the major European states. Global powers may impose their will on smaller states and other actors, but generally through means other than overt military force. The "imperialism of free trade" was as potent as military force in establishing British dominance in far corners of the globe.[38] In any case, the role of small states is not directly relevant for testing balancing hypotheses or balance of power theories more generally.

Thus, global powers historically defined their interests on a global scale and had fewer incentives to expand their influence in Europe. They appeared less threatening to European great powers and were consequently less likely to trigger balancing coalitions. This does not imply that they had no stake in what happened on the European continent. Global powers often perceived that their overall interests would be seriously threatened if any single state achieved a hegemonic position in Europe, because such a position would provide the resources that would enable the continental state to mount a serious challenge to the dominance of the leading global power. Thus, the leading global power often played a central role in balancing coalitions against potential European hegemons. It is not an accident that the global leader in economic and naval power historically played the role of the "balancer" in balance of power theory.

Britain, as the leading global economic and naval power, had the most to lose from the extension of the balance of power concept beyond Europe to include the balance of naval and economic power on a global scale. It is no coincidence that Britain was the strongest proponent of balance of power theory. It is also no surprise that much of the balance of power literature is British (and now American) or that Britain has long defined its interests in terms of pursuing a balance of power on the continent but a preponderance of naval and colonial power on a global scale. Much of the theory and practice of maintaining the balance of power in Europe helped preserve the relative security of the naval and economic strength of the global power.

The Vienna Settlement is often interpreted in terms of the balance of power, for instance, but the system emerging from Vienna constrained France and possibly Russia while doing nothing to limit British naval or colonial power. As Roger Bullen notes, "the concept of the balance of power was hardly ever used except by British governments. The continental powers certainly did not consciously seek to uphold it." British leaders advocated a balance on land while preferring hegemony at sea, and the two are not unrelated. As Quincy Wright argued, "Each statesman considers the balance of power good for others but not for himself. Each tries to get out of the system in order to 'hold the balance' and to establish a hegemony, perhaps eventually an empire, over all the others." Similarly, Nicholas Spykman argued, "The truth of the matter is that states are interested only in a balance which is in their favor. Not an equilibrium, but a generous margin is their objective . . . there is security only in being a little stronger. . . . The balance desired is the one which neutralizes other states, leaving the home state free to be the deciding force and the deciding voice."[39]

Continental statesmen and scholars, on the other hand, were often quite skeptical about the idea of the balance of power and its use by the British. As one French writer pointed out, "[T]he English, while pretending to protect the balance on land which no one threatens, are entirely destroying the balance at sea which no one defends." Both German and French writers argued that the balance of power should apply to colonial and maritime power as well as to the territorial balance of power in Europe. Such arguments themselves contained an important rhetorical component because they helped to rationalize the repeated charges that their states' own efforts to acquire territories and influence beyond Europe were being blocked by Britain and rival global powers.[40]

The fact that balance of power theory contains certain normative biases and a strong rhetorical component will lead some to conclude that a scientific evaluation of the validity of the theory is impossible, but that would be pessimistic in the extreme. All theories contain normative biases to one degree or another, and to conclude that this precludes scientific analysis would leave us unable to test any of our theories or historical interpretations. Instead, we must recognize, as Popper did, that the logic of confirmation is distinct from the logic of discovery, that it does not matter how we generate our theoretical ideas as long as we are as careful and scientific as possible in testing them against the evidence.[41]

Contemporary Implications

This reinterpretation of balance of power theory suggests that the tendency to treat the theory and its propositions as universal is misleading because it fails to account for the scope conditions inherent in a long tradition of

Western writing on the balance of power. The theory grew out of the experience of the European great-power system, where sustained land-based hegemonies did not form and where potential threats of hegemony generated great-power balancing coalitions. The Eurocentric origins and orientation of balance of power theory have a number of important implications for the contemporary world.

One implication is that the absence of a great-power balancing coalition against the United States is not the puzzle that some have claimed. Balancing coalitions did not generally form against leading maritime powers in earlier international systems, and given the U.S. status as the dominant maritime power in the contemporary global system, we should not necessarily expect anti-American balancing coalitions to form.[42]

The logic of my argument does not imply that balancing coalitions never form against leading maritime or global leaders, only that the threshold for balancing is much higher. I can certainly imagine the United States behaving in such a way as to threaten the interests of other great powers and eventually provoking a balancing coalition, but we are currently far from that point, and the trigger would involve specific behavior that threatens other great powers. While the threat from continental hegemons derives from who they are, the threat from global hegemons derives from what they do.

Some will argue, however, that we are living in a new kind of system, that the United States is a new kind of hegemon, and that the old rules of international politics no longer apply. Among other things, the ability of the United States to project its naval and military power on a global scale dwarfs anything that Britain was able to do at the peak of its global dominance, which should lower the threshold for balancing compared to that for previous global leaders. This was also true in the period immediately after World War II, of course, and it is revealing that a great-power balancing coalition formed not against the United States but instead against the Soviet Union. Still, the 2003 American invasion of Iraq provides clear evidence that the United States has the capability of posing a far greater threat to the territorial integrity of other states than have maritime powers of the past.

This line of argument suggests that one important task for future research is to specify the types of American behavior that are likely to trigger a countervailing balancing coalition. Another task, given the importance of alternative forms of resistance that fall short of formal military alliances, is to theorize about a broader range of strategic reactions to the dominant state in a unipolar global system.[43] My argument is that traditional balance of power theory, with its focus on land-based power in Europe or perhaps in other continental systems, provides little guidance here and that we need new theoretical categories and approaches. Among the new theoretical categories that are needed is one for the United States, which is neither a traditional continental power like Napoleonic France nor a traditional maritime power like Britain.

Similar logic applies to the generalization of balance of power theory to contemporary regional systems, including the Middle East, Africa, Central Asia, and elsewhere.[44] While these efforts constitute important contributions to the literature, my argument about the scope conditions of traditional balance of power theory implies that we need to be careful in applying a theory that is drawn from the experience of the great powers to regional systems in which some of the theory's key assumptions might not fully hold.

In particular, the assumption of anarchy—the absence of a higher authority and of any mechanism for enforcing agreements within the system—is not fully satisfied in regional systems. There are likely to be differences in the dynamics of power in autonomous systems like the pre-20th century European great-power system as compared to the dynamics of power in nonautonomous systems, such as regional systems that are often influenced by powerful external states. This does not mean that we cannot talk about balancing in regional systems, only that we cannot assume that traditional balance of power theory can be automatically applied in such systems. Here again, we need new theorizing, not only about balancing behavior in particular regions of the contemporary international system but also about the theoretical dynamics of power politics in any set of nested systems. Several of the other chapters in this volume have taken an important first step in that direction.

Notes

1. David Hume, "Of the Balance of Power," in Paul Seabury (ed.), *Balance of Power* (San Francisco: Chandler, 1965), 32–36; Glenn H. Snyder, "Balance of Power in the Missile Age," *Journal of International Affairs* 14 (1961): 21–24; Hans Morgenthau, *Politics Among Nations,* 4th ed. (New York: Knopf, 1967); Henry A. Kissinger, *A World Restored: Metternich, Castlereagh and the Problems of Peace* (Boston: Houghton Mifflin, 1973).

2. Morgenthau, *Politics Among Nations;* Edward V. Gulick, *Europe's Classical Balance of Power* (New York: Norton, 1955); Inis L. Claude Jr., *Power and International Relations* (New York: Random House, 1962); Ludwig Dehio, *The Precarious Balance: Four Centuries of the European Power Struggle* (New York: Random House/Vintage, 1962); Kenneth N. Waltz, *Theory of International Politics* (Reading, Mass.: Addison-Wesley, 1979).

3. Richard Cobden, *The Political Writings of Richard Cobden* (London: Unwin, 1969; originally published 1903). On the ambiguities of balance of power theory, see Ernest B. Haas, "The Balance of Power: Prescription, Concept, or Propaganda?" *World Politics* 5 (1953): 442–77; Claude, *Power and International Relations;* Michael Sheehan, *Balance of Power: History and Theory* (New York: Routledge, 1996); Jack S. Levy, "Balances and Balancing: Concepts, Propositions, and Research Design," in John A. Vasquez and Colin Elman (eds.), *Realism and the Balancing of Power: A New Debate* (Upper Saddle River, N.J.: Prentice Hall, 2002), 128–53.

4. Fareed Zakaria, "America's New Balancing Act," *Newsweek,* August 6, 2001; G. John Ikenberry, "Introduction," in G. John Ikenberry (ed.), *America Unrivaled* (Ithaca: Cornell University Press, 2002), 3.

5. This section draws on Jack S. Levy, "The Causes of War: A Review of Theories and Evidence," in Philip E. Tetlock, Jo L. Husbands, Robert Jervis, Paul C. Stern, and Charles Tilly (eds.), *Behavior, Society, and Nuclear War,* vol. 1 (New York: Oxford University Press, 1989), 228–43; Levy, "Balances and Balancing," 130–33.

6. Although some theorists treat balance of power theory as synonymous with realist theory, that is misleading. Realist international thought includes both *balance of power realism* and *hegemonic realism.* The latter posits that hegemony or hierarchy, not balance, is commonplace. It does not regard the avoidance of hegemony as a high-ranking state goal for which states are willing to fight, and it does not predict balancing against extreme concentrations of power. Consequently, the falsification of aspects of balance of power theory does not necessarily falsify realist theory. We should focus our theoretical and empirical efforts on falsifiable theories (such as balance of power) rather than on non-falsifiable paradigms (such as realism). On the distinction between hegemonic realism and balance of power realism, see Jack S. Levy, "War and Peace," in Walter Carlsnaes, Thomas Risse, and Beth A. Simmons (eds.), *Handbook of International Relations* (London: Sage, 2002), 350–68.

7. The main exception is Waltz's neorealism, described in his *Theory of International Politics,* which presents an integrated theory.

8. For an alternative interpretation of balance of power theory, one that emphasizes its liberal foundations, see Deborah Boucoyannis, "Balance of Power: The International Wanderings of a Liberal Idea," unpublished paper, Harvard University, 2003.

9. Claude, *Power and International Relations,* 55; Arnold Wolfers, *Discord and Collaboration* (Baltimore: Johns Hopkins University Press, 1962), chap. 8.

10. Gulick, *Europe's Classical Balance of Power*; A. F. K. Organski, *World Politics,* 2nd ed. (New York: Knopf, 1968), chap. 14; Waltz, *Theory of International Politics*; R. Harrison Wagner, "Peace, War, and the Balance of Power," *American Political Science Review* 88 (September 1994): 593–607; Robert Jervis, *System Effects* (Princeton: Princeton University Press, 1997), 131; Geoffrey Blainey, *The Causes of War,* 3rd ed. (New York: Free Press, 1988), 112; Sheehan, *Balance of Power*; Kissinger, *A World Restored.*

11. It is true that the *power parity hypothesis* predicts that an equality of power between two states is likely to lead to peace, and that the *power preponderance hypothesis* predicts the opposite (with most of the evidence supporting the latter). But these are dyadic-level hypotheses that assume that alliances play no role, while balance of power theory is a systemic-level theory in which alliances are central and in which the outcome of any particular dyadic-level balance of power between two states is theoretically indeterminate. On power parity, see Jacek Kugler and Douglas Lemke (eds.), *Parity and War* (Ann Arbor: University of Michigan Press, 1996).

12. Polybius, *The Histories,* vol. 1, trans. W. R. Paton (Cambridge, Mass.: Harvard University Press, 1960); Emmerich de Vattel, *The Law of Nations,* trans. Charles Fenwick (Washington, D.C.: Carnegie Institution, 1916; originally published 1758).

13. Note that maintaining the independence of one's own state is an irreducible national value, whereas maintaining the independence of other great powers is a means to that end, not an end in itself. Balance of power theorists often blur this distinction.

14. Claude, *Power and International Relations*; Waltz, *Theory of International Politics,* 119; Wolfers, *Discord and Collaboration,* 83; Morton A. Kaplan, "Balance of Power, Bipolarity, and Other Models of International Systems," in James N. Rosenau (ed.), *International Politics and Foreign Policy* (New York: Free Press, 1961), 346; A. J. P. Taylor, *The Struggle for Mastery in Europe, 1848–1918* (Oxford: Clarendon, 1954), xx. Also on automatic and manual conceptions of balance of power, see Colin Elman, "Introduction: Appraising Balance of Power Theory," in Vasquez and Elman, *Realism and the Balancing of Power,* 1–22.

15. Crowe cited in Claude, *Power and International Relations,* 47; Winston S. Churchill, *The Gathering Storm* (New York: Bantam, 1948), 207.

16. Claude, *Power and International Relations,* 49.

17. Morgenthau, *Politics Among Nations,* 208–15; Paul W. Schroeder, "The Nineteenth-Century System: Balance of Power or Political Equilibrium?" *Review of International Studies* 15 (April 1989): 135–53.

18. Morgenthau, *Politics Among Nations,* chap. 14; Gulick, *Europe's Classical Balance of Power,* chap. 1; Stanley Hoffmann, "Balance of Power," *International Encyclopedia of the Social Sciences,* vol. 1 (New York: Macmillan, 1968), 506–10; Quincy Wright, *A Study of War,* 2nd ed., rev. (Chicago: University of Chicago Press, 1965), chap. 20.

19. Waltz, *Theory of International Politics,* 168; Gulick, *Europe's Classical Balance of Power,* chap. 3.

20. Waltz, *Theory of International Politics;* Stephen M. Walt, *Origins of Alliances* (Ithaca: Cornell University Press, 1987); John J. Mearsheimer, *Tragedy of Great Power Politics* (New York: Norton, 2001).

21. There is in principle a fourth path to non-hegemonic outcomes: no state has an interest in achieving a dominant position in the system, even if it were unconstrained by the military power of others or by the fear of triggering a counter-hegemonic coalition. Few balance of power realists would accept such a possibility, however, and many liberals would agree with them. Immanuel Kant, for example, who is often identified as one of the founders of liberal international theory, argued that "it is the desire of every state, or of its ruler, to arrive at a condition of perpetual peace by conquering the whole world, if that were possible." Cited in Martin Wight, *Power Politics,* 2nd ed., eds. Hedley Bull and Carsten Holbraad (Harmondsworth, England: Penguin, 1986), 144.

22. Jack S. Levy, "The Theoretical Foundations of Paul W. Schroeder's International System," *International History Review* 16 (November 1994): 715–44.

23. This selection bias is evident in many of the articles in the symposium on balancing published in the *American Political Science Review* 91 (December 1997); reprinted in Vasquez and Elman, *Realism and the Balancing of Power,* part 1. The need to look at cases of unobserved balancing will be clear to anyone familiar with Sherlock Holmes' discussion of the importance of the dog that did not bark. "Negative" outcomes can be as important as "positive" outcomes.

24. U.S. military spending is as large as that of the next fourteen countries combined; the U.S. economy is as large as the next three countries combined; and U.S. spending on research and development, which is one indicator of future military power, is 80 percent of the world's total. See Stephen G. Brooks and William C. Wohlforth, "American Primacy in Perspective," *Foreign Affairs* 81 (July/August 2002): 20–33; Ikenberry, *America Unrivaled,* 1–2; Ikenberry, "Strategic Reactions to American Global Predominance: Great Power Politics in an Age of Unipolarity," unpublished manuscript, Georgetown University, 2002.

25. This section builds on Levy, "Balances and Balancing."

26. As I have argued in two earlier studies, a serious flaw in the literatures on polarity and war and on hegemonic war is their failure to identify the system under consideration and the basis of power in that system. Jack S. Levy, "Theories of General War," *World Politics* 37 (April 1985): 344–74; Jack S. Levy, "The Polarity of the System and International Stability: An Empirical Analysis," in Alan Ned Sabrosky (ed.), *Polarity and War: The Changing Structure of International Conflict* (Boulder, Colo.: Westview, 1985), 41–66.

27. For evidence of systematic (but not deterministic) patterns of balancing against potential European hegemons, but the absence of such patterns against maritime hegemons, see Jack S. Levy and William R. Thompson, "Hegemonic Threats and Great Power Balancing in Europe, 1495–2000," paper presented at

the annual meeting of the American Political Science Association, Boston, Mass., August 29–September 1, 2002; and Levy and Thompson, "Balancing at Sea: Do States Coalesce Against Leading Maritime Powers?" paper presented at the annual meeting of the American Political Science Association, Philadelphia, Penn., August 28–31, 2003.

28. Inis L. Claude, "The Balance of Power Revisited," *Review of International Studies* 15 (April 1989): 77–85; Waltz, *Theory of International Politics,* 72–73; Mearsheimer, *Tragedy of Great Power Politics*; Leopold von Ranke, "The Great Powers," in Georg G. Iggers and Konrad von Moltke (eds.), *The Theory and Practice of History* (Indianapolis: Bobbs-Merrill, 1973; originally published 1833), 65–101; Taylor, *Struggle for Mastery in Europe,* xix. On formal balance of power theories, see Emerson Niou, Peter Ordeshook, and Gregory Rose, *The Balance of Power* (New York: Cambridge University Press, 1989); Wagner, "Peace, War, and the Balance of Power"; Robert Powell, "Stability and the Distribution of Power," *World Politics* 48 (January 1996): 239–67.

29. Morton A. Kaplan, *System and Process in International Politics* (New York: Wiley, 1957), 23. Gulick, *Europe's Classical Balance of Power,* chap. 3.

30. Waltz, *Theory of International Politics,* is an exception and defines stability as the persistence of key structural features of the system.

31. Sheehan, *Balance of Power,* 115.

32. Wright, *Study of War,* chap. 20; Morgenthau, *Politics Among Nations,* chap. 14; Gulick, *Europe's Classical Balance of Power,* chap. 1; Hoffmann, "Balance of Power," 507.

33. Charles I became Charles V when he was elected Holy Roman Emperor.

34. Gulick, *Europe's Classical Balance of Power*; Dehio, *The Precarious Balance*; Claude, *Power and International Relations*; Morgenthau, *Politics Among Nations*; Raymond Aron, *Peace and War,* trans. Richard Howard and Annette Baker Fox (Garden City, N.Y.: Doubleday-Anchor, 1973); Paul Kennedy, *The Rise and Fall of the Great Powers: Economic Change and Military Conflict from 1500 to 2000* (New York: Random House, 1987); Churchill, *The Gathering Storm,* 207–08; Kenneth N. Waltz, "Evaluating Theories," *American Political Science Review* 91 (December 1997): 913–17.

35. Robert O. Keohane, *After Hegemony* (Princeton: Princeton University Press, 1984); Organski, *World Politics;* William R. Thompson, *On Global War* (Columbia: University of South Carolina Press, 1988).

36. Jonathan Israel, *Dutch Primacy in the World Trade, 1585–1740* (Oxford: Clarendon, 1989); Levy, "Theories of General War," 368.

37. John A. Vasquez, *The War Puzzle* (New York: Cambridge University Press, 1993); Paul K. Huth, *Standing Your Guard: Territorial Disputes and International Conflict* (Ann Arbor: University of Michigan Press, 1996); Paul R. Hensel, "Territory: Theory and Evidence on Geography and Conflict," in John A. Vasquez (ed.), *What Do We Know About War?* (Lanham, Md.: Rowman & Littlefield, 2000), 57–84.

38. John Gallagher and Ronald Robinson, "The Imperialism of Free Trade," *Economic History Review* 6, 2nd series, 1953: 1–25.

39. Roger Bullen, "France and Europe, 1815–48: The Problem of Defeat and Recovery," in Alan Sked (ed.), *Europe's Balance of Power, 1815–48* (London: Macmillan, 1980), 122–45; Wright, *Study of War,* 759; Spykman cited in Haas, "Balance of Power," 321.

40. The Duc de Choiseul, quoted in Sheehan, *Balance of Power,* 115.

41. Karl R. Popper, *The Logic of Scientific Discovery* (New York: Harper Touchback, 1959).

42. It is true that the emergence of unrivaled American unipolar hegemony has been associated with various forms of resistance, but we cannot classify this resistance as traditional great-power balancing behavior. We have seen terrorist acts against both the American homeland and its interests abroad, but these acts have been initiated by weaker actors, not by other leading powers. True, other leading powers, including America's closest allies, have not cooperated with the United States on a number of key issues, including the 2003 war in Iraq; but this kind of "soft balancing" falls in a different category than defensive military alliances or massive arms buildups, which are central to traditional balance of power theory. On soft balancing see T. V. Paul's introductory chapter to the present volume; and Robert Pape, "Soft Balancing Against the United States," paper presented at the annual meeting of the International Studies Association, Montreal, Canada, March 17–20, 2004.

43. For a useful first step in this direction see Ikenberry, "Strategic Reactions to American Global Predominance."

44. Walt, *Origins of Alliances*; Eric J. Labs, "Do Weak States Bandwagon?" *Security Studies* 1 (Spring 1992): 383–416. On the application of power transition theory to regional systems, see Douglas Lemke, *Regions of War and Peace* (Ann Arbor: University of Michigan Press, 2001).

CHAPTER 2

Great Powers in the Post-Cold War World: A Power Transition Perspective

DOUGLAS LEMKE

In spite of seemingly widespread agreement that world politics is undergoing an important period of change and adaptation, no one argues that the actions of the great powers are unimportant. Consequently, theories purporting to explain great-power behavior are still a central focus of academic research about world politics. The more accurately a given theory describes such behavior, the more useful it is.

Tradition accords importance to the balance of power between states, and consequently any argument advanced as "balance-of-power theory" enjoys automatic prestige. There are as many balance-of-power theories, however, as there are balance-of-power theorists. Consequently, comparing power transition and balance-of-power theory either requires one to hit a moving target, or forces one to select a specific balance-of-power theory to be analyzed.

This chapter therefore focuses on one balance-of-power theory, offensive realism. Offensive realism is a logical point of comparison to power transition theory because of its contemporary prominence. A recent book on offensive realism by John Mearsheimer is trumpeted as the long-awaited successor to the groundbreaking earlier works of Hans Morgenthau and Kenneth Waltz.[1] Prominent summaries of offensive realism in *Foreign Affairs* and reviews in the *New York Times* demonstrate that offensive realism's arguments have generated popular and scholarly interest, making it a good candidate for comparison.

The chapter unfolds by first describing offensive realism. It then describes power transition theory. The chapter next turns to an empirical consideration of great-power behavior since the end of the Cold War. It concludes by suggesting that offensive realism is largely inconsistent with what the great powers have done in the past decade or so (or, conversely, is unable to be inconsistent with any alternative outcome). In contrast, power transition theory's expectations are generally consistent with great-power behavior over this time period (and, importantly, could have been inconsistent).

Offensive Realism

Over the past decade offensive realism has emerged as a coherent subset of realist theory about world politics. It is usually juxtaposed with a rival variant, defensive realism.[2] An important source of divergence between offensive and defensive realism concerns the distinction between the *possibility* and the *probability* of war; offensive realists are concerned primarily with the former.[3] Under anarchy, war is always a possibility because power shifts constantly and uncertainty about intentions is unavoidable. As a result, states, which are intent on survival, must make every effort to maximize their power, subject only to the dictates of prudence. To survive, states must be wary, paying ceaseless attention to the balance of power, and must remain ready to seize any advantage that arises. In such a world, a state can only be satisfied with its share of power if it becomes a hegemon, for only then would it have sufficient power to guarantee survival.[4] Consequently, states are always looking for opportunities to eliminate their rivals, or to otherwise subordinate or subjugate them. In short, states are always on the offensive, hence offensive realism's name.

Two scholars offer empirical investigations of offensive realist propositions. Erik Labs investigated four cases of great-power war, asking whether the aims of participants in those wars expanded or contracted as prospects of victory approached or receded.[5] If states are ever-conscious of their need for more power, then as victory in war nears, the expansion of war aims would seem an obvious way to take advantage of an opportunity to gain resources for the future. Labs claims the ebb and flow of wartime opportunity corresponded consistently with the expansion and contraction of Prussian war aims in 1866 and 1870, with British war aims in World War I, and American war aims in Korea. Similarly, John Mearsheimer offers a general survey of various great powers' foreign policies over long swathes of time, concluding that:

> The nuclear arms race between the superpowers and the foreign policy behavior of Japan (1868–1945), Germany (1862–1945), the Soviet Union

(1917–91), and Italy (1861–1943) show that great powers look for opportunities to shift the balance of power in their favor and usually seize opportunities when they appear.[6]

Mearsheimer's book is widely seen as the most important statement of offensive realism.[7] Of critical importance are Mearsheimer's arguments about the circumstances under which threatened great powers will balance against potential hegemons and those under which they will pass the buck. This issue is central because it bears directly on what offensive realism predicts is the most likely course of great-power behavior since the Cold War's end.

Mearsheimer describes that when threatened, great powers are likely to balance or to buck-pass. Since the end of the Cold War, the United States has been the world's strongest state, arguably without peer. Because no other great powers can be assured of U.S. intentions, presumably they have been balancing or buck-passing since the Cold War ended. According to Mearsheimer, "with balancing, a great power assumes direct responsibility for preventing an aggressor from upsetting the balance of power" while "a buck-passer attempts to get another state to bear the burden of deterring or possibly fighting an aggressor, while it remains on the sidelines."[8] Actions that qualify as balancing include explicit threats made against the potential hegemon, the construction of defensive alliances targeting the potential hegemon, and internal balancing, whereby the balancer boosts its military power by increasing its production of military hardware or enlarging its armed forces. There are four buck-passing tactics: pursuing cordial relations with the potential hegemon, maintaining cool relations with the potential buck-catcher, building up one's military so as to make the potential buck-catcher a more attractive target for the potential hegemon, and allowing, or even facilitating, the growth in power of the potential buck-catcher so that it can more effectively contain the potential hegemon.

Mearsheimer describes buck-passing as a more attractive strategy than balancing. The incentive to buck-pass is as strong in great-power relations as is the incentive to free ride in collective action situations, and for the same reason: rational self-interest. In other words, it makes no sense to pay for common goods if others are willing or are unable to avoid footing the bill. But as attractive as buck-passing is, it may not be the right strategy for some great powers. For example, if one is physically adjacent to a potential hegemon, buck-passing is much riskier than is the case if one is located far from the potential hegemon.

Other balance-of-power authors suggest threatened states might band-wagon.[9] By bandwagoning, weaker states ally themselves with the strong, either because they recognize it would be futile to resist the stronger state, or because they expect to profit from their alliance with the potential hegemon as it conquers others. Mearsheimer maintains, however, that offensive realism rules out bandwagoning by great powers.[10] By definition, great powers have the ability to resist aggression by the potential hegemon and so have no need to join it. Bandwagoning states, in Mearsheimer's view, also implicitly give up the quest for more power. This fundamentally contradicts offensive realism's emphasis on the ever-present quest for additional power.

If offensive realism is an accurate theory of great-power behavior, great powers should be consumed by a desire for more power even though the Cold War has ended. What's more, because American relative power is so pronounced, other great powers should balance against the threat of potential and emerging American hegemony. Mearsheimer himself voices this expectation, when he writes: "the more relative power the potential hegemon controls, the more likely it is that *all* of the threatened states in the system will forgo buck-passing and form a balancing coalition."[11] Mearsheimer's justification for this unusual state preference for balancing over buck-passing follows:

> Threatened states are reluctant to form balancing coalitions against potential hegemons because the costs of containment are likely to be great; if it is possible to get another state to bear those costs, a threatened state will make every effort to do so. The more powerful the dominant state is relative to its foes, however, the less likely it is that the potential victims will be able to pass the buck among themselves, and the more likely it is that they will be forced to form a balancing coalition against the aggressor.[12]

Ten years after the collapse of its Soviet superpower rival, the United States finds itself in a position of unrivaled global dominance. Offensive realism thus predicts that balancing behavior should dominate world politics.

Power Transition Theory

Power transition theory describes the international system as a hierarchy dominated by one power, the strongest state in the system.[13] Being the strongest state is desirable, because the dominant power establishes the international status quo—the set of formal and informal rules governing international interactions in economics, politics, and military spheres.

The United States has been the dominant power in world politics since the end of World War II. The status quo it has promulgated includes an international financial system comprising the International Monetary Fund (IMF), the World Bank, and the World Trade Organization. Commercial capital markets, stock exchanges, and communication networks are among the informal elements of this system. These financial institutions provide resources (credit, capital, relief from trade disputes) disproportionately to states that organize their domestic economies in accordance with American concepts of market capitalism, free trade, and respect for liberal democratic norms of conduct and human rights. There are obvious benefits to the United States in such arrangements. Because its economy is the largest in the world, it reaps much from interaction with other economies. The more open those other economies become, the more the United States can gain from interaction with them. The IMF, World Bank, and international capital markets are more likely to provide loans and credit to states that have open and capitalist economies, thereby providing a material incentive for states to arrange their domestic economic affairs in accordance with American preferences.

The global status quo also has political elements. The premier international political body is the United Nations (UN). Like the U.S. domestic polity, the UN is organized as a democracy, which in itself forces states that would participate in it to accept American political practice. This serves to validate the structure of America's domestic political regime in the eyes of other nations, and as in the economic sphere, encourages emulation.

Some states will benefit from the existing status quo and others will not. Centrally planned economies will have a very difficult time securing capital from international institutions like the World Bank or from private lenders in international markets. Generally speaking, the more similar a state's domestic institutions are to those of the dominant power, the more likely that state is to expect benefits from the status quo (if only in comparison to the "benefits" they might anticipate from an alternate status quo), and importantly, the more likely it is to be *satisfied* with (supportive of) the status quo. The more dissimilar a state's domestic institutions are from those of the dominant power, the less likely it is to benefit from the status quo and thus the more likely it is to be *dissatisfied* with the dominant power's regime.

Levels of national satisfaction matter because dissatisfied states want the status quo to change. The dominant power prefers to maintain the status quo. If a dissatisfied state achieves sufficient power so that it believes it has the ability to change the status quo, power transition theory anticipates that the dissatisfied state would act on its perception. This leads to the main hypothesis of power transition theory, that when a dissatisfied great-power challenger achieves parity with the dominant power, the probability of international war rises dramatically. The joint presence of parity and dissatisfaction is thus central to power transition theory's expectations about when wars are likely. Parity between a satisfied great power and the dominant power is not likely to lead to war. Even a transition of power in which a satisfied challenger surpasses and succeeds the dominant power as the international system's leader is not anticipated to involve war, for the new dominant power simply maintains, perhaps with some minor alterations, the status quo instituted by the former. The former dominant power also would have little motivation to challenge a new system leader that championed a status quo to its liking.

According to power transition theory, preponderance of power at the hands of the dominant power augurs well for the avoidance of international conflict. So long as the dominant power remains notably stronger than any dissatisfied challengers, the international system is anticipated to remain stable, that is, great-power war is unlikely. An important distinction between power transition theory and some balance-of-power theories regards the potential for war created by power imbalances. According to power transition theory, a power imbalance in which the dominant power is preponderant will be peaceful. In contrast, a situation of rough equality, or parity of power between the dominant power and a dissatisfied challenger augurs a high probability of war. Accordingly, power transition theory suggests the Cold War remained cold because the Soviet Union never achieved parity with the United States.[14]

The distribution of attitudes toward the status quo is as important as the distribution of power when it comes to estimating international stability. Power transition theory suggests that the way great powers react to potential hegemons will depend on their views of the status quo. States with similar views of the status quo will not be threatened by each other's rise in power, because they do not think that increased power will be used against them. States with disparate evaluations of the status quo, however, are very concerned about each other's increases in power. In contrast to traditional balance-of-power notions, power transition theory suggests that satisfied states do not worry about the intentions of other satisfied states. They do not balance or buck-pass in an effort to constrain rising satisfied states. When states differ in their evaluations of the status quo, however, all of the security dilemma-like fears central to balance-of-power arguments apply.[15]

Power transition theory suggests that the way the great powers have behaved in the post-Cold War era is a function of their relative capabilities and evaluations of the status quo. Great powers with domestic institutions similar to those of the United States should benefit from the status quo, will more likely be satisfied, and consequently will spend little or no time or effort balancing against the United States. In fact, it is likely that satisfied states would bandwagon with the United States to bolster the existing status quo. Great powers with domestic institutions dissimilar to America's (for example, command economies or totalitarian regimes) are less likely to benefit from the international status quo, are more likely to be dissatisfied, and thus are more likely to take steps antagonistic to continued U.S. dominance of international affairs. Should such states enjoy parity with the United States, great-power war would be likely.

Post-Cold War Great-Power Behavior

Before discussing whether great-power behavior is consistent with one theory or another, it is necessary first to identify the great powers. Mearsheimer writes: "Great powers are determined largely on the basis of their relative military capability. To qualify as a great power, a state must have sufficient military assets to put up a serious fight in an all-out conventional war against the most powerful state in the world."[16] He then provides a list of great powers. Mearsheimer claims his list overlaps significantly with standard social science data sets (such as that of the Correlates of War Project). But standard lists include the United Kingdom and France as great powers after World War II, and accord China great-power status from 1950 onward.

Mearsheimer's definition has intuitive appeal but is troublesome operationally and not especially well related to his list. Surely China "put up a serious fight in an all-out conventional war" against the United States in Korea in the early 1950s. Yet China was not a great power, according to Mearsheimer, until 1991. Similarly, France's fight against Nazi Germany in 1940 was no more serious than was Poland's in 1939. If France was a great power in 1940, why not list Poland as a great power in 1939? Furthermore, why does North Vietnam not qualify as a great power in the 1960s, or Afghanistan as one in the 1980s? Perhaps, Mearsheimer might argue, everyone *believed* France would be able to put up a serious fight in 1940, but did not believe Poland would be able to put up a serious fight in 1939. Perceptions of great-power status might be important (they clearly are important in the Correlates of War project's great-powers designation because it is based on the subjective consensus of historians). But if Mearsheimer's definition is accepted, those perceptions must be of the potential great power's ability to "put up a serious fight." Well, in 1990 many estimated that the Iraqi army would be able to put up significant resistance against a U.S.-led coalition.[17] Based on ex ante perceptions of combat capability, Iraq qualifies as a great power in the early 1990s.

Mearsheimer is right to suggest that reevaluating each potential great power's status as a great power would be very time consuming. He claims to accept standard great-power designations, but then subjectively reevaluates Britain, China, and France's status after World War II. Partial reevaluations always are suspect—after all, Mearsheimer does not reevaluate any other state's status. Rather than follow his lead, I employ the standard great-power designation offered by the Correlates of War Project.[18] Accordingly, the great powers after the Cold War are Britain, China, France, Germany, Japan, Russia, and the United States. Relations among these states are most important when it comes to assessing whether great powers conform to offensive realist or power transition expectations. In the following section I briefly consider the defense and foreign policies of each great power and then evaluate this evidence from the perspectives of the two theories.[19]

BRITAIN

Since the Cold War's end, Britain has been a steadfast American ally. British forces fought alongside Americans in Iraq (twice), Yugoslavia, and Afghanistan. Britain has not removed itself from the North Atlantic Treaty Organization (NATO), has not undertaken any extensive military buildups, has not formed or even discussed counterbalancing alliances to offset American hegemony, and has not adopted any policies that might be interpreted as either balancing or buck-passing. At times, British officials act as spokes-people for joint U.S.-British positions on such important topics as interna-tional terrorism, Iraqi failure to comply with UN mandates, or potential military operations. If any behavior accurately categorizes British activity since the end of the Cold War, it would seem to be bandwagoning.

CHINA

Unlike Great Britain, China's government has not sent its armed forces to participate alongside Americans in any post-Cold War U.S. operations. Beijing abstained in the Security Council vote that authorized military force to remove Iraq from Kuwait in 1990, bitterly opposed NATO actions against Yugoslavia in 1999, provided only tacit support for American actions in Afghanistan since 2001, and threatened to veto the use of force against Iraq in 2003. The Chinese military has been undergoing restructuring and aug-mentation, featuring acquisition of new generations of fighter aircraft and warships. China's leaders regularly express dissatisfaction with American hegemony and have explored the possibility of constructing a balancing coalition with Russia against the United States. Although Beijing was unsuc-cessful in constructing a counterweight to American power, it is not difficult to interpret China's post-Cold War behavior as consistent with the dictates of offensive realism.[20]

FRANCE

Like their British allies, French units fought alongside American forces in Iraq in 1991 and Yugoslavia, and the French sent naval units to aid the United States in its war against the Taliban in Afghanistan. France has been a leader in efforts to develop an independent European military in the form of the so-called European Rapid Reaction Force. French efforts to organize an armed force for Europe, however, cannot be interpreted as a counterbal-ance to NATO or the United States. The Rapid Reaction Force is too small to serve as a counter to U.S. military power and French officials have stated repeatedly that NATO will remain Europe's primary defense organization. Until recently, France had, if anything, increased its ties with NATO since the Cold War's end. However, France is increasingly critical of American for-eign policy, specifically with respect to the 2003 war against Iraq. Even with strident verbal criticism by France's political elite, there is no evidence of French efforts either to balance or buck-pass when it comes to American preponderance. By the same token, it cannot be said that Paris wholeheartedly bandwagons with the United States.

GERMANY

Following its reunification in 1990, Germany did not remove itself from NATO, has not formed military alliances outside of NATO, and is not exploring the possibility of forming alternative alliances with other states. Instead, until recently German-American relations remained cordial, although the Germans remain extremely averse to the prospect of war anywhere. Despite this, Germany participated with American forces in NATO's air war against Serbia in 1999. Overall, Germany has bandwagoned with the United States. The only exception was strong vocal criticism of American and British military efforts against Iraq in 2003, but even then German opposition was limited to verbal complaints. Admittedly, it would be very hard for German leaders to undertake military action against American interests given that substantial numbers of American troops remain stationed on German soil, but the important aspect of the U.S. military presence in Germany is that it remains by mutual agreement. As demonstrated by forced withdrawals from the Philippines in the early 1990s, the United States will remove troops from overseas bases if the host country wants them to go. Germany apparently still desires an American military presence.

JAPAN

Japan, like Germany, is host to tens of thousands of American troops and consequently it might be hard to think of ways that Japan's government could undertake substantial steps to offset American military power. As the Cold War was ending it was common for scholars to identify Japan as the next likely great-power challenger to America's preeminent status.[21] Compared to the other great powers, however, Japan's economy has been losing ground since the end of the Cold War. A decade's worth of recession has stifled speculation that Japan would soon be in a position to challenge the United States.

Despite, or perhaps because of, its declining economic strength, Japan's behavior offers scant evidence of balancing or buck-passing. Japan has not formed any anti-U.S. alliances and has shown no interest in discussing such possible agreements. Similarly, Japan has not undergone any major military buildup, nor has it used its superior technological capability to assist any state other than the United States in its military acquisition programs. Nevertheless, the Japanese have not structured their diplomacy such that they are cordial with the United States but cold to potential buck-catchers. Indeed, in the post-Cold War world the Japanese government has felt quite free to complain about American policy at various stages. Like the Germans and British, the Japanese are most easily seen as bandwagoning with the United States, even going so far as to initiate a theater missile defense project jointly with their American allies. If the Japanese feared American power, surely they would not cooperate in efforts to develop systems intended to safeguard America from enemy missiles.

RUSSIA

Since the end of the Cold War, the Russians have undergone transformations arguably more profound than those of any other state. The Soviet Union was replaced by a much smaller Russia, with a significantly weakened economy and a pseudo-democratic government. The largest similarity between Russia now and the Soviet Union then is the persistence of a large nuclear arsenal. Although Russian officials have at times voiced concerns about NATO activities, the muted Russian response to NATO expansion flies in the face of offensive realist predictions. Aside from a nebulous "treaty of friendship" with China in the summer of 2001, there has been no Russian effort to balance American power or that of the expanded NATO alliance. Similarly, unless one interprets arms sales to various states as an effort to bolster those states' military capacities so they can balance the United States, Russia has failed to buck-pass. The closest the Russians have come to active disagreement with the United States arose with Russian threats of a Security Council veto against UN military action in Iraq. But when the United States and Britain attacked Iraq in March 2003, the Russians neither counterattacked the coalition nor assisted the Iraqis in other ways.

Since the Cold War's end Russia has, however, accepted enormous amounts of formal and informal American financial assistance. The formal assistance has been in the form of loans, approval of IMF stabilization programs, and debt forgiveness. The informal assistance is represented by the millions of dollars of investment American business has made in Russia. Incorporated into Western institutions to an extent unimaginable during the Cold War, Russia has been added to the G7 (now G8) and enjoys observer status at NATO headquarters. Cooperation between the United States and Russia in the war on terrorism has been extensive, including Russian acquiescence to the stationing of American military forces on bases in former Soviet Central Asian republics. It is hard to interpret this behavior as either balancing or buck-passing. It more closely resembles bandwagoning.

THE UNITED STATES

Since the end of the Cold War, the United States has fought two wars against Iraq, an air war against Serbia, and a multifront war against global terrorism, primarily in Afghanistan. With the exception of Iraq in 1991, these American targets have been weak states or non-state actors that would not increase America's relative international position by adding significantly to existing U.S. military, political, or economic capability. The United States also has expended much effort to advance the scope and effectiveness of international economic and security organizations. It took a lead role in the creation of the North American Free Trade Agreement (NAFTA), thus substantially linking its economy to those of Canada and Mexico. The United States also was a central player in moves to replace the General Agreement on Tariffs and Trade with the World Trade Organization, and then supported Chinese membership in the new trade organization. The United States championed the expansion of NATO to include Poland, the Czech Republic, and Hungary. In terms of military power, the United States substantially reduced its military expenditures after the Cold War: before the war on terrorism, U.S. defense spending was only two-thirds of what it had been in the late 1980s. In cooperation with Russia, the United States also has made massive cuts in its nuclear arsenal and has stopped all of its strategic nuclear modernization programs.

It is possible to consider the expansion of NATO as a power-maximizing move by the United States. It also is possible to interpret NAFTA in the same way, because America's large economy should disproportionately benefit from a free trade agreement with Mexico and Canada. It is very hard, however, to interpret America's "wars" against Serbia or Afghanistan as reasonable ways to maximize power. Furthermore, it is impossible to identify any state the United States would be trying to balance with an expanded NATO, for no state is more powerful than the United States. It also is impossible to represent American efforts to incorporate Russia and China into Western economic and security institutions as either balancing or buck-passing or power maximizing. Similarly, it is impossible to describe reductions in American defense spending, cuts in the strategic nuclear arsenal, or sharing of sophisticated military technologies such as stealth aircraft (with Britain) and missile defense (with Japan) as balancing, buck-passing, or power-maximizing behavior.

In effect, with the possible exception of China, there is little evidence of balancing, buck-passing, or power-maximizing behavior among the great powers. Instead, the dominant policy of these states since the end of the Cold War has been to maximize participation in the existing international economic and political order, led by the United States.

Offensive Realism Versus Power Transition Theory

Even a cursory account of great-power behavior since the end of the Cold War raises serious questions about offensive realism's accuracy. Although there have been great-power actions consistent with offensive realist expectations, the vast majority of great-power activities do not conform to the theory. Instead, they conform much more closely with the expectations of power transition theorists. American hegemony has (with the exception of the 2003 attack on Iraq) been peaceful, at least among the great powers. Satisfied great powers (for example, Britain, Germany, Japan) have cooperated with the United States, while dissatisfied ones (for example, China) have not. The dissatisfied great powers have not found themselves at war with the United States, however, because parity does not exist.

Both offensive realist and power transition theorists offer interpretations of recent great-power history from the perspective of their theory; interested readers are referred to those works.[22] Rather than reiterate all that material, this section focuses on five specific issues as points of comparison between the two theories: great-power bandwagoning, the American failure to take advantage of Russian or Chinese relative weakness, NATO expansion, nuclear disarmament, and offensive realism's non-falsifiability.

GREAT-POWER BANDWAGONING

It is easy to interpret British, German, Japanese, and to a lesser extent, French behavior toward the United States as bandwagoning. Recall, offensive realism specifically describes bandwagoning as unlikely among great powers, because such behavior indicates those doing the bandwagoning have given up, if only temporarily, the goal of power maximization.

But unless one assumes that the other great powers have given up power maximization, it is difficult to explain the fact that these other great powers are not abandoning NATO and are not undergoing massive military build-ups to offset America's enormous military advantages. Even with the dramatic example of European weakness compared to American capability in the air strikes against Serbia in 1999, these other great powers are not taking steps to offset American power by either forming counterbalancing coalitions or increasing their own military capability.

By contrast, British, Japanese, German, and even French behavior can easily be explained by power transition theory. The economic and political institutions of these states have much in common with the United States. They benefit from American maintenance of the international status quo while the United States benefits from their support of its institutions. These states consequently share affinity, which accords with those instances in which they cooperate (for example, in repelling Iraqi aggression against Kuwait or rooting the Taliban out of Afghanistan). These great powers also trust that the United States harbors no aggressive intentions against them. The French may use violent expressions to condemn American foreign policy viz Iraq, yet no Frenchman fears violent American reprisals in retaliation.

AMERICAN FAILURE TO TAKE ADVANTAGE OF RUSSIAN
OR CHINESE RELATIVE WEAKNESS

According to offensive realism, a state never has enough power. Only a global hegemon can be satisfied with the distribution of power, and thus only a global hegemon can enjoy the luxury of leaving the distribution of power unchanged. Other states always aspire to hegemonic status and therefore seek to accumulate more power. Weak great powers need more power to ensure their survival. Regional hegemons need more power so they can more efficiently perform their important role of being offshore balancers against aspiring regional hegemons elsewhere. Mearsheimer is very clear that, according to offensive realism, great powers will strive to dominate world politics:

> The overriding goal of each state is to maximize its share of world power, which means gaining power at the expense of other states. But great powers do not merely strive to be the strongest of all the great powers, although that is a welcome outcome. Their ultimate aim is to be the hegemon—that is, the only great power in the system.[23]

Given this fundamental alleged tenet of great-power behavior, why did the United States not invade the Soviet Union as it crumbled in the late 1980s? Why would the United States negotiate with the Chinese, rather than attack, over disputes about spy planes? What restrains the United States from seizing oil fields in Central or South America?

Even more telling is the fact that the United States has not sought to limit its most likely potential rivals and has instead actively aided the economic advancement of both Russia and China after the Cold War. America's strategies of embracing Russian democracy and of targeting massive amounts of aid to assist Russia's recovery from the economic turmoil following the Soviet Union's dissolution seem impossible to justify based on offensive realism. One would have to make the suspect argument that the United States is trying to buck-pass to the Russians the task of countering the growth of Chinese power. This idea is flatly contradicted by the fact that while the United States has been a strong financial supporter of Russia's recovery, it also has been a staunch proponent of increased economic interaction between China and the West. By repeatedly granting China most-favored-nation status and by supporting Chinese entry into the World Trade Organization, the United States aids and abets the growth of Chinese potential military capability. If the United States is bolstering Russia in hopes it will catch the buck of Chinese future aggression, why has the United States simultaneously bolstered China? Is this a bait-and-bleed strategy?[24]

From the perspective of power transition theory, American policies to engage Russia and China are easily understood. The United States is not interested in bolstering Russian or Chinese military forces so that they can offset each other in some hypothetical future war. Rather, the United States selectively, some might say perniciously, intercedes in Russian and Chinese domestic affairs in ways designed to promote the emergence of democratic and market-based institutions. The United States encourages trade with China due to a belief that this will make China's political elite dependent on continued economic expansion. Such expansion is most easily achieved by engaging with the increasingly global economy. But in order for China to continue to enjoy the prosperity associated with foreign trade and investment, China's internal legal climate must be transformed. Currently, Western firms aggrieved with their Chinese joint-venture partners have no legal standing within China from which to bring suit for damages. This limits the exposure foreign firms are willing to risk in China. If the Chinese want more business with these foreign firms, they will have to change how they interact with them. It is not hard to imagine legal reform of this nature increasing the probability of democratization within China. A democratic and capitalist China would increasingly benefit from the status quo, would increasingly be satisfied with its international position, and would consequently be able to avoid war with the United States when and if parity is attained. Similarly, American influence in Russia has been geared toward enhancing Russian economic and political openness. A democratic and capitalist Russia would easily integrate into Europe, thus heightening Russian satisfaction with the status quo and bolstering U.S. foreign and economic policy.

NATO EXPANSION

In 1999 NATO expanded by adding the Czech Republic, Hungary, and Poland to the alliance. Russian officials complained bitterly at the time about what they perceived to be an American attempt to extend influence into the previously Russian sphere, while many in the West worried NATO expansion was an unnecessary risk, bringing little additional power to the alliance while potentially inflaming Russian fears of encirclement. From the perspective of offensive realism, NATO expansion raises a number of problems. First, why would the other great powers already in NATO (Britain, France, and Germany) agree to NATO expansion? Because it strengthened U.S. power vis-à-vis a potential rival, America's NATO partners might be expected to protest the addition of other members. Additionally, why would NATO continue to exist after the common Soviet threat that motivated NATO's creation disappeared? Mearsheimer writes: "alliances are only temporary marriages of convenience."[25] If this is so, why has NATO not proven temporary and disappeared with the demise of Soviet power? Third, what is the United States hoping to gain by championing NATO expansion? Greater power? If the United States were truly interested in greater power, the addition of these three members requires more explanation. None of them is a significant military actor, and as weak frontline states that must be defended, they might actually constitute a net reduction in military capability for the United States in any conflict with Russia. If NATO expansion is instead an attempt by the United States to construct a larger balancing coalition against Russia, offensive realism must explain why the sole superpower would feel the need to balance against a weaker state.

Given the obvious significance of an expansion in the world's most powerful military alliance, it is unsurprising that offensive realists have offered an account of such activity consistent with their theory. Christopher Layne contends that NATO expansion is part of America's quest for global hegemony. In his analysis NATO is essentially a tool of American dominance over Europe, as well as a tool with which to prevent any rejuvenation of Russia.[26] Admittedly, there is a certain plausibility to this interpretation of American gains from NATO, and it might serve to explain why America favors NATO expansion. But Layne's account cannot then satisfactorily explain what existing partners, and especially the new NATO members, gain from NATO expansion and thus cannot account for why they cooperate.

Mearsheimer too has attempted to explain NATO expansion from an offensive realist perspective.[27] Rather than suggest NATO expansion conforms with offensive realist expectations, however, Mearsheimer contends that NATO expansion is both unimportant and temporary. He believes NATO is coming apart at the seams due to European fears of American power.[28] Admittedly, recent strains in the alliance over the 2003 war in Iraq might prove Mearsheimer right. If the alliance is falling apart, however, it seems odd there is no current evidence of any steps to withdraw military personnel, markedly reduce budgets, or curtail planned joint exercises. In sum, in spite of any confirming evidence and their different interpretations, both Layne and Mearsheimer predict NATO will not last.

Russia's reaction to NATO expansion is not as straightforwardly negative as often portrayed. Yes, Russians did complain about the prospect, but once expansion took place, the Kremlin did nothing to counteract it. Russia did not withdraw from any international organizations in protest nor issue any threats. It did not form a counterbalancing coalition (even though one appears available by allying with China). What's more, complaints about

NATO expansion by Russian leaders may have been window dressing. In a comprehensive survey of Russian public opinion, William Zimmerman reports: "The first wave of NATO expansion did not produce the adverse policy reaction Western critics of expansion had considered probable; indeed there was about as much support among [Russian] mass publics for joining NATO in response as there was for, for instance, canceling various key arms control agreements. Even the sharp response to NATO intervention in Kosovo muted noticeably after a period of months."[29]

International reaction to NATO expansion is consistent with power transition theory. America's great-power allies remain in NATO because they are interested in preserving the status quo, even in the absence of a Soviet threat to European security. NATO is the premier organization supporting the security status quo in the world. Consequently it is still relevant. NATO expansion to new members strongly reinforces the transformation of their societies from communist states to democratic, capitalist members of the satisfied coalition. Steps to enhance the satisfied coalition are perfectly reasonable under power transition theory.

NUCLEAR DISARMAMENT

Mearsheimer interprets the development of large nuclear arsenals by the United States and Soviet Union during the Cold War as evidence strongly consistent with offensive realism's claim that great powers never stop striving for more power.[30] The obvious problem, and one Mearsheimer fails to discuss, is that both Russia and the United States have substantially *reduced* their nuclear capabilities, sometimes even through unilateral initiatives, since the end of the Cold War. One might imagine a cessation of further weapons development and acquisition to be consistent with offensive realist dictates, much like American quiescence as it digested its 19th century territorial gains. But the actual de-targeting, decommissioning, and disposal of significant numbers of nuclear weapons defies offensive realism's explanations.

From the perspective of power transition theory, both the development of huge nuclear arsenals during the Cold War and the disarmament that followed the end of the Soviet-American confrontation are easily understood. For much of the Cold War, the Soviet's relative power position vis-à-vis the United States was improving. Some strategists on both sides of the Cold-War divide even conceived of a future transition point at which both states would be roughly equal, the Soviet Union dissatisfied, and war likely. To enhance the prospects for victory in such a war, the two sides sought to out-pace each other in types and numbers of nuclear weapons, although it proved impossible to find an escape from mutual assured destruction that would make victory in a full-scale nuclear war possible. With the end of the Cold War, however, Soviet and now Russian decline is obvious, and conse-quently there is no need to maintain enormous nuclear arsenals designed to prevent a breakout from the situation of mutual assured destruction. Even with further sharp reductions now being planned, the United States will retain more than enough weapons to ensure deterrence against rising states like China. A direct benefit of nuclear disarmament is that it removes ex-Soviet weapons from circulation. This limits the dangers of accidents and reduces the chance that nuclear weapons or nuclear materials will fall into the hands of terrorists or rogue states. At the same time, the process of mutual disarmament builds trust between the United States and Russia, and enhances the prospects of a satisfied Russia emerging after the post-Soviet transition and recovery.

OFFENSIVE REALISM'S NON-FALSIFIABILITY

The greatest shortcoming of offensive realism as a guide to understanding great-power behavior is that it is so vaguely stated that history can always be interpreted in a way consistent with the theory. In essence, it suggests noth-ing more than that great powers are always interested in power relationships, and consequently when the distribution of power changes, or threatens to change, they react in some way. This indeterminacy is complicated by Mearsheimer's discussion of different strategies states might pursue while reacting to changes in the distribution of power. He describes multiple behaviors that could be seen as either balancing or buck-passing. One of the possible actions they might take would be to do nothing (a form of buck-passing). Thus, both acting and not acting are consistent with his theory.

For example, consider Mearsheimer's discussion of great-power behavior in Europe leading up to World War II. He suggests that "both France and the Soviet Union went to considerable lengths in the 1930s to maintain armies that could stand up to the Wehrmacht. They did so to increase the likelihood that buck-passing would work."[31] At the same time (indeed, on the same page) he claims that "the United Kingdom decided not to build an army to fight alongside France on the continent. Indeed, the British cabinet decided to starve the army of funds, a move that was certainly consistent with a buck-passing strategy." Here we see both military buildups *and the absence of* military buildups as buck-passing. Doing something and doing nothing are consistent with the theory. The example raises other questions of non-falsifiability because elsewhere Mearsheimer defines building up one's military as a quintessential *balancing* activity.[32]

A second example from the same era concerns France's many alliances with central European states. Mearsheimer writes: "Those alliances remained in place after 1933, which might seem to indicate that France was not buck-passing but was committed to building a balancing coalition against Nazi Germany. In reality, however, those alliances were moribund by the mid-1930s, in good part because France had no intention of coming to the aid of its allies."[33] Not content to dismiss just France's little ententes, Mearsheimer also dismisses French efforts to secure an Anglo-French alliance with the claim that France "prized an Anglo-French alliance because it would increase the likelihood that their buck-passing strategy would work."[34] Apparently France was bolstering its *buck-passing* by trying to build a *balancing* coalition.

What about the post-Cold War world? It is possible to describe China as attempting to balance, and the other great powers as trying to buck-pass to the Chinese by doing nothing, even though this interpretation of great power behavior contradicts offensive realism's prediction that in a situation like the post-Cold War world, where the United States is nearly hegemonic, balancing by *all* threatened great powers is expected. That might make the course of post-Cold War great-power behavior consistent with offensive realism. But what could have been inconsistent with offensive realism?

What if the Soviet Union had started World War III instead of accepting the peaceful reunification of Germany within NATO? That too would have been consistent with offensive realism because it considers war one of the prime ways for a state to increase its power. What if NATO had unraveled after the Cold War and the Europeans had formed an anti-U.S. alliance? That too would be consistent with offensive realism's hypothesis of balancing in such situations. What if the United States had taken advantage of its potential hegemony by attacking the Russians, or the Chinese, before their economic recovery and growth in military capability made such an attack likely to fail? That too would be consistent with offensive realism because war can enhance a state's power and states always desire more power. I may be insufficiently creative, but I find it impossible to imagine a scenario that would be inconsistent with offensive realism.

A critic of power transition theory might claim that the absence of an agreed-on measure of whether a state is satisfied with the status quo makes that theory indeterminate. A variety of measures do exist, including alliance portfolio similarity, military buildups, money market discount rates, and disagreement about territorial boundaries.[35] But arguments over how to measure the relative satisfaction of states with the status quo have not rendered power transition theory non-falsifiable. Statistical evaluations that have used different status-quo measures (that is, alliance portfolios and military buildups) have found both evaluations to be statistically significant predictors of war. But more to the point, clear hypothetical post-Cold War scenarios have been inconsistent with power transition theory.

For example, if the Soviet Union started a war rather than merely observe German reunification, this would have been inconsistent with power transition theory because it would have been a war fought when the United States and the Soviet Union were not at parity. Similarly, if the United States attacked the declining Soviets in the late 1980s or the suffering Russians in the 1990s, this would have run counter to power transition expectations. If the United States waged a preventive war in the 1990s against a rapidly growing China, that too would have been an event contrary to power transition theory predictions. The dissolution of NATO and formation of anti-U.S. alliances among former U.S. allies would have been consistent with power transition theory only if major regime changes occurred within those old NATO states. Only then would their evaluations of the status quo have been expected to change. In short, almost any post-Cold War scenario other than what actually happened would challenge power transition theory's accuracy.

Conclusion

Do great powers behave as balance-of-power arguments suggest they should? Not if we define offensive realism as representing those arguments. Does this mean balance-of-power theory should be discarded? Perhaps surprisingly, my answer is no. Because there are as many balance-of-power theories as there are balance-of-power theorists, it would be a mistake to ignore balance-of-power considerations based on the inability of offensive realism to account for recent events.

Works by William Wohlforth and Randall Schweller differ markedly from offensive realism.[36] Their version of balance-of-power theory is quite consistent, in various ways, with power transition theory. For example, Schweller and Wohlforth argue that power transition theory and balance-of-power theory are complements rather than competitors. They describe balance-of-power theory as consistent with states engaging in peaceful and cooperative ways (as power transition's satisfied states do), of preponderance as stable and peaceful, and of unipolarity as enduring without extensive balancing. Research about great-power behavior, whether based on power transition theory or balance-of-power theory, is important. But theory, to be useful, must give at least a plausible account of recent events while offering propositions that are falsifiable. We will never develop perfectly accurate theories, and so getting the facts wrong in any specific case is not invalidation of a theory but an opportunity to explore why general patterns in world politics did not happen to materialize in a specific case. Theories, however, should be right most of the time, and we must be careful to avoid tautology by ensuring there are conditions under which our theories could be wrong.

Notes

1. John Mearsheimer, *The Tragedy of Great Power Politics* (New York: Norton, 2001); Hans Morgenthau, *Politics Among Nations,* 6th ed. (New York: Knopf, 1986); and Kenneth Waltz, *Theory of International Politics* (Reading, Mass.: Addison-Wesley, 1979).

2. A list of offensive realist work includes Erik Labs, "Beyond Victory: Offensive Realism and the Expansion of War Aims," *Security Studies* 6 (Summer 1997): 1–49; Christopher Layne, "The Unipolar Illusion: Why New Great Powers Will Rise," *International Security* 17 (Spring 1993): 5–51; and Layne, "U.S. Hegemony and the Perpetuation of NATO," *Journal of Strategic Studies* 23 (September 2000): 59–91; John J. Mearsheimer, "Back to the Future: Instability in Europe after the Cold War," *International Security* 15 (Summer 1990): 5–56; Mearsheimer, "The False Promise of International Institutions," *International Security* 19 (Winter 1994/95): 5–49; Mearsheimer, *Tragedy*; and Fareed Zakaria, *From Wealth to Power: The Unusual Origins of America's World Role* (Princeton: Princeton University Press, 1998).

3. Reviews of the two schools of realist thought are offered by Benjamin

Frankel, "Restating the Realist Case," *Security Studies* 4 (Spring 1996): ix–xx; and Stephen G. Brooks, "Dueling Realisms," *International Organization* 51 (Summer 1997): 445–77.

4. Offensive realists are divided about hegemony. Mearsheimer (*Tragedy*, 2) writes: "There are no status quo powers in the international system, save for the occasional hegemon." In contrast, Layne, ("U.S. Hegemony," 65) contends: "Hegemons cannot be status quo powers."

5. Labs, "Beyond Victory."

6. Mearsheimer, *Tragedy*, 232.

7. Evidence is offered not only by the testimonials promoting the book, but the prominence of reviews and review essays already in print. For example, see Glenn H. Snyder, "Mearsheimer's World—Offensive Realism and the Struggle for Security: A Review Essay," *International Security* 27 (Summer 2002): 149–73; and Richard N. Rosecrance, "War and Peace: Tragedy of Great Power Politics," *World Politics* 55 (October 2002): 137–66.

8. Mearsheimer, *Tragedy*, 156–58.

9. Randall L. Schweller, "Bandwagoning for Profit: Bringing the Revisionist State Back In," *International Security* 19 (Summer 1994): 72–107; and Stephen M. Walt, *The Origins of Alliances* (Ithaca: Cornell University Press, 1987).

10. Mearsheimer, *Tragedy*, 162–63.

11. Ibid., 268, emphasis added.

12. Ibid., 271.

13. Power transition theory was introduced in A. F. K. Organski, *World Politics* (New York: Knopf, 1958), first tested empirically in A. F. K. Organski and Jacek Kugler, *The War Ledger* (Chicago: University of Chicago Press, 1980), extended and elaborated in Jacek Kugler and Douglas Lemke (eds.), *Parity and War* (Ann Arbor: University of Michigan Press, 1996), and applied to American foreign policy concerns by Ronald Tammen, Jacek Kugler, Douglas Lemke, Allan Stam, Carole Alsharabati, Mark Abdollahian, Brian Efird, and A. F. K. Organski, *Power Transitions: Strategies for the 21st Century* (New York: Chatham House, 2000).

14. Douglas Lemke, "The Continuation of History: Power Transition Theory and the End of the Cold War," *Journal of Peace Research* 34 (February 1997): 23–36.

15. Power transition theory thus differs from other hegemonic theories, such as Gilpin's theory of hegemonic war. For that other theory, see Robert Gilpin, *War and Change in World Politics* (Cambridge: Cambridge University Press, 1981). Empirical evidence that status-quo evaluations are not systematically related to a state's power level is offered by Douglas Lemke and William Reed, "Power Is Not Satisfaction," *Journal of Conflict Resolution* 42 (August 1998): 511–16. Similarly, power transition theory differs from hegemonic stability theory, since power transition theory does not regard the dominant power's status quo as necessarily being a collective good. For hegemonic stability theory, see Robert Keohane, *After Hegemony* (Princeton: Princeton University Press, 1984).

16. Mearsheimer, *Tragedy*, 5.

17. Evidence is offered by Bob Woodward, *The Commanders* (New York: Simon and Schuster, 1991), 207.

18. The Correlates of War great-power list is available at <http://pss.la.psu.edu/intsys.html>.

19. A more detailed and better-documented discussion of these states' behavior can be found in John M. Owen, "Transnational Liberalism and U.S. Primacy," *International Security* 26 (Winter 2001/2002): 117–52.

20. This offensive realism–friendly interpretation of China's foreign policy is contradicted by at least one prominent China scholar. For an alternative view, see Alastair Iain Johnston, "Is China a Status Quo Power?" *International Security* 27 (Spring 2003): 5–56.

21. An offensive realist prediction of Japan's rise is offered by Layne, "The Unipolar Illusion."

22. See, for example, Mearsheimer, *Tragedy*, esp. chap. 9; and Tammen et al., *Power Transitions*, esp. chaps. 4 through 8.

23. Mearsheimer, *Tragedy*, 2.

24. Described as a strategy "whereby a state tries to weaken its rivals by provoking a long and costly war between them" in ibid., 139.

25. Ibid., 33.

26. Layne, "U.S. Hegemony."

27. Mearsheimer, *Tragedy*, chap. 10.

28. Ibid., 391.

29. William Zimmerman, *The Russian People and Foreign Policy* (Princeton: Princeton University Press, 2002), 189.

30. Mearsheimer, *Tragedy*, 224–32.

31. Ibid., 309.

32. Ibid., 157.

33. Ibid., 310.

34. Ibid., 313.

35. For alliance portfolio similarity, see Woosang Kim, "Alliance Transitions and Great Power War," *American Journal of Political Science* 35 (October 1991): 833–50; for military buildups see Douglas Lemke, *Regions of War and Peace* (Cambridge: Cambridge University Press, 2002) esp. chap. 4; for money market discount rates see Bruce Bueno de Mesquita, "Pride of Place: The Origins of German Hegemony," *World Politics* 43 (October 1990): 28–52; and for territorial boundaries see Arie Kacowicz, "Explaining Zones of Peace," *Journal of Peace Research* 32 (August 1995): 265–76.

36. See William C. Wohlforth, "The Stability of a Unipolar World," *International Security* 24 (Summer 1999): 5–41; and Randall L. Schweller and William C. Wohlforth, "Power Test: Evaluating Realism in Response to the End of the Cold War," *Security Studies* 9 (Spring 2000): 60–107.

CHAPTER 3

The Political Economy of Balance of Power Theory

MARK R. BRAWLEY

Does the theory of balance of power offer guidance for conducting economic policy? Realist proponents of the theory appreciate the importance of economics as the mainspring of military power, but they have failed to integrate fully the effects of economic cooperation and competition into their theoretical framework. The economic components of balancing, bandwagoning, or buck-passing—key concepts used to describe balance of power politics—have not been described by existing theory. This omission highlights a serious shortcoming in the theory that leads to indeterminate predictions about state behavior. By failing to integrate an important aspect of national policy into their theory, realists also have failed to take advantage of an opportunity to better understand how states deal with the current balance of power and anticipated changes in the economic and military capabilities of potential competitors and allies.

The limitations of using balance of power theory to understand world politics or to offer guidance concerning national strategy are evident in today's foreign policy debates. Realists, for example, often have difficulty articulating exactly why they oppose current U.S. economic policy toward China. Offensive realism, as laid out by John Mearsheimer, identifies several policy options in addition to balancing.[1] As he defines it, offensive realism is a minimal (or essential) version of realism. In an anarchic international system, each state must fear that another state will accrue enough power to dominate the international system. If one state does rise to a dominant position, all other states will lose their independence. To prevent such an outcome, great powers that anticipate the rise of another state will wish to aggregate sufficient power to stop the ascending great power, either through deterrence or through war.

Early versions of balance of power theory maintained that great powers had no choice but to balance against potential threats. This could be accomplished by enhancing power in one of two ways: by forming an alliance (external balancing) or by harnessing additional domestic resources (internal balancing). Yet theorists also realized that it might make little sense for a weak state to join an alliance if it did not contribute enough power to make balancing effective. Instead, it might try to join the power aspiring to dominate the system, a policy referred to by theorists as bandwagoning. Bandwagoning, however, is rarely a preferred strategy because bandwagoners lose their freedom to maneuver—if not their sovereignty—to the aspiring dominant power.

Theorists have identified two other options great powers have pursued—though realists consider these also to be quite risky. The first is buck-passing. In an anarchic setting, a great power may choose not to balance or to bandwagon, if it anticipates that others will act to deter or prevent the ascending power from gaining hegemony. This is risky because a buck-passer places its own long-term interests in the hands of others and its faith in its own ability to calculate the interactions of other great powers. The second alternative strategy is appeasement, whereby a great power provides concessions to the rising power, in hopes of satisfying the aspirant's desires short of systemic dominance. Given their assumptions about the desires of great powers, realists generally deem this option foolhardy.

Realists argue implicitly that economic policy decisions are related to balance of power politics and policies. Yet they rarely develop a comprehensive understanding of how well their concepts translate into the economic realm. Indeed, realists often have trouble moving from broad logical constructs of strategy to specific military postures or diplomatic positions—a problem that confronts many of the authors in this volume. Not surprisingly then observers typically disagree when evaluating the purpose or impact of specific economic policies pursued today. Their differences arise from unspoken assumptions about the relationship between economics and power. By making these unspoken assumptions explicit, and by then introducing them into balance of power theory, I will identify the international economic policies associated with the five essential balancing strategies: external balancing, internal balancing, bandwagoning, buck-passing, and appeasement. I also identify the conditions that lead states to pursue such strategies. These conditions highlight the sources of indeterminacy in the theory.

Many theorists agree that the theory does not perform well in the post-

Cold War era, though that evaluation may change in light of diplomatic maneuvering during the run-up to the U.S. war against Iraq. Most responses to this assessment, however, have been to generate rival theories, add ad hoc addenda to the theory's core assumptions, or modify those assumptions significantly. Such responses represent a "degenerative problem-shift" in Lakatosian terms. In this chapter, I seek to add elements to the theory that are consistent with its realist origins, but help specify how states manage their power. This modification is merely one possible political economic interpretation—others remain possible.[2]

The Relationship Between Power and Wealth

Difficulties in constructing links between the strategic options in balance of power theory and particular economic policies arise for two reasons. First, economic interaction between states is usually thought to be mutually beneficial. Economic studies focus on the creation and distribution of wealth. Unlike realists who are concerned with the effects of relative changes in military and economic power, economists generally think of wealth in absolute terms. To know whether a state is becoming richer or poorer, economists measure its ability to consume goods and services over time, rather than compare it vis-à-vis other states. By contrast, realists argue that accumulating wealth should never be a state's primary goal, although they concede that wealth accumulation is a legitimate and likely goal of governments. Wealth is important in so far as it is a critical component of power.[3] For realists, power is the commodity that states should pursue and value over all others.

Second, economic gains can be made through international economic cooperation, but the gains are likely to be reaped by all participants. In the simplest realist arguments, states therefore should forego all external economic contacts, or structure their international economic ties in such ways that they ensure that they alone reap benefits. Realists would suggest that states should be wary of interactions that produce absolute gains, especially if potential competitors reap greater relative gains from economic interaction. In other words, realists suggest that under certain circumstances, states should pass up the potential economic gains possible through international trade and instead focus on internal economic development. Since few economic interactions distribute returns equally, one partner would always have a reason to refuse participation, under simple versions of realism. Internal efforts are more predictable and—unlike external economic cooperation—are not likely to produce benefits that the state cannot capture for itself. (This provides the link between realism and imperialism.) While this sounds costly, when relative gains are crucial, the self-imposed costs may be less than the costs inflicted on others. The logic rests on two elements of realism that flow from the assumption of anarchy in the international system: a state cannot rely on any other for assistance, and all other states pose at least a potential threat.

Balance of power theory, however, does not exclude the possibility of international cooperation. In fact, it rests on the assumption that some states share an interest in defeating a common threat (see Levy, this volume). States will therefore band together to assist one another under certain conditions. Thus, another economic policy consistent with realist thinking is for states to engage in trade and investment with their probable allies, not their potential enemies.[4] Either economic strategy—denying trade to everyone, or focusing only on likely allies—may support balancing strategies. The first fits nicely with internal balancing and the second with external balancing. Deciding how to achieve a balance depends first and foremost on the availability of allies—if there are no likely allies, external balancing is not an option.

When considering which economic policy will match a specific balance of power strategy, policymakers also must take into account that wealth does not perfectly translate into power. The two may be coincident over the long run, or they may not.[5] Simple conjectures on this relationship are not likely to be confirmed through empirical studies, since the correlation has changed considerably over the last few centuries. In the mercantilist era (prior to the early 19th century), wealth could be used to purchase power "off the shelf" in the form of armies for hire. Major powers competed fiercely for gold and silver, because these precious metals paid for armed forces. Not until the Napoleonic Wars introduced mass armies motivated by nationalism did the relationship between wealth and power begin to change. Although wealth remained important, population and the land to support it became critical economic components of state power. The ability of states to collect taxes and borrow from their citizens created new, stable internal sources of wealth, while the industrial revolution allowed for mass production of weapons and ammunition to arm the new conscript armies. Increasing specialization and sophistication in production created greater wealth and new technologies, but also introduced new complications into the effort to convert wealth to military purposes. Leaders now had to anticipate which new technologies would have the greatest impact on the battlefield, especially by countering the technologies and weapons their likely opponents preferred.

The rate at which economic capacity can be converted to military power also has varied. Calculations about the effectiveness of economic policies in balancing must include a sense of the time required to convert wealth to power. In World War II, new fighter aircraft could be brought onto the design table, developed, tested, and put into production in a few short years. If one began to design a new aircraft today, however, it would not likely be in service for another decade, and would be expected to remain in service for at least two decades after that. By contrast, advances in computer and communications technologies mean that new weapons can be developed and fielded relatively quickly. One therefore needs to consider the economics behind military power in terms of the mix of three parts. First is the overall investment in the economy. If a state diverts too much money to defense expenditures today, that investment could become a drag on economic growth in the longer run. Second, a state must invest in weapons design and production facilities in the medium term to ensure production capacity in the future. Third, a state must consider the short-term relationship between economics and military power: it must pay for current military production and deployment.

Since wealth spent on military arms today cannot be invested to generate more wealth for the future, converting economic resources into power is impossible without an assessment of *when* one wishes to maximize power and how long it will take to field the most effective weapons. Predicting (or evaluating) the economic component of a balancing strategy, therefore, depends on factors typically missing from the balance of power theory. A complete balance of power theory must include not only information about the distribution of power in the international system, but also assumptions about the specific time when a balance is needed, as well as an understanding of the rate at which wealth can be transformed into power. Otherwise theories of balancing provide no real guidance on how to manage political and economic policies needed to sustain specific balance of power strategies.

EXTERNAL BALANCING

When we think of balancing in international relations, external balancing is the first image that comes to mind. Theory predicts that before one state can rise to the preeminent position in the international system, other states will band together to prevent such an outcome. If the rising power's ambition is to "divide and conquer," the potential victims must "unite and resist." Alliances are the key tool for states to guarantee their survival, thereby preventing the emergence of a global hegemon that would replace the anarchic international system.

Alliances can harness the mutually beneficial aspects of international economic policies to make themselves more successful and more militarily powerful. If trade or international investment makes both parties better off, then such activities should be diverted from the threatening power. External balancing strategies should redirect trade toward alliance members. In the Cold War, the United States organized economic activities along these lines,[6] and there is broad empirical support for the notion that free trade is more likely within alliances.[7] Balancing alliances may support trade and investment links among themselves as a way to make the alliance more credible, since economic ties solidify domestic constituencies supporting the alliance.[8]

INTERNAL BALANCING

Since the early 19th century, national unification and economic growth have arguably been a greater sources of change in the distribution of power than the shuffling of alliance memberships, hence the interest in power transitions. (See Lemke this volume.) In the aftermath of the industrial revolution, countries had the option to rearrange their internal economic and political practices to divert more wealth than ever before to the production of military capability.

Whereas external balancing is associated with alliances, internal balancing is linked to arms races. The implication is that states seeking to dominate their rivals are unlikely to develop greater power through external means because potential allies in their effort to seek domination will be hard to find. Increases in a nation's aggregate power must therefore come from harnessing domestic sources. The best way to harness a national economy to increase military capability, however, is unclear. Should a state immediately convert economic resources into military assets? Or would it be wiser to invest in greater economic potential, so as to have greater resources available in the future? Whereas external balancing alters the distribution of power quickly (and less permanently, since alliances can shift with the stroke of a pen), internal balancing is a way to alter the distribution of power over the long term.

The international economic policies that complement internal balancing emphasize the relative gains associated with international trade and investment. Each country must pay close attention to where the relative gains from international economic activity accumulate. If trade generates wealth for all participants, then states seeking to balance through internal means must ensure that they gain more from that trade than do any potential adversaries. The same holds for international investment, though here the guidance is clearer—invest in your own economy rather than others'.[9]

BANDWAGONING

If a great power cannot hope to tilt the distribution of power in its favor through either external or internal balancing, it may find it wiser to try to ally with the coalition of the great power aspiring to dominate the system. Joining the weaker coalition would not be rational if there were no hope that doing so would deter the rising power. This theory is usually associated with Stephen Walt's analysis of the behavior of lesser powers, but examples can also be found of great powers behaving along these lines, especially once war between other great powers has broken out.[10]

Bandwagoning by small powers makes sense. By definition, their size makes it unlikely that their weight in a coalition would be capable of tilting the balance of power one way or the other. Understanding why great powers might bandwagon, however, requires the introduction of conditional factors that determine the availability of useful allies. If a major power lacks available allies, then external balancing is not an option. Similarly, if great-power allies are available, but are unlikely to do more than deter the dominant power from exercising its preponderant capabilities, then perhaps even a great power may decide to bandwagon rather than balance. A great power geographically isolated from potential allies, for example, may not believe that the others will be able to rescue it from the dominant power's attack. In such a situation, the deterrent effect of the balancing coalition can only be made credible through very binding alliances.[11] Internal balancing remains an option, however, even for an isolated great power.

The international economic policy equivalents of bandwagoning have rarely been discussed. If we interpret bandwagoning loosely ("if you can't beat 'em, join 'em"), then bandwagoning would mean abandoning the balancing strategies described above in order to build greater economic ties with the dominant power. Incorporating both an economic element *and a time element* into the logic of the strategy helps us make sense of why bandwagoning would ever appeal to a great power. Since economic ties can deliver benefits to both parties, the weaker power might hope to survive in the short run by allying with the hegemonic power, but add to its current economic base as well. If current economic gains can be converted to military power in the future, the bandwagoning state might improve its power potential so that it could reassert its autonomy at some point in the future.

BUCK-PASSING

Buck-passing occurs when a great power declines membership in the balancing alliance out of the belief that this coalition already has aggregated enough power to deter or defeat the dominant power, or is likely to act even without its participation. Rather than commit itself to this alliance, the great power leaves it up to others to protect the international system from dominance by a single power. It is "shirking" in terms of providing for its own defense. Realists typically criticize states for having employed buck-passing in the past. It is clearly a risky strategy. But under what conditions would this strategy be rational?

Since converting economic wealth into power is costly, avoiding those costs through buck-passing may be sensible if the state believes it is not under immediate threat, or if it requires time to invest in its own economy to develop the capacity to produce military forces. Joining a balancing alliance means nothing unless the state also contributes credible forces to that alliance. Indeed, if the state does not provide enough additional military power, it can actually be a drag on the alliance by stretching defensive forces further. By passing the buck, a great power might hope to delay the need to convert wealth into power. It may avoid maximizing its power in the short run in favor of enhancing its wealth and therefore its power for the future.

At first glance, the economic analogue of buck-passing appears to be obvious: "free-riding" on collective action. In terms of trade and international investment, however, it is much more difficult to identify a set of policies that would be distinct from some of the policies already mentioned. One would need to evaluate the mix of military and economic policies employed. For example, a great power that chose to buck-pass on military alliances also could try to redirect international economic policy toward its probable future allies. Buck-passing on military matters while trying to balance internally makes less sense, and states would be unlikely to buck-pass on the military side while either bandwagoning in economic relations or attempting external balancing.

APPEASEMENT

Appeasement refers to the granting of concessions to the great power threatening to gain ascendance over others in the international system. Historically, such concessions have been offered in hopes that the power aspiring to dominance will be satiated and cease making demands or aggregating power. Realists are usually extremely critical of this logic because they do not believe that states could ever be satisfied short of attaining complete dominance.[12] While one could challenge this logic on a variety of grounds, it underscores a vital issue: how does one determine what would actually satisfy the rising power? The decision makers adopting appeasement typically cannot provide this critical bit of information, since the theories they rely on do not provide compelling counters to realist ideas.

The economic equivalent of appeasement would be to redirect trade and investment to benefit the aspiring hegemonic power in such a way that it became satisfied. The trade and investment might benefit both the weaker power and the ascending great power in terms of wealth, or perhaps one might gain relatively more—would one outcome be more satisfactory to the aspiring hegemonic power than any others? We must once again face the problem that realism offers no clear guidance on this matter, other than to criticize the whole approach, since realists hold that domination of the entire system is the only thing likely to satiate a great power.

Appeasement, even in economic terms alone, does not make much sense in combination with a separate military posture. Economic appeasement combined with military balancing makes sense only if policymakers have a sense of when balancing might better occur; in this case appeasement repre-

TABLE 3.1

Shorthand/Typology of Policy Options

	Economic Components	Military Components
External Balancing	Strengthen oneself and one's allies through trade; exclude enemies.	Find allies; join weaker alliance
Internal Balancing	Strengthen oneself through economic development; exclude all others.	Arms race
Bandwagoning	Develop ties to dominant power; wait for future.	Join dominant power's alliance
Buck-Passing	Free ride —increase one's wealth, not power, in short run.	Neutrality
Appeasement	Make concessions while building oneself up for the long run.	Make concessions

sents a choice not to balance today, but perhaps to place the state in a better position to balance in the future. In such a situation, however, policies that would build up potential allies would make more sense. Even buck-passing would be a preferable policy. Appeasement is the least likely way a great power would buy time in the hopes of accruing wealth and power for the future, because appeasement eventually could eliminate the state's ability to act independently in the face of the insatiable and ever more powerful hegemon. (See Table 3.1.)

The Importance of the Calculus of the Transformation of Wealth

When would states be expected to initiate one or another balancing strategy? Realists such as Mearsheimer argue that balancing is always the best policy; situational factors dictate only whether internal or external balancing should be pursued. There is little evidence, however, of a coalition forming against the United States in the aftermath of the Cold War. Those who suggest some forms of balancing are occurring look less at present-day strategies, and more at how present investments and economic restructuring could create a different (that is, more balanced) distribution of power in the future. The determination of whether preparations for future balancing are occurring depends on the answers to two questions: what are states' estimates of whether and when balancing will have to occur, and how long will it take to transform wealth into military capability?

Identifying the point in time at which a state wishes to create the balance of power is crucial to knowing whether balancing is under way or contemplated. The correct military and economic strategy for constructing a balance twenty years from now may not be the same strategy for creating a balance today. Assumptions about time often have shaped grand strategy decisions in the past. Realists, however, too often overemphasize the degree of threat in a state's immediate security environment. On the contrary, states often are less concerned about their survivability today, and instead are looking well into the future when considering the likelihood of external threats. This may make policies other than balancing—even appeasement—less risky than realists fear.

An emphasis on the role of timing in the decision to balance implies that policymakers have some sense of the location of the threat, as well as its nature and intensity. The theory of balance of power, however, tends to focus solely on the distribution of power for locating both interests and capabilities. In my estimation this is highly unrealistic and is not consistent with the historical record.[13] This logic would imply that states respond to threats only after they fully materialize and would not respond to anticipated loss of relative strength. Estimates must also be made about the rate at which economic resources can be transformed into military power. If leaders believe that economic assets can be converted into military strength quickly, then economic policies have to reflect relative-gains concerns. In this case, states may feel less secure relying on allies, and therefore prefer self-reliance. If a state needs a longer time, or if its transformation of resources into military power is costly, then economic policy might stress investment and higher levels of inter-alliance trade.

Adding in these two new pieces of information—when to balance and how long it takes to arm—provides us with a better sense of the appeal of balancing versus its alternatives. Table 3.2 illustrates how these two variables determine which of the policies is rational when a major power is confronted with a dominant power that it considers to be a threat in the short run. In

TABLE 3.2

Conditions Shaping the Choice of Strategy: *Balance Now*

Rate of Transformation of Wealth to Power	AVAILABILITY OF ALLIES	
	Yes	*No*
Rapid	External balancing plus arms race	Internal balancing plus arms race
Slow	External balancing, invest in allies	Internal balancing, invest at home *or* bandwagon

Table 3.3, the interaction of the same factors is illustrated in a situation where states decide the dominant power is not an immediate threat, and they can afford to balance over the long term.

In the scenarios represented in the top two boxes in Table 3.2, the ability to convert wealth to power quickly drives states to spend resources on arms in the short term. Arms races result, whether or not allies are available. These outcomes are consistent with the more dire realist assumptions. But note what happens when we broaden assumptions about the time it takes to convert wealth to power. In this case, economic calculations address the longer term. A state that can pursue external balancing (because allies are available) will do so, but the economic calculations mandate that the state invest in itself as well as its probable allies. Although international economic activity could enhance the wealth of the state's allies as well as itself, concerns about the relative gains from overseas trade or investment are muted. If other major powers are not available as alliance partners, however, then it becomes harder to calculate the logical path for states to take. Investing in the home economy would be the best way to maximize potential power for the future (since there are no alternatives). Yet since we are assuming the threat must be responded to in the short run, bandwagoning is also an option.

Table 3.3 illustrates what happens when the first assumption—the need to strike a balance immediately—is relaxed. A shift in this part of the time calculation brings it into play with the second time factor, the time needed to convert economic resources into military power. If a state can convert economic assets to military power quickly, should it invest in its own econ-

TABLE 3.3
Conditions Shaping the Choice of Strategy: *Balance Later*

Rate of Transformation of Wealth to Power	AVAILABILITY OF ALLIES	
	Yes	*No*
Rapid	?	Bandwagon, invest at home
Slow	Buck-pass, invest for long term	Appease, invest at home

omy, or in the economies of its allies? Should the state, rather than invest, instead spend on either its own weapons programs or those of its allies? Once the need for an immediate balance is lifted, these choices become indeterminate. Investing at home is a much more obvious choice when wealth can be switched to power quickly and there are no allies available. A state may have to bandwagon in the short run while building up assets, but since we have assumed no immediate threat, even appeasement becomes a viable option.

By contrast, buck-passing makes sense if a state believes that it is wiser to invest in one's own economic base for a future conflict, leaving others to deter or defeat the aspiring dominant power today. Appeasement is an appealing choice when the offer of concessions to the dominant power (which would add to its power in the short run) can be traded off for additional time to increase one's own strength to achieve a balance in the future.

Applying the Findings

Although the links between the military and economic components of various balancing strategies reflect economic and strategic logic, they also must contribute to our understanding of history to be of practical value. To demonstrate their validity, I compare the framework described in the previous section to several critical decisions great powers made in selecting grand strategy. The cases are familiar, and therefore the descriptions are brief. They are intended to illustrate how crucial assumptions about timing and the relationship between power and wealth influenced the way states selected among the various strategic options identified by balance of power theory.

U.S. POLICIES DURING THE COLD WAR

In 1950, the Truman administration produced National Security Council Planning Document 68, often referred to as NSC 68, which reflected a critical turning point in American policies toward the Soviet Union after World War II. NSC 68 evaluated the Soviet Union's role in the international system, described the nature of the threat it posed to U.S. interests, and proposed a U.S. response. The memorandum, in evaluating the relative strength of Soviet and U.S. armed forces, judged that the Soviets had continued to maintain large military forces after the end of World War II, and predicted that the strength of the Soviet military would increase in the future.

Most significantly, NSC 68 identified a critical time frame within which the United States needed to create forces to counter the Soviet threat, given American beliefs regarding its own ample resources. American decision makers pinpointed "a year of maximum danger," 1954, when Soviet power would peak. In other words, NSC 68 suggested that the United States would have to prepare to balance Soviet power quickly. Weapons procurement and operational readiness were geared toward meeting Soviet power in the short term. As the balance of power framework would predict, this estimate, reinforced by the outbreak of the Korean War, led U.S. leaders to bolster a policy of external balancing by transforming the North Atlantic Treaty Organization (NATO) from a political alliance into a standing military organization. The United States also entered into formal alliances with other states outside NATO, for example, the Australia-New Zealand-United States (ANZUS) pact. In terms of economic policy, the Marshall Plan, General Agreement on Tariffs and Trade (GATT), and export controls by NATO members had the effect of strengthening economic ties among NATO members and excluding the Soviet Union from the economic benefits produced by this increased trade. These outcomes are consistent with the predictions contained in the lower right box in Table 3.2.

The next big shift in American strategy began to take shape in early 1953, when the Eisenhower administration rejected Harry Truman's approach to containing Soviet power. The key change in American thinking was not a reevaluation of the distribution of forces, Soviet intentions, or possible alliance members, but rather a new estimate of the *time frame* for achieving a balance. If the competition between the superpowers were to persist beyond 1954, perhaps into the foreseeable future, maximizing combat power by devoting U.S. resources to strengthen allies quickly was no longer an optimal strategy. President Dwight Eisenhower believed the economy needed to be managed for competition over the long haul; as he put it in his campaign speeches, "security" had to be matched with "solvency." This new thinking was implemented in NSC 162/2, better known as the basis for the "New Look" strategy.

The Eisenhower administration turned away from fulfilling the expensive NATO conventional military buildup agreed to during the alliance's 1952 Lisbon meeting, and instead chose to respond to the long-term Soviet threat through internal balancing. Relatively inexpensive U.S. nuclear forces would expand in size and capability to balance Soviet conventional superiority in Europe. The New Look thus capitalized on advances in nuclear technology and long-range aviation that could be developed more quickly and cheaply than the conventional capability of the NATO alliance. In economic terms, the shift to internal balancing was accompanied by a change in U.S. economic policy. The Eisenhower administration made fewer concessions to its allies on trade and aid than had its predecessor. Although it still sought to exclude likely enemies from participating in the trade and international investment regimes led by Washington, the administration attempted to devote more economic resources to long-term U.S. economic development, and abandoned plans to devote massive resources to its allies to strengthen their military capabilities quickly.

Subsequent changes in the mix of U.S. economic and military strategy also correspond to the economic logic outlined in the earlier sections of the chapter, although the theory can become indeterminate when policymakers estimate that they can achieve a military balance over the long term. The Nixon administration attempted to bolster its strength by creating a de facto alliance with the People's Republic of China, while also engaging in a policy of détente with the Soviet Union. These efforts reflected waning domestic support for America's foreign policy, but were also meant to buy time to restore the country's economic health. The United States matched a perceived increase in Soviet capability by adding a great-power ally, China, and not by diverting additional economic resources to the military competition with the USSR. Nixon's was a sophisticated effort to balance through external means at least in the short run, but it emphasized economic development to strengthen U.S. capabilities in the long run. Economic ties to the Soviet Union were opened, but only in ways meant to make it dependent on the United States. This set of decisions highlights how different strategies can be used to effect balancing in different periods. A short-term balance is achieved through the alliance posture, while the longer-term balance is achieved through economic policies.

Ronald Reagan abandoned the balancing strategy the Nixon administration initiated by increasing short-term military investment. This shift was prompted by the dual perception that Soviet military capability was on the rise and that the United States had the economic strength needed to compete effectively with a faltering Soviet economy. Disputes between the United States and its allies over economic ties with the Soviet bloc heightened as the Reagan administration sought to limit the economic contacts with the Soviets that had been formed during the period of détente. Governments in Europe and Japan resisted American efforts, both because they disagreed about the level of the threat coming from the Soviet side and because they were unwilling to give up the benefits of economic trade with the Soviet bloc. To create military capability quickly, the United States was willing to "go it alone" by increasing short-term expenditures (and increasing debt), which also had the effect of ratcheting up pressure on the Soviet-bloc economies.

American policies in the Cold War illuminate the importance of estimates about the timing of military threats when leaders make strategic choices. The most rational policy to pursue, among variants of balancing and its alternatives, depends not only on the availability of allies, but also on decisions concerning whether to achieve a balance today or to increase future capabilities to meet potential threats. The ability to convert resources into military power rapidly also shapes decisions concerning the mix of alliance and economic policies implemented.

BRITAIN'S CRITICAL POLICY DECISIONS

Britain's strategic and diplomatic history often is referred to as one of the best examples of a state's commitment to the pursuit of balancing. When considering British actions in the years leading up to World War I and World War II, however, it is clear that the United Kingdom employed several different kinds of policies. Beginning in the late 1880s, Britain engaged in an arms race against Germany. Britain did not match this internal balancing, however, with exclusionary economic policies. Moreover, Britain was unsure of the location of threats—were France and Russia just as likely to be enemies? Once the British government settled its differences with these countries through diplomacy, it was able to join them to balance against Germany, although it chose to do so out of the public eye. While Britain balanced through both external and internal means from 1907 on, it did not exclude others from developing ties to its economy. This strategy is largely consistent with the upper-right box in Table 3.2.

In the interwar period, Britain began to implement exclusionary trade and investment policies. But as the Great Depression spread, this behavior was more a response to the economic policies of others than a conscious effort to boost British military might. The British treasury in fact used the "Ten-Year Rule" until 1932 to provide justification for a cap on military expenditures. The Ten-Year Rule held that another major war was not likely for ten years, and thus assumed that the need for balancing (or for military expenditures) lay only in the future. Given this strategic assessment and the fact that it would take time to convert the peacetime economy to a war footing, buck-passing became the most logical strategy for Britain to follow. British investment in the domestic economic base, to increase wealth for the future, steadily intensified through the 1930s. Expenditures on actual forces also increased in the late 1930s, once the Ten-Year Rule was abandoned. Britain chose to appease Nazi Germany in 1938 only because the British military leadership declared the country unprepared to fight, and political leaders feared balancing would polarize diplomacy, leading to war sooner rather than later.[14] British political leaders also may have lacked faith in their allies. The critical factor that led to a policy of appeasement concerned the time required to convert economic assets into military capability, given the near certainty that such capability would be needed in the future—few doubted Nazi intentions or the military threat that Germany could pose to Britain.

Britain's policies in the late 19th and early 20th centuries illustrate again the crucial role that assessments of the time available to balance and required to arm play in selecting balancing strategies. The need to achieve a short-run balance against Germany determined strategy in the years leading up to World War I, including the naval arms race. In the 1920s and 1930s, the Ten-Year Rule dominated strategic thinking. The perception that military threats lay somewhere in a distant future made it possible for the British to give priority to building up their country's economic base.

In sum, estimates about time played a critical role in the decisions made by British and American statesmen about the balancing option that best fit their current and future strategic circumstances. Achieving a sufficient degree of power to deter an enemy was always their goal, but the most rational means to that end depended very much on assumptions about *when* the threat would be greatest and how long it would take to convert economic power to military capability. Changes in these two assumptions about timing, which most balance of power theorists have ignored, can explain shifts in the balance of power policies followed by the United States and Great Britain in the 20th century.

What Are Major Powers Doing Today?

What balancing policies are major powers implementing today? Are they following the precepts of balance of power theory? The answers to these questions hinge on the assumptions each power makes about timing. The United States presently is the world's dominant power. Are there any major powers that believe they are immediately threatened by the United States? Most possible contenders—the European Union, Japan, or even India—probably do not perceive the United States to be a threat to their survival in the short or even medium term. Russia and China, however, might feel threatened by American power in the short term. Do the policy decisions made in Moscow and Beijing support the notion that they are preparing to match America's overwhelming power quickly? What about the policies being followed by other potential great powers such as India, Japan, and the European Union?

To simplify matters, the analysis will assume that it takes time to convert economic assets into military might, that is, the normal ten-year delay between design and deployment of major weapons systems. The options contained in the upper two boxes in Tables 3.2 and 3.3 therefore won't be relevant to this section. Chinese, Russian, Japanese, Indian, and European officials thus have three remaining scenarios on which to base their choices. First, they might believe that they need to balance the United States or another great power in the short run. Second, policymakers might believe that they need to achieve a balance some time in the future, but useful allies will not be available. Third, leaders might desire to achieve a balance in the future, and they believe that potential allies will be available.

CHINA

The prime candidate for balancing the United States today or in the medium term is China. As one of the few great powers to have remained outside of formal American alliances for a long time, and with an economic platform that could challenge U.S. dominance in the long run, it alone has both the potential might and the political motivation to confront American dominance. Yet, what mix of economic and military strategies has China followed since the end of the Cold War? Do these strategies demonstrate that it is preparing to balance against the United States?

For the purpose of balancing over the short run, China lacks available allies to strike up a balancing coalition. Russia is not likely to add to China's military strength, especially if the Russian nuclear arsenal continues to shrink in size; instead it would be a drag on Chinese power. Europe and Japan are formally aligned with the United States. India might be a potential ally, although India's leaders likely fear China more than they fear the United States. Without viable allies, China must choose between trying to achieve a balance alone through internal measures or bandwagoning.

If we consider the next scenario, where the aim is to create a balance in the future without viable allies, then the rational choice for China would be to appease the United States while continuing to build up its economic resources. Even if possible allies exist, the framework predicts that China will pass the buck and concentrate on bolstering its economy. In each case, China's dominant strategy is to concentrate on internal economic development, if it ever hopes to balance against the United States. It is therefore perhaps not surprising that China is in fact promoting stronger economic ties with the United States.

American policy toward China, by contrast, is based on the very different assumption that the internal politics of the People's Republic can be transformed through political and economic interaction. U.S. officials generally hope that this transformation will convert China into a status-quo power, although some voice concerns that American companies are providing China with the rope it needs to "hang" the United States. Mearsheimer, for example, notes that "Whether China is democratic and deeply enmeshed in the global economy or autocratic and autarkic will have little effect on its behavior."[15] In Mearsheimer's view, increasing economic ties with China is likely to increase that country's wealth, but that will only make it stronger, not more satisfied. This makes American policy similar to appeasement, though Mearsheimer does not use that word. By contrast, others argue that the United States should take the risk that economic engagement will transform China because China could not hope to match the American economy for several decades to come (see Ross, this volume).

RUSSIA

In contrast to China, Russia is still in an economic decline that began more than a decade ago (see Wohlforth, this volume). Russia might be able to turn to Europe or China for alliance partners that would add to its strength, although it is more likely to be a drain than an asset to any alliance it joins. Russia's weakness also makes it unlikely that others will wish to have it as an ally. Instead, major powers will probably pander to Russia diplomatically in the short term, while in general considering it the weakest of the major powers.

If it feels threatened by the United States in the short run, Russia is likely to search for external allies, hoping to develop economic ties with them. Russia would be willing to help arm its allies, since it has the remnants of a military-industrial complex that can still produce deadly, if not exactly state-of-the-art, weapons. Russia is more likely, however, to concentrate on re-building its economy or bandwagoning with the United States. If Russian leaders do not perceive an immediate threat from the United States, then they probably will concentrate on buck-passing. Long-term economic recovery remains the primary driver of Russia's short- and medium-term policies.

JAPAN

Japan and the European allies of the United States were buck-passing during the last decades of the Cold War. They let the United States carry the chief burdens of defense against the Soviet threat, while investing great amounts of wealth in their own economies. They assessed the Soviet threat differently than did their American allies, seeing it as a long-term danger that, after the first decades of the Cold War, never became acute. Japan may still need to balance against China and may still turn to the United States to pass the buck. Even though any threat posed by China lies primarily in the future, as this danger begins to materialize Japan undoubtedly will seek a closer security arrangement with the United States. It would thus maintain the option of buck-passing until the threat becomes short term, when it would then seek more traditional forms of balancing. In any case, the Japanese will continue to emphasize their economic goals and worry less about near-term military balancing.

EUROPEAN UNION

The European Union (EU) clearly does not feel threatened by the United States. If it did, Europeans would be demanding the withdrawal of American armed forces from Europe. Instead, recent years have seen the expansion of NATO membership, missions, and activities. While it seems apparent the EU is bandwagoning with the United States, some might say that it is appeasing Washington by going along with actions its members do not wholeheartedly support.

In terms of its economic interests, the EU is searching for ways to develop its capacity to compete against America (see Art, this volume.) This strategy also means amassing enough economic power to move out from under the shadow of the United States, or at least become a capable partner. European aspirations to parity with the United States, however, are limited to the economic sphere—there is no chance that Europe could gain such a position militarily in the next decade. Union members show no sign of investing in the military research and development needed to eliminate their security dependence on the United States even two or three decades from now. Like Japan, Europeans are more likely to expect external threats to manifest in a fairly distant future. For Europe, NATO is a device to pass the buck in the short term, while providing insurance in case a threat does arise in the future.

INDIA

During the Cold War, India cast about for possible allies to balance American power. Since India currently may reckon that China is more of a threat to its interests than the United States, it has very few potential allies to draw on. The Soviet Union was previously available as a balancer against China and the United States, but Russia may not be of much assistance today. India therefore would probably to try to pursue internal methods to balance against local threats, while seeking to appease the United States for the time being. India's only realistic option at this moment is to devote its energies to building up its internal economic capabilities.

In the long run, India must still be concerned about identifying the location of the threat: will it be coming from the United States or China? Once the primary threat is identified, the other great power could then be called on as an ally. Given these threat perceptions, India is more likely to buck-pass until the chief threat makes itself obvious.

In sum, the only major powers likely to feel threatened by the United States have little hope of achieving a balance quickly. Most do not feel as threatened by the United States as they do by other major powers. With limited alliance possibilities, a long time horizon for achieving a balance, and a relatively slow ability to convert wealth to military power, most major powers are likely to choose between appeasing the United States and buck-passing. In other words, most states will hope that someone else will deter the United States from threatening the sovereignty of other states or exercising its power in unconstrained ways. Major powers will voice opposition to American actions, yet they will fail to use force or economic sanctions to oppose the United States. Under these circumstances, it is unlikely that coalitions will form to balance American power.

Conclusion

Three conclusions arise from this characterization of the current behavior of great powers. First, intentions figure mightily in actual policymaking. Europeans are not responding to American superiority by balancing because they do not fear U.S. dominance. They behave as if they are unable to tilt the balance of power, even though they have the economic resources and population that would in fact allow them to balance against the United States. Bandwagoning makes it possible for them to add to their relative economic strength, so that they could steer an independent course at some point in the future, if the need arose.

Second, economic strategizing tends to emphasize domestic growth rates. Trade and investment policies influence growth trends, but are merely two factors among many. The United States posted stronger growth rates than Japan or West European countries in the last twenty years, even as those states have been buck-passing or bandwagoning. American investments abroad have continued for more than a quarter-century after Gilpin condemned them as unwise for American strategic purposes.[16] Still, the United States continues to develop cutting-edge technology and enjoys a relatively strong economy.

Third, the balance of power theory is typically too parsimonious to be of great use. Although balance of power theorists argue that they do not need to evaluate the location of threats in the system by any other means than the distribution of power, such a theory is necessarily incomplete. Time introduces a critical element into the management of economic resources. An estimate of who poses a threat is not complete without an assessment of *when* the threat will arise and how long it will take to arm. Indeed, decisions about the mix of economic and military policies hinge on assumptions about the speed at which one believes economic resources can be changed into military force. Without a consideration of time constraints, any behavior could be claimed to be logically consistent with balance of power theory. The theory can never be very useful as a tool for evaluating past behavior, for predictions, or for offering policy prescriptions if a relevant time frame is not specified. Power maximization itself has little meaning as a concept without knowing when policymakers believe power must be maximized. If the theory of balance of power is to be of any use as a guide, realists need to rectify its shortcomings and accord economics due consideration.

Notes

1. John Mearsheimer, *The Tragedy of Great Power Politics* (New York: Norton, 2001).

2. Unsurprisingly, most political economic analyses create rivals to this realist theory. Those that do attempt to work within the theory's strictures often focus on issues concerning alliance formation and burden sharing. The classic piece is Mancur Olson and Richard Zeckhauser, "An Economic Theory of Alliances," *Review of Economics and Statistics* 48 (August 1966): 266–79. Other important contributions in this area in recent years have been made by several authors. See James Fearon, "Bargaining, Enforcement and International Cooperation," *International Organization* 52 (Spring 1998): 269–306, and "Signaling versus Balance of Power and Interests: An Empirical Test of a Crisis Bargaining Model," *Journal of Conflict Resolution* 38 (June 1994): 236–69; Russell Hardin, *Collective Action* (Baltimore: Johns Hopkins University Press, 1982); and Todd Sandler, "The Economic Theory

of Alliances: A Survey," *Journal of Conflict Resolution* 37 (September 1993): 446–83, among others.

3. Following the industrial revolution, strategists sometimes used the term "war potential" to describe the capacity of a state to transform economic capability into military capability. Production of steel, chemicals, the state of transportation networks, and fuel supplies were often used as measures of a nation's war potential.

4. Joanne Gowa, *Allies, Adversaries, and International Trade* (Princeton: Princeton University Press, 1994); Edward Mansfield, *Power, Trade, and War* (Princeton: Princeton University Press, 1994); and Paul Papayoanou, *Power Ties: Economic Interdependence, Balancing and War* (Ann Arbor: University of Michigan Press, 1999).

5. Mearsheimer incorrectly cites Jacob Viner's classic piece on mercantilism to emphasize one interpretation of this relationship. Viner, however, was arguing only that mercantilists in earlier centuries had maintained that wealth and power were interchangeable; Viner did not conclude that this relationship was static. See Mearsheimer, *Tragedy*, 46; and Jacob Viner, "Power Versus Plenty as Objectives of Foreign Policy," *World Politics* 1 (October 1948): 1–29.

6. Michael Mastanduno, "Trade as a Strategic Weapon," in G. John Ikenberry, David Lake, and Michael Mastanduno (eds.), *The State and American Foreign Economic Policy* (Ithaca: Cornell University Press, 1988), 121–50.

7. Gowa, *Allies, Adversaries*.

8. Papayoanou, *Power Ties*.

9. Robert Gilpin, *U.S. Power and the Multinational Corporation* (New York: Basic, 1975).

10. Stephen Walt, *The Origins of Alliances* (Ithaca: Cornell University Press, 1987).

11. Katja Weber, *Hierarchy Amidst Anarchy* (New York: SUNY University Press, 2000).

12. Realists, however, regularly flip-flop on this matter. For instance, Mearsheimer says that only the hegemonic power favors the status quo, while all other powers are revisionists, though elsewhere he argues that hegemonic powers also wish to extend their lead over others. See Mearsheimer, *Tragedy*, 46.

13. Mark Brawley, "Political Leadership and Liberal Economic Sub-Systems: The Constraints of Structural Assumptions," *Canadian Journal of Political Science* 28 (1995): 85–103.

14. Correlli Barnett, *The Collapse of British Power* (London: Eyre Methuen, 1972).

15. Mearsheimer, *Tragedy*, 4.

16. Gilpin's logic rested on the assertion that growth rates vary in predictable ways based on foreign investment patterns, an unproven relationship.

PART II

New Security Challenges and Balance of Power

CHAPTER 4

The War on Terrorism and the Balance of Power: The Paradoxes of American Hegemony

CHRISTOPHER LAYNE

Has the war on terrorism altered our understanding of balance of power as the basic analytic tool of Realist international relations theory? Did September 11, 2001, usher in a new grand strategic era in which terrorism and "asymmetric" warfare strategies will displace traditional forms of balancing? How does the American response to September 11 fit into current scholarly debates about contending balance of power theories, and the parallel debate about the merits of American hegemony?

To address these questions, the chapter first examines two key concepts at the heart of Realist analyses of the balance of power: hegemony and balancing. Second, it discusses terrorism, and asks whether terrorist violence constitutes an "asymmetric" form of balancing by non-state actors. Third, it explores the implications for balance of power theories of the war on terrorism and America's post-Cold War hegemonic grand strategy by asking two questions. In the long term, will U.S. preponderance prompt counter-hegemonic balancing against the United States in the form of rising new great powers? In the short term, will regional powers and potential peer competitors employ "asymmetric" strategies against the United States as a counter to American preponderance?

The argument presented in this chapter is straightforward. Contrary to the conventional wisdom that September 11 "changed everything," from a geopolitical perspective, the attacks launched by Osama bin Laden changed virtually nothing. Before September 11, the main debates for policymakers, and for students of international relations theory and strategic studies, centered on the issue of American hegemony.[1]

Could the United States prolong its global preponderance? Was the United States a benign, or benevolent, hegemon? During the decade since

the Cold War's end, why had others not balanced against American hegemony? Would new great powers emerge to contest American hegemony?
Underlying these questions is one of the key unresolved debates among
scholars: are peace and stability more likely to be fostered by an equal distribution of material capabilities among several great powers (a multipolar balance of power), or by an *im*balance of power in favor of a single dominant
state (a unipolar, or hegemonic system)? Many of these questions remain relevant today, despite the best efforts of al-Qaeda to transform the international political landscape.

The Balance of Power and Balancing in Realist Theory

There are many varieties of Realism, but all Realists agree on several fundamental assumptions about the nature of international politics.[2] First, international politics are state-centric, because politics are about relations
between organized social groups, and states are the primary organized social
groups in the modern world. Second, international politics take place under
the condition of anarchy. Rather than denoting chaos or rampant disorder,
"anarchy" in international politics refers to the fact that there is no central
authority capable of making and enforcing rules of behavior on the international system's units (states). Third, the international political system is a
self-help system, in which states can only rely on their own devices to guarantee their security and to make sure other states honor existing agreements.
Fourth, international politics involve an ongoing struggle among states for
power and security. Robert Gilpin has distilled these core assumptions into
a pithy explication of Realism's essence. Realism, he says, assumes that "the
fundamental nature of international politics has not changed over the mil-
lennia. International politics continue to be a recurring struggle for wealth
and power among independent actors in a state of anarchy."[3]

　　In international politics, the basic goal of each state is to survive—to preserve its sovereignty and autonomy. As Kenneth Waltz observes, states may
have many goals other than survival, but survival is the prerequisite to attaining them.[4] International politics takes place under the shadow of war,
because, with no overarching law enforcement agency to prevent others from
using military force against it, each state itself must be prepared to use military force to defend itself and ensure its survival. Where anarchy and self-help

are the hallmark of politics, Waltz says, "the possibility that force will be used by one or another of the parties looms always as a threat in the background. In politics force is said to be the *ultima ratio*. In international politics force serves, not only as the *ultima ratio*, but as the first and constant one."[5]

The individual efforts of states to ensure their own survival give rise to the so-called security dilemma: under anarchy, even if self-defense is the motive for building up its military forces, a state's upgrading of its capabilities may be regarded by others as a threat to their security.[6] In an anarchic, self-help system, a state's defensive search for security can have the perverse effect of leading to greater insecurity by triggering an open-ended cycle of moves and countermoves, because when a state increases its military capabilities, prudence constrains others to respond in kind. International politics thus are a ceaseless search for power and security that requires states to pay constant attention to the relative distribution of power among them.

One of the major fault lines in Realism is between those who believe that the dominance of a single power (a hegemon) leads to peace and stability in the international system, and those who believe that multipolar systems— in which material capabilities are evenly distributed among several great powers—are more peaceful and stable. Traditional Realist theory, and Neorealism, adopt the latter position, claiming that, because states seek to preserve their sovereignty and autonomy, power balances will form to prevent a single state from attaining hegemony. Rather than aligning with the most powerful state in the system—"bandwagoning"—other states "balance" against it by increasing their own relative capability. A state that attained hegemony would gain security for itself, but would threaten the security of others. Thus, according to traditional Realists and Neorealists, for other states in the international system, a hegemon's rise is the most acute manifestation of the security dilemma. To prevent the emergence of a hegemon, states balance either by building up their own military capabilities (internal balancing), by forming alliances with others (external balancing), or by combining these two forms of balancing. On the other hand, both Offensive Realists and proponents of power transition theory argue that hegemonic systems are more peaceful and stable.[7] The crux of their argument is that when power is equally distributed, wars are more likely because states will calculate that their chances of winning are good. Wars are unlikely in a hegemonic system, because the disparity of power in the hegemon's favor deters others from challenging it.

Non-State Actors and American Hegemony: Is Terrorism Balancing?

The attacks on the World Trade Center and Pentagon seemed to confirm the arguments of those who have claimed that the forces of globalization and the rising influence of non-state actors have challenged Realism's state-centric focus and transformed the nature of war. These claims are overblown. There is a lot less to globalization than meets the eye: reports that "the state is dead" are greatly exaggerated, and there is little reason to believe that postmodern warfare will replace great-power rivalries and security competitions as the most salient phenomenon of international politics.[8] At the same time, September 11 made plain that new security challenges exist for the United States and the world side-by-side with more traditional forms of great-power politics.

To be sure, the use of organized violence by non-state actors—whether by terrorists, national liberation movements, or the Barbary pirates in the early 19th century—is not new. But it also is clear that the globalization of trade, finance, technology, and culture has expanded both the reach and capabilities of terrorist groups like al-Qaeda. Like goods, in an interconnected world people (including terrorists) move freely. Computers and the Internet enable organizations like al-Qaeda to adopt decentralized ("networked") organizational structures, and yet still coordinate the activities of their geographically dispersed cells. And the worldwide diffusion of military technology and weaponry enables terrorists to augment their striking power, possibly even by acquiring nuclear, chemical, or biological weapons.

There are many forms of terrorism, but here I am concerned only with a specific variety: the use by non-state actors (though sometimes supported indirectly by states) of violence targeted at American interests (at home and abroad) for the purpose of affecting U.S. foreign policy.[9] How does this kind of terrorism fit into traditional concepts of the balance of power? Can terror attacks such as those mounted against the United States by al-Qaeda be classified as a form of balancing? At first blush, the answer would seem to be "no," because in Realist theory, balancing behavior is a form of *state* behavior. At its core, the concept of balancing expresses the idea of a counterweight, specifically, the ability to generate sufficient material capabilities to match—or offset—those of a would-be, or actual, hegemon. Strictly speaking, balancing is a great-power phenomenon, because only great powers can prevent one among them from attaining geopolitical predominance.[10]

If we adhere to this strict (and correct) definition of balancing, non-state terrorist organizations like al-Qaeda simply lack the material capabilities to engage in balancing. Yet, at the same time, it is clear that the behavior of organizations like al-Qaeda reflects some key attributes of balancing. After all, beyond connoting the idea of counterweight, balancing also signifies opposition, or resistance, to a hegemon. Terrorists cannot balance against a hegemon, but they can engage in a related form of behavior aimed at *undermining* a hegemon such as the United States politically or by raising the costs of maintaining hegemony.

Although al-Qaeda is a non-state actor, its activities are recognizable as a kind of political behavior frequent in international politics: the use of armed violence against a state (or states) to attain clearly defined political objectives. Indeed, the use of violence in the pursuit of political objectives is the hallmark of terrorism. As Bruce Hoffman says, terrorism is "about power: the pursuit of power, the acquisition of power, and use of power to achieve political change."[11] Terrorism, moreover, is fundamentally an asymmetric form of conflict, because it is a means that the weak use against the strong.[12]

From this perspective, the assault on America was not a random, senseless, "irrational" act of violence. Despicable and brutal though it was, it was undertaken with cool calculation to achieve well-defined geopolitical objectives. Specifically, al-Qaeda wants to compel the United States to remove its military presence from the Persian Gulf (and, in particular from Saudi Arabia), and force Washington to alter its stance on the Israeli-Palestinian conflict. Al-Qaeda's leaders also apparently hoped that the September 11 attacks would provoke a U.S. overreaction, and thereby trigger an upsurge of popular discontent in the Islamic world that would lead to the overthrow of the Saudi monarchy and other pro-American regimes in the Middle East (Egypt, Pakistan, and Jordan, for example), and their replacement by fundamentalist Islamic governments.[13] In other words, al-Qaeda has sought to undermine U.S. hegemony, and thereby compel changes in America's grand strategy in the Middle East and Persian Gulf.

If we are able to step back for a moment from our horror and revulsion at the events of September 11, we can see that the attack was in keeping with the Clausewitzian paradigm of war: force was used against the United States by its adversaries to advance their political objectives. As German military strategist Carl von Clausewitz himself observed, "war is not an act of senseless passion but is controlled by its political object."[14] September 11 represented a violent counterreaction to America's geopolitical-cultural hegemony. As Richard K. Betts, an acknowledged expert on strategy, presciently observed several years ago in an article in *Foreign Affairs*, "It is hardly likely that Middle Eastern radicals would be hatching schemes like the destruction of the World Trade Center if the United States had not been identified so long as the mainstay of Israel, the Shah of Iran, and conservative Arab regimes and the source of a cultural assault on Islam."[15] U.S. hegemony fuels terrorist groups like al-Qaeda and fans Islamic fundamentalism. In other words, although it is not balancing in the strict sense of the term, terrorist actions of this sort are a form of "blowback" against America's preponderant role in global affairs.

As long as the United States maintains its global hegemony—and its concomitant preeminence in regions like the Persian Gulf—it will be the target of politically motivated terrorist groups like al-Qaeda. But the terrorist threat does not, in itself, compel a rethinking of traditional notions of the balance of power and balancing. Terrorist organizations, even the most sophisticated and capable, lack the material power to constitute a counterweight to a rising, or actual hegemon. Only a peer competitor can do that. Even if terrorists obtain, and are willing to use, weapons of mass destruction (WMD), the amount of damage they can inflict does not even begin to approach the level of harm great powers can inflict on each other. Terrorists can cause pain in the form of civilian casualties, sow fear and havoc, and cause some economic disruption. By so doing, they may hope to force a hegemon to alter its policies, though they are unlikely to succeed if the hegemon believes its vital interests are at stake. Less directly, terrorists might succeed in triggering a chain reaction of events culminating in the overthrow of regimes allied to a hegemon.

As the war on terrorism has dramatized, however, there is a vast disparity between the military capabilities of a hegemonic power like the United States, and those of al-Qaeda (and of states that sponsor terrorism). The United States has a number of options for dealing with terrorism. It has the diplomatic clout to organize coalitions against terrorism (and strong states share a common interest in suppressing non-state actors that challenge the state's monopoly on the use of force). The United States, acting alone or with others, has the economic resources to try to alleviate the root conditions of terrorism in failed states. And the United States has impressive military and intelligence-gathering capabilities. Although terrorism cannot be eradicated, the United States can inflict considerable destruction on terrorist organizations, and thus hold the terrorist threat to an acceptable level. For a hegemonic power like the United States, groups like al-Qaeda have the capacity to wound and harass, but they pose neither an existential threat, nor a fundamental challenge to American preponderance.

The War on Terrorism and American Hegemony: Implications for the Balance of Power

Terrorism does not compel the revision of traditional approaches to the balance of power. But the war on terrorism mounted by the United States raises important questions that go to the heart of scholarly controversies about balance of power. Since the Soviet Union's collapse and the Cold War's end—which left the United States as the sole remaining great power in the international system—U.S. grand strategy has aimed deliberately at preserving America's hegemonic world role. The war on terrorism has given fresh impetus to America's hegemonic ambitions. The question posed thereby for scholars and policymakers alike is whether the United States can be a successful hegemon and avoid the fate that has befallen previous contenders for hegemony.

EXPLAINING AMERICAN GRAND STRATEGY: OFFENSIVE REALISM

Offensive Realist theory explains why great powers seek hegemony and why American grand strategic behavior since the Cold War's end conforms with Offensive Realism's predictions. Offensive Realism actually has two distinct, though closely related, variants, characterized here as Type I and Type II.

Type I Offensive Realism's main claim is that as a state gains in relative power, its grand strategic interests expand. Type I Offensive Realism advances two explanations for this phenomenon. First, states' interests expand as their relative power increases because capabilities drive intentions. Moreover, an increase in a state's relative power not only causes an expansion of its external interests, but also results in the broadening of the state's *perception* of its interests and security requirements. Second, a state's interests expand as its power increases, because the anarchic nature of international politics makes every state insecure. The best antidote to insecurity is for a state to maximize its relative power, because the most promising route to

security is for a state to increase its control over the international environment through the steady expansion of its political interests abroad.[16]

Type II Offensive Realism posits that attaining hegemony is—or should
be—the ultimate aim of a state's grand strategy. Dominance, or hegemony,
is the logical outcome of a grand strategy that seeks to maximize the state's
relative power (or influence). For Type II Offensive Realists, there is only one
way for a state to break out of the security dilemma, and thus to attain lasting security: by becoming the most powerful state in the international system. As John Mearsheimer puts it: "states quickly understand that the best
way to ensure their survival is to be the most powerful state in the system."[17]
A state becomes a hegemon either by eliminating its rivals, or by adopting
strategies that subjugate or subordinate them.

There are three reasons why hegemony is Type II Offensive Realism's preferred grand strategy for states that possess sufficient resources. First, Type II
Offensive Realism depicts multipolar international systems as inherently less
peaceful and stable than bipolar or unipolar systems. Second, a hegemon
gains security when the distribution of power is skewed decisively in its
favor, because others will be deterred from attacking it. Third, hegemony is
the best grand strategic response to a state's uncertainty about others' intentions, and about others' present and future capabilities. States strive for superiority, not equality, as a hedge against miscalculating both the present and
future distribution of power between them and their rivals.

Even if a state attains hegemony, however, its quest to maximize its relative power does not stop. Hegemons cannot be status-quo powers, because
they want to maintain their predominance and they fear the emergence of
new rivals who could challenge their preeminence. A paradox of hegemony
is that hegemons invariably believe their dominance is tenuous. Hence, the
hegemon must constantly increase its power simply to hold on to what it
has. As the Athenian leader Alcibiades recognized, the imperatives of security compel a hegemon constantly to seek to expand its power and influence:
"We cannot fix the exact point at which our empire shall stop; we have
reached a position in which we must not be content with retaining what we
have but must scheme to extend for, if we cease to rule others, we shall be in
danger of being ruled ourselves."[18] For hegemons, the injunction seems to be
that they must expand their power or die.

U.S. foreign and defense policies and behavior since 1989 correspond with
Offensive Realism's predictions. First, consistent with Offensive Realism's

core insight, the United States has sought security by maintaining, and bolstering, its post-Cold War hegemony. America's post-Cold war grand strategic ambitions were initially set out in the first Bush administration's draft Defense Planning Guidance (DPG) for Fiscal Years 1994–1999, which stated that the key aim of U.S. grand strategy would be to maintain America's preponderance by preventing the emergence of great-power rivals.[19] Although the language about unipolarity was deleted from the DPG's final version because it proved controversial, it is evident that the draft DPG accurately reflected not only the first Bush administration's notions about unipolarity, but also the Clinton and second Bush administrations' views of the preferred U.S. approach to world affairs.[20] Since the Cold War's end, American grand strategy has reflected Offensive Realist theory's key premises: hegemonic systems are peaceful and stable (at least when the United States is the hegemon), and multipolar systems are unstable and war-prone.

By removing America's only peer competitor from the geopolitical equation, the Soviet Union's collapse caused a major accretion in America's relative power. Offensive Realist theory predicts that following the Cold War's end, the United States would seek to maintain its hegemony, and that the scope of America's interests would expand, both geographically and ideologically. From the Cold War's end until September 11, U.S. grand strategy conformed to these predictions. The United States sought to preserve its hegemony by maintaining American military capabilities at a level that could not be matched (that is, balanced against) by any other state. Prior to September 11, for example, the U.S. defense budget exceeded the combined defense budgets of Russia and the People's Republic of China, the most likely potential peer competitors. One of the key aims of the National Missile Defense program, and the development of theatre missile defenses, is to ensure that no regional power will be able to frustrate American military intervention in East Asia or the Middle East by acquiring nuclear weapons and long-range delivery systems. Geographically, the expansion of American interests was reflected in the Persian Gulf War, which established the United States as the preponderant power in the Gulf region; in the first round of NATO enlargement; and in U.S. military intervention in the Balkans. Ideologically, the post-Cold War expansion of U.S. objectives was manifested in the policy of democratic enlargement and in the assertion of Washington's prerogative to intervene in the internal affairs of states that treated their own citizens in ways that offended America's ideals.[21]

September 11 reinforced the hegemonic impulses that already were driving U.S. grand strategy, and the war on terrorism has been invoked as justification for American hegemony by its proponents. The five-year defense buildup that the second Bush administration proposed after September 11, if implemented, would see the U.S. Department of Defense outspending the combined military outlays of the rest of the world. The administration's September 2002 National Security Strategy of the United States declared that U.S. strategy would seek to prevent any other power from surpassing, or even equaling, American military capabilities, and its 2002 Nuclear Posture Review, and the incorporation into its national security strategy of preventive war and preemptive strikes, evidence a clear determination to maintain the military capabilities requisite to maintaining U.S. hegemony. Geographically, the reach of American interests continues to expand with a second round of NATO enlargement, and in plans to establish a permanent U.S. military presence in Central Asia. The administration also has picked up where its predecessors left off by seeking to expand the reach of American values, especially in the Islamic world. The spring 2003 Iraq War illustrated concretely America's commitment to extending its hegemonic power, and its willingness to use military power preventively for that purpose.

AMERICA AS A BENEVOLENT HEGEMON? HEGEMONIC STABILITY THEORY AND BALANCE OF THREAT THEORY (AND LIBERALISM)

If international politics are about power, then logically the United States should seek to amass as much power as possible. If an international system comprised of other great powers would endanger U.S. interests, it would make sense for the United States to seek to preserve its preponderant power. Yet, although Offensive Realism's logic has a seductive simplicity, the historical record shows that states that have sought hegemony have not done well. Since the beginnings of the modern international system, there have been successive bids for hegemony by the Habsburg Empire under Charles V, by Spain under Philip II, by France under Louis XIV and Napoleon, and by Germany under Hitler (and, some historians would argue under Wilhelm II). Each of these hegemonic aspirants in turn was defeated by a counterbalancing coalition of states that feared the consequences for their security if a hegemonic aspirant succeeded in establishing its predominance over the international system. "Hegemonic empires," Henry A. Kissinger has observed, "almost automatically elicit universal resistance, which is why all such claimants sooner or later exhausted themselves."[22] Can the United States avoid the fate of previous hegemonic contenders? Notwithstanding the seeming lessons of the past, many scholars and policymakers have invoked hegemonic stability theory, balance of threat theory, and the Liberal approach to international relations to support the proposition that the United States can be a successful hegemon.

Hegemonic stability theory is usually associated with international political economy. The core of traditional hegemonic stability theory is that to function effectively, the international economic system needs a dominant power to perform key tasks: to provide a stable reserve currency and international liquidity; to serve as a lender of last resort; to act as a market of last resort; and to make and enforce "rules of the game."[23] For most theorists interested in the international political economy, the existence of a hegemon—or at least a Liberal hegemon—is seen as a good thing, because the hegemon's actions confer system-wide benefits. The logic of hegemonic stability can be extended from the realm of political economy to other aspects of international politics. As Robert Gilpin argues in *War and Change in World Politics*, a hegemonic power establishes the rules and norms of international order, and acts to provide security and stability in the international system.[24] According to both variants of hegemonic stability theory, others will cooperate with a benign hegemon because they benefit from the collective goods the hegemon provides.

Stephen Walt's balance of threat theory purports to explain why others can perceive a hegemonic power as benevolent, rather than threatening. Balance of threat theory is frequently invoked to support the claim that the United States can follow policies that will allay concerns about America's overwhelming power.[25] In contrast to Waltz's Neorealist theory, which argues that states balance against *power* (and hence would balance against a hegemon), Walt claims that others balance against the state that poses the greatest *threat* to their security.[26] The essence of balance of threat theory is the claim that the mere asymmetry of power in a hegemon's favor does not, ipso facto, constitute a threat to others' security. That is, the state posing the greatest threat to others is not necessarily the strongest state in the system. According to Walt, threat is a function of several factors, including a state's aggregate power (determined by population, and economic, military, and technological capabilities); geographical proximity to others; possession of offensive military capabilities; and the degree to which it exhibits aggressive intentions (or, more correctly, to which others *perceive* that the state harbors aggressive intentions).[27]

According to Walt, the nature of a state's domestic political system is a crucial factor in determining whether a state appears threatening to others. Thus, balance of threat theory serves as the intellectual bridge connecting Defensive Realism to Liberal approaches to international relations theory.[28] Liberal scholars advance two claims to support their contention that the United States can succeed where others have failed because it is a qualitatively different kind of hegemon—a *Liberal* hegemon. First, Liberals like Joseph S. Nye Jr. contend that America's "soft power," that is, its ideals, political institutions, and culture, will attract other states into Washington's orbit.[29] Because America's power is regarded as soft, Nye asserts, "others do not see us as a threat, but rather as an attraction."[30] Second, Liberal institutionalists like G. John Ikenberry and John G. Ruggie argue that other states acquiesce in U.S. hegemony because America exercises its predominance through international institutions, rather than acting unilaterally. Because others can use the international institutions (that is, the World Bank, the United Nations) that the United States helped create to influence and to even constrain its foreign and defense policies, they are willing to live with America's global dominance.

Awareness of America's "hegemony problem" (others' fear of U.S. power) has become more widespread in the aftermath of September 11 and the Iraq War. By synthesizing hegemonic stability theory, balance of threat theory, and the Liberal approach to international politics, however, proponents of U.S. hegemony assert that Washington can defuse fears of American preponderance, and thereby negate the incentives to balance against the United States. Nye, for example, asserts that the United States can preserve its preeminent position in international politics by providing international public goods—maintaining the balance of power in key regions, promoting an open international economy, taking the lead on global environmental issues, strengthening international institutions, assisting economic development, and acting as the organizer of coalitions and mediator of disputes—and by acting multilaterally rather than unilaterally.[31] Similarly, while acknowledging that others are very ambivalent about America's post-September 11 preeminence in world politics, Walt claims that the United States can make its hegemony more acceptable to the rest of the world by acting multilaterally, and acting "with greater forbearance and generosity in its dealings with other states."[32] Echoing Nye and Walt, Liberal scholars contend that by voluntarily accepting constraints on its own power, the United States reassures others that they need not fear American hegemony. As Ikenberry puts it: "American domination or hegemony is unusual . . . American hegemony is reluctant, open, and highly institutionalized—or, in a word, liberal. This is what makes it acceptable to other countries that might otherwise be expected to balance against hegemonic power, and it is also what makes it so stable and expansive."[33]

The Balance of Power Beyond September 11: The Illusion of American Hegemony

Notwithstanding the predictions derived from hegemonic stability theory, balance of threat theory, and the Liberal approach to international relations, it is doubtful that America's hegemony will endure. Neorealist theory predicts that states will balance against hegemons, even those like the United States that seek to maintain their preeminence by employing strategies based more on benevolence than coercion. As Kenneth N. Waltz says, "In international politics, overwhelming power repels and leads other states to balance against it."[34] In contrast to international political economy, in the realm of security hegemony causes *in*stability, because the existence of a single dominant state poses a threat to others' security. In unipolar systems there is no clear distinction between balancing against threat or against power, because the threat inheres in the hegemon's power. In a unipolar world, others must worry about the hegemon's capabilities (which, more or less, are knowable), not its intentions (which are difficult to ascertain and always subject to change). It is a pretty safe bet that the United States will not be able to escape the fates of previous contenders for hegemony. Consistent with Neorealist theory's expectations, we should expect to see American power balanced either by the emergence of new great powers, or the formation of counter-hegemonic alliances directed against the United States, or both.[35]

WHO CAN BALANCE AND HOW?
THE ROLE OF ASYMMETRIC STRATEGIES

For balancing to occur, other actors in the international system must be able to match U.S. military, economic, and technological capabilities. Although it is easy to pinpoint those with the potential to emerge as peer competitors to the United States—China, a resurgent Russia, the European Union (or a Germany hegemonic in Europe), Japan, India—to date no rival to the United States has emerged. Some theorists suggest the present-day distribution of capabilities in the international system is unprecedented, and likely to remain so, because America's economic and technological lead over potential great-power rivals is insurmountable.[36] And, indeed, given the immense *im*balance of power in America's favor, "catching up is difficult."[37] In the short term (the next decade), no state will emerge as America's geopolitical peer. Even for the People's Republic of China—the consensus pick as the state most like to acquire peer competitor status—it will take more than a decade to close the gap between itself and the United States with respect to material capabilities.[38]

In the interval during which they are making the transition from potential to actual peer competitor, how will rising great powers counter American hegemony? Given that the Iraq War has demonstrated U.S. willingness to use preventive war or preemptive strategies to counter *future* threats, rising great powers will have good reason to view the transitional interval as one during which they will be vulnerable. And how will regional powers, which by definition are incapable of engaging in true balancing against the United States, resist perceived American threats to their security? Both rising great powers and regional powers likely will be attracted to asymmetric strategies as a means of offsetting superior U.S. military capabilities.

The terms *asymmetric warfare, asymmetric threats*, and *asymmetric strategies*, have become buzzwords much favored by policymakers and analysts. A little bit of perspective is in order. When discussing asymmetric state responses to U.S. hegemony, it is first necessary to specify the level of analysis being discussed. At the grand strategic level, research on the initiation of asymmetric conflicts suggests that weaker powers often rationally pick fights with stronger powers for a number of reasons.[39] For example, such states may calculate that although the overall material distribution of power is adverse to them, they can still hope to prevail by using clever strategies (for example, pursuing a "limited aims" strategy), and because the "balance of resolve" favors them. The balance of resolve reflects asymmetries in motivation: if the stakes are greater for the weaker power, it may be prepared to take greater risks, and pay higher costs than a defender who regards the stakes as less than vital to its own security interests.[40] Similarly, weaker powers will try to develop methods of war fighting that neutralize the quantitative or qualitative advantages enjoyed by a stronger adversary. At the operational and tactical levels, asymmetric responses by others to a hegemon may be manifested in the weaker power's choice of weapons systems, operational doctrine, and tactics. Here, U.S. difficulties in occupied "postwar" Iraq surely will prompt other militaries to revisit the merits of guerilla warfare as an asymmetric response to American power.

There is nothing novel about asymmetric responses, which are as old as war itself. If its strategists are smart, a weaker power in an asymmetric contest will not attempt to slug it out with a stronger foe. As Edward Luttwak has noted, the essence of strategy always has been the ability to identify, and exploit, the opponent's political, operational, and tactical vulnerabilities.[41] From this perspective, it is understandable that regional powers, unable to match U.S. high-tech conventional capabilities, would seek to acquire nuclear and chemical weapons to deter the United States from using military force against them.[42] It remains an open question, however, whether states like Iran and North Korea actually would use nuclear or chemical weapons in a conflict with the United States once their deterrence strategy failed.[43] The answer, in part, may hinge on how such states perceive Washington's aims.[44] In this respect, the second Bush administration's willingness to use military power in pursuit of regime change—demonstrated by the Iraq War—could have unintended consequences. For example, if the U.S. explicitly goes to war to overthrow regimes such as Iran or North Korea, a "use it or lose it" dynamic that perversely increases the chances that nuclear or chemical weapons would be used against American forces could be created.

Short of using nuclear, biological, or chemical weapons, regional powers— or a state like China that possibly is striving for, but has not yet attained, great-power status—can employ other asymmetric means to offset superior U.S. capabilities.[45] For example, because American forces often depend on basing facilities provided by allies in key regions, weaker adversaries might use ballistic missiles or special operations forces to deny the United States access to these facilities in the event of conflict, or at least to disrupt U.S. force deployments. Regional adversaries also could seek to drive a wedge between Washington and key regional allies, to deny the United States the use of allied territory as a staging area to project American power into a theater of operations. The mere threat that they are at risk of attack by a hostile regional power's ballistic missiles (possibly carrying nuclear, biological, or chemical warheads), could be sufficient to cause allied states to dissociate themselves from the United States in the event of a regional conflict. Similarly, although unable to match the United States in key leading-edge military technologies (command, control, communications, real-time recon-naissance and surveillance), non-peer competitors might acquire low cost technologies and information warfare capabilities that could disable the satellites and computers on which the American military depends for its battlefield superiority. In sum, even if others lack the capability to "balance" against American hegemony in the traditional sense, the very fact of U.S. preponderance gives them strong incentives to develop strategies, weapons, and doctrines that will enable them to offset American capabilities.

THE RETURN OF GREAT-POWER POLITICS

In the wake of America's diplomatic and battlefield success in the opening phase of the war on terrorism, and in the Iraq War, some doubtless will con-clude that victory has confirmed America's permanent global preeminence. The United States, after all, stands at the zenith of its military, diplomatic, and economic power. When even potential rivals like China and Russia have been drawn into the U.S.-led coalition against terrorism, it is tempting to conclude that American hegemony is unassailable, and that, as Stephen G. Brooks and William C. Wohlforth suggest, the only questions now are how long U.S. hegemony will last and how global dominance will shape American foreign policy.[46] Appearances can be deceiving, however, and the coalition Washington mobilized to fight al-Qaeda collapsed during the run-up to the Iraq War, which was opposed vehemently by France, Germany, and Russia.

It is far from clear, however, that the outlook for American primacy is quite so rosy. In the short term, both state and non-state actors will be able to respond only asymmetrically to U.S. hegemony. Over the medium term— twenty years from now—Neorealist theory's prediction that new great pow-ers will rise to counterbalance American hegemony seems certain to be fulfilled. Indeed, there are many signs that this process is under way.

Well before September 11 and the Iraq War—indeed, throughout most of the past decade—there has been a strong undercurrent of unease on the part of other states about the imbalance of power in America's favor. Russia, China, India, and even West European allies like France and Germany feared that the United States was seeking to maintain its global military dominance through unilateral policies. And, as Neorealist theory predicts, others responded to American hegemony by concerting their efforts against it. Russia and China, long-estranged, found common ground in a nascent alliance that opposed U.S. "rogue hegemonism" by promoting reestablishment of a multipolar world. Similarly, America's European allies were openly expressing the view that something must be done geopolitically to rein in a too-powerful America. French President Jacques Chirac and his Foreign Minister, Hubert Vedrine, gave voice to Europe's fears by describing the United States as a "hyperpower."

In the Iraq War's aftermath, it is apparent that the anti-terrorism coalition forged by Washington after September 11 did not represent a permanent accommodation by others to American hegemony. There was no reason to believe it did. After all, alliances and coalitions are never more than marriages of convenience. Western Europe, Russia, China, and India all had reasons of their own to join with the United States in fighting terrorism. None of them, however, has an interest in the expansion of America's hegemonic reach. In this regard, the U.S. decision to wage a unilateral, "preventive war" against Iraq underscored for others the expansive nature of America's hegemonic ambitions. As such, in coming years, the Iraq War may come to be seen as a pivotal geopolitical event that heralded the beginning of serious counter-hegemonic balancing against the United States.

Flushed with (apparent) triumph in Iraq and the awesome display of American might, U.S. policymakers may believe that American hegemony is an unchallengeable fact of international life. Other states, however, will draw the opposite conclusion: that the United States is too powerful and that its hegemony must be resisted. Although American policymakers have convinced themselves that the United States is a benign hegemon, there is no such animal in international politics. And even if U.S. foreign and defense policies remain relatively benign, other states always will fear that such benevolence might disappear in the wink of an election.

Conclusion

In the wake of September 11, American hegemony has had paradoxical effects. On the one hand, its immense military, economic, technological, and financial capabilities have enabled the United States to organize a broad international coalition against terrorism and to achieve significant military successes in Afghanistan and Iraq. On the other hand, however, the United States was a target on September 11 precisely because of its hegemonic role in international politics, and its concomitant geostrategic preeminence in the Persian Gulf. Moreover, the war on terrorism has fueled America's expansionist grand strategic proclivities while simultaneously underscoring the magnitude of U.S. power. Thus, one of the long-term consequences may be to accelerate counter-hegemonic balancing directed at the United States. Finally, there is the risk—seldom acknowledged by American hegemony's proponents—that the United States may succumb to the "hegemon's temptation" to overreach.

Precisely because it is so unconstrained geopolitically, its military superiority may lure the United States to intervene promiscuously in conflicts abroad. The cumulative costs of fighting asymmetric conflicts against terrorists (and waging a possibly prolonged guerilla war in occupied Iraq), regional powers, and "near peer" competitors could erode America's relative power (especially if the United States suffers setbacks in future conflicts, especially with China). At the end of the day, hegemons are defeated not just by the counter-hegemonic behavior of other states, but by mounting internal economic, political, and social weaknesses caused or exacerbated by the strains of hegemony. That is, hegemons fall victim to what Paul Kennedy called "imperial overstretch." In fact, a causal relationship exists between the external and internal roots of hegemonic decline, because, as overextension leads to enervation—and a consequent decline in the hegemon's relative power—the gap between the hegemon and others begins to narrow. The closing of the relative power gap makes it more feasible for others to engage successfully in counter-hegemonic balancing.

Far from rendering balance of power theories irrelevant as the key analytical tool in the study of international politics, asymmetric challenges—from terrorism, regional powers, and rising peer competitors—have underscored their salience. American hegemony poses important questions for international relations theorists, policy analysts, and policymakers. In the realm of policy, debate in coming years will focus even more intently on whether the United States can be a successful hegemon, or whether it should adopt offshore balancing—a more traditional balance of power approach—as its grand strategy.[47] This debate on American grand strategy will overlap the debate among international relations theorists about which balance of power theories have the most robust explanatory and predictive value. In coming years, the real world of international politics will furnish an interesting field test of Offensive Realism versus Defensive Realism, and of those theories that claim that hegemony produces peace and stability (hegemonic stability theory, balance of threat theory, and power transition theory), and of those that argue that hegemonic systems are war-prone and unstable (Neorealist theory and classical balance of power theory). The bet here is that the core predictions of Neorealist theory and classical balance of power theory will be validated.

Notes

1. For representative arguments in favor of American hegemony, see Zbigniew Brzezinski, *The Grand Chessboard: American Primacy and Its Geostrategic Imperatives* (New York: Basic, 1997); Stephen G. Brooks and William C. Wohlforth, "American Primacy in Perspective," *Foreign Affairs* 81 (July/August 2002): 20–33; Robert Kagan and William Kristol, "The Present Danger," *The National Interest* No.59 (Spring 2000): 57–69; William Kristol and Robert Kagan, "Toward a Neo-Reaganite Foreign Policy," *Foreign Affairs* 75 (July/August 1996): 18–32; Zalmay Khalilzad, "Losing the Moment? The United States and the World after the Cold War," *Washington Quarterly* 18 (Spring 1995): 87–107; Charles Krauthammer, "The Unipolar Moment," *Foreign Affairs* 70 (1990/91): 23–33. For critiques of the strategy of preponderance, see Samuel P. Huntington, "The Lonely Superpower," *Foreign Affairs* 78 (March/April 1999): 35–49; Christopher Layne, "Rethinking American Grand Strategy," *World Policy Journal* 15 (Summer 1998): 8–28; Charles William Maynes, "The Perils of (and for) an Imperial America," *Foreign Policy* No. 111 (summer 1998): 36–49.

2. Core Realist works include, E. H. Carr, *The Twenty Years' Crisis, 1919–1939: An Introduction to the Study of International Relations* (New York: Harper Torchbooks, 1964); John J. Mearsheimer, *The Tragedy of Great Power Politics* (New York: Norton, 2001); Hans J. Morgenthau, *Politics Among Nations: The Struggle for Power and Peace*, 6th ed. revised by Kenneth W. Thompson (New York: Knopf, 1986); Kenneth N. Waltz, *Theory of International Politics* (Reading, Mass.: Addison-Wesley, 1979). For useful discussions of Realism, see Benjamin Frankel, "Introduction: Restating the Realist Case," *Security Studies* 5 (Spring 1996): ix–xx; Robert G. Gilpin, "No One Loves a Realist," *Security Studies* 5 (Spring 1996): 326; Robert G. Gilpin, "The Richness of the Tradition of Political Realism," in Robert O. Keohane (ed.), *Neorealism and Its Critics* (New York: Columbia University Press, 1986), 301–21; Jack S. Levy, "The Causes of War: A Review of Theories and Evidence," in Philip E. Tetlock, Jo L. Husbands, Robert Jervis, Paul C. Stern,

and Charles Tilly (eds.), *Behavior, Society, and Nuclear War,* vol. 1 (New York: Oxford University Press, 1989), 209–333.

3. Robert Gilpin, *War and Change in World Politics* (Cambridge: Cambridge University Press, 1981), 7.

4. Waltz, *Theory of International Politics*, 91–92. Robert Gilpin also notes that unless it first assures its security and survival, a state will not be able to pursue other goals that it values. Gilpin, "Richness of Political Realism," 305.

5. Waltz, *Theory of International Politics*, 113.

6. John Herz argued that the "power and security dilemma" was Realism's core insight. John Herz, *Political Realism and Political Idealism* (Chicago: University of Chicago Press, 1951), 24. Also, see Robert Jervis, "Cooperation Under the Security Dilemma," *World Politics* 30 (January 1978): 167–214.

7. On Offensive Realism, see Mearsheimer, *Tragedy;* Fareed Zakaria, *From Wealth to Power: The Unusual Origins of America's World Role* (Princeton: Princeton University Press, 1998); Eric J. Labs, "Beyond Victory: Offensive Realism and the Expansion of War Aims," *Security Studies* 6 (Summer 1997): 1–49; and Christopher Layne, "'The Poster Child of Offensive Realism': America as Global Hegemon," *Security Studies* 30 (Winter 2002/3), 120–64. On power transition theory, see A. F. K. Organski, *World Politics* (New York: Knopf, 1968); A. F. K. Organski and Jacek Kugler, *The War Ledger* (Chicago: University of Chicago Press, 1980); Jacek Kugler and Douglas Lemke (eds.), *Parity and War: Evaluations and Extensions of the War Ledger* (Ann Arbor: University of Michigan Press, 1996).

8. Perhaps the best-known argument that traditional forms of warfare between states will be displaced by low intensity conflicts, including terrorism, waged by non-state actors is Martin van Creveld, *The Transformation of War: The Most Radical Reinterpretation of Armed Conflict Since Clausewitz* (New York: Free Press, 1991).

9. For a very useful discussion of terrorism and its different manifestations, see Bruce Hoffman, *Inside Terrorism* (New York: Columbia University Press, 1998).

10. Although lesser powers—regional powers, for example—often imitate the balancing behavior of the great powers (to prevent nearby rivals from attaining regional hegemony, or to prevent distant great powers from establishing regional preponderance), they operate under different constraints than great powers. Thus, it is not uncommon for non-great powers to eschew balancing strategies in favor of bandwagoning.

11. Hoffman, *Inside Terrorism*, 14–15. See also, James D. Kiras, "Terrorism and Irregular Warfare," in John Bayliss, James Wirtz, Eliot Cohen, and Colin S. Gray (eds.), *Strategy in the Contemporary World: An Introduction to Strategic Studies* (New York: Oxford University Press 2002), 228–29.

12. John Arquilla, David Ronfelt, and Michele Zanini, "Networks, Netwar, and Information Age Terrorism," in Ian O. Lesser, Bruce Hoffman, John Arquilla, David Ronfelt, and Michele Zanini (eds.), *Countering the New Terrorism* (Santa Monica, Calif.: RAND, 1999), 39; Ian O. Lesser, "Countering the New Terrorism: Implications for Strategy," in Lesser et al., *Countering the New Terrorism*, 85.

13. Along these lines, during the U.S. bombing of Afghanistan in fall 2001 and winter 2002, the Taliban regime disseminated false accounts of civilian casualties to the Islamic world in the hope of fomenting widespread public unrest against the United States. David Zucchino, "In the Taliban's Eyes, Bad News Was Good," *Los Angeles Times,* June 4, 2002, online at <http://www.latimes.com/news/printedition/asection/la000039059jun03.story?coll=la%2Dnews%2Da%>.

14. Carl von Clausewitz, *On War,* Michael Howard and Peter Paret, eds. and trans. (Princeton: Princeton University Press, 1976), 92.

15. Richard K. Betts, "The New Threat of Mass Destruction," *Foreign Affairs* 77 (January/February 1998): 26–41. Betts was referring to the first attack on the World Trade Center in 1993.

16. Zakaria, *From Wealth to Power,* 20.

17. Mearsheimer, *Tragedy,* 33.

18. Robert B. Strassler (ed.), *The Landmark Thucydides* (New York: Free Press, 1996), 372.

19. Patrick E. Tyler, "U.S. Strategy Plan Calls for Insuring No Rivals Develop," *New York Times,* March 8, 1992, A1.

20. For example, see Undersecretary of Defense (Policy), *1991 Summer Study,* organized by the Director, Net Assessment, held at Newport, R.I., August 5–13 1991. Also, see the 1997 *Quadrennial Defense Review* (Clinton administration), and 2001 *Quadrennial Defense Review* (second Bush administration). The 1997 *QDR* makes it clear that the objective of U.S. grand strategy, and the military posture that underpins it, is to keep things just the way they are geopolitically by "discourag[ing] a prospective challenger from initiating a military competition with the United States." And the 2001 *QDR* states (12–13, 15) that the United States seeks to maintain "favorable power balances" in key regions like East Asia, the Persian Gulf, and Europe. Washington will accomplish this aim by maintaining overwhelming military superiority to "dissuade other countries from initiating future military competitions" against the United States, and, if necessary, to "impose the will of the United States . . . on *any* adversaries." Also revealing is the admission by the primary author of the draft FY 94–99 *DPG,* Paul Wolfowitz (back in the Pentagon in the second Bush administration as deputy secretary of defense) that the *DPG's* grand strategic objective was to maintain a Pax Americana. Paul Wolfowitz, "Remembering the Future," *The National Interest* (Spring 2000): 86.

21. What subsequently became known as the "Clinton Doctrine" was in place as early as April 1993, when President Clinton stated:

During the Cold War our foreign policies largely focused on relations among nations. Our strategies sought a balance of power to keep the peace. Today, our policies must also focus on relations within nations, on a nation's form of governance, on its economic structure, on its ethnic tolerance. These are of concern to us, for they shape how these nations treat their neighbors as well as their own people and whether they are reliable when they give their word." President Bill Clinton, "Remarks to the American Society of Newspaper Editors," Annapolis, Md., April 1, 1993.

Similarly, in January 2000 Deputy Secretary of State Strobe Talbott declared that, "the way a government treats its own people is not just an 'internal matter;' it is the business of the international community because there are issues of both universal values and regional peace at stake and also because true security and stability in Europe can only come when those commodities exist within society as well as between states." Deputy Secretary of State Strobe Talbott, "Robert C. Frasure Memorial Lecture," Tallinn, Estonia, January 24, 2000, State Department Web site. <http://www.state.gov/www/policy_remarks/2000/000124_talbott_tallinn .html> accessed 1/14/03.

22. Henry A. Kissinger, "The Long Shadow of Vietnam," *Newsweek*, May 1, 2000, 50.

23. On hegemonic stability theory see Gilpin, *War and Change in World Politics*; Gilpin, *U.S. Power and the Multinational Corporation: The Political Economy of U.S. Foreign Direct Investment* (New York: Basic, 1975); Charles P. Kindleberger, *The World in Depression, 1929–1939* (Berkeley: University of California Press, 1973).

24. See footnote 3.

25. For example, see Michael Mastanduno, "Preserving the Unipolar Moment: Realist Theories and U.S. Grand Strategy," *International Security* 21 (Spring 1997): 49–88.

26. Ibid., 21.

27. Ibid., 22–26.

28. Walt, *War and Revolution*, 19, 339.

29. On the role of soft power in American grand strategy, see Joseph S. Nye Jr., *Bound to Lead: The Changing Nature of American Power* (New York: Basic, 1990).

30. Joseph S. Nye Jr., "The Power We Must Not Squander," *New York Times*, January 3, 2000, online archive search result at <http://query.nytimes.com/gst/ abstract.html?res=FB0E16FC395C0C708CDDA80894D8404482> accessed January 14, 2003. In a similar vein, see G. John Ikenberry and Charles A. Kupchan, "The Legitimation of Hegemonic Power," in David P. Rapkin, ed., *World Leadership and Hegemony* (Boulder, Colo.: Lynne Rienner, 1990).

31. Joseph S. Nye Jr., *The Paradox of American Power: Why the World's Only Superpower Can't Go It Alone* (New York: Oxford University Press, 2002), esp. chaps. 1 and 5.

32. Stephen M. Walt, "Beyond Bin Laden: Reshaping U.S. Foreign Policy," *International Security* 26 (Winter 2001/2002): 59–62, 76.

33. G. John Ikenberry, "Institutions, Strategic Restraint, and the Persistence of Postwar Order," *International Security* 23 (Winter 1998/99): 76–77.

34. Kenneth N. Waltz, "America as a Model for the World? A Foreign Policy

Perspective," *PS* (*Journal of the American Political Science Association*) 24 (December 1991): 669.

35. For a detailed explanation of the theoretical and empirical foundations of this argument, see Christopher Layne, "The Unipolar Illusion. Why New Great Powers Will Rise," *International Security* 17 (Spring 1993): 5–51.

36. William C. Wohlforth, "The Stability of a Unipolar World," *International Security* 24 (Summer 1999): 4–41.

37. Kenneth N. Waltz, "Globalization and American Power," *The National Interest* 59 (Spring 2000): 54.

38. There is disagreement among analysts about China's prospects for emerging as a true peer competitor of the United States. See Thomas J. Christensen, "Posing Problems without Catching Up: China's Rise and Challenges for U.S. Security Policy," *International Security* 25 (Spring 2001): 5–9.

39. The key work is T. V. Paul, *Asymmetric Conflicts: War Initiation by Great Powers* (Cambridge: Cambridge University Press, 1994).

40. In his classic study, Andrew Mack demonstrates that weaker powers often count on favorable asymmetries in motivation to offset an unfavorable asymmetry in material capabilities. Specifically, weaker powers often calculate that if the stakes in the conflict are vital to themselves but peripheral to a more powerful defender, domestic political factors ultimately will constrain the stronger power from incurring high costs to defeat the weaker power. See Andrew Mack, "Why Big Nations Lose Small Wars: The Politics of Asymmetric Conflict, " *World Politics* 27 (January 1975): 175–200.

41. Edward Luttwak, *Strategy: The Logic of War and Peace* (Cambridge, Mass.: Belknap Press of Harvard University Press, 1987), 16.

42. For a discussion of the Iraqi and Iranian cases, see Timothy V. McCarthy and Jonathan B. Tucker, "Saddam's Toxic Arsenal and Biological Weapons in the Gulf Wars," and Gregory F. Giles, "The Islamic Republic of Iran and Nuclear, Biological, and Chemical Weapons," in Peter R. Lavoy, Scott D. Sagan, and James J. Wirtz (eds.), *Planning the Unthinkable: How New Powers Will Use Nuclear, Biological, and Chemical Weapons* (Ithaca: Cornell University Press, 2000), 47–78, 79–103. It should be noted that the "American threat" is not the only motive for regional powers to acquire nuclear, biological, or chemical weapons. For example, Iran and Iraq are locked in an intense security competition with each other, and both regard Israel—a nuclear power—as a security threat.

43. For a counterfactual analysis that seeks to shed light on this question, see Barry R. Posen, "U.S. Security Policy in a Nuclear-Armed World (Or: What If Iraq Had Had Nuclear Weapons?)," *Security Studies* 6 (Spring 1997): 1–31.

44. James J. Wirtz, "Counterproliferation, Conventional Counterforce and Nuclear War," *Journal of Strategic Studies* 23 (March 2000).

45. For an analysis of how a China that failed to achieve peer competitor status might nonetheless prevail (or perceive that it could prevail) in an asymmetric

conflict with the United States fought over the fate of Taiwan, see Christensen, "Posing Problems without Catching Up."

46. Brooks and Wohlforth, "American Primacy in Perspective," 21.

47. For fuller descriptions of offshore balancing, see Christopher Layne and Benjamin Schwarz, "A New Grand Strategy," *Atlantic Monthly* 289 (January 2002): 36–42; Christopher Layne, "From Preponderance to Offshore Balancing: America's Future Grand Strategy," *International Security* 22 (Summer 1997): 86–124; Christopher Layne, "American Grand Strategy After the Cold War: Primacy or Blue Water?" in Charles F. Hermann (ed.), *American Defense Annual 1994* (New York: Lexington, for the Mershon Center, Ohio State University, 1994); Layne, "The Unipolar Illusion"; Mearsheimer, *Tragedy,* esp. chaps. 7 and 8.

CHAPTER 5

The Balance of Power Paradox

JAMES J. WIRTZ

Balancing behavior is important in world politics because it can deter conflict, at least according to its leading proponents and theorists. It is not just
the presence of an international coalition ready to use diplomacy or violence
that deters aggression, but the possible emergence of states willing to resist
aggression that must be taken into consideration by leaders contemplating
the use of force to achieve their objectives. As Jack Levy notes in this volume,
"potential hegemons anticipate that expansionist behavior would lead to the
formation of a military coalition against them and refrain from aggression for
that reason." Indeed, one security motivation behind the formation of the
United Nations, and the North Atlantic Treaty Organization, for that matter, was to create standing coalitions to demonstrate to potential trouble-
makers that significant forces will respond to threats to international peace or
to the security of member states. Collective security organizations are not
supposed just to respond to war, they also are supposed to deter aggression.

By suggesting that balancing behavior can serve as a significant mechanism to deter war, however, balance of power theorists face an embarrassing
anomaly: war often erupts between great powers and very weak states.
Whatever theoretical school one follows—in other words, whether one
believes that a parity in the balance between states preserves the peace or that
a preponderance of power deters hostilities—the outbreak of war between
states with gross disparities of military, economic, or diplomatic resources
defies the expectations of balance of power theorists.[1] Disagreement about
relative strength has been identified by Geoffrey Blainey as a cause of war,
but the fact that this disagreement can emerge when both states apparently
recognize that significant military, economic, or demographic disparities
exist between them has received less attention.[2] It also defies the expectations
of deterrence theorists, who predict that the awareness of a potential oppo-

nent's overwhelming military capability, combined with its stated willingness to use force, should deter a grossly inferior competitor from initiating hostilities. Deterrence theorists also would suggest that in circumstances where extreme disparities in capabilities exist, compellent strategies adopted by the stronger party should succeed in achieving their objectives short of war. Leaders equipped with even limited rational insight should comply with the demands of a greatly superior opponent. One would therefore think that the demands of a universal coalition of states would be irresistible.

Although few scholars have addressed the anomaly inherent in these "asymmetric conflicts," past efforts have focused on identifying the circumstances under which a weaker party might decide to initiate hostilities. By using the expected-utility model, for example, T. V. Paul has explained how weaker powers might initiate hostilities to obtain limited objectives, such as breaking a deadlock in negotiations or to highlight some perceived injustice in the status quo.[3] James Fearon also notes that states often are influenced by "private information" about the existing military balance and have incentives to hide information about their military capabilities and intentions, producing disagreements about relative strength that can lead to war.[4] Theorists, however, usually focus on the reasons why unexpected outcomes occur, rather than on how the expectations of both sides can lead to war.[5] They fail to explain the calculations made by the stronger actor in the asymmetric conflict and why its balancing behavior or its deterrent or compellent policies fail. Asymmetric conflict would be better explained if viewed as a strategic interaction that produces a balance of power paradox: the tendency of war to erupt during confrontations between weak and strong states—wars that strong states should strive to avoid and weak states cannot realistically expect to win. A complete explanation of the paradox would have to take into account the behavior of both sides in a conflict and how their interaction produces war.

In contrast to previous suggestions that weaker powers generally fight much stronger powers over limited objectives or that private information, denial, and deception cloud what should be a relatively clear assessment of the strategic balance, the argument advanced here is that weak powers engage in conflicts with enormously superior opponents because their leaders believe that the great power will not be able to bring its full force to bear in the conflict. Leaders of weak countries tend to focus on the constraints imposed by the balance of power on the stronger opponent (for example, the danger that another great power will be drawn into the conflict on the weak power's behalf). By contrast, leaders of the stronger side focus on the relative power imbalance between themselves and the weaker opponent. They fail to recognize that extremely weak opponents sometimes see reasons for optimism beyond a specific bilateral relationship. Because the strategic effect of the balance of power paradox is to make both sides extremely risk acceptant, conflict breaks out in crises that theory and logic would suggest should be resolved short of war. There is a clear pattern of bias in ex ante estimates, and this bias is shaped by the very structure of the conflict (that is, strong state versus weak state) itself. Those who focus on how human cognition limits the prospects of rational choice can use this argument to predict which analytical lenses or types of wishful thinking are likely to shape the ex ante assessments of the opponent's willingness to engage in war.

A host of psychological explanations, not to mention an even more vexing array of idiosyncratic developments, could thus explain the immediate outbreak of asymmetric conflicts or the inner workings of the balance of power paradox. But this chapter will suggest that these wildly divergent perspectives about the relative power positions held by both sides in an asymmetric conflict are inherent in balancing behavior. By focusing on only one facet of the balance, leaders tend to perceive the constraints facing their opponent, while their own strengths are highly salient to them. Leaders of strong powers thus take an "attritional" view of conflict, taking full measure of how their superior capabilities will clearly and inevitably crush weak challengers. By contrast, leaders of weak powers are likely to adopt an "asymmetric" view of conflict because they tend to believe that their strategies will prevent the stronger power from bringing its full weight to bear in a conflict. In other work I have identified the crucial role surprise plays in the calculations of weaker states planning to attack strong states.[6] Here I identify the way balance of power calculations themselves can create the balance of power paradox—the eruption of war between strong and weak states.

To address this issue, the chapter will first use Kenneth Waltz's *Theory of International Relations* to explain how the balance of power paradox leads to indeterminate predictions of the behavior of weak and strong states in a bipolar system. Waltz's argument does so by examining the way balance of power considerations affected American and North Vietnamese perceptions of their relative positions during the Vietnam War. This chapter will then explore the recent failures of deterrent and compellent strategies in the 1991

Gulf War, to demonstrate how the conflict represents a transition point between the constraints created by the Cold War and a new situation that reflects more "soft balancing." This chapter is ambitious in the sense that it identifies not only the forces that shape the balance of power paradox, but also the forces that continue to foster it at a time when the United States enjoys a position of increasing military, economic, and diplomatic dominance in world politics.

The Balance of Power Paradox in a Bipolar World

In a bipolar system, the two dominant powers, which were referred to as superpowers, were preoccupied with one another's activities. "In the great-power politics of bipolar worlds," according to Waltz, "who is a danger to whom is never in doubt."[7] Because of the enormous conventional and nuclear arsenals possessed by both superpowers, only the United States and the Soviet Union could mortally threaten each other's survival. Moreover, because of the enormous gulf between the capabilities and resources possessed by the superpowers and their nearest rivals, American and Soviet desires to strengthen themselves vis-à-vis their main competitor were best realized through internal efforts. Under these circumstances, allies objectively added little to the security of the superpowers, and even major changes in alliances had little effect on the existing military, economic, and political equilibrium between the United States and the USSR. To highlight this point, Waltz cited the minimal systemic effect produced by Beijing's withdrawal from the American "alliance" in 1949, and the de facto Sino-American alliance that emerged during the 1970s. In other words, if the world's most populous country could change sides during the Cold War without altering the balance of power significantly, then changes among lesser allies and rivals could not alter the equilibrium of a bipolar world.[8]

Given these structural realities, Waltz would suggest that both superpowers could be expected to shun military involvement in peripheral conflicts in the Third World. In 1967, for example, Waltz noted:

> Two states that enjoy wide margins of power over other states need worry little about changes that occur among the latter. . . . Because no realignment of national power in Vietnam could in itself affect the balance of

power between the United States and the Soviet Union—or even noticeably alter the imbalance of power between the United States and China—the United States need not have intervened at all.[9]

At best, involvement in the periphery represents a "side show" that could do little to affect the balance of capabilities between the superpowers in a bipolar world. At worst, peripheral involvements could drain vital resources needed to maintain a superpower's position vis-à-vis its main rival.[10]

Conversely, bipolarity can provide superpowers with an incentive to become embroiled in peripheral conflicts. In a bipolar world, according to Waltz, great-power leaders tend to view international relations as a zero-sum situation. Regardless of the causes of a particular setback, losses to one superpower are often interpreted to be a direct gain for its main rival. This zero-sum view increases both sides' preoccupation with changes affecting allies, lesser rivals, and nonaligned nations, despite the fact that these changes have little direct impact on the superpower competition. "Bipolarity encourages the United States and the Soviet Union to turn unwanted events into crises," according to Waltz, "while rendering them relatively inconsequential. . . . Both gain more by the peaceful development of internal resources than by wooing and winning—or by fighting and subduing—other states in the world." Because of this zero-sum view of the world, according to Waltz, "the U.S. has responded expensively in distant places to wayward events that could hardly affect anyone's fate outside of the region."[11]

Thus, when the great powers in a bipolar world face "wayward" events in the periphery, Waltz's theory leads to two opposing propositions about their response. First, the two superpowers will avoid involvement in unrewarding peripheral conflicts to husband their resources for the paramount great-power competition. This first proposition assumes that policymakers will be sensitive to the systemic constraints that they face and are reluctant to exploit the constraints—by definition, relative military inferiority—faced by weaker rivals. Second, faced with disagreeable, albeit relatively inconsequential, events in the periphery, the two superpowers will rush to intervene in less than vital regional disputes, to prevent even incremental gains by the rival superpower. This proposition supposes that policymakers are not sensitive to the systemic constraints that they face and are instead anxious to exploit the weaknesses of lesser rivals.

How will weak states behave toward antagonistic superpowers? Waltz's analysis does not directly address this question, but a response can be deduced from his theory and the work of other balance of power theorists. Weak states, like the great powers that loom over them, face their own array of incentives and constraints, leading to indeterminate predictions of their behavior during confrontations with a superpower in a bipolar world.

Unlike the rough equilibrium that characterizes the relationship between the superpowers in a bipolar setting, the competition between the great powers and peripheral states was one-sided. The superpowers possessed over-whelming nuclear, conventional, economic, manpower, and natural resources when compared to weak states. Although there is often a discrepancy between the appearance of power and its reality in international relations, the gross disparity in capabilities between the superpowers and weak states is too overwhelming to misunderstand or ignore.[12] It would be unlikely, indeed quite foolhardy, according to many balance of power theorists, for weak states to risk a major confrontation with a great power. "Clearly," explained Inis Claude, "a potential aggressor is likely to be deterred more effectively by confrontation with preponderant, rather than merely equal power."[13] Given the superpower tendency to view changes in the periphery in zero-sum terms, Moscow and Washington could be expected to respond to even minor challenges made by weak states. From this perspective, the combination of the superpowers' enormous capability and willingness to respond to changes in the periphery should pose a strong deterrent to provocative behavior by the weak state. According to Klaus Knorr, because of the overwhelming power great powers possess, weak states do "not even consider certain courses of action because it is obvious that they are likely to incur the displeasure of a . . . very superior state."[14]

If they focus on the systemic constraints faced by the great powers, however, policymakers in weak states will view their insignificant position in a bipolar world not as a liability, but as a major advantage. Bipolarity can offer weak states increased freedom of action, especially in risking potential conflict with a great power. Because the superpowers can be expected to concentrate primarily on the bipolar competition, weak states might calculate that the great powers would be unlikely to expend resources on trivial developments in the periphery. In the words of Arnold Wolfers, small states possess the "power of the weak."[15] Even though the great powers could easily crush them, weak states could gamble that they just are not worth the effort, and thus pursue their own policies regardless of superpower displeasure.

WHY DOES THE PARADOX LEAD TO WAR?

The very existence of the balance of power paradox suggests that war is possible, but not inevitable. Thus, a parsimonious specification of balance of power theory cannot predict whether leaders will find their constraints or their opponent's constraints most compelling during a confrontation. For example, even though Waltz maintains that great powers will probably intervene in peripheral disputes to prevent cumulative, potentially significant losses, war is risky and could weaken a superpower, leaving it vulnerable to its main competitor.[16] Conversely, weak states also might engage in provocative activities to obtain limited objectives, but this generates the graver risk of superpower intervention. For the paradox to produce war, the leaders of both weak and strong states must believe that they can avoid the systemic constraints they face while their opponent cannot escape the constraints their relative power position creates.

The divergent ways that leaders of great powers and weak states perceive a brewing conflict can propel them to war. Leaders in strong states tend to take an attritional view of warfare, focusing on the overwhelming advantages they enjoy against weaker competitors and how this military superiority will inevitably produce a victory once battle is joined. Leaders in weaker states, however, take an asymmetric view of the coming conflict. They believe that it will be possible to avoid the full brunt of their opponent's superior capability and thus achieve their objectives. For instance, surprise is often attractive to the weaker party in the conflict because it allows the weaker state to present a stronger opponent with a fait accompli without first having to do the impossible: defeat a much stronger opponent in attritional warfare. Similarly, John Mearsheimer suggests that policymakers are more likely to challenge conventional deterrence if they believe they possess a strategy that allows them to prevail quickly over their opponents with minimal cost. Mearsheimer's argument suggests leaders of weak states will ignore the systemic constraints they face when they believe they possess an asymmetric strategy, a strategy that allows them to prevail quickly and cheaply in a conflict without facing the full military might of a vastly superior opponent.[17]

Key to this analysis is that this divergence in perception tends to mask the systemic constraints faced by both strong and weak powers in a brewing conflict. By focusing on the attritional aspects of a brewing conflict, stronger powers overestimate the effectiveness of their deterrent, compellent, and war-making potential, or at least they overestimate the effect their capabilities will have on their weaker adversaries. The leaders of weaker powers, by focusing on the opportunities created by asymmetric strategies, contemplate provocative moves because they believe that they can avoid the full weight of the great power's military capability.

VIETNAM: UNLIKELY WAR, UNLIKELY OUTCOME

Given the gross disparity in resources, it is surprising that the regime in Hanoi could ever have hoped to challenge the United States militarily in South Vietnam and succeed. Given the low position of Vietnam on a long list of American strategic priorities, it also is surprising that the United States—despite claims, made from divergent political outlooks, concerning falling dominoes or the importance of Vietnam as a source of raw materials—ever devoted significant resources to stop North Vietnam's efforts to unify the country. Indeed, the so called Big-Unit War, which erupted between the Viet Cong (VC) and their North Vietnamese allies and the Saigon regime and its American supporters, actually proved to be an unwelcome development from the perspective of both the victors and the vanquished. Even though North Vietnam eventually succeeded in uniting the country, the communist leadership in Hanoi initially expected to achieve their objectives without having to fight an enormously destructive war.[18] Conversely, the members of President Lyndon Johnson's administration did not initially expect to fight, and certainly not to lose, a long, costly war to preserve the Saigon regime, a war that would hurt America's global economic position and its military standing vis-à-vis the Soviet Union.

THE VIEW FROM HANOI

Because the communists eventually won in Vietnam, scholars have a tendency to underestimate the problems confronting North Vietnam following American intervention in the ground war. Yet the challenge posed by U.S. intervention loomed large in the minds of communist leaders, political cadres, and soldiers. Indeed, a wave of "defeatism" swept the ranks following American intervention as the communists encountered the mobility, firepower, and motivation of highly trained and well-equipped American forces. According to Patrick McGarvey: "The move that caused the greatest anxiety among Vietnamese Communist leaders—if the sheer volume of writing is an accurate gauge—was the sudden influx of American ground forces in South Vietnam in mid-1965."[19]

Decisions made by North Vietnam to escalate its involvement in the south evolved over time. Following the renewal of guerrilla warfare in South Vietnam during the late 1950s, provoked by Ngo Dinh Diem's successful anticommunist campaign, members of the Viet Cong petitioned the Hanoi leadership to aid them in their fight for survival. In response, North Vietnam provided "regroupees," southern communists who had fled north following the 1954 Geneva accords, to support the Viet Cong. This relatively limited North Vietnamese aid had a significant impact on the battlefield. Prior to Diem's overthrow in November 1963, the South Vietnamese military position had deteriorated. In the aftermath of the Diem coup, however, the South Vietnamese position collapsed as Army Republic of Vietnam (ARVN) units and their commanders became caught up in the struggle to control the government in Saigon. The North Vietnamese, following a December 1963 meeting of the Central Committee of the Vietnamese Worker's (Communist) Party, decided to capitalize on this turmoil by escalating their involvement in the south. North Vietnamese Army (NVA) units were soon streaming down the Ho Chi Minh Trail.[20] By 1963, harassment of an American client had escalated to the point of a direct North Vietnamese threat to the continued existence of South Vietnam.

In acting provocatively, were the North Vietnamese so obsessed with the goal of unifying Vietnam that they were oblivious to the systemic constraints they faced? The answer to this question is no. North Vietnamese officials realized that the U.S. possessed overwhelming resources; they recognized that they faced systemic constraints. This awareness was a tacit product of their Marxist-Leninist ideology. Characterized as the "leading imperialist power," the U.S. enjoyed certain advantages, among them overwhelming military and economic resources. Marxism-Leninism, however, also identified the systemic constraints faced by the United States. Writing in September 1967, long after the Johnson administration had demonstrated its willingness to intervene massively in the war, General Vo Nguyen Giap noted that America's global commitments limited the resources it could devote to the conflict: "The U.S. imperialists must cope with the national liberation movement [in countries other than South Vietnam], with the socialist bloc, with the American people, and with other imperialist countries. The U.S. imperialists cannot mobilize all their forces for the war of aggression in Vietnam."[21] Giap was referring to the systemic constraints created by bipolarity as a factor that would limit the U.S. response in Vietnam. Even though their ideology identified the systemic constraints that they faced, as well as those of their opponents, in December 1963, communist leaders chose to emphasize the obstacles confronting the United States. In deciding to escalate the conflict in the south, they estimated that the United States probably would not respond massively to overt North Vietnamese intervention. At worst, the North Vietnamese predicted that the Americans might send 100,000 troops to support their Vietnamese clients, but they considered this eventuality to be unlikely.[22]

The North Vietnamese saw recent history as a reflection of the systemic constraints the United States faced. In their view, Americans had a tendency either to abandon clients or compromise in the face of concerted challenges to "imperialism." North Vietnamese leaders pointed to the U.S. decision not to save Chiang Kai-Shek's regime in China as an example of the American tendency to walk away from "no-win" situations. They regarded U.S. acceptance of a compromise settlement of the Korean War in the same light, despite the fact that the Chinese communists, who relied on a different interpretation of the Korean analogy, continuously warned them of the danger of provoking a massive American response in Southeast Asia. Even though many North Vietnamese officials blamed their Soviet and Chinese allies for the "sell-out" that produced the 1954 Geneva accords, the agreements in their view again pointed to an American preference for compromise settlements. Finally, the North Vietnamese saw the 1961 agreement on the neutralization of Laos as further evidence of American reluctance to interfere in Asia. Given their reading of recent events, the communists apparently believed that if they could convince U.S. officials that the situation in Saigon had deteriorated significantly, Americans either would accept a political settlement of the war or would simply withdraw from South Vietnam. In order to trigger the expected American response to a deteriorating situation, the North Vietnamese escalated their involvement in the south.[23]

In the minds of Hanoi strategists, the People's War would largely negate the advantages enjoyed by the leading imperialist power, by allowing the North Vietnamese to control the level of violence in any confrontation with the United States. By shifting their *dau tranh* (struggle) to liberate the south toward the political realm, they could reduce casualties and increase the duration of the war, thereby denying Americans a quick military victory. In other words, the North Vietnamese believed that they possessed a military strategy that would raise the stakes enough to force American officials to withdraw from Vietnam or risk wasting resources that needed to be preserved for the main contest with the Soviet Union.[24] Systemic constraints would prevent the United States from bringing its full power to bear in Southeast Asia.

THE VIEW FROM THE POTOMAC

Prior to their decision to intervene in the ground war, members of the Johnson administration failed to realize that they ran the risk of becoming embroiled in a lengthy war that could reduce America's standing vis-à-vis the USSR. Warnings existed, however, about the gravity of the task they contemplated. France's unhappy experience in Indochina could not be ignored, even though many Americans denied its relevance as a guide to policy.[25] After all, as William Bundy noted in a November 1964 memorandum to the National Security Council (NSC) working group on Southeast Asia, "the French also tried to build the Panama Canal."[26] A war game, code-named SIGMA I, conducted during late 1963, also suggested that after a ten-year commitment of 600,000 U.S. combat troops, the VC would continue to expand their control of the South Vietnamese countryside. The participants in the exercise, with even more exact foresight, concluded that the American public would grow tired of such a costly, drawn-out conflict. Yet the lessons offered by SIGMA I failed to have any discernible impact on the policies the Johnson administration adopted.[27] Members of the Johnson administration were not particularly concerned about the systemic constraints they faced in contemplating intervention in Vietnam.

In contrast, members of the administration were alert to the possibility that not acting to stop the communists might produce negative consequences for the United States. They believed they needed to maintain their reputation as a faithful ally. Since the administration's rhetoric highlighted the American commitment to South Vietnam, administration officials believed that U.S. policy toward Southeast Asia would be interpreted as a test case of American resolve. As John McNaughton's July 13, 1965, memorandum to Secretary of Defense McNamara demonstrates, the administration's goals in Southeast Asia were intended:

70%—To preserve our national honor as a guarantor (and the reciprocal: to avoid a showcase success for Communist 'wars of liberation'?)

20%—To keep SVN (and their adjacent) territory from hostile expansive [sic] hands -

10%—To "answer the call of a friend," to help him enjoy a better life.

Also—To emerge from crisis without unacceptable taint from the methods used.[28]

If the United States backed away from it commitment to South Vietnam, there was concern that it might damage "Free World" solidarity vis-à-vis the Soviet bloc. For many members of the Johnson administration, a quick humiliation in Vietnam, not a drawn-out war, was interpreted as the more conceivable threat to American standing in the global competition with the USSR. Ironically, systemic constraints were offered as a justification for intervention in Vietnam. A U.S. failure to respond to the communists was seen to lead to prompt negative consequences, while the long-term threat of becoming embroiled in a quagmire appeared less salient to policymakers.

The objectives behind the American decision to respond to the NVA invasion of South Vietnam closely matched their perception of the way the international system constrained their Vietnamese opponents. The purpose of American policy toward Southeast Asia was not to win the war in Vietnam, but to demonstrate to the North Vietnamese that they could not obtain their objectives militarily. The Americans believed that if their actions could increase the salience of the systemic constraints faced by the North Vietnamese, in this case military inferiority, then the communists would abandon their quest to unite Vietnam through military action. Commenting on the conclusions reached by senior officials during an April 1965 meeting in Honolulu, McNamara noted that the American goal in Vietnam was "to break the will of the DRV/VC by depriving them of victory."[29] In the words of Maxwell Taylor, "a demonstration of Communist impotence . . . will lead to a political solution."[30] Years later, Taylor elaborated on the expectations held by American officials at the time:

In 1965 we knew very little about the Hanoi leaders other than Ho Chi Minh and General Giap and virtually nothing about their individual or collective intentions. We were inclined to assume, however, that they would behave about like the North Koreans and Red Chinese a decade before; that is, they would seek an accommodation with us when the cost of pursuing a losing course became excessive.[31]

American policymakers believed that officials in Hanoi had somehow experienced a strategic or intelligence failure, and had underestimated the potential forces that could be arrayed against them. By engaging in a gradual escalation of the conflict and by introducing combat forces into South Vietnam, the Americans expected that they would be able to compel Hanoi to abandon their effort to unify Vietnam through the use of force. If Ho Chi Minh and his follows had miscalculated, then a demonstration of force would bring them to their senses by highlighting the systemic constraints (that is, their military inferiority) they faced. Two American mistakes thus smoothed the path to a disastrous conflict: (1) they failed to realize that North Vietnamese leaders believed they would not have to face the full brunt of American military power; and (2) they did not anticipate North Vietnamese willingness to suffer when the United States actually intervened in force. As Taylor noted in 1972, "the North Vietnamese proved to be incredibly tough in accepting losses which, by Western calculation, greatly exceeded the value of the stake involved."[32]

The Balance of Power Paradox and the End of Bipolarity: The 1991 Gulf War

If the North Vietnamese could look to the Soviet Union to constrain the United States, what force today prevents the United States from using its overwhelming military capability to punish or coerce weak states? Indeed, the balance of power paradox is even more perplexing in the aftermath of the Cold War because weak states can no longer hope that the remaining superpower will be constrained by a great-power competitor. Nevertheless, U.S. deterrent and compellent threats have failed repeatedly since the end of the Cold War (for example, the 1999 war in Kosovo, or a near-decade-long terrorist campaign launched by al-Qaeda), leading to brief conflicts between the United States (usually accompanied by many allies) and grossly inferior opponents. From a systemic perspective, the United States, as the sole surviving superpower, faces few constraints, which should leave weak states little hope of avoiding the full brunt of its military capability. Yet, weak states and groups continue to confront, defy, and even attack the United States and its interests, while hoping to avoid defeat or even retaliation. In all cases, none of America's opponents doubted that the United States enjoyed significant military capability. Instead, they all believed that U.S. officials, for one reason or another, would not be willing to use that power effectively.

The Iraqi invasion of Kuwait in August 1990 and the subsequent international effort to liberate the small nation occurred at the very moment the old bipolar order was crumbling; the conflict began during the Cold War but at its end only one superpower remained. It also represents both a failure of deterrence, in that the United States did not prevent the Iraqi invasion, and a failure of compellence in the sense that Saddam Hussein did not withdraw from Kuwait but instead chose to battle a global coalition that was determined to eject Iraqi forces from the emirate. Although the Iraqi invasion of Kuwait is a poor case to assess deterrence theory because U.S. officials failed to make a clear deterrent threat prior to the invasion, it does illustrate the fact that Saddam Hussein was not particularly concerned about the prospect of intervention.

THE FAILURE OF DETERRENCE

By all accounts, Iraq's invasion of Kuwait was prompted by a fundamental and well-understood motivation: money. With its economy wrecked by the Iran-Iraq war, with international creditors beginning to back away from loans, and with hundreds of thousands of veterans wanting to return to the good life that would follow their "victory" against Iran, Iraq was in dire straits. Saddam Hussein turned to extortion to shore up his economy and preserve his regime by putting pressure on Kuwait for territorial concessions, access to Kuwaiti oil reserves, and an outright gift of $10 billion. The war also highlighted rifts among members of the Organization of Petroleum Exporting Countries (OPEC), between those who championed long-term policies of price stabilization and those who sought quick profits by manipulating oil markets or at least increasing their production quotas. Ironically, the Gulf War was in fact all about oil, but it was driven by Saddam Hussein's unscrupulousness and OPEC disarray.

Critics might charge that the United States never really suffered a deterrence failure prior to the Gulf War because officials in the George H. W. Bush administration failed to appreciate the nature of the threat posed by Iraq until just hours before the invasion. In the months leading up to the crisis, U.S. officials were preoccupied with the collapse of Soviet power in Europe, German unification, and devising a way to support newly liberated states in Eastern Europe. Nor, in the weeks leading up to the crisis, was the gravity of the impending threat appreciated by the international community, thanks to a highly effective denial and deception campaign undertaken by Baghdad, which convinced all concerned that the crisis would be resolved after the Kuwaitis offered up some minimal concessions, or would terminate in some sort of small Iraqi land grab in Kuwait.[33] Although the United States did manage to issue some warnings to Baghdad before the invasion, the Bush administration, following requests made by friendly governments in the region, toned down its deterrent rhetoric to allow Arab mediation to settle the dispute.

Of crucial importance, however, is Saddam Hussein's estimate of the likely U.S. response to the invasion of Kuwait. Hussein clearly believed that the United States could respond to Iraqi aggression, but he estimated that the Bush administration would choose not to expend blood and treasure to defend Kuwait. He even went so far as to make this assumption plain to the U.S. ambassador to Iraq, April Glaspie, that the Americans did not share Iraq's willingness to lose 10,000 people per day in battle, and that they risked terrorist attacks within the United States itself if they interfered in the dispute with Kuwait.[34] Hussein also might have hoped that the Soviet Union would act to restrain the United States, but as Lawrence Freedman and Efraim Karsh argue, the Iraqi dictator probably recognized that Soviet influence and power were fading rapidly. Other Arab states were beginning to reorient their foreign policies in response to the loss of their superpower patron; it is possible that Hussein saw a narrow "window of opportunity" in the summer of 1990 and decided to act before the Soviet Union disappeared from the scene.[35] In a speech delivered to the Arab Cooperation Council in Oman in July 1990, for example, Hussein noted that unless Arab states asserted themselves, Soviet decline would leave the United States as the dominant power in the Gulf.[36] Hussein also apparently believed that he could paralyze any potential Arab response to his seizure of Kuwait by linking his move to the "Israeli" issue. Without Arab acquiescence, he estimated that U.S. policymakers would be unlikely to intervene in the Gulf. And for their part, Arab leaders initially were eager to find an "Arab solution" to the conflict—not out of some feeling of Islamic solidarity, but to forestall an increase in the military presence of the great powers in the region. In effect, Hussein was not deterred because he correctly estimated that he could seize Kuwait easily and then present the world with a fait accompli that would be difficult, albeit not impossible, to overturn. The Arabs would never form a common front with the West, the Americans did not have the guts to fight, and the Soviets might see the crisis as a way to reassert their fading influence in world affairs.

THE FAILURE OF COMPELLENCE

The failure of the international effort to compel Iraq to leave Kuwait without having to resort to war underscores the difficulty of creating and maintaining a solid international front against aggression. This problem was compounded by Saddam Hussein's ability to exploit every opportunity to sow dissension among his opponents, and the tendency of the Iraqi dictator to grasp at straws even as a global coalition massed overwhelming forces against him. The international coalition that slowly gathered strength during the second half of 1990 with the purpose of expelling Iraq from Kuwait nevertheless offers a textbook case of compellence.[37]

The international forces arrayed against Baghdad were indeed impressive. Iraq faced an economic embargo that was facilitated by its reliance on oil as its sole source of hard currency. Without oil exports, Iraq lacked the cash needed to entice officials or black marketeers to risk breaking the UN economic sanctions that were imposed just days after the invasion of Kuwait. Hussein attempted to torpedo the international coalition forming against him by playing the "Public Opinion," "Third World," "Arab," and Soviet cards. He seized hostages to split the coalition, offering to return nationals to visiting dignitaries who pleaded for their safety if only their governments would break ranks with the UN. He treated western hostages better than those from the developing world, while simultaneously making overtures to governments of poor countries that he thought had common cause with them in their struggle against imperialism. (These efforts to manipulate public opinion, however, backfired as images of Hussein interacting with hostages, especially children, produced universal revulsion and anger.) He berated his Arab neighbors with the warning that any war among Muslims only strengthened Israel. Most Arab governments agreed with that sentiment, but they universally blamed Saddam Hussein for creating the conflict in the first place. And in a strange twist, Hussein taunted Soviet officials by noting that their failure to come to Iraq's aid demonstrated to all concerned that they were a state in demise:

He who represents the Soviet Union must remember that worries and suspicions about the superpower status assumed by the Soviet Union have
been crossing the minds of all politicians in the world for some time. . . .
Those concerned must choose this critical time and this critical case in
order to restore to the Soviet Union its status through adopting a position
that is in harmony with all that is just and fair.[38]

None of these gambits significantly disrupted the coalition forming
against Hussein or the universal call for Iraq to withdraw from Kuwait. In
fact, each of Iraq's moves actually hardened international public opinion in
its opposition to the Iraqi occupation of Kuwait. In the end, Iraqi officials
became highly dismissive of Soviet efforts to convince Hussein that they
would not support him in his effort to hold onto Kuwait. Soviet Foreign
Minister Eduard Shevardnadze noted that Saddam Hussein's response to an
August 23 letter from Soviet President Mikhail Gorbachev, advising him to
comply with UN resolutions, was not even worth a comment.[39]

Compellence began in earnest following the Bush administration's
October 31, 1990, decision (which was announced on November 8) to begin
to deploy forces necessary not just to deter and defend against an Iraqi drive
into Saudi Arabia, but also to expel Iraqi occupation troops from Kuwait by
force.[40] UN Resolution 678 was passed on November 29, 1990, authorizing
member states to "use all necessary means" to gain Iraqi compliance with all
eleven previous resolutions regarding Kuwait. The deadline stated for Iraqi
compliance was January 15, 1991.[41] Resolution 678 constituted an *international* ultimatum to Saddam Hussein to withdraw from Kuwait. Although a
steady stream of official, semiofficial, and private initiatives to find a peaceful solution to the crisis were taken in the weeks and days leading up to the
outbreak of hostilities, most of these emissaries reiterated the fundamental
demand advanced by the United Nations: Iraq must withdraw from Kuwait
before any of Iraq's demands would be addressed. The massive movement of
coalition forces to the Persian Gulf accompanied this diplomatic activity. In
the penultimate diplomatic meeting before the war on January 9, 1991, U.S.
Secretary of State James Baker attempted to deliver a letter to Saddam
Hussein that clearly spelled out the size and nature of the military forces
arrayed against him, made veiled threats about the "strongest possible
response" that would follow any Iraqi use of chemical or biological weapons
in the coming conflict, and the fact that Iraq would be left "weak and backward" following the terrible beating it would take in the coming war. Baker

told Tariq Aziz, the Iraqi foreign minister, that if Saddam Hussein would not comply with the demands of virtually the entire international community, Iraq would suffer decisive defeat in a short war. Baker's warning to Aziz should not have been news to Iraqi officials. In the months leading up to the war, Soviet envoy Yevgeny Primakov repeatedly told Saddam Hussein that U.S. military capabilities were vastly superior to anything in Iraq's arsenal.[42]

Although Aziz refused to deliver President Bush's letter to Saddam Hussein, he responded to Baker's brief by stating that it was the Americans and their allies who were in for a long and bloody conflict. He told him that the Arabs in the coalition would never fight alongside the United States, and that no Arab leader had ever been hurt by standing up to the West. In the days leading up to the war, Iraqi officials including Saddam Hussein harped on this theme, replete with references to America's inability to tolerate casualties and references to the U.S. experience in Vietnam. Iraqi officials were banking on the notion that the coalition could not withstand the negative political pressures generated by coalition losses in battle or the loss of civilian life from missile attacks on cities. Sometimes Iraqi officers actually claimed that the coalition lacked the necessary forces (3 million troops) to prevail over the Iraqi military, which was 1 million strong.[43] But more often they claimed that the coalition might be impressive on paper, but would in the end lack the stomach for war.

Conclusion

Although they debated different issues and in different strategic settings, the policymakers on both sides of the Vietnam and Gulf War conflicts shared remarkably similar views of their prospects in the conflict. In one case, the great-power leaders' predictions of the likely outcome came to pass: Iraq suffered a quick and decisive defeat during the Gulf War. In the other case, the limits of American power were reached in a long and bloody attritional war in Southeast Asia—a war that was won by the weaker party. In both cases, the balance of power produced war, even though Vietnam occurred at what might be considered the peak of bipolarity, while the Gulf War occurred at a time when the Soviet Union was no longer capable of acting, or willing to act, like a superpower that faced a threat to one of its clients.

In both instances, officials in the great power adopted an attritional view of war, in the sense that they focused on the gross differences between the military capabilities of the parties in the conflict and the fact that the weaker party had little prospect for victory in the event of war. The compellent strategies adopted by American policymakers thus focused on changing the perceptions of their opponents, to communicate missing information some-how about the true weakness of their military forces vis-à-vis the great power. In Southeast Asia, members of the Johnson administration hoped that mil-itary demonstrations in the form of air strikes or the deployment of ground forces would force the North Vietnamese to recognize both their military inferiority and the U.S. commitment to save the regime in Saigon. Prior to the Gulf War, officials in the first Bush administration thought that Saddam Hussein had never been given the unvarnished truth by a staff of sycophants who feared bringing the dictator an honest appraisal of Iraq's strategic prospects in the event of war. Baker's last-minute meeting with Aziz to deliver a letter from the president was intended to make sure that an honest appraisal of Iraq's prospects reached Hussein. The potential weaknesses in their position never dominated the view of the impending conflict held by leaders of the superpower.

While North Vietnamese and Iraqi officials recognized the overwhelming superiority of their potential superpower antagonist, leaders from both nations believed that the United States would not be able to bring the full weight of its military power to bear in a conflict. Leaders in Hanoi believed that America's worldwide commitments and the need to keep substantial forces in reserve to deal with a possible conflict with the Soviet Union, would limit the resources Washington could devote to blocking the unification of Vietnam under communist rule. Hanoi never really expected to defeat U.S. forces on the battlefield, but sought to confront U.S. officials with a long war that would end in a negotiated settlement favorable to the North Viet-namese. Similarly, Saddam Hussein saw the Soviet Union and an unwilling-ness to spend blood and treasure as restraints on the U.S. inclination to interfere with his plans for Kuwait. When the Soviets joined the global coali-tion to compel Iraq to abandon Kuwait, Saddam berated Moscow for its fail-ure to play its traditional superpower role by restraining the United States. And, like Hanoi, he assumed the weakest of asymmetric strategies: he will-ingly engaged the United States in an attritional campaign in an effort to get at what he perceived was the Western Achilles heel, an aversion to casualties.

What is clear in both conflicts is that American officials always framed the war in terms of a clash of military forces that the weaker party had virtually no prospect of winning, while the weaker party expected that for one reason or another the stronger party could not bring its full force to bear in a conflict. Both parties in both conflicts chose to fight instead of limit their demands—the stakes always involved who would control South Vietnam and Kuwait. But it is not surprising that a preponderance of power fails to generate a deterrent or compellent threat when it involves risk acceptant opponents, especially one that views the conflict from an asymmetric perspective and one that views the conflict from an attritional perspective. Both see their opponent's weaknesses through a different lens, and both see paths to victory.

Since 1991, other conflicts between extremely strong and extremely weak opponents have occurred in Panama, Kosovo, and Iraq that exemplify this paradox. Events in the post-Cold War era do not support the notion that states rarely challenge a superior power as balance of power theory would predict. Indeed the theory argues that parity preserves peace and under preponderance, it is the strong that attack the weak. In these cases, the weak show the inclination to challenge the status quo even when an opposing state or international coalition is overwhelmingly preponderant. The implications of this paradox for U.S. hegemony in the 21st century are enormous; both state and non-state actors can be expected to challenge the United States using asymmetric strategies. Although these challenges are rare, they still form significant anomalies to the balance of power theory.

Notes

1. George Liska, *International Equilibrium: A Theoretical Essay on the Politics and Organization of Security* (Cambridge, Mass.: Harvard University Press, 1957); Inis L. Claude, *Power and International Relations* (New York: Random House, 1962), 56.

2. Geoffrey Blainey, *The Causes of War* (New York: Free Press, 1973).

3. T. V. Paul, *Asymmetric Conflicts: War Initiation by Weaker Powers* (New York: Cambridge University Press, 1994).

4. James D. Fearon, "Rationalist Explanations for War," *International Organization* 49 (Summer 1995): 379–414.

5. Ivan Arreguin-Toft, "How the Weak Win Wars: A Theory of Asymmetric Conflict," *International Security* 26 (Summer 2001): 93–128; and Andrew Mack,

"Why Big Nations Lose Small Wars: The Politics of Asymmetric Conflict," *World Politics* 27 (January 1975): 175–200.

6. James J. Wirtz, "Theory of Surprise," in Richard K. Betts and Thomas G. Mahnken (eds.), *Paradoxes of Strategic Intelligence* (London: Frank Cass, 2003), 101–16.

7. Kenneth N. Waltz, *Theory of International Politics* (Reading, Mass.: Addison-Wesley, 1979), 170.

8. Waltz, *Theory of International Politics*, 169.

9. Kenneth N. Waltz, "International Structure, National Force, and the Balance of Power," in James Rosenau (ed.), *International Politics and Foreign Policy* (New York: Free Press, 1969), 310.

10. Waltz's students were quick to build on this point. See Stephen Van Evera, "American Strategic Interests: Why Europe Matters, Why the Third World Doesn't," *Journal of Strategic Studies* 13 (June 1990): 1–51.

11. Waltz, *Theory of International Politics*, 172.

12. According to Arnold Wolfers: "There are several reasons for the frequent discrepancies between the appearance of power and its actual performance: one is the relativity of power, another is the gap between the estimate of power and its reality, and a third is the specificity of power, which means that it takes specific types of power to bring results under specific circumstances." Arnold Wolfers, *Discord and Collaboration* (Baltimore: Johns Hopkins University Press, 1962), 110–11. The point made here, however, is that the difference between the capabilities of the superpowers and weak states is so large that leaders of weak powers have ample reason to expect that the great powers will be able to confront a challenger with overwhelming resources.

13. Inis Claude, *Power and International Relations* (New York: Random House, 1962), quoted in Robert Art and Robert Jervis (eds.), *International Politics* (Boston: Scott Foresman, 1985), 117. For a similar perspective, see A. F. K. Organski, *World Politics* (New York: Knopf, 1958), 293; Robert G. Gilpin, *War and Change in World Politics* (Cambridge: Cambridge University Press, 1981), 50–105; and, K. Edward Spiezio, "British Hegemony and Major Power War, 1815–1939: An Empirical Test of Gilpin's Model of Hegemonic Governance," *International Studies Quarterly* 34 (June 1990): 169–70.

14. Klaus Knorr, *The Power of Nations: The Political Economy of International Relations* (New York: Basic, 1975), 10. The suggestion of an "implied" or "general" deterrent situation between the superpowers and weak states would be rejected on the basis of a strict definition, offered by Ned Lebow and Janice Gross Stein, of deterrence: "Deterrence requires that the 'defender' define the behavior that is unacceptable, publicize the commitment to punish or restrain the transgressors, demonstrate the resolve to do so, and possess the capabilities to implement the threat." In other words, the definition of deterrence offered here would only encompass the last two criterion suggested by Lebow and Stein. For a critique of this kind of "nebulous" deterrence theorizing, see Richard Ned Lebow and

Janice Gross Stein, "Deterrence: The Elusive Dependent Variable," *World Politics* 42 (April 1990): 336–69.

15. According to Wolfers, "[W]henever two great powers are locked in serious conflict they can spare little if any of their coercive strength to deal with minor offenders and to impose their will on them over issues that have no direct bearing on the major struggle in which they are involved with their equals." See Wolfers, *Discord and Collaboration*, 111–12.

16. Waltz, *Theory of International Politics*, 172.

17. John J. Mearsheimer, *Conventional Deterrence* (Ithaca: Cornell University Press, 1983), 23–24, 63–64.

18. William J. Duiker, *The Communist Road to Power in Vietnam* (Boulder, Colo.: Westview, 1981), 189.

19. Patrick McGarvey, *Visions of Victory* (Stanford: Hoover Institution on War, Revolution and Peace, 1969), 5.

20. William J. Duiker, *Vietnam: Nation in Revolution* (Boulder, Colo.: Westview, 1983), 54; Duiker, *Road to Power*, 183–93; Gabriel Kolko, *Anatomy of a War: The United States, and the Modern Historical Experience* (New York: Pantheon, 1985), 99–101; and U. S. Grant Sharp and William Westmoreland, *Report on the War in Vietnam* (Washington, D.C.: U.S. Government Printing Office, 1968), 81, 92.

21. Vo Nguyen Giap, "The Big Victory, the Great Task," Nhan Dan and Quan Doi Nhan Dan (September 14–16, 1967), contained in McGarvey, *Visions of Victory*, 237.

22. Duiker, *Road to Power*, 221–23, 226; and Stanley Karnow, *Vietnam: A History* (New York: Viking, 1983), 327, 329–30.

23. Duiker, *Road to Power*, 226.

24. Duiker, *Road to Power*, 127–31; Douglas Pike, *PAVN: People's Army of Vietnam* (Novato, Calif.: Presidio, 1986), 213–53; Douglas Pike, *Viet Cong* (Cambridge: MIT Press, 1966), Appendix A: "NLF Accounts of Dich Van Struggle Movements," 385–97.

25. Douglas Blaufarb, *The Counterinsurgency Era: US Doctrine and Performance* (New York: Free Press, 1977), 49–50.

26. "Memorandum for the Chairman, NSC Working Group on Southeast Asia (Mr. William P. Bundy, Department of State)," November 10, 1964, Document #228, contained in *The Pentagon Papers, The Senator Gravel Edition* vol. 3 (Boston: Beacon, 1971), 625.

27. Andrew Krepinevich, *The Army and Vietnam* (Baltimore: Johns Hopkins University Press, 1986), 133–34.

28. McNaughton's memorandum quoted in George McT. Kahin, *Intervention: How America Became Involved in Vietnam* (Garden City, N.Y.: Anchor, 1987), 357.

29. McNamara quoted in Kahin, *Intervention*, 319.

30. Taylor quoted in Kahin, *Intervention*, 319.

31. Maxwell Taylor, *Swords and Ploughshares* (New York: Norton, 1972), 401.

32. Taylor, *Swords*, 401.

33. Richard Russell, "CIA's Strategic Intelligence in Iraq," *Political Science Quarterly* 117 (Summer 2002): 191–207.

34. Iraqi transcript of the meeting between President Saddam Hussein and U.S. Ambassador April Glaspie, *New York Times*, September 23, 1990, p. A 19.

35. Lawrence Freedman and Efraim Karsh, *The Gulf Conflict, 1990–1991* (Princeton: Princeton University Press, 1993), 13–18, 52.

36. Janice Gross Stein, "Deterrence and Compellence in the Gulf, 1990–1991: A Failed or Impossible Task?" *International Security* 17 (Autumn 1992): 158.

37. For the textbook, see Thomas Schelling, *The Strategy of Conflict* (New Haven: Yale University Press, 1966).

38. Saddam Hussein quoted in Freedman and Karsh, *The Gulf Conflict*, 164.

39. Freedman and Karsh, *The Gulf Conflict*, 149.

40. Michael Gordon and Bernard Trainor, *The Generals' War* (Boston: Little, Brown, 1995), 153–56.

41. Freedman and Karsh, *The Gulf Conflict*, 233–34.

42. Stein, "Deterrence and Compellence," 174.

43. Freedman and Karsh, *The Gulf Conflict*, 279–80.

CHAPTER 6

A World Not in the Balance:
War, Politics, and Weapons of Mass Destruction

EDWARD RHODES

This volume aims to explain the theory and practice of power "balancing" in the 21st century. This particular chapter, however, suggests reasons why we should be dubious about such an effort and recommends abandoning, rather than searching for ways to rehabilitate, the "balancing" metaphor and the logic that flows from it. This chapter argues that both of the basic propositions of balance of power theory—that states pursue, or ought rationally to pursue, a military balance of power and that military balances are likely to emerge—are premised on assumptions about warfare and politics that are implausible in the contemporary period. Both of these propositions have long and distinguished intellectual lineages, and both have been widely accepted in elite and popular discourse. In these early days of the 21st century, however, there is no logical reason to expect either of these propositions to hold true, and there are strong reasons to anticipate that neither will. Simply put, "balancing" has become a wildly misleading metaphor. Efforts to understand national security policy choices and the functioning of the international system that are based on this metaphor are likely to prove woefully off the mark. Today, states do not face a logical imperative to balance each other's military forces, and there is no reason to expect balances, rather than huge imbalances, of military or politico-military power to emerge.

Given the central place of "balancing" and balance of power theory in Realist accounts of foreign policy and international relations, this chapter may be read as a criticism of much of the Realist literature. Alternatively, it may be read as a plea for greater realism in Realism, especially for greater sensitivity to the assumptions on which particular theoretical claims are based and for greater historical awareness of how, over time, underlying realities increasingly depart from those assumed. This chapter's analysis underscores the importance of recognizing the changing, socially constructed nature of political actors and of the institutions, such as war, through which they interact. It concludes that scholarly and political "realism" that ignores the socially constructed dimensions of political reality, and that mistakes the logic of one historical set of circumstances for a universal law, risks going dangerously awry.

This chapter's argument is based on two simple observations. The first is that the impulse to "balance" another state's military forces exists only if conflict is expected to take on a trinitarian form. Only in a world of trinitarian wars do militaries need to "balance" militaries; only in such a world is the rational measure of military sufficiency calculated by reference to other states' military capacity. For a variety of political and technological reasons, during the modern era (roughly, from the Peace of Westphalia in 1648 to the mid-20th century) Western societies generally conceived of "war" as a trinitarian exercise. In today's increasingly postmodern world, however, "war" has escaped the trinitarian straitjacket. The destruction of the World Trade Center, the subsequent American campaign against "tyrants and terrorism," and the attention now devoted in Washington to the problem of defending American civilians against nuclear, chemical, and biological attack all illustrate the non-trinitarian nature of today's warfare.

The second observation is that states face an imperative to balance power only if they believe that *any* state, if too powerful and unchecked by other states, would threaten the sovereignty of the other states in the system and that *all* states are vulnerable to being deprived of their independence by stronger neighbors. In other words, the logic of pursuing a balance of power is based on the double assumption that states believe that *every* state is by its own nature and the nature of the international system a potential predator, restrained from its carnivorous impulses only by its weakness relative to the coalition that might form against it, and that they believe that *every* state is potential prey, surviving to live another day only because of the existence of a balance in the system that holds potential predators in check. All states are seen both as desiring, or being driven by the logic of the system, to reduce others to servitude if the opportunity were to arise, and as inherently vulnerable. As an "ideal type," this description is a vaguely plausible, if admittedly oversimplified, model of the European system in the 17th and 18th centuries. But the assumption that every state lives in fear of the imperial ambitions of every other state is simply ludicrous in the present age, when wealth and power are tied more intimately to technology, education, and social cohesion than to territory or population; when nationalism is seen as creating a substantial obstacle to imperial expansion; when liberal norms have diffused widely and institutions and amities binding together particular nations have grown strong; and when nuclear arsenals give great powers reassurance of the ultimate invulnerability of their sovereignty.

Thus, both war and politics have changed over the centuries since the metaphor of military "balancing" was popularized. They have changed not because some sort of political millennium has arrived or because the nature of human beings has altered, but because both war and political structures are socially constructed, and, for better or worse, social evolution is an inevitable and ongoing process. Ours is a world in which war is less and less likely to be conceived of in trinitarian terms. And—fortunately for the United States, whose hegemonic military power is patently unbalanced in today's world—most of today's great and middling powers do not assume that their existence, much less the survival of the sovereign-state system, is threatened even by gross imbalances in military might.

This chapter begins its critique of the metaphor of "balancing" by examining the trinitarian image of war and investigating why "war" has ceased to be constructed in trinitarian terms. It then explores why the assumption of trinitarian war is essential to the logic of military balancing and why, in a world in which non-trinitarian war has become the expectation rather than the exception, states are indifferent to calculations of balance. Finally, the chapter considers why states no longer see the state system as highly vulnerable and are largely unconcerned that an imbalance of military power might lead to imperium.

Trinitarian and Non-Trinitarian Constructions of War

To Carl von Clausewitz we owe recognition of war's compositional trinity of politics, passion, and reason. With each of these attributes of war, Clausewitz observed, one could loosely associate the different estates whose participation was necessary for a state to wage war: the state's political authorities, its people, and its military establishment. Writing in the transitional period of the early 19th century and struggling to understand and explain the nature of war as it was and as it should be, Clausewitz with this trinitarian distinction implicitly grasped the peculiar essence of war and politics as they had been practiced in Europe in the century and a half following the Thirty Years War.[1] As the great state builders and wagers of dynastic war of the 17th and 18th centuries recognized, for war to be a meaningful political act, limited in its scope and controlled and tailored to serve a political purpose (and not simply an exercise in senseless, wanton destruction or an uncontrolled emotion-driven orgy of violence), each of these three actors had to be confined to its appropriate role. True, states were not always successful—and not even always wholeheartedly or completely committed—in this effort to define and distinguish these roles. And outside the "civilized" confines of Europe, "war," even when waged by European powers, took on very different forms and was fought by very different rules. Thus, trinitarian war was always an imagined ideal type and never a perfect description of reality. Nonetheless, both as a first-order model and as a normative aspiration, "war" in Europe in the 17th and 18th centuries can reasonably be analyzed and discussed in trinitarian terms.

In the trinitarian schema, political leaders were responsible for deciding when war was to be undertaken; for determining the political objectives of the war and calculating what terms were to be demanded in return for a cessation of hostilities if military victory were achieved; and for determining if or when the war was lost and the conditions that might be accepted in defeat. The general population provided the war-making resources demanded by the state's leadership—money, materiél, and manpower. The people's passion and energy provided the fuel for the violence inherent in war, the violence that required the direction and restraint provided by political leadership if it were to be turned to political purpose. The role of the state's armed forces was to transform this popular passion and energy into an employable tool that could be put to the political purposes identified by the political leadership, and then use this tool to do battle against opposing states' armed forces when, and for as long as, directed to do so by the political leadership.

This trinitarian framework holds out the potential for significantly constraining the scope of death and destruction in war. Neither state leaders nor ordinary folk are a legitimate target of violence. To the contrary, they are to be protected from the harm and destruction associated with warfare. The state's armed forces—its armies and navies—are expected not only to be observably distinct from the political leadership and ordinary civilians, but to act violently *only* against the similarly distinct and distinguishable armed forces of the adversary state. Military personnel are not to use their capacity for organized violence as a means to support themselves through the pillage or plunder of either their own or an opposing state's population, since a state's people at the direction of the political authorities willingly provide the resources these armed forces require. Nor is the military establishment to use its power as a means to challenge the competence of the state's political leaders to make *political* decisions—including when to wage war and when to halt it. The populace, protected from depredations of its own state's and adversary states' armies, is barred both from undertaking violence itself (that is, from infringing on the legitimate sphere of the armed forces) and from exercising political judgment about when to fight and when to cease fighting (that is, from infringing on the legitimate sphere of the state's leadership).

That warfare in today's world should fail to fit the trinitarian ideal of late 17th- and 18th-century European conflict is hardly surprising. There are, as historians such as John Keegan and Martin van Creveld have elegantly argued, any number of forms that warfare may take, of which trinitarian war is but one.[2] "War" in any society or any age is by its nature a social construction. What "war" involves—who we do or do not harm, the kinds of harm we are willing to inflict, the kinds of weapons we are willing to employ, and when we begin and end this activity—depends on the meaning our societies read into organized violence. "War" is a highly complex form of social interaction and the nature of this interaction rests on an implicit but fundamental social agreement regarding appropriate behavior and the meaning ascribed to that behavior. The prevalence in the 17th, 18th, and even 19th centuries of trinitarian wars, or of wars that to a recognizable degree approached this ideal type, was a reflection of a widely shared, socially accepted belief in the Western world that "war" *was* trinitarian war—it was a social activity in which imagined political units called "states," under the direction of political leaders recognized as legitimate, raised and equipped visibly distinct bands of men called "armies" from the masses and directed these forces to undertake particular kinds of ritualized violent actions against each other to ascertain the winner. At least within the society of European states, unorganized or nonpurposive violence, or other types of organized, purposive violence (for example, guerrilla warfare by nonuniformed fighters, campaigns of plunder or pillage by uniformed soldiers, or deliberate campaigns of terror or genocide authorized by political leaders), were seen as violating critical social norms.

The prevalence of trinitarian war, or of any particular mode of war, thus rests on a social construction of the concept of war. This social construction is mutually constituted with the day's other political institutions and, like them, is rooted in and consistent with the technological and physical realities of the day. To paraphrase Marx, we construct our own wars, but not according to our own choosing. The social construction of a fundamental human activity such as war is not a matter of will or of whim—nor, however, is it a matter of material dialectics. To the contrary, it is an integral part of our culture, an integral part of the socially shared telos we construct to help us make sense of our material realities and of our interaction with these realities and with each other. As such it is an embedded structural element in the political architecture we create to order our social lives (that is, it and our other political institutions are mutually constituted) and is consistent with our understanding of the objective facts and technologies of our age and society.

Although admittedly an ideal type, trinitarian war provides a reasonable description of the dominant European social construction of war in the period between the Peace of Westphalia and the outbreak of the French Revolution. The physical realities and political institutions that coexisted with this social construction of war, however, have been steadily eroding ever since. Even when Clausewitz was writing, he was describing more accurately what war had been (and, he may be interpreted as implying, what it needed to once again become) than what it was. Already in the early 1800s, European societies were conceiving of war and fighting it—that is, they were constructing it through discourse and praxis—in ways that departed substantially from the trinitarian ideal type.

Democracy, Nationalism, Industrialization, Computerization, and War

Trinitarian war rests on political institutions that separate the ordinary citizen both from political power and from violent action. Democracy undercuts the former: if political power (indeed, in some formulations, sovereignty itself) ultimately resides in the hands of the people, then the people become an extraordinarily attractive target for violence. "Making Georgia howl," in William Tecumseh Sherman's famous phrase, makes sense if and only if the citizens of Georgia possess political institutions that give them power over their leaders and, at least indirectly, over their state's armed forces. Making Georgia *bleed* might make sense in the absence of institutions that empower ordinary civilians if it weakened Georgia's war-making capability, but making it *howl*—making its people suffer, even if this has no impact on the war-making capacity of the state's armed forces—is rational only in a world in which civilians have meaningful political capacity.[3]

Just as democracy undermines the separation between ordinary people and political leadership, nationalism undercuts the separation between citizens and soldiers. Ultimately, the assumption that the ordinary civilian and the combatant can be differentiated, and that each will be willing to keep to his or her proper sphere, rests on the presumption that ordinary people do not care very much about who wins the war. Once they care, then the civilian's temptation to join in the struggle becomes overwhelming. Unfortunately for trinitarian war, in a world in which national identities not only matter but have become fused with the state, ordinary citizens are likely to see their prosperity, their sociocultural way of life, their ego and emotional well-being, and their individual and collective survival jeopardized by the defeat or capitulation of their nation-state, and so they are likely to care very, very much whether their state wins or loses. Thus, in an era of nationalism, civilians routinely resort to violence against other states' military forces, or even against other states' people. Military reprisals can be used to attempt to restore trinitarian behavioral boundaries, coercing those civilians who are tempted to transgress into remaining within their "proper" sphere. Ironically, however, these efforts by militaries to use terror to cow defeated populations into accepting defeat in themselves reflect a breach of the trinitarian rules. Equally to the point, military reprisals are likely to further convince civilians that their personal security and well-being require the defeat and expulsion of the invader, making civilians believe even more strongly in the importance of their state's ultimate victory and to make them even less likely to passively accept its defeat. The rise first of democracy and later of nationalism thus eroded the basis for a trinitarian construction of war. The gradual construction of national-democratic political institutions logically and necessarily implied the reconstruction of war in increasingly non-trinitarian terms.

Technological developments have only accelerated this trend. It would be easy to single out nuclear weapons as the technology that laid to rest trinitarian war. But a far broader range of technological developments has critically affected the social construction of war. Advances in nonmilitary technologies have eroded the potential for trinitarian conceptions of war as much as have revolutions in military technologies.

Trinitarian thinking about war is inescapably rooted in preindustrial technological and social conditions. The industrial revolution undermined the trinitarian construction of war by creating tighter links between the civilian and military elements in the trinity, blurring the distinction and narrowing the separation between combatants and noncombatants. A preindustrial military was reliant on the civilian population, but not in any immediately critical way. The primary linkage was through finance: ultimately the populace would have to provide political authorities with the financial resources necessary to support the military establishment. The army and the people were thus not yoked very tightly together. Even in the long run the military required only the grudging support of the civilian population. In the short run it could do without any civilian backing or civilian economy at all. While in the end the civilian population would have to produce the wealth, and pay the taxes, necessary to support a war, prudent political leaders would have sufficient financial reserves (or the ability to raise short-term capital through foreign borrowing) to make it possible for the military to continue to operate even if the functioning of the civilian economy, or the taxing capacity of the political leadership, was temporarily disrupted. Typically, therefore, there was little reason for a military establishment to attack "the enemy's" civilians, or for political leaders to direct it to do so.

In the industrial age, however, the civilian economy was much more integrally involved in the military effort. To wage war effectively—to produce the vast quantities of weapons, ammunition, and other military matériel that modern, industrial-age warfare consumed at a prodigious rate—the state needed to transform the civilian economy into a war economy and this economy had to continue to function. The "civilian" economy thus became civilian in name only. It was not only the financial foundation for the military effort but also its vital logistics element. In the industrial age, the notion of "a nation in arms" reached its full realization: both the military and the populace were *directly* and *immediately* engaged in the war effort.

In the preindustrial age, the distinction between civilian and soldier was relatively easy to maintain because the contribution of the civilian to the war effort, at least in the short run, was so small that he or she was viewed as qualitatively different from a soldier. Killing civilians would do nothing to affect the outcome of the current war. In the industrial age, by contrast, the contribution of a civilian, particularly a skilled, urban worker, to the war effort could have a significant impact on the current war effort. Strategic bombing attacks on key industries or their workforces might well be a more effective use of munitions than tactical bombing of soldiers or their bases.

Just as the civilian economy's importance in warfare grew as a consequence of the industrial revolution, so too did its vulnerability to attack. Built in large measure on the concepts of comparative advantage and specialization, the industrial revolution generated increasing interdependence both within nations and between nations. This interdependence, of course, created exploitable vulnerabilities. Henry V's England could not be starved by a blockade. George V's England could. Industrialization and the loss of self-sufficiency, at both the household and national levels, meant that relatively modest attacks on key nodes in the civilian economy might yield enormous consequences. The temptation to abandon trinitarian norms and strike at civilians, either directly (for example, by seizing, bombing, or sabotaging factories, or by trying to kill or terrorize urban-industrial workers) or indirectly (by cutting off the flow of food or raw materials) became nearly irresistible. Both the military and the political logic of war in the industrial age dictated attacks on civilian targets.

The revolution in computers, information technology, telecommunications, and education of the last several decades has further undercut the physical realities on which trinitarian politico-military logic and the trinitarian social construction of war were built. It has done so, however, in ways very different from the first industrial revolution.

The logic of the trinitarian model of war assumed a meaningful difference between the uniformed military's capacity for violence and the violence that civilians, acting individually or in small bands, would be able to do. In an era when the epitome and measure of military power was the regiment—a highly disciplined, highly drilled, well-equipped military force that could be produced and maintained only by a large, centralized, hierarchic bureaucracy—and even more in an era when the greatest tool of violence was an armored division, an aircraft carrier battle group, or a wing of advanced aircraft, military establishments possessed an overwhelming capacity for violence that civilians could not hope to match. Regardless of motivation, an ordinary civilian, or even an entire civilian community, had little prospect of standing up to one of Marlborough's regiments, Patton's armored divisions, or LeMay's air armies, or of inflicting harm on anything like the scale that these were capable of imposing.

Changes in communications and information processing technology—in particular when coupled with the technology for producing weapons of mass destruction—have drastically reduced this disparity in the ability to use violence. Ordinary civilians, acting individually or in relatively small, relatively nonhierarchical groups, are now able to master and muster violence in ways and at levels that make it a potent political tool. Today, a terrorist or even a cyber-terrorist can inflict or threaten to inflict millions or billions of dollars of damage and to take hundreds, thousands, or tens of thousands of lives. While the ability of such non-state groups to take on a *military* establishment is still limited (though long-standing civil wars and the occasional attack on a military installation by a terrorist group remind us that it exists), their ability to hurt civilians or political authorities is substantial. As the capacity to produce chemical, biological, or radiological weapons diffuses to the civilian world, these abilities grow. And given that they possess, or might plausibly possess, the leverage that flows from such significant levels of "military" capability, politically dissatisfied civilians are unlikely to willingly forego tools of violence and to accept the politically disempowering limits on their behavior dictated by historic trinitarian distinctions. In turn, military establishments cannot ignore civilians as they might have done in an earlier age. Having lost the natural monopoly on violence that the preindustrial and industrial ages had endowed them with, military establishments in the postindustrial age must forcefully defend their monopolistic ambitions against civilian challengers.

The second consequence of today's revolution in information technology and education is that, at the same time they have begun to rival the military in terms of ability to undertake politically significant violence, ordinary people have also begun to rival political leaders in their capacity for analysis and communication.[4] Just as it implicitly assumed that the military would be qualitatively better equipped than civilians to use violence, the trinitarian model assumed that political leaders would be qualitatively better able than ordinary folk to make and communicate decisions. In a world in which the effective collection, analysis, and dissemination of information required a large, bureaucratic, hierarchic structure (that is, required the state or some sort of similar corporate organization), this assumption was fairly reasonable. New data-gathering, analysis, and communication technologies, however, have reduced the need for large bureaucracies to process data and communicate over long distances. In the Internet age of computer-literate and highly networked ordinary civilians, the relative ignorance of the public, and consequently its willingness to accept authority, is undermined. The dark side of individual empowerment, and of the postindustrial age's mantra to question authority, is an unwillingness to accept the subservient role inherent in the trinitarian differentiation of responsibilities. People are less willing to defer to political leaders or to accept decisions with which they disagree, even on matters such as war and peace. Technology has thus made possible and encouraged the social reconstruction of political institutions including war. In the end, the ability of the civilian to infringe on the domain of the political leadership, by acting individually or in coordinated small groups without guidance from political authorities, makes the civilian a potentially legitimate, and at times even a necessary, target of political violence, since it can no longer be assumed that compelling political leaders to surrender or sue for peace will be sufficient to end the war.

Vulnerable Cities and Invulnerable Militaries

Of course the erosion of the trinitarian construction of war has occurred not simply because of changes in political institutions (democracy, nationalism) and civilian technology (industrialization, computerization). It also reflects developments in military technology that profoundly altered the physical realities on which the trinitarian conception of war was based.

The notion that war's actual fighting ought to be limited to a state's armed forces was encouraged in part by the pre-democratic, pre-national, preindustrial, precomputer perception that no great advantage (and, at least in the long run, tremendous cost) was associated with fighting wars any other way. After all, if the masses lacked political power, were unmotivated to take any active part in war, and did not contribute very immediately or very significantly to the war effort, then they might as well be left alone (especially if plundering them would invite similar behavior by one's adversary, thus destroying the economic resources that both states needed for their long-term survival). But the trinitarian construction of war also rested on the fact that there was no easy alternative. Doing violence against the adversary state's population or against its leadership would, in general, require first defeating the adversary state's military forces. If achieving military victory—using one's own military establishment to defeat or destroy the opponent's military establishment—were a necessary and sufficient precondition for hurting the adversary state's people and leadership, then actually hurting the people and leadership would not, in a war between rational leaders, ever be necessary, since as soon as one state's military achieved victory over the other state's military, the political leaders of the two sides would sit down and negotiate.

Of course, raids that avoided the opponent's military forces and struck at civilians or leaders had always been possible, at least where population densities were low and it was therefore not possible to provide an effective military shield. Wars between American Indians and European settlers typify this sort of counter-societal war, in which raids against ordinary folk were the norm. But in "civilized" (that is, relatively densely populated) contexts, a military shield was in fact usually available: major gains would require major military operations, and these could be countered by the opposing side's military force, thus necessitating military versus military contact. The most significant exception, as Germany demonstrated during the two world wars, was at sea, where force-to-space ratios were low (especially when convoys were not used to increase population densities artificially), and where submarines and surface raiders could therefore operate fairly freely.

Advances in military technology, however, opened up new opportunities for counter-societal warfare. Graphically, one could imagine a representation of war in a trinitarian world as two triangles, each of which represented the trio of Clausewitzian actors in an opposing state. In the world of the late 17th, 18th, and 19th centuries, the two triangles would be aligned so that the military apex of each triangle pointed at the military apex of the other. The political and civilian apexes of each triangle were discreetly and safely hidden in the rear. The violent collision of the two triangles—war—would bring the military in contact with the military. Technology, however, reoriented these triangles. Suddenly, it was possible, even easy, to strike at the opponent's leaders or civilian population. Thanks to airpower, it was possible to bypass the military units that served as a shield.

What airpower made possible, nuclear, chemical, and biological weapons made cost effective. Indeed in our current age, the practical realities that underlay a trinitarian construction of war have now been stood on their heads. In the nuclear age it has become relatively easy to reach and hurt large numbers of civilians or the opposing state's political leaders. At the same time, it has become extremely hard to strike at the most important elements of the opponent's military. The other side's nuclear forces, for example, are likely to be placed in hardened silos, explicitly designed to make a military versus military engagement impossible by making the missile stored inside invulnerable to military attack, or hidden at sea specifically so they can not be found and engaged by opposing military forces, or (during the height of the Cold War) kept aloft or placed on rapid alert status so that they could evade engagement. In other words, nuclear arsenals have been designed to make trinitarian conflict impossible. Indeed, in today's world even conventional military forces are increasingly difficult for an adversary to find and fight: one of the touted advantages of sea power, for example, has been its mobility and relative invisibility, giving it the capacity to strike at critical political command nodes and at the civilian, industrial vitals of an opposing nation while dodging the counterblows of the opponent's military. By contrast to military targets, urban civilian populations are large, in fixed locations, and soft: they are easy targets for nearly all types of conventional and nuclear, chemical, or biological weapons. And political leaders and institutions, despite efforts to increase security, remain perpetually vulnerable, particularly to a surprise attack.

That nuclear weapons changed the physical realities of large-scale war, and reversed trinitarian assumptions about the relative vulnerability of military forces and civilian targets, was acknowledged during the Cold War. Indeed, this new, non-trinitarian conception of war was codified in pacts that sought to make virtue of necessity. The Strategic Arms Limitation Treaties (SALT) deliberately guaranteed that civilians would remain easy targets and that key elements of the military structure would remain effectively invulnerable. SALT thus involved a construction of war that represented the complete negation of Clausewitzian thinking: it sought to make it *impossible* for the superpowers to fight a large-scale trinitarian war. This reconstruction of "war" meant, and was understood by both sides to mean, that a major war between the superpowers could *not* be a rational continuation of politics by other means.

To be sure, in its "New New Look" of the late 1950s, the Eisenhower administration talked seriously about a tactical nuclear war waged between nuclear-armed armies; in the 1970s, the Carter administration's theorizing about "countervailing" in strategic exchanges hypothesized a nuclear war fought as a duel between nuclear missile forces; and in the 1980s, the Reagan administration raised the possibility of military forces shielding the nation against a nuclear blow from the skies, much as conventional forces shielded terrestrial borders against incursions. But plans for massive societal destruction—threats to kill tens of millions of ordinary civilians—dominated American thinking about nuclear weapons. When ordinary Americans and their elected leaders constructed a nuclear war in their minds, what they imagined was devastating attacks deliberately targeted on civilians. And in all likelihood this is in fact what a nuclear war would have involved. Indeed, even the term "weapons of mass destruction" illustrates the non-trinitarian nature of war in the nuclear age: these were weapons of *mass* destruction—weapons to destroy the masses, not simply their military guardians.

Even warfare with conventional weapons has ceased to be trinitarian in any meaningful sense. To be sure, U.S. policymakers may nostalgically slip back into old habits of trinitarian thinking when they imagine a quick war in Iraq, in which a superior American army bests an inferior Iraqi one, the Iraqi political leadership capitulates, and the Iraqi masses placidly accept a new, better government. These, however, are daydreams and exercises in wishful thinking, and, except in certain rarefied inner circles of government, are generally recognized as such. The reality is painfully non-trinitarian. It involves paramilitary Baathist snipers and civilian Shiite mobs attacking U.S. soldiers, terrorist bombings in Baghdad that kill civilians and UN officials, and a gun battle in Mosul that pits U.S. troops against holdout political fugitives Uday and Qusay Hussein, leaving these two dead. This—and Afghanistan and Somalia and Lebanon and Kosovo—is "war" as America's military forces, political leaders, and, increasingly, citizens are experiencing it.

The impact of the current "revolution in military affairs"—improvements in sensors, communication technologies, and computerization—on America's capacity to wage trinitarian war and recreate a trinitarian world is double-edged. On the one hand, it improves the precision of warfare, reducing collateral damage. It means that the United States is better able to target exactly what it wants—whether that is enemy soldiers, key civilian targets, or political institutions. On the other hand, by making American forces increasingly distant, mobile, and otherwise invulnerable, it also makes it increasingly impossible for adversaries to fight by trinitarian rules even if they so desired.

The thinking of America's likely opponents seems not only to have kept up but raced ahead. It has long been fashionable to describe the likely strategy of America's potential adversaries as "asymmetric." This description sometimes implies an asymmetry in the adversary's choice of weapons—for example, instead of using tanks against tanks, an adversary might use computer or biological viruses to incapacitate communications or soldiers. Other times it is meant to imply an asymmetry in targets. Instead of targeting American tanks, an adversary might target the American populace or leaders. Asymmetry can also embrace both of these: an adversary might use computer or biological viruses against the American people or its leaders, neither investing in tanks of its own nor paying much attention to American tanks. To the degree that we anticipate adversaries will be asymmetric in their targeting, we are acknowledging that they will embrace non-trinitarian war. In fact, this is precisely why we suspect and fear that potential U.S. adversaries will acquire nuclear, biological, or chemical weapons: we suspect that they may be imagining a war that is non-trinitarian in form, and intend not only to avoid investing in tanks, aircraft, and warships but also to ignore U.S. investment in these and instead focus their destructive energies on America's vulnerable people and leaders.

The Balancing Metaphor in a Non-trinitarian World

What does the end of trinitarian warfare mean for "balance" as a metaphor, and what does it imply about the relevance of the logic that flows from this metaphor? Balance as a metaphor or analogy only makes sense if we are balancing military forces against military forces. Thinking in terms of balance or balancing only makes sense if the sufficiency of one's military forces is measured in terms of, or as some proportion of, the adversary's military forces.

In a world of trinitarian wars, trying to ensure a balance in military forces makes sense. How many soldiers or tanks or warships a state needs depends on how many its opponents have, because soldiers, tanks, and warships are going to fight soldiers, tanks, and warships. Thus, in a trinitarian world, it is logical for states to monitor each other's military preparations and to react to increases in strength, either by building up their own forces or by entering into alliances.

Even in the now-passed age of trinitarian war, of course, the metaphor of balancing provided only a rough guideline for behavior. Differences in geography meant that "balancing" did not imply the two sides needed exactly equivalent forces (whatever the metric for measuring this would be). Two sides might be "in balance" when one side had substantially larger forces.

More important, even in the trinitarian age "balancing" was a metaphor of uncertain utility because the scale on which the weighing took place was at times enormously insensitive and at other times hypersensitive to variations in military power. Whether the balance was sensitive or insensitive depended on whether the offense or the defense was perceived as dominant. Technological or geographic conditions that were viewed as favoring the defense over the offense (widely assumed to be the normal situation) implied a relatively insensitive scale on which the military balance was weighed. For example, if offense required a three to one numerical advantage to succeed, then any weighing of forces from a one to three disadvantage to a three to one advantage would not shift the scale's reading: over this wide range, for practical purposes the scale would show equivalency. Neither side could win a war and jeopardize the other's sovereignty. By contrast, in situations in which the offense was perceived as having an advantage over the defense, *any* weighing of forces would result in an inequality—the scale would tip to whichever side put its forces onto the scale first (or, to mix the metaphor, to whichever side was first to roll the dice of war). Only a heavy external hand (of international society or of third parties), ready to add its weight to the lighter side of the scale and forcefully hold the balance at equilibrium, could prevent an offense-dominant scale from tilting out of control.

Thus, in a world of trinitarian conflict, the image of balance needed to be modified to take into account geography and the defense- or offense-dominated character of the balance. But it still made some sense.

In a world in which wars are no longer trinitarian, however, the image of balancing an adversary's military forces makes no sense *because militaries no longer fight militaries: they fight opposing populations or leadership.* When we think about WMD, for instance, the metaphor of balancing almost certainly leads us astray. In gauging the sufficiency of a nuclear arsenal, "enough" is not logically measured as a multiple or a fraction of the adversary's nuclear or other military forces. The question is not whether one state's military forces have a sufficient stockpile of nuclear weapons to defeat the other state's military forces, because these nuclear arms are not meant to be used to fight the other state's military forces. The question is whether one state has a sufficient nuclear arsenal to inflict unacceptable damage on the other side's civilian population and political leadership, or to protect its own people and leaders. *These calculations are largely insensitive to the size of the adversary's forces.*

Consider: if a state has 100 cities each of which it regards as vital and its adversary has one invulnerable nuclear warhead, the state needs to shelter or plan the evacuation of the population of all 100 of these cities. Its necessary level of effort is not dictated by its opponent's level of effort but by its own vulnerabilities. If the number of vital cities doubles, the level of effort must double; if it declines by half, the level of effort can decline by half. By contrast, if the adversary doubles its military capability to two warheads, or even if it increases it tenfold or a hundredfold, it has no significant impact on the task confronting the defending state. Similarly, if a state perceives the need to destroy or to threaten to destroy 100 of the adversary's cities, it is this fact, not the size of the adversary's military force, that dictates the size of the force that needs to be acquired. If the state changes its estimate of what is necessary for deterrence—setting the goal at, say, 10 vulnerable cities or 1,000, rather than 100—then it must change its level of military effort. But so long as its nuclear forces are invulnerable, its necessary level of military effort is insensitive to changes in the size of the adversary's military forces. Given the non-trinitarian nature of a nuclear war, it is each side's political calculation about the civilian losses it is willing to suffer, and about the civilian losses it believes it would be necessary to inflict on an adversary, *not a concern with balancing the adversary's military preparations*, that determines how much is enough. There is no reason why adversaries should seek to balance each other or for them to end up with "balanced" forces.

Similarly, when we think about wars against today's most plausible adversaries—rogue states and terrorists—the image and logic of balancing are again inappropriate. No one doubts that the United States is vastly stronger, militarily, than any rogue state or terrorist group. Rogue states and terrorist groups have no prospect of balancing American military power. In fact, the whole world in coalition might not, at the moment, be able to balance American military power. And yet, the absence of an ability to balance U.S. military superiority is politically irrelevant. It is irrelevant because rogue states and terrorists are unlikely to choose to wage a trinitarian war. In a world of non-trinitarian wars, what is relevant is how vulnerable American cities and political leaders are to attack.

In other words, it is absolute, not relative, military capabilities that matter. In a confrontation with a rogue state or terrorist group, the fact that the United States may have a thousand to one military superiority and an unquestioned ability to win a fair military versus military fight is unimportant. What is important is that the adversary might have the capacity to kill thousands or millions of American civilians.

Neither the United States nor the state or non-state actors it confronts care in the least about some nuclear, chemical, or biological balance, or even about a conventional military balance. The *relative* size of arsenals and capabilities does not matter. *Absolute* capabilities, by contrast, matter a great deal to all involved. The United States does not seek a balance against rogue states and terrorist groups and is unlikely to believe that a world in which it and its allies have a parity of power with the "Axis of Evil" would be a safe or stable one. Indeed, the Bush administration argued that *any* Iraqi WMD capability was unacceptable, regardless of the size of the forces placed in the balance against Iraq. By the same token, rogue states and terrorist groups do not seek to create a "balance" against the United States. They do not aspire, or see the need to aspire, to military parity or equilibrium. Nor do they engage in classical "balancing" behavior. They do not see the need to ally to each other to increase their relative capabilities vis-à-vis the United States or more closely to approach a balance. Given the vulnerability of American society and leaders, a militarily trivial capacity may be sufficient for their purposes. Equally to the point, rogue states and terrorist groups are likely to be insensitive not only to the balance but to changes in the balance. Doubling or quadrupling the American nuclear arsenal or army would neither spur terrorists and rogue states to greater effort nor convince them to yield; cutting American nuclear or conventional forces would be similarly irrelevant.

Of course, to the degree that military establishments still fight military establishments, calculations of sufficiency must still take the absolute size of the adversary's military force, among other things, into account. During the Cold War, fears that the Soviet Union might attack U.S. missile bases helped to justify demands for more survivable basing of U.S. missiles and for missile defenses. Similarly, if the United States chooses to go militarily mano a mano with terrorists, hunting down and killing them one at a time rather than intimidating the leaders and populations that shelter and support them, the size of the American military force structure may depend on whether there are 1,000 terrorists or 100,000. Even in this case, though, the fact that the adversary is not intending to wage a trinitarian war means that "balancing" is a woefully misleading metaphor. While the United States may well respond to the acquisition of new capabilities by potential adversaries, it will do so not with an eye to balancing them but with an eye to negating them. The American objective is *not* to balance Iraq or North Korea or al-Qaeda. It is to render them harmless. And the end result may well be a situation of gross imbalance in capabilities and forces.

It is equally clear that America's potential adversaries also have no interest in balancing the United States. What they seek are the military capabilities that would permit them to threaten the United States with mass civilian or leadership casualties, and thereby extract concessions. This is likely to lead them to seek military weapons, like WMD, that could "make Georgia howl." As the United States, in turn, takes steps to negate these capabilities, either politically or militarily, America's potential adversaries will seek more or different asymmetric means of inflicting pain. A strategic interaction is likely to emerge. This action-and-reaction cycle may reach a stable equilibrium (in which both sides are simultaneously able to meet their political goals, or one side gives up trying), or it may not. In neither case, however, does the balancing metaphor provide an accurate description of what is occurring.

The irrelevance of the traditional military balance and of concerns about relative capability becomes self-evident when one observes what really worries the United States and the other great powers. What drives American military preparation is not the action of other great powers. Rather, it is concerns about the possible actions of some of the weakest of the weak: third-world rogue states and terrorist groups. The United States has increased its defense spending not because the strong are increasing their forces, as balance of power theory would predict, but because the trivially weak are acquiring very basic capabilities. Similarly, if Britain, France, Germany, and Russia increase their military spending in coming years, it is unlikely to be because of a perceived need to balance the United States, but rather because they too are concerned by security threats from the weak. And, contrary to balance of power predictions, this increase in the military strength of other great powers would be applauded by the United States, not viewed with alarm—and it would likely cement the alliance between these great powers and the United States, not cement a "balancing" alliance against the last superpower.

Reliance on the metaphor of balancing leads not only to erroneous expectations about state behavior but to erroneous predictions about the behavior of the international system. An equilibrium in power, some balance of power theorists have reasoned, ought to reduce the likelihood of war; the preponderance of one state or coalition of states ought to increase the system's instability and propensity toward conflict. In a world in which international violence could be expected to take on trinitarian form, this reasoning flowed logically. But in a world in which war does not necessarily involve militaries fighting militaries, there is no reason to expect any relationship between military parity and *either* war or peace. Assuming rationality, peace will exist when no player sees a net gain from war—but in a non-trinitarian world a parity of military power is neither a necessary nor a sufficient condition for this.

A non-trinitarian perspective on war also raises doubts about another of balance of power's core propositions, that balancing alliances tend to form when one state begins to build its military capability. In a world of non-trinitarian wars, the problem for balance of power logic is not simply that the relevant measure of sufficiency is absolute, rather than relative, military capabilities. It is also that, measured in terms of political output, military power is increasingly nonadditive. In a world of trinitarian wars, adding Britain's military might to France's was likely to make a significant difference, politically as well as militarily, if either confronted, say, Russia. When militaries fought militaries, doubling the size of one's army by adding that of an ally was likely to have a significant impact on military outcomes, on political calculations, and on political outcomes. At a minimum, it was likely to provoke the opponent to consider increasing the size of its military effort or to seek additional allies. In a world of non-trinitarian wars, however, joining Britain and France in an alliance makes surprisingly little difference. Above a threshold, additional military capabilities do not translate into additional political or even military power. There are, of course, a variety of reasons why states may still choose to ally: there are all sorts of shared problems that an alliance may help them resolve. But in a world in which war takes on non-trinitarian forms, states and other political actors are unlikely to enter into alliances to balance the military capabilities of potential opponents, or in response to increases in opponents' military capabilities.

Aside from raising false expectations about international stability and state behavior, there is a danger that relying on the balancing metaphor may lead to adoption of misguided or counterproductive policies. On the one hand, the balancing metaphor may lead us think—and to behave as if—we are more powerful than we are. The fact that the United States may soon spend more on its military than the rest of the world combined, or that by some calculations it already has more military power than all of its potential adversaries combined, does not necessarily mean that the United States can deter or defeat its adversaries, much less win a war in any meaningful sense, since America's adversaries are unlikely to accept an American offer to fight by trinitarian rules. A focus on balancing, or a belief that a calculation of military balance tells us much that is useful, may thus lead the United States to undertake conflicts that it cannot win, or cannot win at an acceptable cost. If one looks at the military balance between the United States and anti-American political groups in Iraq, one would predict a quick and easy victory—just as one would have if one had examined the military balance between the United States and Vietnam or between the Soviet Union and Afghanistan.

On the other hand, the balancing metaphor also may lead us to spend excessively on military capability or to maintain forces in excess of actual needs. Although there may be interesting political reasons for pursuing a bilateral or multilateral framework for arms reductions rather than reducing U.S. forces unilaterally based on its own calculation of sufficiency (including tying America's hands against future domestic political pressures or demagoguery, and trying to tie other states' hands against similar pressures to behave irrationally), the Bush administration's position with regard to nuclear arms has been logically correct: how big the U.S. nuclear arsenal needs to be does not depend on the size of the Russian arsenal, at least within the range of Russian forces that now seems plausible.

In today's political environment, the "balancing" metaphor when applied to nuclear issues is dangerous also because it misdirects our attention, leading us to try to solve less pressing problems through measures that may well exacerbate more urgent problems. Because it rests on Clausewitz's assumption that war will be a rational act—an extension of politics—balancing misses the more critical nuclear problem for American security, that nuclear weapons will be used accidentally or irrationally. In today's world, a rational decision by a great power to launch a nuclear attack on the United States is highly unlikely: there are no political issues of contention between the United States and any of the great powers that would remotely justify the costs that even a limited nuclear war would certainly entail. And yet the danger of a nuclear exchange has not disappeared. On the contrary, the decay of Russian early warning and command-and-control facilities may well be heightening these dangers, as may Russia's increased reliance on nuclear weapons to compensate for its disintegrating conventional capabilities. It is only by disabusing ourselves of the Clausewitzian notion that war is an extension of politics, an extension that can be avoided through intelligent balancing, that we can come to grips with the most significant nuclear threats now facing the United States.

Why Great Powers Are Unlikely to Care About the Nuclear Balance

As this chapter has argued, the first reason why the metaphor and logic of balancing lead us astray is that they rest on an assumption that war will be a trinitarian exercise, and in today's world it is not. The second reason they lead us astray is that they rest on an assumption that all states fear for their sovereignty and perceive all other states as potential imperial predators. This assumption, too, is false in today's world.

Perhaps the clearest exposition of the logic that is presumed to lead states to balance is Edward Gulick's.[5] The core of Gulick's argument is that only by preserving the sovereign state system can states ensure their individual survival; preserving this state system in turn depends on states balancing to prevent the emergence of a power strong enough to overturn that system. Thus, Gulick points out, balancing was a response not to immediate disputes but to the generalized fear that if any state were to become powerful enough, it would reduce the sovereign state system to empire. In this conception of interstate politics, every state is perceived as a potential threat to the system and every state fears the loss of sovereignty.

In today's world, however, this is not the situation. The great powers may dislike and distrust each other. They may even have disputes—over trade, markets, borders, or international regimes—of such significance that they would risk or undertake war. The great powers in the post-Cold War world, however, do not see each other as threats to the system: they do not believe each other to seek imperium. The states of the European Union may resent U.S. tendencies toward unilateral action and disagree vehemently with the United States on a wide range of issues, from how to deal with terrorism to tariffs on bananas. But European states do not suspect the United States of seeking to reduce Europe to vassalage. Though they may seek the economic and military power that would permit them to get their way on the issues on which they and the United States disagree, the European powers do not perceive a need to build, through their own efforts or through alliances with outside powers, a military force equivalent to America's.

There are two reasons why they do not feel such a need. The first is that it is implausible to them that a liberal, democratic nation-state such as the United States would seek to overturn the sovereign state system and conquer Europe. The second is that two Western European states possess what they regard as absolute guarantees of their sovereignty—a secure capacity to inflict what would appear to be unacceptable damage on any adversary that attempted to eliminate their sovereignty.

Just as the evolution of political institutions and physical realities undercut the conditions on which the trinitarian conception of "war" was socially constructed, the evolution of political institutions and physical realities also has served to undercut the conditions that led 17th-, 18th-, 19th- and even 20th-century states to believe that balancing was necessary for the survival of the system and the preservation of their own individual sovereignty. Two developments have been key to the decline in the perceived necessity of balancing.

The first has been the rise of Liberalism and liberal political institutions. Liberalism has had two consequences: to make balancing more difficult and to make it less necessary. Liberalism made balancing more difficult by ruling out the tools on which balancing relied. Liberalism's support for national self-determination interfered with the adjustment of state borders for balancing purposes. Liberalism's demand that state policies receive popular endorsement or legitimation seriously constrained the creation of flexible alliances and the implementation of domestically unpopular military buildups. And Liberalism's objections to war gravely reduced the ability of states to use what was ultimately a critical tool in maintaining a balance.

At the same time, Liberalism created a network of institutions for resolving interstate disputes, reassuring states of their sovereignty, and ensuring the flow of raw materials and finished goods necessary for the prosperity of national economies. Empire thus became unnecessary: liberal great powers do not believe that it would be in their interest to replace the sovereign state system with an empire were it within their power to do so. More important,

they understand that other liberal states face the same incentives and constraints, incentives and constraints that will lead them, too, to eschew the
pursuit of empire.

This, of course, does not mean that conflicts of interest are absent or that
war is impossible. It does, however, mean that key players on the world stage
no longer assume that other key players on the world stage have imperial
motivations that pose a threat to the state system. Thus, unless these powers
have active disputes with each other, large disparities in military power can
be tolerated. In other words, imbalances in power are no longer per se dangerous. The generalized fear of systemic instability that Gulick identified as
the root cause of balancing no longer exists. The danger of war still exists, of
course, and states can be expected to take steps to mitigate or protect themselves against the threats they perceive. But these dangers and threats now
stem either from specific disagreements or from specific actors who are
regarded as non-liberal or as irrational. So long as the system's most powerful members are liberal, democratic, status-quo nation-states with whom
one has no fundamental unresolved disputes, imbalances of military might
are not a source of concern to liberal great powers.

The second development contributing to diminished concerns about the
possible rise of an imperial power is the nuclear revolution. States armed
with invulnerable nuclear forces of sufficient size to inflict grievous harm on
an adversary do not worry about preserving their sovereignty. They may still
worry about their physical survival, should an all-out nuclear war irrationally
occur. And they may still worry that the rules of the international system will
be changed in ways not to their liking, or that they will have declining
influence outside their borders. But they do not need to fear that their sovereignty will be taken away. Again, therefore, while they may be concerned
about the absolute military power of states they regard as irrational or with
whom they have disagreements, they will not necessarily be concerned with
growing systemic imbalances.

In sum, Liberalism and nuclear weapons mean that states will not seek to
balance power—though of course states will still desire to eliminate or render harmless the military capabilities possessed by particular states they see
as dangerous. The perceived systemic imperative that motivated the classic
European balance of power no longer exists. What remains is the fear that
states and other political actors that are irrational or dissatisfied with the status quo will attempt to use the military capabilities at their disposal to cre-

ate or compel change. It is the absolute military capabilities and asymmetric strategies of these irrational or dissatisfied actors, not the fear of imperium, that stimulates military buildups and alliance formation. Because war is not a military versus military duel, protection from these irrational or dissatisfied actors cannot be achieved by maintaining some sort of balance, parity, or equilibrium.

Living Without Balance

As the events of September 11, 2001, drove home, we live in a dangerous world. To protect our security it is necessary to understand this world. Reliance on the simple metaphor of balancing does not help us develop this understanding. To the contrary, it leads us to expect state behavior and international outcomes that are not occurring and that are unlikely to occur.

If war today were something that militaries did to militaries, and if today's liberal democratic great powers feared that other liberal democratic great powers had imperial ambitions that would ultimately threaten their own sovereignty, then logically states would—or should—indeed attempt to balance each other's military capabilities. But war in today's world is a nontrinitarian affair. It is waged against civilians and leaders. As a consequence, what matters is the absolute military capability political actors possess, not their relative capability. Further, not every state is perceived as posing a potential threat to the sovereign state system, and some states do not fear for their survival even when faced with an imbalance of military power. There is thus no logical reason why states should necessarily respond to increases in the military power of other great powers either by increasing their own military power or by forming balancing alliances.

This deduction comes as something of a relief, because even the most cursory look at the empirical evidence would seem to suggest that balancing is not the norm in today's world. During the Cold War it was possible (though difficult) to argue that the behavior of great powers such as Britain, France, Japan, Italy, and West Germany did in fact represent balancing—and some Realist scholars did in fact try to fit the facts into this Procrustean bed. But the absence of balancing behavior, on a global level, since the end of the Cold War is hard to deny. The growth of U.S. military power has not prompted other great powers, with the possible exception of China, to increase their military efforts. Nor has it resulted in alliances against the United States.

To suggest that the present is different from the past is to invite accusations that one possesses a naive view of human nature or has succumbed to liberal millenarianism. I plead innocent to such charges. My argument does not assume that the human leopard has changed his spots, that war and violence are obsolete, or that we have reached some sort of end of history. My argument is simply that the evolution of social institutions, such as war and the liberal democratic nation-state, and changes in technology mean that the logical imperative for states to balance military power no longer exists.

If we are to develop sensible security policies and if we are to understand the dynamics of world politics, we need to begin by abandoning the outdated metaphor of balancing. Balance of power theory needs to be taken not as an article of faith but as an explanation of behavior and outcomes under certain highly circumscribed social and technological conditions. Realist scholars and policymakers who assume that 21st-century states will pursue military balances of power, or that balances of military power will tend to emerge, are mistaking the logic that flowed from a particular construction of "war" and a particular set of political conditions in a particular historical era for an unchanging, universal truth. Understanding *why* states balanced and *why* balances tended to emerge—that is, understanding why balancing makes sense if and only if "war" is a trinitarian exercise and all states assume they must fear all other states—allows us to understand why we should not expect balancing today.

Notes

1. Carl von Clausewitz, *On War* (London: Penguin, 1968), 101–38, 367–410. See also Peter Paret, "Clausewitz," in Peter Paret (ed.), *Makers of Modern Strategy from Machiavelli to the Nuclear Age* (Princeton: Princeton University Press, 1986), 200–202 and Martin van Creveld, *The Transformation of War* (New York: Free Press, 1991), 33–42.

2. See, for example, John Keegan, *A History of Warfare* (New York: Knopf, 1993), 3–60; and van Creveld, *Transformation of War*, 33–42, 192–223.

3. Thomas C. Schelling is generally credited with developing the distinction between coercive uses of power, based on the imposition of pain, and direct uses of it, based on the seizure or destruction of resources. See Schelling, *Arms and*

Influence (New Haven: Yale University Press, 1966), 2–11. For an extended discussion of competing counter-military and counter-societal social constructions of "war," see Edward Rhodes, "Constructing Peace and War," *Millennium Journal of International Studies* 24 (Spring 1995): 63–66; or Edward Rhodes, "Sea Change: Interest-Based Vs. Cultural-Cognitive Accounts of Strategic Choice in the 1890s," *Security Studies* 5 (Summer 1996): 108–18. Clausewitz, of course, explicitly considers the possible advantages to be gained by occupying a territory and destroying its capacity to support the adversary's armed forces, particularly in forcing a reluctant opponent to do battle at a time and in a place of one's own choosing. See Clausewitz, *On War*, 127.

4. On the parametric change in human capabilities and the resulting turbulence this causes in political relationships, see James N. Rosenau, *Turbulence in World Politics* (Princeton: Princeton University Press, 1990), 10–20.

5. Edward Vose Gulick, *Europe's Classical Balance of Power* (New York: Norton, 1967), 30–51.

PART III

Regional Subsystems and Balance of Power

CHAPTER 7

Europe Hedges Its Security Bets[1]

ROBERT J. ART

Introduction

Since the end of the Cold War, Europe has experienced a significant number of changes in its security environment, most but not all of which have been beneficial. The Soviet Union broke up, the Warsaw Pact collapsed, and all the Central European states have set themselves on the path of democratic reform and most have joined NATO. Russia for the most part remains militarily weak, Germany has been reunified and peacefully integrated in Europe, the European Union is in the process of expanding and deepening, and the Balkans, after a succession of wars, appear quiescent.

Does balance of power theory help us understand how the Europeans have dealt with these momentous events? My short answer is "yes, to a degree." Balance of power theory cannot explain every twist and turn in Europe's posture as a whole, nor can it account for every action taken by each state in the region. After all, balance of power is more a theory about the outcomes of state interaction than a theory of foreign policy. Although it does not explain everything, balance of power theory can shed light on how and why Europeans reacted to the end of the Cold War and the significant events that followed in its wake.

This chapter applies two versions of balance of power theory to explain recent events in Europe. Traditionally, balance of power theory, together with Stephen Walt's important amendment to it (balance of threat theory), predicts that a state or group of states, facing another state or group of states whose power is growing and is judged to be a threat, will act to offset the growing strength of the threatening party.[2] Essential to this conception of balance of power are two elements: a perception that a clear threat to a state's physical security exists and a belief that more economic and military resources must be deployed to counter it, to be mustered either through internal efforts (a state devotes more of its resources to military armaments), or through external means (a state aligns with other states), or both. This is the concept of "hard" balancing referred to in the introduction to this volume.

A looser version of balance of power, however, can be used to explain developments in Europe. It is not quite equivalent to the "soft" balancing concept described in the introduction, but is close to it. In this looser version, a state does not fear an increased threat to its physical security from another rising state; rather, it is concerned about the adverse effects of that state's rise on its general position, both political and economic, in the competitive international arena. This concern also may, but need not, include a worry that the rising state could cause security problems in the future, although not necessarily war. The justification for employing this second version of balance of power is that it is rooted in the neorealist view that relative power considerations count heavily in state calculations, that perceived and actual changes in relative power rankings do affect state behavior, and that states do care about how they fare politically and economically, even when their physical security is not at immediate risk. This wider balance of power lens sensitizes us to state actions motivated by relative power considerations.

When these two lenses of balance of power theory are applied to Europe from 1990 to 2003, the following results become apparent:

— There has been no "hard" balancing by Europe against the United States because the United States does not represent a direct military threat to Europe's security. The United States is, after all, Europe's ally and protector.[3]

— There has been some soft balancing against the United States, first by the French alone, then by the French together with the British, and most recently by the French together with the Germans.

— Fear of American abandonment and the need to provide a hedge against that eventuality, Europe's desire for a degree of autonomy vis à vis the United States, Europe's desire to gain more influence over the United States, and the perceived need to produce a more coherent foreign and security policy for the European Union—these have been the prime factors that have given impetus to the development of the European Security and Defense Policy (ESDP).

— Europe, including France, has favored the maintenance of the North Atlantic Treaty Organization (NATO) in order to keep U.S. forces in

Europe as insurance against the reemergence of a powerful and hostile Russia, as a potential counterweight to a united Germany, and as a mechanism to avoid Europe's descent into nationalistic and competitive security policies.

The best way to illustrate the accuracy of these propositions is to analyze four national security issues that Europeans dealt with from 1990 to 2003. They were the most important security decisions that the Europeans had to face during this period, and, in one fashion or another, all were affected by the changes in the balance of forces that were taking place both within Europe and between Europe and the United States. They are therefore good tests of the above propositions. The four issues are the political struggle to devise a post-Cold War security order for Europe in the immediate aftermath of the Soviet Union's fall, a struggle that lasted from 1990 through 1995; the expansion of NATO into Central Europe from 1994 to 1999; the planning for, and conduct of, the Kosovo War in 1998–1999; and the effects of the second Gulf War on European-American relations and on the cohesiveness of the European Union in foreign and military affairs in 2002–2003.

This chapter first places the above issues in a broader political context. It then explores each issue in turn, and concludes with some observations about the future of the ESDP.

The Political Context of European Balancing

Three factors had a profound influence on Europe's security policies during the 1990–2003 period. First is the simple fact that many actors were involved in formulating these policies. Second is the fact that Europe, despite its considerable success in economic integration, nonetheless remained a collection of sovereign entities with different perceptions, fears, needs, and desires. Third are the hedging policies that Europe pursued as a consequence of the powerful influence that the United States, Russia, and Germany have exerted on Europe.

MULTIPLE ACTORS

Europe's security and defense policies had to take account of multiple factors and actors: the United States, its prime ally and protector, whose reliability, staying power, and multilateralist tendencies varied; the North Atlantic Treaty Organization, the key embodiment of America's security commitment to Europe and Europe's prime security institution, which underwent a major transformation in both role and size and whose future remains problematic; Russia, which although neither an adversary nor an ally, is contiguous to Europe and will greatly affect Europe's future security policy; the European Union, which remains in the process of widening and deepening and whose ultimate shape is both uncertain and controversial; Germany, Europe's most powerful state and largest economy, whose balancing of European and national interests tilted more toward the latter than the former since the Cold War's end; and the ESDP enterprise and its prime embodiment, a rapid reaction force of 60,000, to which Europe is strongly committed in rhetoric but to which it has not yet committed the necessary resources to make fully effective. All these actors and forces influenced events throughout the period under review, but they varied in their relative importance and often worked at cross purposes, producing a complex set of European responses and, in turn, varied American reactions to Europe's policies.

Although multiple factors were at play in European politics, two clear periods stand out during these thirteen years, and the concerns that predominated during the first period (1990–1997) differed dramatically from those that characterized the second (1998–2003). Germany's unification and Russia's transition to democracy were the paramount concerns up to 1997; both produced a strong desire among Europeans, including the French, to have the United States remain as Europe's protector. In the second period, worries about American power came to the fore. These worries included a concern about whether the United States could be counted on to help solve problems on Europe's eastern border and about the vast military gap between the United States and Europe. European leaders questioned what that gap might portend for Europe's role in Washington's global strategy and for the unilateral exercise of American power. During the first period, uncertainty about Germany and Russia made most Europeans ardent suitors of American power; in the second, alarm over increasing American military strength caused many Europeans to worry about its unbridled use. Because Kosovo was the first conflict to demonstrate clearly and dramatically the vast gap that had opened up between U.S. and European capabilities, that war, not the second Gulf War, represents the turning point in the thirteen-year security history of post-Cold War Europe.

DIFFERENT INTERESTS

In assessing the effects that changing balances had on European nations, we must remember that there is as yet no single entity called Europe that speaks with one voice on foreign, security, and defense policy. Unlike in the economic arena, there are no strong supranational institutions and, consequently, no common European foreign and security policies, and certainly no truly European defense force. On these issues, Europe still remains a set of nations that retain individual control over their foreign policies and defense establishments and whose national interests on these matters differ.

The contrast between the economic and the foreign-security-defense areas could not be starker. In the former there are a single European currency, a single European central bank, and qualified majority voting. In the latter, although there is currently a European Union foreign policy minister (named the High Representative for Common Foreign and Security Policy), he still has to compete with national capitals on foreign and defense issues, and manage the requirement for unanimity in voting on these matters. (As of this writing, the draft constitution for the European Union may envision a single European foreign minister, but the requirement for unanimity on foreign policy, not qualified majority voting as in economic and trade matters, still obtains.) Although the United States may have to negotiate with Europe as a whole on trade relations, it still deals with national capitals bilaterally on foreign policy, security, and defense. On the economic side, there is now a powerful supranational institution that coexists with strong national institutions; on the foreign policy, security, and defense side, there is only a weak supranational institution that competes poorly with strong national ones.[4]

National differences within Europe remain important to foreign and security policymaking, and these differences have marked effects on what Europe as a whole can do. For example, the British and French may share imperial memories and have proud traditions of independence in foreign affairs, but they have been at loggerheads as much as they have cooperated on foreign and defense matters. The British have been the most insistent that NATO remain the prime venue for security discussions and the central security institution for Europe; the French have been the most insistent on forging a European identity and defense entity distinct and separate from NATO. The Germans have usually found themselves caught between these two positions, trying to satisfy each but often aggravating both of their allies. The smaller states of Europe are not interested in a Franco-German condominium in foreign and defense policy and want to see the United States remain as a counterbalance to these two powers. The Central European states, the newest entrants into NATO, have remained the most committed to an American military presence and the traditional collective defense function of the alliance because they share common concerns about Russia's future course. Thus, in foreign and defense policy, there is rarely a single European point of view, but, instead, many national points of view, and they are not harmonious.

HEDGING POLICIES

Even though it often speaks with a cacophony of voices on foreign and military policy, Europe does on occasion look more like a single actor. This most often occurs when it confronts powerful or potentially powerful opponents, thus illustrating the importance that power considerations have had on European behavior. In their policies toward Germany, Russia, and the United States, the nations of Europe have generally hedged their security bets by utilizing both balancing and integrating mechanisms.

Europe's policy toward Russia has been both to balance against the possibility of its aggressive resurgence and to integrate it into European institutions. Europe overall has favored the maintenance of NATO as a residual guarantee—and means to hard balance—against the revival of an aggressive, powerful Russia, but Europeans also have supported Russia's integration into Europe through closer economic interactions and quasi-security institutions because they have a vital interest in seeing its successful transition to a democratic, market-capitalistic state with close ties to the West. Apart from the Organization for Security and Cooperation in Europe, NATO has been the most important institutional means to do this. The NATO link has taken two forms: the Permanent Joint Council and its successor, the NATO-Russia Council. These two provide for formal relations between NATO and Russia, giving Russia access to NATO and some sense of participation in NATO matters, but without a veto over them and without membership in the organization. Through both, the European nations, along with the United States, tried to square the circle: keep NATO as a residual protector against a potential Russia gone bad, and use NATO to bring Russia into security cooperation with Europe. The United States led the way in creating both these mechanisms, but they resonated quite well with the Europeans because they fit nicely into Europe's dual approach toward Russia. Europe lives next to a Russia that is neither enemy nor ally. As long as its future path is still to be written, it is as sensible for Europe to make provision against a bad Russian landing, even though that looks less likely now than it did in the early and mid-1990s, as it is for Europe to help produce a good one.

Similarly, Europe hedged its security bets toward a united Germany. Germany's neighbors did not welcome its unification, and France and Britain even tried to avert it, or at least slow it down. Once the United States came out unequivocally for a single Germany, however, they could do little to prevent it. Germany's neighbors were concerned about what a more powerful Germany might mean for them politically, economically, and militarily, and sought institutional fixes to constrain it. At the same time, they sought to harness German power, especially the German economy, to advance European integration.

The dual motives of balancing and integrating produced two main institutional responses: Europe's desire for NATO's continuance and Europe's move toward greater political integration. Even though the Cold War ended, NATO persisted because the Europeans wanted it to remain a hard-balancing mechanism against the possibility, no matter how remote, that a Germany reunited might revert to its more nationalistic past. (The actual balancing mechanism is the U.S. presence in Europe, but NATO represents the political framework for the U.S. presence.) In fact, Germans themselves wanted NATO as a guard against the same possibility. Europe's desire for a hard-balancing mechanism was matched by its equally strong desire to tie a united Germany more deeply into Europe. Hence, German unification was almost immediately followed by moves, launched by the Germans and the French, to deepen European political cooperation in the foreign and security policy realms. Europe's Common Foreign and Security Policy (CFSP) was born in the early 1990s out of this desire to bind a united Germany more deeply into Europe by widening and deepening those institutions. Just as with Russia, so, too, Europe followed balancing and integrating strategies toward Germany; and by remaining a European continental military power, the United States was central to both efforts.

Finally, the Europeans hedged their security bets vis-à-vis the United States. They took steps to prevent the United States from abandoning

Europe to its fate, but also tried to make contingency plans should that happen. They have been more successful with the former than with the latter. As was the case during the Cold War, European nations made moves that appeared to do more for their own defense and address American concerns, especially those voiced in Congress, about burden sharing and free-riding, in order to dampen America's isolationist impulses. These moves were also intended to give Europe more autonomy from, and more influence over, the United States should U.S. forces remain in Europe, and to provide the foundation, although not the entire edifice, for its own defense should the United States leave Europe. In pursuit of these objectives, the Europeans invented and reinvented various institutional formulas for greater European cooperation in foreign, security, and defense affairs: the European Political Union (EPU), Common Foreign and Security Policy (CFSP), European Security and Defense Identity (ESDI), the Franco-German Eurocorps, the Rapid Reaction Force (RRF; also called the ERRF, European Rapid Reaction Force), and European Security and Defense Policy (also called CESDP, for Common European Security and Defense Policy). None of these as yet has amounted to much, but all have been designed both to keep U.S. forces in Europe and to hedge against its departure.

These three factors—the multiple actors bearing on Europe's security policies, the importance of national interests and differing perspectives, and the hedging policies toward the United States, Russia, and Germany—represent the important underlying forces that have shaped balance of power considerations in Europe's security policies since 1990.

The Empirical Record

Between 1990 and 2003, the Europeans faced four security challenges critical to their relations with the United States, with Russia, and with one another. First, they had to decide on a new security order for Europe in the immediate aftermath of the Cold War, a decision complicated by the onset of the Bosnian War in 1992. Then, they had to deal with America's determination to expand NATO eastward. Next, they were forced to confront Yugoslav President Slobodan Milosevic's aggression in Kosovo and the Kosovo War, and, finally, they had to face Washington's unilateralism in its determination to unseat Saddam Hussein.

Balance of power theory can help us understand some of the major concerns Europeans shared and actions they took on these issues, although it cannot explain everything the Europeans thought and did. With regard to security, Europe as a whole wanted NATO to remain in place as a residual hard balancer against Russia and a united Germany. In addition, France wanted to deepen the European Union both to bind Germany's enhanced power more tightly into Europe's institutions and to obtain more autonomy vis-à-vis the United States. The European nations, however, were either lukewarm toward, or opposed to, NATO's expansion. They worried that expansion, by taking in new, less militarily capable members, could dilute NATO's military effectiveness and degrade its hard-balancing role, or that expansion could alienate Moscow and strengthen its hardliners, thereby endangering Russia's experiment with democracy and peaceful integration into Europe. When the conflict in Kosovo broke out, the Europeans, especially the British, quickly realized that they could do little to end the fighting without relying heavily on the United States. This realization led to the Franco-British agreement at Saint-Malo, France, in 1998 to cooperate on building a more robust European defense capability, one that could provide a degree of military autonomy vis-à-vis the United States. In the run-up to the second Gulf War, concerns about U.S. unilateralism led to soft balancing by the French and the Germans in order to restrain the United States. The balance of power prism in both the hard and softer versions helps us comprehend some of Europe's key motivations and actions on these central issues.

THE POST-COLD WAR SECURITY ORDER, 1990–1995

Three factors—Germany's unification, Russia's uncertain course, and Europe's concern about the solidity of Washington's commitment to its security— shaped the 1990–1995 debate over the security order that Europe should construct for itself following the Cold War.[5] The first two factors caused the third: a newly reunited Germany and the potential for a resurgent Russia caused many European states to favor a continued U.S. military presence on the continent. The Bosnian War of 1992–1995 reinforced this desire because it showed the Europeans that they were collectively unable or unwilling to deal effectively with conflicts on their eastern border.

In late 1989, the prospect of Germany's unification provoked unease among its neighbors, an unease most clearly articulated in France and

Britain.[6] At the end of October 1989, West German Chancellor Helmut Kohl had proposed a confederation for the two halves of Germany. French President François Mitterrand's response was to fly to Kiev in early December to consult with Soviet President Mikhail Gorbachev on how to slow down, if not totally prevent, such a confederation. At a meeting in early December in Brussels between U.S. President George H. W. Bush and the European Union heads of state, British Prime Minister Margaret Thatcher took the position that Germany should not be reunified for ten to fifteen years at the earliest. She subsequently met twice with Mitterrand to discuss ways to thwart Kohl's confederation plans. French-British efforts were for naught because President Bush in early December unequivocally came out in support of German unification.

Subsequently, French and British strategies differed on how to deal with the prospect of German unification, especially once it became clear in early 1990 that it would happen rapidly. Thatcher herself nicely summarized this difference: Mitterrand chose the path "of moving ahead faster towards a federal Europe in order to tie down the German giant" rather than returning to the path "associated with General Charles DeGaulle—the defense of French sovereignty and the striking up of alliances to secure French interests."[7] (Former French President Valery Giscard d'Estaing put the French strategy more bluntly: "We need an organized Europe to escape German domination."[8]) In other words, the French sought to bind a reunited Germany more tightly to Europe by strengthening European-wide institutions; the British, to balance Germany by making certain that the NATO alliance, and the American military presence in Europe, were preserved.

French moves to strengthen Europe's institutions came in two stages. The first was short-lived, from the fall of the Berlin Wall in early November 1989 until mid-March 1990; the second commenced in April 1990 and lasted for a few years. Mitterrand took advantage of the prospect of German unification, which initially he and others viewed as inevitable but not immediate, to push European Monetary Union (EMU) on Kohl, who had been resisting the idea for several years. In return for French support of Germany's eventual reunion, Kohl agreed to EMU in early December 1989.

The second stage commenced after the 1990 March elections in East Germany made clear that Germany would unify rapidly, not slowly. EMU now looked to Mitterrand and to Kohl, who also favored embedding a reunited Germany in a stronger and deeper Europe, as insufficient by itself to bind Germany tightly enough into Europe. On April 19, therefore, Mitterrand and Kohl endorsed a second intergovernmental conference on European political union to complement the one created earlier on monetary union. The central purpose of political union was to deepen European integration even more than would be obtained through EMU, and one way to achieve such deepening was to create a common foreign and defense policy. Hence, with European Political Union, the European Defense Identity (EDI) was born.[9] EDI would have a second advantage for the French: it would enable Europe to develop a more coherent security policy and a bigger defense capability, thereby giving Europe more autonomy and independence from the United States, a goal the French had favored for a long time. Hence, with German unification looming, French moves to enhance Europe's foreign and defense capabilities would not only reduce Germany's freedom for independent action, it also would lessen Europe's reliance on the United States.

While the French sought to entangle Germany in a strengthened Europe, Britain balanced against it by working to keep the United States military engaged in Europe.[10] This meant preserving NATO as the prime security organization in Europe. With the United States militarily present in Europe, a united Germany would loom less large, and an additional benefit would be protection against the residual possibility of a bellicose, resurgent Russia. Consequently, the British undertook to deflect the Franco-German call for EDI into a path that would be "NATO-friendly," and the device they settled on was the Western European Union (WEU), a largely moribund organization born in 1948 with the Brussels Treaty. The WEU had two advantages: it was not a part of the European Community but was free-standing, and it was organically tied to NATO but had historically been subservient to it. The latter attribute was especially advantageous; the 1954 Protocol that amended the 1948 Brussels Treaty clearly stated that the WEU would not duplicate the military staffs of NATO, but instead would rely on NATO. Here was an institutional solution that suited British interests: channel any European defense effort that might emerge into an organization that had had a secondary position to NATO, thereby ensuring the latter's primacy.

The Germans found themselves caught in the middle. They wanted to preserve Franco-German cooperation because it was the engine of European integration, but they also wanted to preserve the primacy of NATO because it was seen as central to Germany's and Europe's security. Kohl, in particular, understood that it was as important for Germany to be embedded in NATO as it was for Germany to be embedded in stronger European institutions; both were necessary to reassure Germany's neighbors about its enhanced power. Consequently, the Kohl government acted to please both the French and the British by trying to split the difference between them. The German chancellor backed France's intention to make the WEU formally part of the newly created European Union (Paris had decided to counter London's strategy by seeking to incorporate the WEU into the European Union), but he insisted that it had to be compatible with NATO. This meant that an enhanced WEU could not duplicate NATO's military command structure and operational planning capability, thereby keeping it secondary to the alliance. Kohl supported France's plan to create a Eurocorps, which was to be the nucleus of a European army, but again insisted that whatever troops Germany assigned to it would be under both NATO and Eurocorps command, thereby effectively rendering the Eurocorps subservient to NATO.[11] With France trying to "Gulliverize" Germany, with Britain balancing against it, and with the other states of Europe warily watching it, Kohl acted to mollify everyone by supporting a meaningful European Defense Identity and a strong NATO and by locking Germany into both.

A compromise between the French and British positions was finally reached at the end of 1993. Although it incorporated elements of the French view, the compromise was closer to what the British wanted, largely because the United States threw its weight behind the British proposals. The WEU would become part of the European Union, which came formally into existence in January 1993, but all agreed that NATO would remain "the essential forum for consultation and venue for agreement" on security and defense matters in Europe.[12] Consequently, the WEU's structure would remain small and not duplicate NATO's, especially NATO's large planning staff at SHAPE (Supreme Headquarters Allied Powers Europe). The modus vivendi between NATO and the WEU was described as "separable but not separate capabilities."[13] This meant that there would be two political decision-making chains (one for the WEU and one for NATO), but only one set of military assets. By relying on NATO's military staff work, command structure, operational planning, logistics, intelligence, and lift, the WEU remained a decidedly junior partner. In short, as long as the WEU did not threaten the primacy of NATO, it would be tolerated.

France's drive to create a more autonomous and more muscular European

Defense Identity failed because its Western European allies wanted the United States to maintain its military presence in Europe, and preserving NATO as Europe's prime security institution was the best way to achieve that goal. Ultimately, the French came around to this point of view, largely as a consequence of the Bosnian War. It convinced the French (at least for a time) that NATO could not be reduced simply to the role of residual protector against a resurgent Russia, but that it had an important role in projecting stability beyond Western Europe's eastern border. For the French and the other Europeans, Bosnia demonstrated that eternal peace had not yet arrived on their continent, that they could not agree on a common policy to end the war, and that they did not have the collective will or capability to intervene forcefully to stop it. Bosnia also held another key lesson for the Europeans: whatever common efforts they could muster would be for naught if the United States opposed their policies and gave parties to the conflict hope that they could gain America's backing. (The United States encouraged the Bosnian Muslims in the early stages of the war not to settle for a deal that the Europeans had worked out, holding out hope that they could gain more territorially if they refused to settle.) The war came to an end only when the United States decided that it was threatening the credibility of NATO and hence America's own position as a European great power. Under belated but forceful American leadership, credible military power was applied, a cease-fire was enacted in September 1995, and in December the war ended with the Dayton Accords.

Bosnia demonstrated to the Europeans their collective impotence, their difficulty in prevailing when the United States opposed their policies, and, consequently, their need for U.S. political participation and military power. And yet, while the Europeans collectively agreed that the United States remained essential to Europe's security, the Bosnian War also taught the Europeans that they must bolster their own military capability. Even though the French may have moved closer to the views of their allies, by the same token they moved closer to the French. The British in particular concluded from the Bosnian War that although the United States remained essential, Europe had to bolster its own defense capability for those contingencies from which the United States chose to remain aloof. Bosnia produced a narrowing between the French and British positions, thereby making it easier for Germany to satisfy both.

In sum, balance of power theory in both its hard and softer versions helps illuminate the European powers' stratagems and actions regarding the security order that they sought from 1990 to 1995. They viewed U.S. might as essential to balance against a reunited Germany and an uncertain Russia and to put an end to the Balkan conflicts, and hence favored a strong NATO even though the Cold War had ended. They also began to see merit in the French view that they needed to work harder on a substantive European Defense Identity, even if they did not agree with the French that it should rival and ultimately supplant NATO.

NATO ENLARGEMENT, 1994–1999

The Europeans had not fully settled the matter of Europe's post-Cold War security order before they had to contend with another issue: America's push to enlarge NATO. The Europeans' initial reactions to this proposal ranged from tepid to opposed. They worried about the impact that enlargement would have on NATO's effectiveness and on Russia's difficult transition to a stable democracy, but, ultimately, the Europeans succumbed to Washington's wishes because they could not resist them. Enlarging NATO became the price the Europeans had to pay if they wanted to keep NATO vibrant and the United States militarily engaged on the continent.[14]

In the United States, as James Goldgeier makes crystal clear, NATO enlargement was very much a decision that emanated from the top.[15] It was not one in which the president was captured by the bureaucracy; rather, it was a decision President Clinton imposed on a bureaucracy that was caught off guard. In October 1993, Clinton and his principal advisors had agreed to offer to the Central European states at the upcoming January 1994 NATO summit a proposal called Partnership for Peace—an ingenious device that would tender various forms of cooperation between NATO and the states of Central Europe, but without giving them NATO membership. Immediately after the Brussels summit, however, Clinton traveled to Prague to meet with Central European leaders and in a prepared statement on January 12 said: "While the Partnership [for Peace] is not NATO membership, neither is it a permanent holding room. It changes the entire NATO dialogue so that now the question is no longer whether NATO will take on new members but when and how."[16] Subsequently, under the determined leadership of National Security Advisor Anthony Lake and Assistant Secretary of State for European Affairs Richard Holbrooke, the U.S. government officially embraced NATO enlargement, even though no formal meeting of Clinton's top foreign policy and defense officials had taken place to debate its merits or even to endorse it. By late 1994, enlargement was the official position of the U.S. government.

Clinton and his advisors had several reasons to push enlargement. The first was to make certain that the former members of the Warsaw Pact would make the transition from authoritarian communism to capitalistic democracy. Unless these states were firmly anchored to the West, it was feared that they might "succumb to creeping authoritarianism."[17] NATO membership would provide the institutional anchor to avert that outcome by giving the democratic forces the security they desired and the encouragement they needed. Furthermore, the pro-democratic forces in these states had to show their publics that there would be concrete benefits if they made the democratic transition, and membership in NATO was one of them. Enlarging NATO to include the newly established democracies of Central Europe also fit nicely into President Clinton's convictions that democracy needed to be expanded.

Equally important was America's desire not to leave Germany facing instability alone on its eastern borders, or to allow Russia and Germany together to deal with Central Europe as they saw fit. Instead, Clinton administration officials believed the solution should be a multinational one, and the NATO alliance represented the best multilateral institution to stabilize Central Europe. In this regard American policy was both anticipatory of, and responsive to, concerns expressed in some German quarters about dealing alone with instability on its eastern borders. This German unease was one of the prime motivations for Volker Ruehe, then Germany's defense minister, to call for NATO enlargement in March 1993, when he delivered the annual Alastair Buchan lecture at London's International Institute for Strategic Studies (IISS), a stance he took without consulting either the German Foreign Office or Chancellor Kohl.[18]

A final reason for enlargement was the Clinton administration's belief that NATO needed a new lease on life to remain viable. NATO's viability, in turn, was important because the alliance not only helped maintain America's position as a European power, it also preserved America's hegemony in Europe.[19] The spread of democracy, the need to fill a power vacuum in Central Europe, and the preservation of America's hegemony in Europe— these were the prime motives for NATO's enlargement.[20]

The Clinton administration's call for enlargement met with an enthusiastic response from the leaders of Central Europe; indeed, they had been calling for it repeatedly.[21] Western Europe's leaders, however, were decidedly unenthusiastic, if not downright opposed. Volker Ruehe may have wanted NATO to expand, but it was not the official position of the German government at the time, nor was his IISS speech well received by those NATO ambassadors from Western Europe who were present. In fall 1993, the governments of Western Europe were as divided on enlargement as was the Washington foreign policy bureaucracy. To the extent that there was a consensus view among the allies, it was for giving the Central Europeans membership in the European Union, not NATO, as the best way to integrate them with the West.

Each major state had its own particular set of concerns. The British worried that NATO expansion would dilute NATO and weaken Washington's security commitment to Europe. The French feared enlargement would strengthen NATO and thereby increase U.S. influence in Europe, as well as slow progress toward European integration.[22] (Enlargement was like "giving NATO vitamins," said one senior French official.[23]) The Germans were especially concerned about the effects of enlargement on Europe's relations with Russia. At his first meeting as U.S. ambassador with German officials in September 1993, Richard Holbrooke reported that Chancellor Kohl and three other top German officials "disassociated themselves from Defense Minister Ruehe's views on NATO's future," and later, at a private dinner, Kohl sent Holbrooke a private message stating: "NATO can exclude taking in countries of Eastern Europe. . . . We must tell these East European countries that they can count on our support, but not membership."[24]

This reluctance persisted. In late January 1995, the U.S. ambassador to NATO, Robert Hunter, reported to Washington: "Few allies are enthusiastic about expansion, and several will drag their feet on getting the necessary work done this year, whether out of inertia or out of a hope that, somehow, they will not have to cross this particular Rubicon."[25] Europe's unease continued into 1996. Chancellor Kohl and President Chirac were particularly concerned about the effects of enlargement on Russian foreign policy and suggested a delay until U.S.-Russian relations were on solid footing.[26] President Clinton persisted in his commitment to enlarge NATO. After Boris Yeltsin was reelected president of Russia in July 1996, Clinton wrote to his European counterparts that he intended to push ahead with enlargement. Europe's foot-dragging finally ended only after Yeltsin had yielded to Clinton's insistence on enlarging NATO at their March 1997 Helsinki summit, and had agreed to negotiate the details of the NATO-Russian agreement, subsequently known as the NATO-Russian Founding Act.[27]

Ultimately, the Europeans agreed, although their reasons differed. The British supported the decision for typically British reasons: even if they thought enlargement a mistake, going along with it would preserve Britain's influence and traditional close relations with the United States. They also wanted any enlargement to be as small as possible.[28] The French went along because they could not stop it, and because they had come to realize the importance of NATO to Europe's stability as a consequence of the Bosnian war. The Germans were the most enthusiastic of the big European powers, and the reasoning of the Kohl government is worth noting, as U.S. Deputy Secretary of State Strobe Talbott recounts his meeting with Kohl in January 1997:

> The chancellor moved quickly . . . to what enlargement would mean for Germany itself. . . . As long as Germany's border with Poland marked the dividing line between East and West, Germany would be vulnerable to the pathologies of racism and the temptations of militarism that can come with living on an embattled frontier. That frontier could disappear, he said, only if Poland entered the European Union. His country's future depended not just on deepening its ties within the EU but on expanding the EU eastward so that Germany could be in the middle of a safe, prosperous, integrated and democratic Europe rather than on its edge.[29]

What light, then, does balance of power theory shed on Europe's reaction to the U.S. push to enlarge NATO? Three points are in order. First, common to all European positions was the fear that enlargement could dilute NATO as a hard-balancing mechanism. Second, common to all European positions was the fear that enlargement could derail Russia's transition to democracy and create a security threat to Europe from a place where it had just ceased to emanate. The first concerned capabilities: could NATO continue to be an effective collective defense mechanism if it grew larger? The second concerned intentions: would NATO's enlargement increase the power of the nondemocratic forces in Russia? These two concerns represent the two faces of a balance of power theory that incorporates the material and the psychological ingredients of power balancing. The final point is simple: power counts for a great deal in international relations, and on the issue of NATO enlargement, the United States was in the driver's seat. If the Europeans wanted NATO to remain viable, then they had to accept America's new definition of NATO as an alliance designed to make Europe "whole and free" again.

In sum, balance of power theory does not explain every twist and turn in the enlargement saga, nor does it account at all for the integrationist designs with regard to Central Europe and Russia shared by both the Americans and the Europeans. What it does do is help us understand European worries that enlargement could weaken NATO and alienate Russia.

THE KOSOVO WAR AND ESDP, 1998–1999

The third major security issue that the Europeans confronted during the 1990–2003 period was violent "ethnic cleansing" in the Serbian province of Kosovo. Dealing with the Kosovo crisis during 1998 and 1999 drove home three tough lessons to the Europeans. First, in contemplating military intervention in the fall of 1998, they realized that they needed U.S. military power, especially the headquarters and planning capabilities of NATO, if they were going to do something effective about Milosevic's depredations in Kosovo.[30] Second, while waging war in the spring of 1999, they learned firsthand that a wide technological gap had opened up between their military forces and those of the United States, and they found themselves both dependent on the United States and unable to interoperate fully with U.S. air power. Third, in retrospect, they realized that Washington's military intervention was a "near miss" and that the United States might not be willing to intervene in the next European crisis.[31] Consequently, Kosovo had the effect of vividly demonstrating to Europe the huge gap in military power between it and the United States, on the one hand, and Europe's utter dependence on the willingness of the United States to solve conflicts on Europe's periphery, on the other. These "faces of Kosovo" pushed the Europeans to become more serious than they hitherto had been about developing a genuine European military capability.

What resulted from this reconsideration of security needs was the European Security and Defense Policy.[32] Its concrete manifestation was the European Rapid Reaction Force, a 60,000 strong force that could be deployed within sixty days of the order to move and sustained in the field for up to one year, with the air and naval assets required to make it effective. The European Union committed itself to the ERRF at its Helsinki summit in December 1999 in what was called the "Headline Goal." For all parties, including the French, ESDP was meant to supplement NATO, not supplant it. As one French ministry of defense official put it: "I don't know of anyone in the French policy mainstream who thinks that the European Union should be a military challenger to NATO."[33] ESDP was to serve double duty: to give Europe the capability to deal with situations where NATO (the United States) chose not to become involved, and to keep the United States in Europe by showing Washington, especially the U.S. Congress, that the Europeans were finally going to pull their own weight. At this time, ESDP was motivated more by Europeans' fear of American abandonment than by their resentment at U.S. overtones of unilateralism during the Kosovo war, although there clearly was some resentment when the United States chose to bypass NATO channels while conducting the air war. Thus, ESDP was both a hedge against U.S. inaction in the next European crisis and a means to persuade the Americans to remain engaged in Europe.[34]

Kosovo may have been the catalyst that forced the Europeans to take more seriously the military force they had committed themselves to in both the Maastricht and Amsterdam treaties, but Prime Minister Tony Blair's Britain was most responsible for bringing about the ERRF. The British, after all, had been the biggest impediment to the development of a European military force because they feared that it would either relegate NATO to second-class status or cause the U.S. military to go home. Consequently, throughout most of the 1990s, the British had used the Western European Union as a means to foil French plans for a more capable European military force. As one high-level British official put it: "Blair thought the WEU was useless and it was. We British used it to prevent an effective European security personality from emerging precisely because it was useless."[35]

Four factors caused Blair to reverse Britain's course and throw its weight behind developing an effective European force. First, he wanted Britain to play a greater role in the construction of the European Union. Because Britain was not a member of the single-currency Euro zone, the only other place where it could play a significant role was in defense, where Britain had considerable assets to bring to the table. Second, the Blair government realized that Europe was going to move ahead on its project of developing a common foreign and security policy with or without London's blessing, and therefore that it was better for Britain to become more deeply engaged to make it come out right. According to a high-level MOD official: "We wanted to construct a new [defense] pillar to protect our interests. We worried that it would come out wrong if we were not involved at the outset. Hence we wanted to control the direction and not lose control. When we launched the new effort [ESDP], we defined the terms and managed to set things on the right course for the European defense entity."[36] Third, Blair was frustrated throughout 1998 in his attempt to develop a policy to get involved in Kosovo, both because the Clinton administration seemed reluctant to deal with the crisis and because the European Union seemed inadequate to the task.[37] At one meeting with his MOD planners, Blair was told that forceful intervention in Kosovo would require that Britain put up 50,000 troops, the United States 100,000, and the rest of Europe 50,000. Clearly, such intervention could not be done without U.S. participation.[38] Finally, Blair wanted the Europeans to develop a greater military capability so that they could have more influence with the United States and within the NATO alliance. He insisted, however, on two red lines: whatever Europe did in the defense area had to be NATO-friendly, and any really large military operation had to be done within NATO.[39]

These considerations pushed the Blair government to take the initiative and work out a rapprochement with the French on defense matters. The result was the Franco-British meeting at Saint-Malo, France, in December 1998, where both states committed themselves to building a more effective European defense capability within the European Union. One key phrase from the declaration summarized this new bilateral understanding: "the [European] Union must have the capability for autonomous action." The declaration made clear, however, that the European Union would take action "when the alliance as a whole is not engaged" and that the assets that the EU developed would occur "without unnecessary duplication" of NATO's capabilities.[40] With the Saint-Malo declaration, the British had moved closer to the traditional French position that Europe needed its own autonomous capability, but the British worked hard in drafting the Saint-Malo accord to make certain that autonomy meant only that the European Union would have the autonomous capability to decide and to act, not to become separate from NATO.[41] In other words, whatever defense capability the Europeans created would be used for both NATO and the EU. Most important, the British insisted that whatever defense institutions the EU developed,

NATO's military operational planning staff at SHAPE, which consisted of about 800 military officers who prepare military contingency plans, would not be duplicated. These understandings were largely accepted by the French, although they did not give up their ultimate, long-term goal of developing a European military capability that could make the EU a global military actor.[42] The provisions were subsequently endorsed by the European Union when it mandated the ERRF at Helsinki in December 1999.[43]

ESDP and ERRF, as originally conceived, are not hard-balancing mechanisms directed at the United States. The best indication that the Europeans did not intend ESDP and its rapid reaction forces to challenge the primacy of NATO was their agreement to limit the size of the ESDP's military planning staff (called the European Union Military Staff, or EUMS, which is to consist of 90–140 staff officers) so as not to challenge NATO's military staff at Brussels and especially NATO's operational planning capability at SHAPE headquarters. They clearly understood that creating a planning staff that could rival NATO's would make the ESDP into a NATO-minus-the-United States organization, something the United States would not tolerate and that risked its military departure from Europe. Instead, ESDP was meant to enhance Europe's influence within the NATO alliance; to enable Europe to act in those instances when the United States chose to sit out a European crisis that required military action, instances that the Europeans hoped would be rare; and to appear to do more burden sharing so as to keep U.S. forces in Europe. At the same time, in agreeing to push for a more capable European defense force, neither the British nor the French intended to give up their sovereignty. As one high-level British official said: "neither government is about to surrender foreign policy to the EU."[44]

Thus, to the extent that balance of power theory helps us understand what the Europeans meant when they initially embarked on ESDP, it was to enhance their political influence within the transatlantic alliance through soft balancing, but not to challenge's America's military hegemony with hard balancing.

THE SECOND GULF WAR, 2002–2003

The final security crisis that the Europeans confronted between 1990 and 2003 was the second Gulf War. Just as the Kosovo War crystallized for Europeans their long-standing dependence on the United States to solve conflicts on their periphery, so, too, the second Gulf War drove home to them, even including those who supported U.S. policy toward Iraq, their inability to restrain Washington's growing unilateralist impulses. If Kosovo demonstrated that the United States might not go to war when the Europeans wanted it to, then the second Gulf War demonstrated that the United States could go to war when the Europeans did not want it to. Together, Kosovo and the second Gulf War demonstrated the two faces of U.S. unilateralism: an overwhelmingly powerful but potentially stand-aloof United States, and an overwhelmingly powerful and highly interventionist United States. Neither unilateralist face pleased the Europeans.

The sources of Europe's concerns about U.S. unilateralism were both structural and issue specific, but they clearly were magnified by the arrogant style and tone of the George W. Bush presidency. The summary rejection of the Kyoto Treaty, the tearing up of the Anti-Ballistic Missile Treaty, the attack on the International Criminal Court, the proclivity of the Bush administration to inform its allies of its policies rather than to consult them, its apparent intolerance for those who disagree with it, and its willingness to punish those who cross it politically—all these created a feeling in Europe (and elsewhere) that the United States was turning from a benevolent hegemon—one that takes other states' interests into account when framing its actions—to a selfish hegemon—one that puts its interests first and tramples on others' when they conflict with its own priorities.[45] Joschka Fisher, Germany's foreign minister, gave vent in early 2002 to the frustrations the Europeans were experiencing with the Bush administration's foreign policy when he pointed out: "Alliance partners are not satellites."[46]

However, the political conflict over Iraq that raged between France, Germany, Belgium, and Russia, on the one hand, and the United States, on the other, during late 2002 and early 2003 ran deeper than the Bush administration's style and tone. At least three structural factors were at work, and they are important because they set the backdrop for understanding the dispute over how to deal with Iraqi dictator Saddam Hussein.

First, the widening gap in military power between the United States and the Europeans, as Robert Kagan cogently argued, has led to a difference in approach to foreign policy and national security.[47] A state as militarily powerful as the United States looks askance at international institutions that can bind its freedom of action and turns to military solutions because it has the military power to move quickly and act unilaterally. In comparison, Europe, which cannot by itself project military power beyond its continent sufficient to deal with large problems like Iraq, and which has been involved in a fifty-year multilateral institutional experiment in devaluing military force, naturally tends to prefer multilateral institutional and political-economic solutions to conflict. Kagan overdraws this difference between U.S. and European approaches, but there is some merit in it.[48] After all, militarily powerful states are more likely to eschew international institutional constraints; weaker states prefer international institutions to check more powerful states.

Second, the end of the Soviet threat removed the "common-enemy cement" that held the NATO alliance together and that kept political disputes within bounds. There was no dearth of such disputes between the United States and its European allies during the Cold War, but the need to maintain a united stance against the Soviet Union worked to keep them manageable. Today, not only is there no threat powerful enough to force the United States and Europe to submerge their differences, but also America's second war against Iraq opened up wide differences between it and Europeans over how to deal with the common threat—Islamic terrorism—that they both face. The events of September 11 made Americans feel vulnerable in a way that they did not for generations. More Americans were killed on September 11, 2001, than died in the Japanese attack on Pearl Harbor on December 7, 1941. By contrast, many European nations have a long familiarity with terrorism, and given that familiarity, they believed that America's war against Iraq increased, not decreased, the Islamic terrorist threat that they confront.[49] Consequently, not only is the powerful restraining effect of the Soviet threat now gone, but 9/11 and 3/11 (the terrorist attack in Madrid on March 11, 2004) have left Americans and Europeans divided over the proper ways to deal with Islamic terrorism.

Third, Europe is a lesser preoccupation for the United States currently than it was in the 1990s, even if it is of no less importance.[50] In many ways, the 1990s were the "decade of Europe." Germany's unification, Russia's transformation, NATO's enlargement, the Balkan wars—all were of central importance to the United States, and these events consumed a large proportion of the time and the attention of the Bush (père) and Clinton administrations. Although not the sole preoccupation of the United States during the 1990s, Europe held pride of place. Now, however, except for some lingering problems in the Balkans, there are no imminent security threats (other than terrorism) to be dealt with in Europe. As a consequence, Europe looms less large on Washington's radar, with the result that the United States gives diminished priority to the concerns and interests of the Europeans. If the 1990s were the decade of Europe, the first decade of the 21st century is likely to be dedicated to dealing with the threats of terrorism and weapons of mass destruction.

These three structural factors create a greater propensity for more built-in U.S.-EU political conflicts that are harder to keep in bounds than was the case during the Cold War. Added to these structural factors have been specific policy disagreements between the United States and most Europeans over Iraq and the Middle East. Unlike the Bush administration, most European governments, except for the British, did not see Iraq as an imminent threat requiring immediate action. Most worried that waging war against Iraq was a diversion from the campaign against terrorism and would, in fact, likely radicalize more Muslims, create more anti-Western sentiment, and would most probably lead to more terrorist attacks. Most thought the establishment of democracy in Iraq a complex problem, fraught with many pitfalls. These governments believed inspections were the right way to deal with Iraq's alleged weapons of mass destruction, and in any case, that they should run their full course before military action was contemplated. Finally, most believed that the long, bloody Israeli-Palestinian conflict deserved higher priority.[51] These views echoed the criticisms leveled against Washington by American opponents of war with Iraq.

The structural factors, the specific policy differences over Iraq and the Middle East, and the Bush administration's overbearing style created fertile ground for the French, who have never abandoned their long-range goal of making Europe a global counterweight to the United States. With his sweeping electoral victory in May 2002, Chirac had a five-year mandate, freed from electoral pressures, to pursue his foreign policy goals. These goals are well described by Pierre Lellouche, a conservative member of the French parliament, who was foreign affairs advisor to Chirac in the early 1990s: "Chirac has a vision of how he'd like the world to be. He sees a multipolar world in which Europe is the counterweight to American political and military power. In Europe, he sees a position of leadership for France. And he sees Europe as a bridge between the developing and developed world."[52]

Once German Chancellor Gerhard Schroeder, partly for electoral reasons but also partly out of genuine policy differences with the Bush administration, declared in late summer of 2002 that Germany would not support war with Iraq under any circumstances, Chirac was given his opening.[53] The dispute over how to deal with Iraq became a tool in Chirac's policy of furthering France's European project and enabled him to use this political dispute to revive the Franco-German alliance.[54] In their retrospective on the run-up to the second Gulf War, two *Wall Street Journal* reporters described what happened: "French officials confirm that Iraq became a test of a much broader question: what international rules should govern when countries—including the U.S.—may go to war? With Germany and much of world opinion weighting against U.S. plans to attack Iraq, the officials say, what better time to try standing up to Washington?"[55]

Chirac's chief diplomatic advisor, Maurice Gorudault-Montagne, visited Washington in mid-January 2003 and reported back to Chirac that he was convinced that the United States would go to war "no matter what."[56] Shortly after, Schroeder visited Paris, and the two leaders made a firm alliance to oppose U.S. military action against Iraq in the United Nations Security Council.[57] Franco-German resistance, bolstered by Russian President Vladimir Putin, prevented the United States and Britain from obtaining Security Council support for a second resolution authorizing the use of force against Iraq. Subsequently, Britain and the United States went to war against Iraq without the legitimacy of a United Nations mandate.

What does the U.S.-European dispute over the second Gulf War mean, both for transatlantic relations and for balance of power analysis? Clearly, it does not mean that Europe as a whole had coalesced against the United States. After all, sixteen European governmental leaders joined Blair and Spanish Prime Minister José María Aznar in signing a letter of support for the United States regarding its Iraqi policy, despite the fact that public opinion in nearly every European country, including those eighteen, was overwhelmingly opposed to war. The other states of Europe resented a Franco-German alliance presuming to speak for all of them. The second Gulf War split official Europe as much as it disrupted transatlantic unity and made a mockery of Europe's Common Foreign and Security Policy.

Clearly, too, the dispute over the second Gulf War did not mean that Europe was engaged in hard military balancing against the United States. There is no evidence that the Europeans viewed the United States as a direct military threat to them, and there is no sign as yet that they have decided to increase their defense budgets significantly to generate the military power necessary to offset U.S. military might.[58]

Instead, what the transatlantic fracture over Iraq meant is that two significant European great powers—France and Germany—came out openly in favor of soft balancing, largely through political-diplomatic means against the United States, but with an apparent renewed commitment to ESDP. France no longer stood alone in its quixotic quest to make Europe a counterweight to the United States; Germany under Schroeder seemingly threw Germany's weight in with the French (although Germany will likely not allow itself to become captive of France's grand designs for European defense). In late 2002, Schroeder began speaking of Germany's *Sonderweg* (special path) in foreign policy, and in April 2003, he was elucidating the need for "more Europe" or a "core Europe," and especially the need to move forward on the ERRF.[59] Germany met with France, Belgium, and Luxembourg at the end of April to discuss the modalities of closer military cooperation (even though the Germans publicly rejected a European army or a defense policy independent of NATO, and even though the French and the Germans together maintained that anything they do will be complementary to NATO, not competitive with it).[60] The best evidence that the Franco-German alliance could trigger a significant diminution of America's political influence in Europe, however, was the fact that the United States took it seriously. According to the *Financial Times*: "US envoys in Europe are putting pressure on European Union countries to weaken the deepening Franco-German alliance, fearing it will lead to a more independent European defense and foreign policy."[61]

Finally, there is no sign that the French and the British have backed away from their 1998 Saint-Malo agreement to create a more effective and robust European defense capability. In spite of their bitter differences over Iraq, they began "drawing up ambitious proposals to put the European Union's defense policy back on track."[62] At their February 2003 summit in Le Touquet, Blair and Chirac agreed that the European Union should be able to deploy land, sea, and air forces within five to ten days instead of the sixty envisioned for the ERRF.[63] Their goal also included plans to have the EU take over NATO's mission in Bosnia in 2004 and to deploy troops to Africa's hot spots.[64]

All this means that Europe's three biggest military powers remain committed to the ESDP project because they share the belief that a more robust European defense capability will give Europe more say over, and more independence from, American policies. Although they differed on the ultimate destination for ESDP, the British, the French, and the Germans nevertheless agreed sufficiently in 2003 to regain momentum on ESDP and ERRF.

Conclusion

To judge how far and how fast the Europeans have moved down the road of more enhanced security and defense cooperation, it is instructive to compare what they have done in this area to what they have accomplished in the economic area. In the latter the Europeans have succeeded in melding their economic sovereignty to a considerable extent by creating a common currency and a single central bank.[65] Three factors impelled them to do so: the desire to create a more effective and efficient common market, the desire to move further down the integrationist path, and the need to meet the economic challenge from the United States and Japan. Economic and financial integration not only would enhance Europe's economic performance, it also would enable it to compete better with the larger and more efficient Japanese and U.S. economies. Integration was thus as much a means to balance against, and better compete with, the external economic competitive threat as it was to make Europeans better off economically.[66]

Europe's integration in defense and non-trade-related foreign policy, by contrast, has moved more slowly and has not gone as far as the economic union. To begin with, Europe started seriously down the path of integration in foreign policy and defense about a decade and a half later than in the economic area—in the late 1990s as opposed to the mid-1980s. One of the reasons for the later start was sheer inertia: it was easier for Europe to rely on the United States for security than to build its own defense structure. Another reason was fear of doing anything that might give the United States cause to leave Europe—the fear that building up a credible defense capability would strengthen those political forces in the United States that wanted to leave Europe. Still another reason is that defense, security, and foreign policy remain the last redoubts of national sovereignty, and they represent areas where the British and the French, in particular, jealously guard their prerogatives. Beyond these factors lies still another: economic and financial integration seemed to be both a more natural evolutionary step in the European integrationist project and to be of greater immediacy and necessity than integration in defense and foreign policy. It would have been difficult politically and institutionally to engage in both integrationist projects at the same time, even though the Europeans had pledged themselves to do so at Maastricht.

Herein lies the key: for the Europeans, greater cooperation in the defense area was, until quite recently, seen as less compelling than was believed to be the case for economic and financial affairs. The lack of an imminent external threat, combined with the ease of continuing to rely on the Americans, meant that Europeans could take a more relaxed approach to defense integration. As a consequence, they have pursued a hedging strategy: continue to rely on the United States but take steps to enhance their own autonomy; do nothing to endanger ties with the former, but build up capability for the latter.

Of late, however, European thinking has showed a marked change. It began with the Kosovo War, as mentioned above, and was given additional impetus by the second Gulf War. Throughout most of the 1990s, enhanced cooperation in defense was seen as necessary largely, although not entirely, for internal reasons: it would help advance the European project by deepening political integration. This motive is still important in Europe's defense, security, and foreign policies, but since 1999 an external dimension has been added: Europe needs to coalesce further in these areas in order to make the United States feel its weight and to offset U.S. power and unilateralism.[67] There is now a clear "make-Europe-stronger-to-offset-the-United-States element" in the ESDP project that had not been previously present, except perhaps among the French.[68] If Europe succeeds in its ESDP project, it represents a weak form of hard balancing, but with the caveat that its purpose is not to protect Europe from a U.S. threat to its security, but rather to give Europe more weight to better influence U.S. policies.[69]

How far Europe chooses to go down the road of a truly common (and effective) foreign and security policy, as well as down the path of defense autonomy, is not yet knowable.[70] An ERRF of sorts will materialize, but it is not likely to be one that will enable Europe to project power on the scale of the second Gulf War. It will therefore not likely be a global competitor to America's military machine, but the more important issue is whether ESDP will be NATO-friendly or NATO-hostile. The answer to that depends critically on the Germans and the British. Traditionally, the Germans have wanted to be both good Europeanists and good Atlanticists and not have to choose between the two. Traditionally, the British have put Atlanticism above the European project. However, Britain under Blair in late 1998 and

Germany under Schroeder in early 2003 moved their countries partly away from their respective traditional positions and toward the Europeanist position, a place traditionally occupied by the French. Later in 2003, however, the British seemed to move back toward their more traditional stance. In considering its position toward the draft European Union constitution, for example, the Blair government stated: "We believe that a flexible, inclusive approach and effective links to NATO are essential to the success of ESDP. We will not agree to anything which is contradictory to, or would replace, the security guarantee established through NATO."[71] If Britain has its way, ESDP will remain subsidiary to NATO. The position of the Schroeder government was not completely clear, although it was on record as saying that it envisioned an ESDP complementary to NATO, not competitive with it, as was made clear earlier. Much will depend for Germany's future course on whether the Schroeder government remains in power and, if not, whether the Christian Democrats follow Schroeder's more pro-French line.

Much, however, will also depend on what the United States does. If it continues on the unilateralist path set by the Bush administration, ESDP will likely to become more ambitious than the British originally favored and more like what the French have sought. If the United States returns to a more multilateral and consensual approach, ESDP will be less ambitious than the French have traditionally sought because the British and the Germans will be more likely to walk France back from its grand design. A more ambitious ESDP would likely be NATO-hostile in the sense that it would become a competitor to NATO and strip the alliance of much of its value; a less ambitious ESDP is likely to be NATO-friendly and not challenge NATO for primacy in European security. Thus, as has been the case since 1945, Europe's future direction in defense matters will be determined as much by what the United States does as by what Europe's own internal integrationist dynamics bring forth.

Notes

1. I thank Seth Jones, Barry Posen, William Wohlforth, Micah Zenko, and the anonymous reviewer of Stanford University Press for helpful comments, and the Center for German and European Studies, Brandeis University, for a travel grant that enabled me to conduct interviews in Europe in June and July 2000.

2. Stephen M. Walt, *The Origins of Alliances* (Ithaca: Cornell University Press, 1987), 17–33.

3. Strictly speaking, they have not bandwagoned either, if we employ the correct definition of bandwagoning: states ally with a state that is considered a threat. Since the United States is not a military threat to Europe, Europe does not bandwagon with it so much as ally with it. See Kenneth N. Waltz, *Theory of International Politics* (Reading, Mass.: Addison-Wesley, 1979), 126; and Walt, *Origins of Alliances,* 32.

4. For a different view, one that stresses that Europe is only in the early stages of greater military cooperation and is in fact making reasonable progress, see Charles A. Kupchan, *The End of the American Era: U.S. Foreign Policy and the Geopolitics of the Twenty-First Century* (New York: Knopf, 2002), 148–53.

5. This section draws from Robert J. Art, "Why Western Europe Needs the United States and NATO," *Political Science Quarterly* 1 (Spring 1996): 1–39.

6. The best source on the diplomacy surrounding the unification of Germany is Philip Zelikow and Condoleeza Rice, *Germany United and Europe Transformed: A Study in Statecraft* (Cambridge, Mass.: Harvard University Press, 1995).

7. Margaret Thatcher, *The Downing Street Years* (New York: HarperCollins, 1993), 798.

8. Quoted in David Marsh, "Final March of the Old Guard," *Financial Times* April 25, 1994, 17.

9. See George Graham, David March, and Phillip Stephens, "Bonn and Paris Move to Speak of European Unity," *Financial Times,* April 20, 1990, 1.

10. This account of British strategy is based on interviews I conducted in London at the Foreign and Commonwealth Office and the Ministry of Defense in June and November 1991 and in January 1992.

11. German policy had always been to keep NATO the prime security institution. The 1963 Franco-German treaty provided for a Franco-German defense union, but Germany had inserted a preamble stating that nothing in the treaty would affect Germany's commitments to NATO.

12. The phrase appears in *Final Communiqué of the Ministerial Meeting of the North Atlantic Council in Copenhagen, June 7, 1991,* paragraph 7, in *NATO Review* 39 (June 1991): 31.

13. The phrase comes from *Partnership for Peace: Declaration of the Heads of State and Government, January 10, 1994,* paragraph 6, in *NATO Review* 42 (February 1994).

14. The two best sources on NATO's enlargement are James M. Goldgeier, *Not Whether But When: The U.S. Decision to Enlarge NATO* (Washington, D.C.: Brookings Institution, 1999); and Ronald D. Asmus, *Opening NATO's Door: How the Alliance Remade Itself for a New Era* (New York: Columbia University Press, 2002). I have relied heavily on these two in the following analysis.

15. Goldgeier, *Not Whether But When,* 153.

16. Quoted in ibid., 57.

17. Asmus, *Opening NATO's Door,* 43.

18. Jonathan Eyal, "NATO's Enlargement: Anatomy of a Decision," *International Affairs* 73 (October 1997): 703; and Asmus, *Opening NATO's Door,* 31–32.

19. Asmus, *Opening NATO's Door,* 25.

20. Domestic considerations—Clinton's need to muster support in the 1996 presidential elections from Poles and other Central European American voters—were also present, but are seen by close observers and participants in these decisions as decidedly secondary. See, for example, Goldgeier, *Not Whether But When,* 10–11, 61–62, 98–101, 166–67.

21. Clinton's meeting in Washington in April 1993 with the leaders of Poland (Lech Walesa), the Czech Republic (Vaclav Havel), and Hungary (Arpad Gonecz) apparently had a deep impact on him. After this meeting, Clinton asked his national security advisor Lake: "Tony, why can't we do this [take these three states into NATO]?" Quoted in Asmus, *Opening NATO's Door,* 24.

22. Ibid., 46–47, 299.

23. Quoted in ibid., 46.

24. Quotes from ibid., 47.

25. Quoted in ibid., 101.

26. Ibid., 142–43.

27. For an account of the meeting between Yeltsin and Clinton, see Strobe Talbott, *The Russia Hand: A Memoir of Presidential Diplomacy* (New York: Random House, 2002), 234–43.

28. Eyal puts the British view well: "The British accepted enlargement as inevitable rather than desirable." Eyal, "NATO's Enlargement," 709.

29. Ibid., 227.

30. I am indebted to Barry Posen for stressing the Europeans' lack of headquarters and planning capabilities outside of NATO.

31. The United States Senate passed a resolution by a vote of only 52 to 47 authorizing NATO's bombing campaign against Serbia; the House of Representatives failed to pass a resolution endorsing the bombing campaign (the vote was 213 to 213), and one month into the war it refused to authorize the spending to send American soldiers to fight in Yugoslavia. See Kupchan, *The End of the American Era,* 205, 213.

32. Both ESDP and ESDI were intended to enhance Europe's defense capabilities, but they differ in the venue under which that enhancement was to occur. ESDI was to take place within NATO; ESDP outside of NATO and under the aegis of the European Union.

33. Interview in the French Ministry of Defense (MOD), June 16, 2000.

34. This view of the functions of ESDP is based on about forty interviews conducted in London, Paris, Berlin, and Brussels in June 2000 with national

security officials in foreign affairs and defense ministries, prime ministers' offices, and with officials at NATO headquarters. For a useful chronology of the evolution of ESDP, see European Union in the United States, "European Security and Defense Policy, at http://www.eurunion.org/legislat/Defense/esdpweb.htm.

35. Interview with a British (MOD) official, London, June 22, 2000. Another high-level MOD official said roughly the same thing: "Yes, we used the WEU in the early 1990s as a firebreak—to prevent a European identity that could challenge NATO from emerging. In short, the WEU had become a joke, and we made it even more of one by using it as a firebreake." Interview with a high-level British MOD official, London, June 23, 2000.

36. Interview with a high-level British MOD official, London, June 23, 2000.

37. Jolyon Howorth, "Britain, France, and the European Defence Initiative," *Survival* 42 (Summer 2000): 33.

38. Interview with a high-level NATO official who was formerly a high-level official in the British MOD during the Kosovo crisis, Brussels, June 21, 2000; and interview with François Heisbourg, Paris, June 19, 2000.

39. Interview with British MOD official, June 22, 2000.

40. Phrases are from *Text of a Joint Statement by the French and British Governments*, Franco-British Summit, Saint-Malo, France, December 4, 1998. Quoted in Robert E. Hunter, *The European Security and Defense Policy: NATO's Companion— or Competitor?* (Santa Monica, Calif.: RAND, 2002), 31.

41. Interview with a high-level British MOD official, June 23, 2000.

42. Interview with an official in the French Minister of Defense's cabinet, Paris, June 19, 2000; and Howorth, "Britain, France," 44–45.

43. See Annex IV (Presidency Reports to the Helsinki European Council on "Strengthening the Common European Policy on Security and Defense" and on "Non-Military Crisis Management of the European Union"), *Presidency Conclusions, Helsinki European Council, 10 and 11 December, 1999*, available at the European Union's Web site.

44. Interview with an MOD official, London, June 22, 2000.

45. The way the United States initially treated its NATO allies in waging war against the Taliban regime in Afghanistan in the fall of 2001 simply reinforced the Bush administration's unilateralist reputation. Not wanting to repeat the "war-by-committee" experience of Kosovo, the Bush administration not so politely told the Europeans that its help was not needed when NATO invoked article 5 of the treaty and offered its assistance, although it did accept a few AWACS planes to patrol in the continental United States. The swift defeat of the Taliban regime gave additional powerful evidence that the Americans could act effectively without the Europeans, at least in defeating a country's military forces. Although the United States later welcomed European forces, especially for peacekeeping, the initial impression of "thanks but no thanks" stuck.

46. Quoted in Ivo Daadler, "The End of Atlanticism," *Survival* 45 (Summer 2003): 160.

47. Robert Kagan, *Of Paradise and Power: America and Europe in the New World Order* (New York: Knopf, 2003). Also see Philip H. Gordon and Jeremy Shapiro, *Allies at War: America, Europe, and the Clash over Iraq* (New York: McGraw-Hill, 2004).

48. See Tony Judt, "America and the World," *The New York Review of Books* 50 (April 10, 2003): 28.

49. This view may be mistaken because al-Qaeda did plan an attack on the European Parliament at Strasbourg in 2001, but it was foiled by European authorities. For European views on the al-Qaeda threat to Europe and the United States, see Harald Muller, *Terrorism, Proliferation: A European Threat Assessment* (Paris: Institute for Security Studies, 2002), 37, 87.

50. See Daadler, "The End of Atlanticism," 2–4.

51. See, for example, the op-ed piece by Jean-David Levitte, "A Warning on Iraq, from a Friend," *New York Times*, February 14, 2003, p. A31. Levitte was France's ambassador to the United States during the second Iraqi war. For Germany's views, see Klaus Larres, "Mutual Incomprehension: U.S.-German Value Gaps beyond Iraq," *Washington Quarterly* 26 (Spring 2003): 24–25. An additional restraining factor on the Europeans could have been the large number of Muslims residing in Europe. France, in particular, has the largest number of Muslims, numbering 5 million. European governments could have been concerned about the spread of anti-Americanism from the Muslim world to their own Muslims.

52. Alan Riding, "With Iraq Stance, Chirac Strives for Relevance," *New York Times*, February 23, 2003, A1.

53. For German attitudes toward the second Gulf War and Schroeder's exploitation of them, see Anja Dalgaard Nielsen, "The Gulf War: The German Resistance," *Survival* 45 (Spring 2003): 99–116.

54. Robert Graham, "Comment and Analysis," *Financial Times*, March 12, 2003, 11.

55. Philip Shiskin and Carlta Vitzhum, "Behind U.S. Rift with Europeans: Slights and Politics," *Wall Street Journal*, March 27, 2003, A7. Also see Marc Champion, "Behind U.K.-French Split on Iraq Are Two Views of Europe's Role," *Wall Street Journal*, March 14, 2003, 5.

56. Shiskin and Vitzhum, "Behind U.S. Rift," A7.

57. John Tagliabue, "France and Germany Draw a Line, Against Washington," *New York Times*, January 23, 2003, A10.

58. Judy Dempsey, "Call for Relaxed EU Rules to Boost Defense," *Financial Times*, May 20, 2003, 6.

59. Larres, "Mutual Incomprehension," 26; and Elaine Scilino, "Europe Assesses Damage to Western Relationships and Takes Steps to Rebuild," *New York Times*, April 2, 2003, B12.

60. This four-nation initiative intended to build a command center near Brus-

sels (in Tervuren) that would give the Europeans the ability to "plan and execute European operations autonomously." Quoted in Craig W. Smith, "Europeans Plan Own Military Command Post," *New York Times*, September 3, 2003, A10. Britain initially strongly resisted this initiative, but by the late fall, it had agreed with the French and the Germans on the need for more enhanced European cooperation on defense and security matters. By the spring of 2004 the European Union had agreed, in the words of Barry Posen, "to augment its military staff rather than to set up a new EU command organization as these four states originally suggested" and that this augmented staff "would coordinate the delegation of operational authority for EU missions to the national operational headquarters that have been developed in Britain, France, Germany, and Italy since the mid-1990s." By augmenting its military staff and relying on national headquarters for military operations, rather than setting up a new command organization, the EU was trying both to strengthen its own operational military capabilities but also not to undermine the earlier agreement with NATO to rely on NATO's planning and command capabilities at SHAPE. See Barry R. Posen, "ESDP and the Structure of World Power," *The International Spectator*," Vol. XXXIX (2004), 11–12. Also see Judy Dempsey, General Set to Lead EU's New Military Planning Cell, *Financial Times*, April 5, 3004, 2; and Jolyon Howorth, *Saint-Malo Plus Five: An Interim Assessment of ESDP*, Groupement D'Etudes and De Recherches (Paris: November 2003), 13–14, available online at http://www.notre-europe.asso.fr/Policy7-en.pdf.

61. Judy Dempsey, "Franco-German Alliance Raises US Defense Fears," *Financial Times*, January 27, 2003, 3. There is also evidence that the United States was playing on European divisions, because, in the words of one senior U.S. lobbyist: "it is more preferable to pick and choose our allies in Europe and reward them accordingly than deal with a united Europe." Quoted in Judy Dempsey, "Member States Remain Split over Security and Relationship with US," *Financial Times*, May 2, 2003, 6.

62. Judy Dempsey, "London and Paris Push Ahead on Common EU Defense Goals," *Financial Times*, March 14, 2003, 3.

63. Steven Everts and Daniel Keohane, "The European Convention and EU Foreign Policy: Learning from Failure," *Survival* 45 (Autumn 2003): 182.

64. Under French leadership the EU deployed troops to the eastern Congo in the summer of 2003 to help keep the peace.

65. Although the Europeans have a common currency for trade within Europe, they have not yet given up national sovereignty over its external management. See Kathleen R. McNamara and Sophie Meunier, "Between National Sovereignty and International Power: What External Voice for the Euro?" *International Affairs* 78 (2002): 849–68.

66. For a full defense of the balancing rationale in EU economic integration, see Wayne Sandholtz and John Zysman, "1992: Recasting the European Bargain," *World Politics* 42 (October 1989): 95–128.

67. Public opinion in Europe mirrored the change in elite thinking, according

to a recent poll. Europeans now "starkly question U.S. global leadership" in the words of the press release about the poll. In 2002, 64 percent of Europeans wanted to see a strong U.S. presence in the world. In 2003, only 45 percent of Europeans favored such a presence, although there was a clear split within Europe between the British, Dutch, and Poles favoring strong U.S. leadership, on the one hand, and the French, German, Italians, and Portuguese opposed, on the other. See the German Marshall Fund of the United States and Compagnia di San Paolo, *Transatlantic Trends 2003*, 7, and the press release accompanying it. Both can be found at http://www.gmfus.org.

68. For a different view, see Seth G. Jones, "The European Union and the Security Dilemma," *Security Studies* 12 (Spring 2003): 1–46. Jones stresses the continuing importance to European cooperation in defense matters of the need to enmesh Germany in European institutions and to prevent security competition among the European states from breaking out. He argues that European defense cooperation has increased as U.S. forces in Europe have gone down. I agree with Jones that these two motives still remain important in understanding European defense cooperation, but I also believe that the desire to offset U.S. power and to better influence U.S. policy have become equally important today.

69. The German Marshall Fund poll (note 67) found that a large majority of Europeans wanted the EU to become a superpower like the United States (if it did not require greater military spending), but the purpose of becoming such was to better cooperate with the United States, not to compete with it. See German Marshall Fund, 9–10.

70. Although it preserved unanimity voting in foreign policy, the EU's draft convention had some ambitious proposals. It made provision for a European foreign minister, a "capabilities agency" to coordinate and harmonize Europe's research and procurement in defense equipment, an avant-garde group of states to collaborate more closely on defense, and a voluntary solidarity clause for mutual defense. The EU also agreed on a security doctrine drafted by Javier Solana, the EU's High Representative for the Common Foreign and Security Policy. See the European Convention, *Draft Treaty Establishing a Constitution For Europe*, part I, chap. 2, articles 39–42, at http://european-convention.eu.int/docs/Treaty/cv00850.en03.pdf; and Javier Solana, *A Secure Europe in a Better World*, European Council, Thessaloniki, June 20, 2003, at http://ue.eu.int/newsroom. For an analysis of the defense provisions of the draft constitution and the Solana security paper, see Everts and Keohane, "The European Convention."

71. Quoted in the draft bill on Britain's negotiating position for the forthcoming Intergovernmental Conference on the EU's draft constitution. See James Blitz and Jean Eaglesham, "UK May Clash with EU Partners over Defense," *Financial Times*, September 10, 2003, 4.

CHAPTER 8

Revisiting Balance of Power Theory in Central Eurasia

WILLIAM C. WOHLFORTH

Post-Soviet central Eurasia presents a bewildering array of constantly shifting state strategies. In the decade after 1991, Russia sometimes seemed bent on forming an anti-U.S. coalition in league with China, India, and Europe, but at other times it cooperated closely with Washington. At times, Moscow's neighbors appeared to be acting vigorously to counter Russian hegemony in the region by rushing to join the North Atlantic Treaty Organization (NATO) or forming their own security alliances. Yet at other times they cooperated closely with Russia and allowed themselves to become dependent on it for markets, energy, or security.

Is this confusing set of strategies the outgrowth of the age-old balance of power imperative? No general theory can explain each subtle shift in every state's strategic behavior. But if balance of power theory captures the core security problem of the region, then the seemingly contradictory and confusing strategic behavior of central Eurasia's newly independent states can be explained as a function of larger forces that international relations scholars have long understood. Armed with the theory, and given certain assumptions about global and regional trends in relative power, we might forecast the future trajectory of the region's international politics.

This chapter assesses the applicability of balance of power theory to post-Soviet Eurasia. It suggests that the theory applies, but very weakly. Russians worry about the continued concentration of power in the United States, and Moscow's neighbors fear Russia's declining but locally formidable capabilities. Many Russian policymakers would prefer a world in which U.S. power were balanced, just as many of Moscow's neighbors would be delighted to see Moscow cut down to size. When push comes to shove, however, policymakers in the region act as if the most serious long-term threat they face is not domination by an aspiring hegemon but poverty and marginalization.

They frequently use balance of power rhetoric to describe policies driven by the desire to enrich their countries—or often themselves and their cronies. Most policymakers in the region would prefer a more even distribution of power. None, however, is willing to pay the economic, political, or military costs of balancing.

Specifying the Theory

Balance of power theory posits that because states residing in global anarchy have an interest in maximizing their long-term odds on survival, they will check dangerous concentrations of power ("hegemony") by building up their own capabilities ("internal balancing") or aggregating their capabilities with other states in alliances ("external balancing"). It predicts that the higher the probability of hegemony, the more likely states are to balance. In his introduction, T. V. Paul argues that scholars tend to formulate the theory too restrictively and thus miss crucial dynamics that might fall within its purview. Here, by contrast, I contend that even the simplest renderings of the theory turn out to be fearsomely complex in practice. In particular, two tasks must be addressed before applying even the sparest version of the theory to any contemporary case.

The first task is to clear away the confusion created by the common conflation of two quite distinct balance of power theories—each with different definitions of "hegemony" and different predictions concerning unipolarity—that are currently in widespread use. Scholars have made much of the distinction between balance of power theory and Stephen Walt's balance of threat theory.[1] Do states balance against power or threat? Many neorealists exclude intentions from their assessment of the probability of hegemony. For these scholars, threat inheres in power alone, and large concentrations of material capabilities should spark balancing behavior regardless of intentions. Thus the debate comes down to whether to include intentions in the calculation of the probability of hegemony; that is, whether balancing only occurs when some state reveals its hegemonic aspirations by the specific policies it adopts.

Less widely recognized but ultimately far more important is a deeper distinction between two kinds of balance of power theories. One is a universal balance of power theory that defines a hegemon as any state with unrivaled power, and thus predicts a general tendency toward equilibrium in any system of states. Kenneth N. Waltz transformed this line of thinking from classical writings into a full-blown social science theory in his 1979 *Theory of International Politics*.[2] Waltz claims that his structural theory explains outcomes, not state strategies. In other words, the theory explains how the willy-nilly pulling and hauling of routine security competition produces equilibrium even if no state actually seeks to balance prospective hegemons.

While classical writers sometimes stated their theory in a universal form, most of them were actually talking about the continental European system. In practice, they described a different balance of power theory in which hegemony meant "a concentration of military power that raises the specter of the conquest of all the other great powers in a given system." The theory is contingent because it expects balance of power dynamics to occur only in regional or contiguous interstate systems. It would not expect powerful "offshore" states like Britain in the 19th century and the United States today to spark counterbalancing coalitions because of the "stopping power of water." Indeed, the failure of other states to balance the British empire simply never presented itself as a puzzle to the classical balance of power theorists. As dominant as such offshore states may be globally, their ability to achieve real mastery over the international system is circumscribed by the difficulty of projecting military power overseas, and so they are unlikely to spark counterbalancing. Because classical writers included intentions in their discussions of the hegemonic threats that elicited balancing reactions, by modern terminology they would be called conditional balance of threat theorists. But a purely power-centric version of the conditional theory survives today. Because of its greater precision, for example, the contingent version is invariably the choice of scholars seeking formal rigor.[3] In addition, John J. Mearsheimer incorporates the contingent balance of power concept into the offensive realist theory presented in his 2001 volume, *The Tragedy of Great Power Politics*.[4]

These definitional distinctions yield the theories mapped out in Table 8.1. They matter for the analysis that follows because scholars' failure to be specific about their theoretical assumptions has generated confusion in post-Cold War debates about balance of power theory and unipolarity. The universal theory presupposes the contingent theory, but not vice versa. If there is a general tendency toward equilibrium, then there must be balancing against regional military hegemons, but regional balancing of military capabilities does not necessarily produce a tendency toward global equilibrium. This is crucial for our case, because the universal theory predicts that Russia

TABLE 8.1

Balance of Power Theories

PROBABILITY OF HEGEMONY FUNCTION	DEFINITION OF HEGEMONY	
	"Ability to conquer all others"	*"Unrivaled power"*
Material capabilities + intentions	Conditional balance of threat (Classical writers: Dehio, Gulick)	Universal balance of threat (Walt)
Material only: military power/ geographical/ technical	Conditional balance of power (Mearsheimer, Levy, Wagner, Powell)	Universal balance of power (Waltz, Layne)

will try to balance the United States, but the contingent theory does not. Even if the stopping power of water did not disqualify the United States as a hegemonic threat, nuclear deterrence would. After all, the theory is based on the assumption that states are security maximizers. By that assumption, existential deterrence must be credible: a would-be hegemon would have to conclude that other great powers would use their nuclear forces if their sovereign existence were ever threatened by territorial conquest. Hence, no rational would-be hegemon, no matter how overwhelming its conventional capabilities, would contemplate the territorial conquest of other nuclear-armed great powers, and no rational, nuclear-armed great power would fear hegemony as contingent balance of power theory defines it.

Before setting forth hypotheses on balancing, however, a second task emerges: to establish clear operational guidelines for distinguishing "balancing" from other routine kinds of security competition. If all security policies are "balancing," then balance of power theory becomes vacuous. Waltz and some of his followers have claimed that their theory explains balanced outcomes without necessarily predicting balancing strategies by states. This argument makes the theory exceedingly general, extremely difficult to test, and impossible to apply to any specific case. Fortunately, we can set it aside, for both Waltz and Christopher Layne have stated clearly that their universal theory predicts balancing against U.S. unipolarity. Hence, they expect that causal mechanism to be in play today, however subtly.[5]

How then do we tell whether states are balancing? While they may part ways on some issues, nearly all balance of power theorists agree that the theory is *systemic*. It is not about dyads. The intellectual history of the balance of power as well as classical and modern efforts to develop it as a theory all testify to the centrality of this systemic element.[6] It follows that *balancing* is action taken to check a potential hegemon. It is action, moreover, that would not have been taken in the absence of a dangerous concentration of power in the system. And it is action that actually has the potential to affect the systemic distribution of capabilities. State behavior unrelated to systemic concentrations of power—and that is arguably much of what goes on in international politics—has nothing to do with balance of power theory. This yields two often-overlooked distinctions that are central to any analysis of balance of power theory in today's unipolar system.

First is the distinction between routine security competition and genuine balance-of-power dynamics. During the Cold War, for example, the United States and its allies frequently disagreed on important policy matters. Often, allies withheld cooperation and even struggled vigorously to get Washington to change course, as in the Vietnam War. For its part, the United States sometimes took very tough action against its own allies, as in Suez. Terrorists repeatedly attacked U.S. interests in the Cold War as well. Truck bombs and other forms of "asymmetric warfare" were employed, as against the U.S. Marine compound in Lebanon in 1982. It rarely occurred to anyone to try to use balance of power theory to explain these phenomena, for the simple reason that a compelling example of real balancing—against the Warsaw Pact—stood right before their eyes.

Today's unipolar system lacks such potent balance of power dynamics, and analysts are consequently tempted to trumpet nearly any action that might complicate U.S. policy as balancing. Some of this behavior is completely unrelated to U.S. power; that is, the states or other actors involved would do much the same thing if the United States were half as strong as it is in reality. And many of these actions are genuine responses to U.S. primacy, but do not have any prospect of affecting the scales of world power. While it may make sense to use terms such as rhetorical, prestige, cultural, or soft balancing, to describe some of these actions, it is important not to confuse them with the real thing.[7]

The second key distinction is between economic growth and internal balancing. Internal balancing is enhancement of a state's power in response to a potential hegemon. Not all shifts in relative power—not even all power shifts that work against the international system's leader—are caused by balance of power dynamics. Most states want their economies to grow rapidly and would prefer their power to increase relative to others whether there is a hegemon on the horizon or not. In other words, internal balancing is the net growth in states' relative capabilities caused by a systemic concentration of power. It may be difficult to distinguish routine increases in states' power from increases specifically sparked by balance of power imperatives. The clearest case is when a state chooses to translate economic potential into military power in order to check another state's bid for mastery of the system. But not all military buildups are necessarily internal balancing.

Russia's Response to U.S. Power

By 1993, Russians realized that the distribution of power had undergone a massive shift yielding a systemic concentration of raw capabilities in the United States that was unprecedented in four centuries of world history. As this realization set in, Russian leaders and policy commentators began to speak incessantly of the need to take action to create multipolarity. By the mid-1990s, there appeared to be a consensus in Moscow on this approach.[8] From 1995 to 2000, Russia's foreign ministry engineered a parade of ostensibly anti-U.S. diplomatic combinations: the "European troika" of France, Germany, and Russia; the "special relationship" between Germany and Russia; the "strategic triangle" of Russia, China, and India; and, most important, the "strategic partnership" between China and Russia. This evidence appears to ratify universal balance of power theory's prediction that Russia will try to balance the United States. But talk is cheap. A close examination of what Russia actually has done to augment its capabilities alone or with others shows that appearances are deceiving.

IS RUSSIA BALANCING?

There is no evidence of Russian internal balancing. On the contrary, between 1992 and 1998, Russia experienced what was probably the steepest peacetime decline in military spending by any major power in history.[9] Despite much loud talk, to date nothing serious has been done to advance real military or defense industrial reform.[10] Russian defense policy appears to have been one of malign neglect—let the military decline until a more propitious moment arrives to begin to construct a modern armed force from the rubble. Even after defense budget increases in 1999, outlays in 2000 remained less than 40 percent of those in 1992. Weapons procurement declined even more dramatically after 1991, and by 2000 only 20 percent of Russia's operational weapons stocks were modern, compared to 60–80 percent in NATO countries.[11] Maintenance and training are dismal; personnel problems are dire and getting worse.[12] Unable to subdue the Chechen rebels, the Russian military is beset by so many problems of such magnitude that virtually all experts agree that major reforms entailing huge expenditures are critically necessary simply to forestall its self-destruction. Hence, increased budgetary outlays and intensified reform efforts are driven by deep problems of decay that are unrelated to counterbalancing U.S. power. If Washington were to cut its defense outlays by two-thirds tomorrow, the pressure on Moscow to forestall further military decline would be undiminished.

Neither did Russia engage in external balancing. Moscow's most widely touted treaty relationships—those with China and India—simply are not power-aggregating alliances. All three states continued to cooperate closely with the United States on a very large range of security and economic matters, behavior bearing scant resemblance to any normal understanding of balancing. The relationship with India amounts to a Soviet holdover based on the Friendship Treaty of 1971, whose language implied weak security obligations even in the Cold War, and a largely symbolic Declaration on Strategic Partnership signed by Putin and Indian Prime Minister Atal Behari Vajpayee in 2000. The Russia-China Treaty on Good-Neighborliness, Friendship, and Cooperation signed in July 2001 capped over a decade of improving bilateral ties, but it similarly lacks anything resembling a mutual defense clause.[13] While the treaty obligates the signatories in a general sense to maintain the global equilibrium and to consult each other in the event of security threats, neither it nor any public Russo-Chinese agreement entails any observable or costly commitment to counter U.S. power.

At the core of Russia's relationships with India and China are major arms sales and extensive military coproduction arrangements. The need to counterbalance U.S. power does not drive Russia's interest in these exports. Rather, they are desperately needed to slow the inexorable decline of Russia's military industrial complex. Given the collapse of domestic orders (in 2001, only 10 percent of Russian defense firms received state orders), Russia's defense sector possesses massive excess capacity.[14] Exports are a crucial life-line for a military industry producing less than one-third of its 1992 output, and rapidly losing technological competitiveness. The defense sector supplies income and welfare services to hundreds of thousands of workers and their families, provides the economic lifeblood of dozens of cities, and enriches numerous managers and public officials. The evidence concerning Russia's major arms relationships overwhelmingly indicates that they have little to do with U.S. power. Again, the United States could cut its defense outlays by two-thirds tomorrow, and Moscow would remain just as eager to sell weaponry to Beijing and New Delhi. Moreover, while arms sales to its Asian clients do alter local power balances, not even the most alarmist interpretation of them suggests that they will provide a genuine counterbalance to U.S. power overall.[15]

The bottom line is that Russia's putative efforts to counter U.S. power fall far short of "hard balancing." Much of Moscow's strategic behavior is driven by security or development concerns that are unrelated to U.S. unipolarity, and so it does not count as "soft balancing." The external-balancing initiatives that Moscow pursued did not hold out even a vague promise of affecting the scales of world power, and the Russians eventually concluded that even that game was not worth the candle. There is simply no evidence that Moscow has been willing to pay any significant costs in order to hasten the end of American primacy. That is, the Russians have done nothing to augment their power that they would not have done in a world without an overpowering United States.

UNIVERSAL BALANCE OF THREAT OR CONDITIONAL BALANCE OF POWER?

Russia's behavior belies universal balance of power theory's prediction of balancing. This result leaves two competing hypotheses derived from the theories arrayed in Table 8.1:

H2 (universal balance of threat theory): Russia is not balancing because the United States has benign intentions.

H3 (conditional balance of power theory): Russia is not balancing because nuclear deterrence and America's offshore location ensure no genuine threat of hegemony.

Which is right? The answer matters not just for academic theory but for policy as well. If universal balance of threat theory is true, only the benign nature of U.S. intentions prevents dangerous counterbalancing. If U.S. behavior gets too threatening, other states will revise their estimates of American intentions and possibly bring unipolarity to an end. If conditional balance of power theory is true, the absence of counterbalancing is driven by material factors unrelated to U.S. intentions, and Washington need not be concerned that overly aggressive or unilateral actions might spark a costly counterbalancing reaction. It is not possible to reject either hypothesis conclusively, of course, but two quick tests are suggestive.

First, H2 predicts that America's benign intentions should figure prominently in Russian assessments of the security environment. In other words, the benign nature of U.S. primacy should be an important reason why Russians do not consider it necessary to counterbalance. In fact, this is not the case. Russia's two post-Soviet presidents (as well as the last Soviet one); all its defense ministers, foreign ministers, chiefs of staff, and national security advisors; and all of its official doctrines on national security, military policy, and foreign policy have stated unequivocally that the military subjugation of Russia by the United States or any other major power is not a concern on the policy-relevant horizon.[16] The main reason given for this state of affairs is nuclear deterrence. In addition, Russian analyses highlight the punishing costs that real balancing would impose, especially the extent to which it would run counter to Russia's aim of integrating itself into the world economy, and the greater salience of local security threats. So their basic argument is that balancing is not critical for Russian security and therefore that the costs outweigh the benefits. Even Russian liberals, who might be expected to highlight the ultimately benign nature of U.S. intentions, do not do so. Rather, they stress the economic opportunity costs argument, as well as the greater long-term threat posed by Russia's erstwhile balancing partner, China.[17]

Second, H2 predicts that a Russian propensity to balance should correlate with aggressive U.S. behavior, which indicates malign or hegemonic U.S. intentions. At the rhetorical level, there is some evidence for this proposition. The best indicator of Russia's propensity to balance is probably its "multipolar" policy line, inaugurated in the mid-1990s by Russian Prime Minister Yevgeny Primakov. It is important to stress that the real goal of the policy was modest: to try in concert with other players to get the United States to alter specific policies. In other words, it was not power balancing,

REVISITING BALANCE OF POWER THEORY IN EURASIA

but policy bargaining, more typical of coalition politics among allies or even in domestic politics than the military balancing of the Cold War or the 19th century. Russia sought to present itself as the linchpin member of global coalitions aimed at countering specific U.S. policies, such as NATO expansion, the maintenance of sanctions against Iraq, intervention in the Balkans, and abandoning the Anti-Ballistic Missile (ABM) Treaty to construct missile defenses. The policy arguably reached its apex during NATO's war in Kosovo. Realist commentators in the United States consequently railed against these expansionary U.S. moves. Their argument appeared to be derived directly from universal balance of threat theory: further expansionary U.S. policies are likely to push Russia toward more, and more consequential, balancing behavior. In other words, if the United States became too militarily active, resistance to its policies would grow.

From 1999 to 2001, however, tough U.S. policies produced effects precisely the opposite of H2. Russian analysts and policymakers became increasingly disenchanted with the multipolar policy. [18] The most important criticism was that the old policy simply did not work. It did not maximize Moscow's bargaining leverage either with Washington or the other main players in the policy counterbalancing game. On each issue with the United States throughout 1993–2000, Russian diplomats stated their opposition in unambiguous terms and then ended up backing down, sometimes in a humiliating manner. By publicly backing down from such clearly stated positions, Moscow squandered its limited prestige and advertised its weakness. The multipolar policy scattered Russia's limited foreign-policy energies around the globe, preventing a necessary concentration on priority issues. It constrained Russia's flexibility, trapping it into taking a lead position in most global anti-U.S. policy coalitions. Other powers, such as France and China— often with greater interests at stake and far greater capabilities—were letting Russia do the dirty work of seeking to constrain the United States, all the while making lucrative deals with Washington on the side. Moreover, critics argued, if relations between any of the other multipolar partners and Washington were to deteriorate seriously—for example, between Beijing and Washington over Taiwan—Russia might have been drawn into a confrontation in which it had no stake and which it could not afford.

The evidence strongly suggests that Vladimir Putin was ahead of the curve on this issue and came into office knowing that most of his military and national security elite were indulging in nostalgic fantasies regarding the real role Russia could play in world affairs.[19] He used the September 11, 2001, attacks on the United States as a pretext to accelerate the strategic shift toward bandwagoning that was already under way. The centerpiece of the effort was a retreat on issues Putin knew Russia would eventually have to compromise on in any case: NATO expansion and the Bush administration's push to abandon the ABM Treaty. Once Russia further softened its stance on these issues, the path was open to major improvements in relations with the United States, signified by Russia's signing of a strategic arms reduction agreement during U.S. President George W. Bush's May 2002 visit to Moscow and St. Petersburg, and formally joining the new NATO-Russia council later that month. Adding weight to these modest policy moves was a dramatic increase in the clarity with which Putin and other top officials described the rapprochement with the West.[20]

This rapprochement took place as the United States embarked on one of the most expansionist periods in its history, inserting military force into Russia's backyard in central Asia and proceeding to vanquish the Taliban in Afghanistan. The new U.S. expansion elicited cries of opposition in Russian military and foreign policy circles, but Putin elected to bandwagon with America's war on terror. Within a year of that decision, universal balance of power theory faced its greatest test: the U.S. war in Iraq. This time, Russia refused to lead the policy coalition against Washington, choosing instead to shelter behind France and Germany. When he could hedge no longer, Putin ultimately decided to support the European powers against Washington. Yet again, even in the face of U.S. expansion far more significant than Kosovo, Russo-American relations never became as tense over Iraq as they had in the Balkans. Moscow's tack toward Europe reminded Washington that the Russians still have some bargaining room, but it did not come at the expense of a working strategic partnership with the United States. As Putin's foreign policy aide Sergei Prikhodko put it: "Our partnership with the United States is not a hostage of the Iraq crisis. There are far too many common values and common tasks both short term and long term . . . our cooperation never stopped, even during the Iraq crisis."[21] And this was not just rhetoric; concrete cooperation continued on intelligence sharing, nuclear arms control, NATO expansion, peacekeeping in Afghanistan, and the North Korea issue. The policy reflected a bet that the Americans would not allow Iraq to derail the most important parts of the new U.S.-Russian relationship—the antiterrorism coalition and managing Russia's further entry into the world economy.

The real story is the opposite of what H2 predicts. Tougher and more imperious U.S. behavior yielded an improvement in Russo-American relations and a reduction in Moscow's opposition to U.S. policies. Ultimately, H3 accords best with the evidence. Russians appear to place less emphasis on U.S. benignity than on a hardheaded assessment of its material capabilities. While most Russians resent U.S. primacy and would love to see it checked, the security problems created by the concentration of power in the United States are often not the most salient for Moscow, and so Russians are unwilling to pay the costs of balancing. Attempting to balance the United States would take resources away from more pressing needs. Indeed, declining relative power has caused Moscow progressively to pare down its security agenda. As a result, the list of issues where U.S. unipolarity appears to threaten Russian interests has grown shorter even as the list of pressing near-term and local threats has lengthened. And, as the example of the war on terror demonstrates, many of those threats require cooperation with—not balancing against—the world's most powerful state.

Central Eurasia's Response to Russian Power

At first glance, balance of power theory appears to apply more directly to the post-Soviet region of central Eurasia, where genuine military hegemony is at least possible. While Russia today is utterly incapable of reconquering its erstwhile provinces, it may someday regain that capability. Russia's underlying superiority is enormous, as Table 8.2 shows.

Not surprisingly, given these power realities, elites and leaders in the newly independent states do discuss the probability of hegemony as realistic, if currently very low. Based on a simple reading of balance of power theories, both the universal and contingent versions should predict that these states would be balancing as hard as they can. Moreover, given Moscow's imperial history and its bellicose behavior throughout much of what Russian officials ominously call "the near abroad," balance of threat theory only reinforces the predictions of balance of power theory.

Unfortunately, however, applying the theory to a specific region is complicated. Even though the probability of hegemony in Eurasia is comparatively high, the theory still does not necessarily yield precise predictions. The reason is that Russia's neighbors are generally so weak that their collective

TABLE 8.2.

Central Eurasia's Balance of Power[a]

	Population		GDP		Defense Expenditures		Military Personnel	
	1995	2000	1995	2000	1995	2000	1995	2000
Russia	50.54	50.38	91.30	88.52	96.24	93.04	63.03	58.24
Armenia	1.17	1.19	*	*	*	*	2.85	2.51
Azerbaijan	2.63	2.66	*	*	*	*	3.51	4.30
Belarus	3.52	3.50	*	*	*	*	4.24	4.94
Estonia	*	*	*	*	*	*	*	*
Georgia	1.85	1.68	*	*	*	*	n.a.	1.00
Kazakhstan	5.76	5.53	1.49	1.34	*	*	1.99	3.81
Kyrgyzstan	1.54	1.62	*	*	*	*	*	*
Latvia	*	*	*	*	*	*	*	*
Lithuania	1.26	1.25	*	*	*	*	*	*
Moldova	1.48	1.51	*	*	*	*	*	*
Tajikistan	2.09	2.15	*	*	*	*	*	*
Turkmenistan	1.43	1.53	*	*	*	*	*	1.04
Ukraine	17.40	17.30	3.06	2.36	1.29	1.71	19.90	18.11
Uzbekistan	7.98	8.44	*	1.4	*	*	1.49	3.3

SOURCE: International Institute for Strategic Studies, *The Military Balance* (London: IISS, 1996, 2002).

[a] Expressed as percentage of total; * indicates less than 1%.

ability to balance Moscow is limited. Hence, they face a strong temptation to pass the balancing buck to others or even to bandwagon actively with the hegemon to curry its favor and derive benefits from Moscow. Referring to great powers, Mearsheimer notes that "threatened states are reluctant to form balancing coalitions against potential hegemons because the costs of containment are likely to be great; if it is possible to get another state to bear those costs, a threatened state will make every effort to do so."[22] If buck-passing temptations appeal to great powers, they are likely to be nearly irresistible to weak regional states whose potential contribution to a balancing coalition is marginal.

Balance of power theorists have long recognized that weak states often cannot respond optimally to balancing imperatives, which is why many of them restrict the theory to great powers. Consequently, they do not provide deductively based predictions of when to expect balancing, buck-passing, or bandwagoning in regional interstate systems. The theory's basic logic, however, suggests three conditional variables that affect the propensity of states to balance in regional systems where the probability of hegemony is comparatively high.

First, the availability of allies will affect any state's strategic choice. By virtue of geography or possession of some strategically valuable resource, some states are better able to secure allies than others. If powerful allies are available, the theory expects neighbors to take advantage of them. Second, the greater a state's relative power (defined as the capability to balance the hegemon), the more likely it is to balance. Only the weakest states whose marginal contribution to containing the hegemon is negligible should bandwagon. For stronger states, bandwagoning materially increases the probability of hegemony and thus the possibility that the state might lose its sovereignty. The strongest regional actors are the most likely to be able to balance. States whose power falls in the middle of this range should prefer to balance, but may not be able to. They can be expected to follow ambiguous hedging strategies that allow them to cooperate with the potential hegemon even as they encourage other states to pay the costs of balancing it. Third, geography affects the choice between balancing and buck-passing. Contiguity lowers the costs and raises the benefits of balancing. By the usual three to one offense/defense rule, a state can balance against a possible offensive by its potentially hegemonic neighbor relatively cheaply. At the same time, contiguity begets balancing because neighbors are the most likely victims of territorial conquest by aspiring hegemons. For all these reasons, buck-passing is hard for states bordering on potential hegemons.

It follows from the foregoing discussion that while the theory predicts that states will want to balance potential hegemons, it cannot predict that balancing will succeed in a particular time or region. In any given region, history and geography might conspire to produce a "natural" hegemon that cannot be balanced no matter how much its regional neighbors might want to. The theory cannot predict success or whether balancing behavior actually will occur; it only can predict the intensity of various states' propensity to balance. Bearing this inevitable limitation in mind, balance of power theory predicts that the most likely candidates for balancing are the most capable regional states that border on the potential hegemon and are lucky enough to find powerful great-power allies. States that have only two of these attributes still might balance. States with one or none have no realistic balancing options and should opt to pass the buck to those that do. Only the very weakest and most vulnerable states should opt to bandwagon.

THE EVIDENCE: HEDGING BALANCING BETS

The evidence since the mid-1990s overwhelmingly indicates that hedging is the dominant strategy among Russia's neighbors. This might seem surprising, given the strong balancing rhetoric emanating from many regional capitals. But, as in the case of Russia's mainly symbolic balancing against the United States, rhetoric is a poor indicator of the strategic realities on the ground in central Eurasia. Three major strains of evidence are most important here.

First, there is no measurable internal balancing. Table 8.2 essentially tells the story. In terms of aggregate indicators of military might, the region is just as primed for hegemony as it was in 1995: none of Russia's neighbors has managed to enhance its relative share of military power to any significant degree. Looking beyond these indicators, Russia's real ability to conquer neighboring lands is far more limited than the numbers suggest. Yet most of Russia's neighbors are even less capable militarily than their miniscule shares of aggregate capabilities imply. They face immense challenges of institution building, and in most cases military reforms have barely begun. Ukraine is an important case in point. Like Russia, Ukraine inherited a seemingly impressive military establishment from the Soviet Union. But the mismatch between that imperial inheritance and the real security needs of a smaller successor state was much greater in Ukraine's case. It presented the Ukrainians with even greater challenges, and exacted greater relative economic costs than those faced by military reformers in Russia. With far greater resource constraints, Ukraine's response has been less coherent than Russia's. While the military has been downsized and partially rationalized, it remains fundamentally unreformed.[23]

Thus, indictors of military power for Ukraine need to be deflated even more than those for Russia. And the same goes for most other former Soviet states. In the central Asian republics, as well as Belarus, Georgia, and Armenia, local militaries not only are struggling with reform, but they remain deeply penetrated by direct and indirect Russian influence. Russia maintains military or naval bases on the territories of Armenia, Georgia, Moldova, Tajikistan, and Ukraine. It has command posts and extensive military cooperation arrangements with Kazakhstan and Kyrgyzstan. It remains the principal arms supplier for most former Soviet republics, whose own defense industrial structures remain vertically integrated with Russia's. Only the Baltic militaries have undergone substantial reforms, and they may well represent capabilities that exceed the impression given by small scores on the indicators of power, but they remain tiny and lack defensible borders.

Second, external balancing in the region is mainly symbolic. The main intra-regional balancing effort is GUAM, a loose political and security grouping formed in 1997 that comprises Georgia, Ukraine, Azerbaijan, and Moldova. (Uzbekistan's brief membership between 1999 and 2001 inserted another "U" into the group's name, but had no lasting consequence.) The group's main purpose is ostensibly to counter Russia diplomatically and politically. But it lacks real institutions and coordinating mechanisms and has had no measurable effect on its members' real capabilities, or even their joint ability to resist Russia politically. As former Georgian president Eduard Shevardnadze put it, "GUAM is an artificial organization . . . [with] rather bleak prospects."[24]

The main problem was that Ukraine, the keystone in GUAM's arch, simply failed to rise to the role of a regional balancer. Other regional governments carefully watched Kyiv's statements and actions in the late 1990s, and what they saw gave them scant comfort: every move against Russia was hedged with a commensurate move accommodating Russia. Faced with a wavering Ukraine whose government contained many pro-Russian elements, weaker members like Georgia and Moldova could hardly be expected to spearhead anti-Russian coalitions. Both of those countries contain territory under Russian military control and are much more vulnerable to Russian pressure than Ukraine. In the end, Azerbaijan proved to be the member state able to take the most consistent anti-Russian stance in regional politics, a bold stance that owed nothing to the Ukrainian-led regional balancing effort and everything to its energy riches and U.S. interest in exploiting them.

Hence, external-balancing action in the region centers on outside powers and especially NATO. The three Baltic states stand out as the region's earliest, most consistent and now successful NATO aspirants. Politically and

TABLE 8.3

Former Soviet States: Bandwagoning, Balancing, or Hedging?

High trade dependence on Russia (c)	High energy dependence on Russia (a)	Dependent on Russian energy transport infrastructure (b)	Russian military base or troops stationed in territory	Member CIS Coll. Sec Treaty	Newly Independent State	Slated to join NATO or strong declared interest in joining	U.S. troops on territory	Standard Score (left side – right side)	Real score (left side–right side, including shaded indicators)
X	X	X	X	X	Belarus			2	4
X	X	X	X	X	Armenia			2	4
X	X	X	X		Moldova			1	4
X	X	X	X	X	Kazakhstan			2	4
X	X	X	X		Ukraine	X		0	3
X	X	X			Latvia	X		-1	2
X	X	X			Lithuania	X		-1	2
X			X	X	Kyrgyzstan		X	1	2
			X	X	Tajikistan			2	2
	X	X	X		Georgia	X	X	-2	2
					Turkmenistan			0	0
X	X	X			Azerbaijan	X		-1	1
X	X	X			Estonia	X		-1	0
X		X			Uzbekistan		X	-1	0

NOTES: (a) High energy dependence means Russia is the main energy supplier. (b) High dependence on Russian energy transport infrastructure means a country's energy imports and exports largely flow through Russian pipelines. (c) High trade dependence means more than 30% of a country's exports or imports are accounted for by Russia.

diplomatically, if not yet militarily, their campaign for NATO membership carried clear costs and risks vis-à-vis Moscow, and promised some benefits. Georgia and Azerbaijan also have stated repeatedly their preference for NATO membership, but their location and fragile political institutions make membership unlikely. Once again, the Ukrainian case is instructive. After spending most of the 1990s hedging its bets, Ukraine finally announced its intention to sign a NATO Membership Action Plan in July 2002. Yet, Kyiv also agreed to join the Russia-sponsored Eurasian Economic Community, and, most important, its demarche occurred only after Russia itself had accommodated NATO. The signing of the new charter on the NATO-Russia Council dramatically lowered the political costs of Ukraine's decision. Indeed, as long as Russia retains a cordial and institutionalized relationship with NATO, the geopolitical significance of expressed intentions to join the organization remains questionable. Ukraine's decision to opt for NATO membership thus did nothing to reduce the studied ambiguity it has maintained in regional alignments.

The third strain of evidence is the most important: the strongest regional balancers remain critically dependent on Russia economically and especially for energy resources. Table 8.3 compares indicators of bandwagoning with Russia on the left side with external balancing with the west on the right side. The shaded areas display indicators of economic dependence often excluded from balance of power analyses. Ignoring those indicators leads to overestimating the degree and success of balancing in the region. The most consistent balancers, the Baltic states, have been unwilling or unable to absorb the economic costs of reducing their deep dependence on Russia for energy (oil, gas, and electricity) and transportation infrastructure, and Russian companies purchase strategic assets in all three countries. Russian influence and Baltic vulnerability continue and in some ways increase, despite NATO membership. In pure strategic terms, ongoing energy dependence could make the three Baltic states very vulnerable to Russia if matters ever came to a real crisis. Even more important, the region's most powerful actor, Ukraine, remains much more dependent on Russia than the tiny Baltics. Ukraine gets over 90 percent of its overall energy supplies from Russia, owes Russia's gas monopoly Gazprom over US$3 billion, is crucially dependent on earnings from transshipping Russian gas to Europe, is in arrears on its electricity debt to Russia's energy giant UES, depends on Russia for key markets, and is a central site for strategic foreign direct investment from Russian companies. These dependencies go a long way toward explaining Kyiv's hedging strategy.

BALANCE OF POWER THEORY IN CENTRAL EURASIA: A BALANCE SHEET

How well does balance of power theory do? Overall, the theory accurately predicts the widespread regional preference for balancing. Most of Russia's neighbors would like to see Russia balanced. Many have pursued allies vigorously, though only the tiny Baltic states have succeeded in joining a significant alliance. Many tried ardently to find allies against Russia, but have simply been unable to do so—Georgia is a notable case in point. The non-shaded areas of Table 8.3 capture the balancing aspirations of states, if not their degree of success. And many states are working to reduce their economic dependence on Russia. Since 1995, the number of states that are trade dependent on Russia has decreased. The region has witnessed intensive efforts to reduce reliance on Russia for energy transportation. Many states are hedging because they have no choice—Moldova is an example. Table 8.3 also indicates that the number of states that have actually *chosen* to bandwagon with Russia by acceding to Moscow's Commonwealth of Independent States Treaty on Collective Security is small. Most of these states are very weak and lack outside allies. Armenia is a prime example that accords with the theory's expectations.

The theory thus captures an important piece of strategic reality in central Eurasia, and it remains a necessary part of the analyst's tool kit. Yet it also faces major limitations. It is of little utility in explaining much of the variation in local responses to Russia. Even when we add conditional variables to the theory to derive more discrete hypotheses, it fails to add much to the explanation of why Kazakhstan is such a faithful bandwagoner despite its proximity to Russia; why Turkmenistan eschews all external balancing of any kind while Tajikistan cozies up to Russia; and why Belarus has been such a faithful bandwagoner despite relative power and a geographical position similar to the Baltics. The answers to these questions lie in local history and politics, in the details of the imperial dissolution rather than the insights from a general theory.

Balance of power theory's predictions utterly fail in the key case of

Ukraine. Ukraine's share of relative power, geographical position, and proximity and attractiveness to outside great-power allies all suggest that it should be more prone to balancing than any of the other successor states. The reasons Ukraine failed to respond to balancing imperatives all center on the classic "weak state" problem: the country lacks effective state institutions and hence cannot act as coherently on the world scene as balance of power theory expects.[25] It is thoroughly penetrated by Russian influence at all levels; it has one of the most corrupt governments in the world; it is currently run by a president who talks and frequently behaves like a gangster.[26] All these factors weigh heavily in Ukrainian policymaking and help account for Kyiv's inability to balance internally, and its reluctance to unambiguously provide leadership to GUAM or to court NATO.

In addition, balance of power theory's myopic focus on the problem of hegemony diverts attention from the varied security agendas of the region's states. That is, while it accurately predicts a widespread preference for balancing, it tends to exaggerate the strength of that preference. For many, Russian hegemony is too far down the list of strategic priorities to warrant expending too much economic or political capital on balancing. For most, the chief threats are internal opponents to the regime, or, more generally, the potential of an internally generated failure to develop and prosper.[27] The balancing preference is thus a weak predictor of what these states will actually do strategically to counter Russia, especially when Russia can offer some economic and (internal and external) security benefits. The problem of hegemony is but one variable in a complex equation of the costs and benefits of cooperating with the local great power.

Uzbekistan is an important case in point. By standard measures, it is the region's third most powerful state after Russia and Ukraine, but unlike the latter it is blessed with energy riches of its own. Hence, the importance attached to President Islam Karimov's decision to join GUAM in 1999. But other concerns than countering Russia drive Karimov, including his own aspirations to be a regional hegemon and his fears of Islamic extremists.[28] The former objective put Tashkent at odds with its central Asian neighbors, and the latter augured for cooperation with Russia. Both of these concerns sapped Uzbekistan's ability to counter Russia. At the same time, Tashkent's local imperialism is an important factor behind the decisions of Kazakhstan and Kyrgyzstan to bandwagon with Moscow.

Conclusion

Revisiting balance of power theory in post-Soviet Eurasia demonstrates old social science truisms. A theory that seems to apply everywhere all the time is likely to be of little practical utility. Any theory worth its salt is likely to be wrong about some things and simply inapplicable to others.

The most ambitious version of balance of power theory, which posits a universal tendency toward equilibrium in all international systems, adds little to the analysis of Russia's response to American primacy. The theory does capture Russian decision makers' subjective preferences: they would rather live in a world with a more equitable distribution of power. But the theory is misleading when it confuses those norms and beliefs with the concrete strategic decisions that Russian leaders are willing to make. In the end, users of the theory show a tendency to shoehorn nearly any Russian effort to aggregate or exercise power into a narrative of balancing the United States. In fact, it is hard to identify any such move that Russia would not have taken even if the United States were not so dominant in the scales of world power. If words could balance, the theory would be accurate and Russia would be the great organizer of a Eurasian anti-U.S. coalition. But Moscow's real strategy has varied between hedging and bandwagoning. As an explanation of real strategic behavior, the universal version falls short in this case.

Balance of threat theory does little better. It might be the case that over the long run Russia's propensity to balance hinges on the benign character of U.S. intentions, as revealed in its policies, rather than the threat inherent in U.S. power. But it is very hard to find Russian analysts who accord much strategic significance to the benign nature of U.S. power or the pacifying influence of its institutions. And the track record so far is the opposite of what balance of threat theory predicted: bellicose and expansionary U.S. policy elicited more cooperative Russian behavior. More bellicose and expansionary U.S. policy in 2001–2003—deploying military forces to central Asia, and forcefully changing regimes in Afghanistan and Iraq—elicited weaker responses from Russia than less threatening policies in the late 1990s.

Regarding Russia's neighbors in central Eurasia, balance of power theory does highlight a real strategic concern that underlies the region's politics. As the theory predicts, Russian hegemony is a background worry, and many local states have tried hard to find allies and reduce their vulnerability to Moscow. But this is hardly a novel insight for which one needs an elaborate theory. A theory that generated discrete hypotheses about balancing versus buck-passing or bandwagoning strategies would be of real utility in making sense of the complex behavior of the region's states. Unfortunately, it is not yet possible to extract such hypotheses from current writings on the balance of power. The only way to make sense of the pattern of strategic responses in the area is to delve deeply into the domestic and local politics of all the actors involved—a task well suited to area experts trained in comparative politics, but to which balance of power theory has little to add beyond common sense. The clearest prediction that current theory can offer is that Ukraine should be the post-Soviet state most prone to balancing. Thus far, Ukraine has not been able to rise to the role the theory assigns to it, mainly because of the standard weak-state reasons with which regional experts are all too familiar.

Ultimately, balance of power theory faces major problems when it is applied to restricted domains. If the theory is divorced from concern with systemic concentrations of power, it becomes a catchall surrogate for any and all security policies. If the theory is specified such that it only deals with hegemonic threats—which is in keeping with the existing literature, can generate falsifiable hypotheses, and is thus what we have done here—then it yields precise predictions only in the rare cases when hegemony is sufficiently probable that it overwhelms other security (and nonsecurity) concerns. For all of the states in central Eurasia, either hegemony is not nearly the most important problem in the near to medium term, or, if it is, there is nothing materially that they can do about it. Under those circumstances, given a trade-off between balancing and economic growth, governments will choose not to balance in the short term in the expectation that enhanced economic growth will put them in a better position to balance—and so maximize their security—in the longer term when and if it becomes necessary or possible. Hence, the conclusion most charitable to balance of power theory is that it does not apply to this group of states at this time.

Notes

1. Stephen M. Walt, *The Origins of Alliances* (Ithaca: Cornell University Press, 1987).

2. Kenneth N. Waltz, *Theory of International Politics* (Reading, Mass.: Addison-Wesley, 1979).

3. For formal treatments that yield the conditional variant, see Morton A.

Kaplan, *System and Process in International Politics* (New York: Wiley, 1957); Emerson M. S. Niou, Peter Ordeshook, and Gregory F. Rose, *The Balance of Power: Stability in International Systems* (Cambridge: Cambridge University Press, 1989); Robert Powell, *In the Shadow of Power: States and Strategies in International Politics* (Princeton: Princeton University Press, 1999); and R. Harrison Wagner, "What Was Bipolarity?" *International Organization* 47 (Winter 1993): 77–106. For a strong argument that the conditional variant is the only testable version, see Jack S. Levy, "Balances and Balancing: Concepts, Propositions, and Research Design," in John A. Vasquez and Colin Elman (eds.), *Realism and the Balancing of Power: A New Debate* (Englewood Cliffs, N.J.: Prentice Hall, 2003).

4. John J. Mearsheimer, *The Tragedy of Great Power Politics* (New York: Norton, 2001).

5. Christopher Layne, "The Unipolar Illusion: Why New Great Powers Will Arise," *International Security* 14 (Spring 1993): 86–124; and Kenneth N. Waltz, "Structural Realism after the Cold War," *International Security* 25 (Summer 2000): 5–41.

6. On the intellectual history, see Martin Wight, *Power Politics* (Leicester: Leicester University Press, 1978); and Herbert Butterfield, "Balance of Power," in Philip P. Wiener (ed.), *Dictionary of the History of Ideas* (New York: Scribner's, 1968).

7. See T. V. Paul's introductory chapter, as well as Stephen M. Walt, "Keeping the World 'Off Balance': Self-Restraint and U.S. Foreign Policy"; and Josef Joffe, "Defying History and Theory: The United States as the 'Last Remaining Superpower,' " both in G. John Ikenberry (ed.), *America Unrivaled: The Future of the Balance of Power* (Ithaca: Cornell University Press, 2002).

8. See the result of a poll of foreign policy elites reported by Gudrun Dometeit, "Vision of Greatness," *Focus* (Munich), June 3, 1996, 235–38, reprinted and translated in *Foreign Broadcast Information Service—Daily Report: Central Eurasia* 96–109; D. Furman, "O veshnepoliticheskikh prioritetakh Rossii," *Svobodnaya mysl'* 2 (1996): 13–18. A comprehensive review is provided by Hannes Adomeit, "Russia as 'Great Power' in World Affairs: Image and Reality," *International Affairs* (London), 71 (January 1997): 35–68.

9. Christopher Hill, "Russian Defense Spending," in United States Congress, Joint Economic Committee, *Russia's Uncertain Economic Future* (Washington, D.C.: Government Printing Office, 2002), 168.

10. See especially Dale R. Herspring, "Recreating the Russian Military: The Difficult Task Ahead," draft report presented at the Liechtenstein Institute on Self-Determination Conference "The Future of the Russian State," Triesenberg, Liechtenstein, March 14–17, 2002.

11. "Only 20% of Russian Arms Are Modern," RFE/RL *Daily Report*, May 21, 2001.

12. "Every Third Potential Conscript Said Not Fit For Military Service," ITAR-TASS, May 23, 2002.

13. For a detailed analysis of the treaty, see Elizabeth Wishnick, "Russia and China: Brothers Again?" *Asian Survey* 41 (September–October 2001): 797–821.

14. Kevin P. O'Prey, "Arms Exports and Russia's Defense Industries: Issues for the U.S. Congress," in Joint Economic Committee, *Russia's Uncertain Economic Future.*

15. The major effect is on the power assessments that overshadow bargaining on the Taiwan issue. See Thomas Christensen, "China," in Richard J. Ellings and Aaron L. Friedberg (eds.), *Strategic Asia: Power and Purpose, 2001–2002* (Seattle: National Bureau of Asian Research, 2001).

16. See, for example, the most recent drafts of the foreign policy concept, the national security concept, and the military doctrine, which are available at the Security Council's Web site: http://www.scrf.gov.ru/Documents/Documents.htm.

17. See Aleksandr G. Yakovlev, "'Tretiya ugroza:' Kitaai—Vrag No. 1 dlya Rossii?" *Problemy Dal'nego Vostoka* (January 2002): 48–61, and sources cited therein.

18. An excellent example of expert criticism of the multipolar line is the Council on Foreign and Defense Policy's "Strategiia dlya Rossii IV," which is available on the council's Web site: http://www.svop.ru.

19. For more analysis and evidence, see William C. Wohlforth, "Russia," in Richard J. Ellings and Aaron L. Friedberg (eds.), *Strategic Asia 2002: Asian Aftershocks* (Seattle: National Bureau of Asian Research, 2002).

20. See, for a good example, the interview with Igor Ivanov reported in Svetlana Babaeva, "Igor Ivanov: Glavnoe-stoby vneshnyaya politika ne privodila k raskolu vnutri strany," *Izvestiya,* July 10, 2002, 1.

21. Quoted in Andrew Jack and Stefan Wagstyl, "Optimism on Russian Postwar Accord with U.S.," *Financial Times,* May 16, 2003.

22. Mearsheimer, *Tragedy,* 269

23. See Walter Parchomenko, "The State of Ukraine's Armed Forces and Military Reform," *The Journal of Slavic Military Studies* 13 (September 2000).

24. Taras Kuzio, "GUUAM Reverts to GUAM as Uzbekistan Suspends Its Membership," *Eurasia Insight,* August 19, 2002.

25. See Randall L. Schweller, "Missed Opportunities and Unanswered Threats: Domestic Constraints on the Balance of Power" (American Political Science Association, 2002).

26. On Transparency International's Year 2000 Corruption Perception Index, Ukraine ranked 87 (tied with Azerbaijan) out of 90 countries. Only Yugoslavia and Nigeria ranked worse. The country has been in political turmoil since the release of secretly recorded audiotapes in November 2000, with the president's voice apparently ordering his Interior Minister to "rub out" Georgy Gongadze, an opposition journalist. Several days prior to the release of the tapes by one of President Kuchma's security guards, Gongadze's decapitated body was found in a forest outside Kyiv, two months after his disappearance.

27. See Stephen R. David, "Explaining Third World Alignment," *World Poli-*

tics 43 (January 1991), 233–56; and Stephanie G. Neuman (ed.), *International Relations Theory and the Third World* (New York: St. Martin's, 1998).

28. See Martha Brill Olcott, *Central Asia's New States: Independence, Foreign Policy, and Regional Security* (Washington, D.C.: United States Institute of Peace Press, 1996); and Olcott, "Central Asia," in Ellings et al., *Strategic Asia.*

CHAPTER 9

The International System and Regional Balance in the Middle East

BENJAMIN MILLER

The international politics of the Middle East are dominated by a variety of regional conflicts, civil wars, and external interventions. The great powers are heavily engaged in the region because of oil, the strategic location of key actors, formal and de facto alliances, and significant economic interests. As a result, great-power involvement in the Middle East makes a major difference in regional politics, especially if great-power involvement takes the form of competitive balancing by a number of states or hegemonic management by a single great power.[1] Competitive intervention by several great powers will lead to a regional balance of power and the prevention of regional hegemony. By contrast, states will tend to bandwagon with a global hegemon that regularly intervenes in the region. Under these conditions, revisionist actors are likely to be contained and marginalized, and their attempts at forming a countervailing coalition are likely to fail.

To explain the current balance of power motivations and behavior in the Middle East, the chapter will first present several propositions about the effects of the international system on the regional balance of power. It then describes balance of power politics in the Middle East during the Cold War, explaining why American exclusionary policies could not succeed in a bipolar situation. The third section explores how the United States has emerged as the Middle East hegemon following the collapse of the Soviet Union and the defeat of Iraq in the Gulf War. The chapter considers the effects of 9/11 and the Iraq War and concludes by describing how the revisionist forces and enduring regional conflicts continue to pose major challenges to Pax Americana in the region.

Theoretical Perspectives on Regional Balances of Power

When scholars talk about international anarchy, they are speaking about the absence of an international government and the lack of effective mechanisms for enforcing international agreements.[2] Yet regional systems are not pure anarchy because of the influence of great powers.[3] Great powers can play the roles of police, protector, guarantor, referee, broker, enforcer, and banker in regional politics.[4] The regional balance of power is not autonomous but heavily depends on the number of great powers in the international system, and on the type of regional involvement (competitive, cooperative, or hegemonic) in which the great powers engage. This dependence leads to the first proposition considered here.

> Proposition 1: Regional balances of power depend on the way great powers are engaged in regional systems.

Only when the great powers disengage from a particular region is an autonomous regional system able to arise. Such regions are likely to be those where no great power has important interests or where interested great powers lack the necessary capabilities to intervene to affect the regional balance of power. In all other regions, the great powers exercise a crucial influence on the regional balance.

As Jack Levy suggests, the great powers do most of the balancing in the international system.[5] The great powers are well equipped for affecting regional balances because of their superior capabilities and the local actors' dependence on stronger allies. Unless the great powers disengage from a region, the regional balance of power is itself dependent on them, especially in regions they consider vital.[6] Great powers seek to affect the local power balance via arms supply (or arms embargoes), economic assistance, investment, sanctions, and technology transfers. The great powers exercise distinctive effects on regional balances in two key types of situations:[7] a global balance of power in which the powers extend their competition to various regions by balancing each other and a global hegemony in which the hegemon is intensely engaged in regions that are important to its interests. This leads to the chapter's second proposition.

> Proposition 2: During periods of global balancing behavior by the great powers and intense great-power regional competition, regional bal-

ances will form among lesser powers and global and regional attempts at hegemony will fail. Such outcomes will persist only so long as none of the great powers is able to reach superiority.

When two or more great powers maintain a global balance of power system, these competitors balance each other to avoid the emergence of a global hegemon. None of the great powers is willing to accept the other's superiority, because such superiority might lead to abuses such as threatening, blackmailing, or coercing weaker parties. This balancing is extended to various regions, especially regions that affect the global distribution of capabilities because of their strategic location or economic importance. When the global rivalry is especially intense, as in bipolar systems,[8] the great-power competitive balancing is extended to the periphery of the international system, that is, to regions considered less than vital by the great powers.[9]

Balancing at the regional level takes place through great-power alliances with local states that involve diplomatic support, financial aid, and military assistance. Arms subsidies make it easier for the regional states to absorb the costs of balancing their regional rivals and to persist in costly protracted conflicts.

Whenever one of the great powers attempts to dominate a region by excluding its rivals from regional affairs, the competing powers tend to increase the assistance they give to local allies, so as to prevent their clients from bandwagoning with the rival great power. Similarly, if a state attempts to dominate other states in the region, usually with the help of its global great-power patron, the patrons of its neighbors will increase aid to their own local allies to prevent their great-power rival's client from becoming locally dominant.

Thus, during the bipolar Cold War, balancing was the norm as great powers and local actors sought but failed to dominate regional systems. The more intense the competition among the great powers in the region, the greater was the autonomy of small states and their ability to manipulate great powers and extract military and economic aid.[10] Because of the keen superpower rivalry during the Cold War, the ability of regional actors to manipulate the great powers grew sharply after 1945.[11]

Hegemonic-stability theory suggests that the production of such "common goods" as peace and stability requires the presence of a single hegemon that has dominant capabilities in important issue areas and is willing to lead (is ready to offer "side payments" to get other states to join it). The leader sees itself as a major long-term beneficiary of regional stability. To promote stability, the hegemon provides a flow of services and benefits to small states: diplomatic "good offices," mediation, security guarantees, construction of arms control and crisis-prevention regimes, and deterrence and compellence of military aggressors. Hegemonic-stability theory is the basis of the third proposition presented by this chapter.[12]

> Proposition 3: Hegemony leads status-quo states to bandwagon with the hegemon and to balance against revisionist threats.
>
> A hegemon is *willing* to invest in regional stability for two major reasons: the intrinsic importance of a region, and a shared threat. A distinction has to be made between different regions according to their standing in the great powers' balance of interests. Intrinsically important regions, whose value for the great powers stems from major material resources and also from geographic proximity to the powers, will draw great-power involvement and attempts at stabilization.[13]

Shared perceptions of threat by a great power and its status-quo clients promote regional engagement to counter the influence of an aggressive revisionist power. The presence of such a shared threat will lead the great power to invest considerable resources in forming and leading a countervailing coalition, in deterrence and compellence of the aggressor, and in promoting acceptance of itself as mediator in disputes among regional states.

As for the ability of great powers to stabilize a region, a hegemon can reduce conflict in regions vital to its interests because hegemony reduces the maneuvering room of regional actors and enables the great powers to exert coordinated moderating pressures (diplomatic, economic, and military) on their regional allies, as well as to broker settlements and mediate between the local parties. As a result, peacemaking efforts by the hegemon will be more effective than in competitive, balance of power situations.

Hegemony of a single great power in a region produces a strategic-economic environment that makes it highly profitable for local actors to bandwagon with the hegemon.[14] Those that bandwagon often are status-quo players, while revisionists reject the regional peace promoted by the hegemon unless the great powers subdue them. Yet revisionists are likely to be in an inferior position because they do not enjoy the support of a countervailing power able to balance the hegemon. Because they lack a great-power supporter to help them balance, the regional states enjoy little freedom to maneuver and a limited ability to manipulate the great powers. As a result, most states are expected to bandwagon with the hegemon, while the revisionists are deterred and contained by the hegemon.

Thus in contrast to the claims of both current variants of realism—the defensive (in the form of Steven Walt's balance of threat theory) and offensive (as expressed by Randall Scwheller's neoclassical realism)—bandwagoning under a benign hegemony is a stabilizing process.[15] Under hegemony, those who oppose the peace promoted by the hegemon are likely to pay a heavy military and economic price so long as they reject domination. Thus many players are expected to become more supportive of the regional peace because of the combined offer by the hegemon of rewards or positive sanctions for those who support the peace, and punishment or negative sanctions to those who oppose it.

During the hegemonic post-Cold War period, bandwagoning by status-quo players with the American hegemon[16] and balancing against revisionist threats therefore should be the norm. The combined effect of this bandwagoning and balancing should lead to the emergence of Pax Americana in regions deemed important by the United States and should be especially evident in the Middle East.

> Proposition 4: In high-conflict regions, states will tend to balance local rivals, especially revisionist states, that pose the greatest threat to other states' security and territorial integrity.

States want to maintain their independence and thus will balance against powerful states that threaten their autonomy or their key security interests, especially their territorial integrity. In regional systems, the balancing is directed against the most threatening states, that is, especially against proximate powers that have offensive capabilities and revisionist intentions.[17] Balancing is particularly intense in regions with dangerous conflicts and states willing to challenge the regional states system and the territorial status quo.

Accordingly, balancing should be a dominant feature of the regional politics of a conflict-prone Middle East. The rise of a global hegemon, which intervenes diplomatically, economically, and militarily in the Middle East, should, however, increase the tendency to bandwagon with the hegemon. At the same time, status-quo states will continue to balance against revisionist regional powers, which pose the greatest threat to their security.

Applying the Propositions to the Middle East

The Middle East is a good example of a "penetrated" regional system, in which the great powers have constantly intervened since at least the Napoleonic era.[18] Based on the logic of capabilities and asymmetric dependence of regional states on the global powers, the type of great-power involvement in the region should have decisive effects on regional balancing behavior. If the objective of balancing is to prevent the emergence of hegemony, the Middle East is a good example of how a balance of power was maintained during the Cold War, both on the superpower and regional state level. With the emergence of U.S. hegemony since the end of the Cold War, several states have begun to bandwagon with the United States. At the same time, rising revisionist threats also have spurred balancing.

THE MIDDLE EAST DURING THE COLD WAR

Various attempts to establish Pax Americana and to exclude the Soviet Union from the international diplomacy of the Middle East failed during bipolariy. Two major examples of such failures are the move in the 1950s to organize the Middle East into an anti-Soviet alliance, and the strategy, especially in the 1970s, to promote the Arab-Israeli peace process under exclusive U.S. leadership. While the first attempt boomeranged by bringing about Soviet penetration to the heart of the Middle East, the second was more successful, though it could be only partially successful so long as bipolarity endured.

THE BAGHDAD PACT

Western efforts in the 1950s to maintain hegemony in the Middle East by establishing military pacts served only to reinforce anti-Western orientations in the Arab world, and thus made it easier for the USSR to balance by forming alliances with radical Arab regimes.[19] The Western powers sought to exclude the Soviets from the region by leaving them out of such agreements as the 1950 Tripartite Declaration that limited arms deliveries to regional states.

The Western strategy of containment focused initially on establishing an anti-Soviet multilateral alliance. The most elaborate endeavor was the Baghdad Pact, which was established in 1955 and comprised Iraq, Iran,

Pakistan, and Turkey. These "northern tier" states, all proximate to the Soviet Union, were intended to serve as a geographic barrier to prevent Soviet penetration into the Middle East. The USSR leapfrogged this attempt by establishing close ties with radical Arab regimes in Egypt and Syria, which regarded local rivals supported by the "imperialist" West as their major threats.[20] The Soviet Union's "leapfrog" over the Northern Tier and its penetration into Arab lands, beginning with the Czech arms deal (1955), increased the freedom of action of Arab states; as a result, Egypt could rebuff Western pressures to join the Baghdad Pact. Moscow provided massive technical, financial, and military aid to the radical states and those that were radicalized by revolution, for example, Iraq in 1958. Moscow's involvement accelerated a polarization of the region from the mid-1950s until the outbreak of the 1973 Arab-Israeli war.

COUNTERBALANCING U.S. EXCLUSIONARY PEACEMAKING IN THE 1970S

Following the 1973 war, the United States changed strategy and brought Egypt back into its orbit by focusing on advancing the Arab-Israeli peace process. This successful maneuver enhanced America's regional position at the expense of the USSR. The "loss" of Egypt, in which the Soviets had invested heavily, and which constituted the centerpiece of their engagement in the developing world, was a severe blow to Soviet standing in the Middle East and a major accomplishment of U.S. power advantages in the region. The region appears to display slowly growing U.S. superiority since 1973— the only real setback being the Islamic Revolution in Iran in 1979. Yet Soviet counterbalancing helped to maintain strong anti-U.S. and anti-Israel coalitions until the end of the Cold War. Until the end of bipolarity, Arab states did little bandwagoning toward the Egyptian-American-Israeli axis, despite the benefits of joining the stronger coalition and gaining access to U.S. economic resources, with its potential leverage on Israel.

Moscow worked hard to obstruct U.S.-led peace initiatives, especially when Soviet leaders were excluded from the process. The Kremlin helped to construct an anti-Camp David coalition by increasing its support of Syria, a pivotal actor whose cooperation was (and is) essential to the achievement of any comprehensive Arab-Israeli peace. Soviet support made it much easier for Syria to balance against the Camp David coalition without risking an inferior military position vis-à-vis Israel or economic decline.[21]

Nevertheless, the failure to construct an American-sponsored regional order cannot be attributed to Soviet resistance alone. Part of the failure has been the result of U.S. clumsiness and ineptitude in conducting the peace process, and the bitter animosity that underlies the Palestinian issue. Under the Reagan administration, the United States also was not consistently prepared to play the role of a hegemon, which required expending resources, including the time and attention of high-level officials, to promote stability.[22] As U.S. Secretary of State Henry Kissinger envisioned, Israel proved to be a diplomatic asset when it came to bringing Egypt back into the American camp. But as an ally able to "penetrate" the U.S. political process by mobilizing sympathetic constituencies, Israel also could influence U.S. diplomatic policies.[23] At the same time, Arab intransigence and inter-Arab rivalries or balancing, notably between Syria, Iraq, and Egypt, have consistently frustrated U.S. attempts to extend the bilateral Egyptian-Israeli peace.

Because of the keen diplomatic and military competition produced by a bipolar world, smaller powers enjoyed a degree of autonomy that was disproportionate to their intrinsic power. This explains why the superpowers were unable to "deliver" their Middle Eastern clients even though they had reached substantive agreements in 1967, 1969–1970, 1972, 1973, and 1977. The superpower rivalry made it easier for determined clients to manipulate their patron's behavior to their own advantage, and to play off the two powers against each other. Israel and Egypt on numerous occasions deliberately obstructed attempts at great-power cooperation at the same time that they, along with Syria, were able to extract great amounts of aid and arms from the superpowers and entangle them in crisis situations.[24]

BALANCING BY REGIONAL STATES

The struggle for local dominance in the Arab world was intensified by the divisive ideology of Pan-Arabism.[25] Pan-Arabism often served as a useful legitimizing force for regional actors that aspired to a dominant role in inter-Arab politics and sought to gain support from other Arab states.[26] Indeed, the outstanding feature of the recent history of inter-Arab relations is the struggle for leadership in the name of Arab unity.[27]

The traditional protagonists vying for Arab leadership were Egypt, Saudi Arabia, and the Hashemites in Iraq and Jordan. A major rivalry burgeoned between Egypt and Iraq,[28] for example, regarding the establishment of the

Baghdad Pact in the mid-1950s.[29] Later, the post-Hashemite regime in Iraq continued to play an important role in the competition, while Jordan's importance declined and Syria's increased.[30] Regional leadership has been an ongoing contest, none of whose contenders has achieved widespread regional acceptance.[31] This is true even of Egypt under President Gamal Abdel-Nasser, when it came the closest of all to obtaining the hegemon's title.[32] Since the decline in Egypt's relative power in the post-Nasser period, none of the other Arab states has filled the vacuum, despite their ambitions.[33]

The competition for hegemony provided incentives for extremism and constraints against moderation. Arab states were pressured by Pan-Arabism to eschew compromise and endorse hard-line positions vis-à-vis Israel. This tendency, far from moderating the competition for leadership, only exacerbated the rivals' controversies and disputes.[34] Arab states used the fight against Israel to buttress their own position in the Arab world. Examples include the 1948 invasion of Palestine, the 1967 Six-Day War, and the October 1973 and 1991 Gulf wars. Widespread intervention by numerous Arab states (and Israel and Iran) in Lebanon exacerbated the domestic conflict there and led to war with Israel in 1982.

THE ARAB-ISRAELI BALANCE

None of the parties in the Arab-Israeli conflict could inflict a total defeat on the other side. On the one hand, Israel could never completely win any conflict because of the vast asymmetry in manpower and territorial space between Israel and its opponents. On the other hand, the Arab states knew that if they moved actually to destroy Israel, the United States might intervene or Israel might use its nuclear arsenal. Thus no war could end decisively because the superpowers would not allow complete surrender. Israel's military superiority, its victorious war record, and its nuclear deterrence probably convinced many Arabs, though not the considerable revisionist forces, that diplomacy is the best way to resolve the Arab-Israeli conflict. Arabs also resorted in the 1990s to nonmilitary efforts to prevent Israeli dominance in the region, such as excluding it from multilateral forums and pressuring Israeli officials to make concessions in the peace process. But the key to the regional changes was the transformation of the global balance of power and its regional manifestations following the end of the Cold War and Iraq's defeat in the 1991 Gulf War.

U.S. Hegemony in the Middle East

U.S. willingness to play the role of hegemon in the Middle East stems from the intrinsic importance of the region to U.S. interests, due primarily to the location of vast oil resources there. As a result, the United States has an important stake in maintaining good relations with the Arab states, but this stake conflicts with the American political and ideological commitment to Israel's security. The United States has tried to reconcile this conflict of interests by advancing the Arab-Israeli peace process. During the Cold War, promotion of peace and stability in the Middle East could serve to reduce the likelihood of an inadvertent superpower clash resulting from a local war. A stable Pax Americana would also ensure that the United States continued to enjoy all the related political and economic benefits of regional dominance, by peaceful means.

U.S. attempts during the Cold War to construct an Arab-Israeli grand alliance against the Soviet Union failed because regional actors tended to focus on local threats, not global ones. Since its 1990 invasion of Kuwait, Iraq has posed a threat to the United States (because of the danger to regional oil resources), Israel, and status-quo Arab states alike. This shared threat enabled the United States to lead a multinational coalition, which included most Arab states, against Iraq, and to bring new life to the Arab-Israeli peace process. Regional dependence on U.S. power created strong incentives for the local actors to moderate their position in the peace process.

The United States has enjoyed several advantages in the Middle East that make it possible for Washington to play a crucial role in regional peacemaking. First, Washington wields much diplomatic leverage in the Middle East, particularly over Israel because of Israeli dependence on American military and economic aid, a dependence further enhanced by the fact that Israel lacked any real option for realignment. Consequently, once Arab states realized that they could not recover the territories occupied by Israel in 1967 by force they turned to the United States as the chief arbiter of the Arab-Israeli dispute. Although Israel is able to mobilize influential allies in the U.S. domestic arena and significantly limit U.S. ability to increase pressure, still, a determined administration is able to influence Israel's behavior so long as it does not put at risk the vital security interests of the Jewish state as they are seen by the majority of the Israeli public (rather than by narrowly based extremist forces).

Second, America's superior economic resources have enabled it to promote peacemaking in the region by providing small states with financial and technological inducements to cooperate. Considerable financial resources have been transferred by the United States to the Middle Eastern states that cooperate in the peace process. For this reason, Egypt and Israel top the list of recipients of U.S. foreign assistance.[35]

Third, the termination of the Cold War and the disintegration of the Soviet Union eliminated the strategic umbrella previously provided by the Soviets to the radical Arab states, notably Syria.[36] During the Cold War, Arab radicals could turn to the Soviet Union for diplomatic assistance and weapons, especially when the tide turned against them in some war. This made it possible for them to persist in their conflict against Israel and to intimidate those who wanted to make peace. The disintegration of the Soviet Union terminated this support and opened a window of opportunity for progress toward a more comprehensive multilateral peace in the region.

The demise of the Soviet Union had major repercussions for specific Middle Eastern states. For example, without the Soviet spare parts and supplies it was used to receiving by grant or credit, the Syrian army found its ability to use military force against Israel severely limited. By 1987, Syrian President Hafez al-Asad realized that the changes in the Soviet Union's global position and its policies in the Middle East, the waning of Soviet-American competition, and the improvement in Soviet-Israeli relations all weakened Syria's standing and compelled Asad to alter his regional policy.[37] The cut in Soviet arms supplies was tangible: it is estimated that by late 1989, arms shipments from the USSR to Syria had dropped more than 50 percent from their 1985 levels.[38] Furthermore, political considerations no longer governed these arms transactions; they became simply commercial transactions. The purchaser now had to pay full price for military hardware, without the benefit of long-term credits from the Russian government.[39]

THE EFFECTS OF THE GULF WAR

The defeat of Iraq in 1991 further weakened the standing of the radical anti-American forces in the Middle East. American resolve to defend its interests provided the United States with the credibility it needed to push new initiatives.[40] A de facto pro-American coalition was established that included all the status-quo actors in the region: Egypt, Jordan, Saudi Arabia and the Gulf states, Syria, Morocco, Tunisia, Turkey, and Israel. The United States has supported this coalition by providing security for some members, economic aid for others, and influence over Israel within the framework of the peace process, a critical resource for Syria and Jordan.[41] The threat of U.S. military action also has prevented Iran and Iraq from forming a countervailing coalition. The defeat of Iraq demonstrated that there was no real option for ex-Soviet clients like the Palestine Liberation Organization (PLO) or Syria to join an anti-U.S. alliance in the Middle East, and that there was no countervailing force to balance against U.S. power in the region.[42]

The need to improve relations with the United States exerted pressure on local Arab states to conclude agreements with Israel, the sine qua non of closer relations with America.[43] There also were specific incentives for Israel's neighbors to seek a rapprochement with the sole global power: if the PLO wanted control over the West Bank or Syria wanted to reclaim the Golan Heights, they needed the United States to put pressure on Israel.[44] Syria's Asad had to conclude that negotiations under American sponsorship remained the only road open to him if he hoped to reach Syria's strategic, territorial, and political objectives. He cannily used the Gulf War to win U.S. recognition of Syria as a responsible power. This can explain why Syria was the first state in the region to respond positively to U.S. Secretary of State James Baker's invitation to the October 1991 Madrid peace conference, while Asad had rejected out of hand the 1973 Geneva negotiations. The rise of American influence in the region also influenced Asad's announcement that he had made a strategic choice to conclude peace with Israel. The loss of its great-power ally and the rise of U.S. power in the Middle East limited other options available to Syria.

The Gulf War also dramatically demonstrated the security dependence of Israel and most Arab states on U.S. military power. The inability of even the stronger Arab states such as Egypt and Syria to defend or later liberate Kuwait from Iraq's army made clear that the oil-rich and militarily weak Gulf states would have to rely on the United States for their security. The Gulf countries in fact preferred de facto American guarantees to Arab ones because they trusted U.S. military capabilities more and feared its political intentions less than those of their neighbors.[45]

When the United States deployed Patriot missile batteries in Israel as a substitute for an Israeli military response to Iraqi Scud missile attacks on Tel Aviv during the Gulf War, Washington showed its ability as well to limit

Israeli military action. Israel also relied on U.S. satellites for early warning data about incoming Iraqi Scuds, and on U.S. nonproliferation and counter-proliferation efforts directed against Iraq's and Iran's nuclear, biological, and chemical weapons programs, to enhance its own security.

PUTTING U.S. LEVERAGE TO WORK:
THE 1991 MADRID CONFERENCE

The American economy gives Washington further important leverage in the Middle East by providing direct financial assistance, credit, and technology transfers to important actors in the region. Israel, for instance, needed loan guarantees to absorb a mass influx of new immigrants from the disintegrating Soviet Union in the early 1990s, while Egypt needed foreign aid to stave off economic collapse threatened by a quickly expanding population and diminishing resources. This aid in turn put the United States in a position to force regional leaders to make the choices Washington believed were most likely to lead to peace, such as participating in the 1991 Madrid peace conference. The ability to provide financial incentives can ease making the painful concessions necessary for peace by bribing states and mitigating the costs and risks involved in the bargain. Financial incentives also create a stake for local parties in a settlement by conditioning the continuation of aid on their adherence to the agreement's terms.

Following the Gulf War, the Palestine Liberation Organization had to accept the American offer to participate only indirectly in the Madrid conference, as part of a joint Jordanian-Palestinian delegation. Yet Israeli opposition to allowing any PLO official into the negotiations, a position backed by the United States, did no more than prevent PLO leader Yasser Arafat from being present personally in Madrid. It is clear that the Palestinian delegation was receiving its orders from the PLO. But the United States also put pressure on Israel to cooperate. It hinted that it might reconsider the loan guarantees and reduce its technical assistance to Israel's anti-ballistic missile development program unless Israel were willing to enter into talks that included a Palestinian presence. The United States also made effective use of security assurances and financial incentives to encourage all sides to accept its mediation.

The United States compensated Israel and Egypt in particular with aid for their acceptance of the Camp David accords. The side payments provided to

Israel in return for its consent to withdraw from the Sinai—a provision of the accords—included a U.S. pledge to finance the transfer of three Israeli military airbases from the Sinai to the Negev desert, inside Israel proper. The cost of these transfers was roughly $3 billion.[46] The military and economic assistance granted to Israel grew conspicuously after the 1979 peace accord, and stabilized at about $3 billion.[47] Following its acquiescence to the Camp David accords, Egypt was cut off from the economic aid that had been offered by the oil-producing states of the Persian Gulf. To compensate for this loss, the United States altered the cost-benefit analysis of Egypt's leaders by institutionalizing an annual aid transfer to Egypt of about $1.5 billion.[48] In the aftermath of the Cold War, these side payments continue to serve as a "base" of U.S. aid to Israel and Egypt, and a powerful source of U.S. influence in both states.

Another positive incentive America presented Israel was a special aid package after the Gulf War ended. Egyptian officials view U.S. aid as an entitlement for having made peace with Israel. The U.S. government also canceled $7 billion of the Egyptian debt as a reward for Egypt's contribution to the Gulf War.[49]

Forty percent of all U.S. foreign aid goes to the Middle East. No other major power comes close to these levels of regional involvement. In addition to the large amounts of aid given to Israel and Egypt, Jordan and the Palestinian National Authority received substantial assistance following the signing of peace agreements with Israel in 1993. In the aftermath of the Gulf War, Jordan faced a very dire economic situation.[50] Interested in both guaranteeing Jordan's stability and encouraging its participation in the peace process, the Clinton administration used U.S. financial assistance to convince Jordan's King Hussein to seek peace and eventually to sign a peace treaty with Israel in 1994.[51] To achieve these objectives, the administration granted Jordan about $200 million annually, and in 1994 offered Hussein's kingdom $700 million of debt forgiveness. In addition, the United States encouraged members of the Paris Club and the International Monetary Fund (IMF) to relieve Jordan's foreign debt by rescheduling and forgiving some of its debt burden. Total debt relief obtained in 1995 through the IMF and Paris Club reached about $1.4 billion.

In the aftermath of the 1993 Declaration of Principles (Oslo 1), the United States again used economic aid to facilitate peace negotiations and the implementation of the accords between Israel and the PLO. American officials pledged to deliver $500 million worth of aid to the Palestinians between 1994 and 1998 to enhance the prospects for Palestinian autonomy.[52] U.S. officials also encouraged other states to donate large sums of money to the Palestinian Authority (PA),[53] including a $600 million EU transfer.[54] In 1995, as economic conditions in the Gaza Strip and West Bank continued to deteriorate due to Israeli border closures, the White House and State Department exerted economic pressure to resolve the dispute. The United States turned to high-visibility projects that could be quickly implemented to demonstrate the benefits of the peace process to the Palestinians.[55] American economic assistance also supported Israel's withdrawal from parts of the West Bank and Gaza. In 1995, the Clinton administration authorized $95.8 million for redeploying troops from Gaza and $240 million to facilitate an Israeli withdrawal from West Bank cities.[56]

RESTRAINING CLIENTS

American efforts to restrain Israel often occurred during Middle East wars, especially when Israel posed a threat to Arab capitals (the 1967 and 1973 wars) or when its use of force might potentially have caused a conflict to escalate (the 1956 war and the Gulf War). As the Cold War bipolar rivalry began to fade, however, the first Bush administration, despite severe disagreements over Jewish settlements in the West Bank, did not try to coerce Israel in its first two years in office (1989–1990). Only following the 1991 Gulf War did American officials use their economic leverage to induce changes in Israel's settlement policy.[57] Washington found that a major point of leverage was American loan guarantees intended to help Israel absorb thousands of new immigrants from the now defunct Soviet Union.

President Bush and Secretary of State James Baker actually placed an ultimatum before Israel: either it would cease any settlement activity in the occupied territories, or desperately needed loan guarantees of $10 billion over the next five years would not be granted.[58] Loan guarantees became the main carrot-and-stick Americans used to transform the harsh Israeli position regarding the settlements into something more acceptable. In response to Israel's refusal to freeze settlement activity, the administration asked the Congress on September 6, 1991, for a 120-day delay before considering an Israeli loan guarantee request.[59] American pressure against the conservative Likud Party government on the issue of the loan guarantees contributed to the eventual defeat of the right-wing coalition in the 1992 elections and the rise to power of a more amenable Labor-led coalition. The United States had skillfully used its hegemonic leverage to alter Israel's policy regarding settlements.[60]

The Emergence of the Revisionist Threat in the Gulf

The 1979 Iranian revolution and the Islamic fundamentalist threat it posed to the stability of Arab regimes constituted the first challenge to America's new Middle East order. A second threat came from the expansionist "Greater Iraq" or Pan-Arabist policy pursued by Iraqi President Saddam Hussein, which culminated in the invasion of Kuwait in 1990. These developments also deeply concerned the status-quo Arab regimes (Egypt, Saudi Arabia, the Gulf states, Jordan and, to a more limited extent, Syria), Turkey, and Israel.[61] The perception of a common threat created a basis for a rapprochement among these countries. This willingness to cooperate began during the Madrid conference partly as a continuation of the balancing coalition against Iraq in the Gulf War, and culminated in bilateral negotiations between Israel and its Arab neighbors, and in multilateral talks that involved most of the Arab states and Israel. Given the remaining distrust and the unresolved issues that divide the states in the region, however, U.S. pressure is essential to move the peace process forward. The United States also plays a crucial role in guaranteeing the security of the Gulf States.

The failure of the regional balance of power to deter Iraq and the inability of local states to establish regional collective security due to the hostility between revisionist and status-quo states in the region, led to the internationalization of security arrangements following the Gulf War. In recent years, U.S. policy toward the Persian Gulf sought to preserve regional stability; prevent Iran and Iraq from enhancing their suspected chemical, biological, or nuclear weapons capabilities; contain Iran's support of radical Islamic forces in the region; and topple Saddam Hussein, although that was not a top priority until the 9/11 attacks. To meet these objectives, the United States employed economic sanctions, United Nations–sponsored weapon inspections, pressures on external suppliers (notably China and Russia), a powerful military presence, "no-fly" zones in northern and southern Iraq, limited military strikes against Iraq, and support for the Iraqi opposition.[62]

COERCION BY SANCTIONS AND USE OF FORCE

The United States has imposed economic sanctions and arms embargoes on states perceived to be hostile toward its regional interests and the advancement of the peace process. Iraq, Libya, Iran, and Sudan, states identified by the State Department as sponsoring international terrorism, often have felt the sting of U.S. sanctions.[63] The United States also has attempted various ways to deter potential threats and to compel states to accept U.S. policy preferences. When these strategies failed to prevent aggression, the United States has demonstrated its willingness to use force to defeat a regional aggressor and to form a global coalition to restore order (e.g., the Gulf War).[64] Since the Gulf War, the United States has deployed forces in the Gulf in reaction to Iraqi troop movements in the direction of the Kuwaiti border and has conducted ongoing military operations against Iraq to punish Iraq for failure to comply with UN disarmament mandates and to enforce no-fly zones over the northern and southern portions of the country.

Although the United States has been relatively successful in its efforts to contain Iraq and in moderating the interstate conflict between its Arab clients and Israel, it has enjoyed less success in its efforts to pacify communal violence between Israelis and Palestinians. The eruption of violence between Israel and the Palestinians in fall 2000 (the second intifada) testifies to the severity of the unresolved problems between them. These issues include the demand of the Palestinians to exercise the right of self-determination in a state of their own, the construction of legitimate boundaries between Israel and the Palestinians, the future of the Jewish settlements in the occupied territories, and especially the status of Jerusalem and the "right of return" of Palestinian refugees. American pressure and influence were incapable of producing a change in the nationalist-religious motivations of the parties, and therefore remained incapable of ending the increasing violence between them.

The United States did, however, help to prevent a regional escalation of the intifada despite powerful domestic pressures on Arab states to join the Palestinian struggle against Israel. U.S. allies in the region, notably Egypt and Jordan, which are heavily dependent on U.S. aid, were strongly encouraged by the United States to oppose a widening of the conflict beyond the Israeli-Palestinian confrontation. Thus neither the Arab League nor the Islamic Conference, their anti-Israeli rhetoric notwithstanding, have adopted extreme resolutions introduced by revisionist forces in the region. Moreover, despite strong domestic pressures against the continuation of peace with Israel, Jordan and Egypt persist in the U.S.-supported "cold peace" with their Jewish neighbor.

In a unipolar world, it is difficult for local actors to escalate regional conflicts without the backing of other great powers that are competing with the United States for dominance in the Middle East. Thus the absence of serious international challengers to the United States helped to prevent the escalation of violence within Israel and the Occupied Territories into a regional war. This was especially important in the case of Iraq. Even before the outbreak of the second intifada, Saddam Hussein had made a series of belligerent speeches, as he did before the invasion of Kuwait in 1990. Iraq also mobilized several divisions on its Western border, offering to step in if Syria needed military help. Yet when the United States was joined by a number of Arab states including Syria in ordering him to pull them back, he did.[65] The U.S.-led international environment also has helped to moderate Iran's behavior in the second intifada. While issuing extreme anti-Israeli statements and calls for volunteers to fight Zionists, Iran's desires to improve its relations with the West and to join the global economy limited the level of Iranian support for the Palestinians to the provision of arms and money to extreme Islamist organizations, eschewing any escalation of its involvement beyond that level. The United States was particularly helpful in preventing escalation along the explosive Israeli-Lebanese border, which could have brought about an Israeli-Syrian war.

On the diplomatic front Syria has continued to be torn between bandwagoning with the United States versus ideological and domestic constraints. The bandwagoning is based on profit maximization: economic and territorial benefits—to get back the Golan from Israel under U.S. brokerage. The tension between the bandwagoning and the domestic constraints is manifested in the peacemaking with Israel. Syria has continued to be interested in making peace with Israel under U.S. auspices. A key objective of this strategy was to pursue a rapprochement with the United States. Yet due to significant ideological and domestic constraints, Syria has continued to insist on unacceptable conditions for Israel: a total Israeli withdrawal to the 1967 lines based on what Syria interpreted as the Egyptian precedent—a peace treaty for full Israeli withdrawal to the 1967 lines. Israel insisted also on normalization of relations and security arrangements, yet Syria did not share the

Israeli view on these issues and also on the timetable for the Israeli with-drawal. Thus no peace agreement was reached,[66] and that was one of the reasons why Syria could not thus far join the pro-U.S. coalition—in addition to its sponsorship of what the U.S. defines as terrorist organizations, including in its client state Lebanon—and its close relations in recent years with the Saddam Hussein's regime in Iraq and with Iran.

While American power and influence are unable to prevent the eruption of communal violence between national groups competing for control of the same territory and its religious-nationalist symbols, it can exercise moderating pressures to prevent the spread of this violence across the region. Moreover, the United States has induced the parties to resume peace negotiations quickly, even before the cessation of violence. President Clinton's active role in these negotiations demonstrated that the United States remains the only reliable broker between Israel and the Palestinians. Thus the United States will likely have to play a leading role in brokering any future peace agreements between the two parties. The dominant role of the United States in the region continues to provide strong incentives to all concerned to pursue peace. The Palestinians realize that once they are ready to make peace with Israel, the United States will provide the most effective avenue for pursuing a land-for-peace formula. The dependence of Arab states on the United States induces them not only to avoid joining the fight alongside the Palestinians, but also to move toward more peaceful positions. The relatively moderate 2002 Saudi plan of swapping land for peace is an example of this type of moderate negotiating position.

Progress in ending the dispute between Israelis and Palestinians will help reduce the overall level of violence in the Middle East. Together with the formation of legitimate boundaries between Israel and Syria, the resolution of these problems will allow the establishment of a comprehensive peace in the Middle East. Even under optimistic scenarios, however, intensive U.S. engagement will be crucial to the creation of an environment conducive to any progress toward peace.

The Effects of 9/11 and the War in Iraq

Although a unipolar world emerged following the collapse of the Soviet Union, the materialization of U.S. hegemony was only partial until 9/11.

While the disintegration of the Soviet Union weakened the constraints on U.S. dominance, the disappearance of the Soviet threat also reduced the motive for an intensive worldwide U.S. engagement.[67] A major manifestation of the partiality of U.S. hegemony in the Middle East was the continued challenge posed by a defiant Saddam Hussein who survived in power in direct contrast to U.S. preferences. Such a signal of the lack of resolve of U.S. hegemony undermined its ability to promote American objectives in the region, notably advancing Arab-Israeli peace.

The 9/11 attacks have changed this situation by increasing the U.S. motivation for a resolute international engagement. Terrorist organizations and regimes that sponsor them, host them, or develop weapons of mass destruction are now perceived by the U.S. administration as posing a major threat not only to regional stability but also to U.S. homeland security. This is the background for the wars in Afghanistan and, more controversially, in Iraq. The removal of Saddam Hussein is expected to weaken the power of the radicals in the Arab world and strengthen pro-Western moderates and thus to increase the prospects for resolving the Israeli-Palestinian conflict and increase regional stability. Radical regimes allegedly sponsor anti-American terrorism while the Palestinian issue supposedly produces resentment against the United States because it supports Israel. Thus the Bush administration hopes that the recent regime changes in Iraq and Afghanistan will weaken the appeal of radical terrorist organizations and make it much harder for them to act in the Middle East, recruit volunteers, and raise funds. The hoped-for result is to eliminate the threat to U.S. national security posed by al-Qaeda and related Islamic radical forces.

Indeed, at first glance it seems that the removal of Saddam Hussein weakened the radical forces in the region and increased the likelihood of progress in the peace process. The Bush administration seemed more determined to promote the process and following the military victory had more leverage to pressure the parties to make concessions. Thus following U.S. pressures both the Palestinians and Israelis endorsed the U.S.-sponsored "roadmap" to peace. The United States also pressed for reforms in the Palestinian Authority and indeed a moderate—Abu-Mazen—became the Palestinian prime minister, even if only temporarily, thus ending the monopoly of policy-making by Arafat who has continuously obstructed peacemaking. Israel is more reassured because the removal of Hussein undermined the so-called Eastern Front that could have potentially posed a major security threat by combining the forces of Syria and Iraq against it. Thus Israel seems now more willing to make concessions under U.S. pressures. The pro-Arab moderates, Egypt, Jordan, Saudi Arabia, and Morocco, are more willing to join again the U.S.-led peace coalition. Even the radicals—Syria and Iran, although hostile to the U.S. war in Iraq and to its continued occupation— seemed recently ready to moderate their challenges to the United States, realizing that they have to take into account the continued heavy military presence of the United States in the region. Syria might also be expecting to gain back the Golan Heights by joining the U.S.-led peace process.

THE CHALLENGES TO U.S. HEGEMONIC MANAGEMENT

The challenges to U.S. hegemony in the Middle East persist and might even be reinforced, in the aftermath of the Iraq War. First, it is inherently difficult for an external power to pacify communal violence like the Israeli-Palestinian clashes or to stabilize, let alone democratize, an occupied country like Iraq with a divided society that was held together for decades by an iron fist. If Iraq continues to be unstable, it will pose a major problem for U.S. standing not only in Iraq but also in the region as a whole. The problems in Iraq have already diverted U.S. attention and energy from the peace process. Second, countervailing forces oppose U.S. hegemony, even though they are still weak militarily: Iran, Islamic forces, and other radical movements including those inside Iraq and Palestine, terrorist organizations like bin Laden's al-Qaeda, and to a lesser extent Syria. In a different way the Europeans, notably the French, also oppose U.S. hegemony and seek a greater role in Middle East diplomacy. At any rate, there is an increasing economic and diplomatic engagement of the EU in the Middle East. Third, there is a rising popular resentment across the Arab world and in the region against the United States and its heavy military presence in the Middle East. This resentment is intensified by what is seen in the Arab world as an unjustified invasion of Iraq and the continuing occupation of the country. Feeling is widespread in the Arab world of a "double standard" in the American attitude toward the Arabs in comparison to Israel, especially following the eruption of the intifada, because of the supposedly pro-Israeli bias of the United States under the influence of its domestic politics. In addition, the United States is seen as supportive of repressive pro-U.S. regimes, notably Egypt and Saudi Arabia. Moreover, the U.S. objectives of "regime change" and "democratization" in Iraq (and in Palestine) not only pose a potential threat to many nondemocratic Arab regimes but are perceived as manifestations of U.S. imperialism in the region. On the other hand, if democratization takes place in Iraq and other Arab states, anti-U.S. Islamist governments might come to power, at least initially.

Conclusion

This chapter shows how the global balance of power influences regional balance in the Middle East, and the state strategies adopted by actors in the region. It also shows the dramatic transformation of the regional balance at the end of the Cold War. During the bipolar Soviet-American standoff, the superpowers balanced each other and supported their regional clients, making it possible for them in turn to balance the clients of the rival superpower. Indeed, attempts at forming hegemony, either through pro-Western alliances or through U.S. exclusionary peacemaking, failed. At the same time, the United States achieved a significant goal when Egypt made its move from the Soviet sphere to the U.S. orbit, culminating in the American-sponsored Camp David accords in the late 1970s. U.S. efforts to extend American influence in the Middle East failed, however, as long as the Soviet Union was a superpower.

Following the Soviet collapse and the Gulf War, most of the states in the region bandwagoned with the United States because of the prospects of financial and territorial gain and the chance to come under the American security umbrella. This bandwagoning helped the Arab-Israeli peace process gain some important achievements. Once placed under the U.S. security umbrella, status-quo states were willing to help contain their revisionist neighbors, Iraq and Iran.

To maintain its influence in the Middle East, the United States uses the traditional tools of military alliances and arms sales, but significantly, also makes extensive use of less threatening, more positive inducements such as economic incentives, diplomatic mediation, and regional security regimes to bolster its influence and to advance its interests in the region. American officials also wield great influence as arbiters and guarantors of agreements between regional actors.

The military victory in the Iraq War bolstered U.S. hegemony in the region by removing from power a key anti-U.S. leader and by showing U.S. commitment and capability to advance its interests even against strong international and regional opposition. The regional balance of power shifted decisively in favor of the pro-U.S. forces. This shift creates a new window of opportunity to advance the American-inspired order in the region by making progress in resolving the Israeli-Palestinian conflict and by stabilizing a more moderate pro-U.S. regime in Iraq. Yet these are very tough challenges even for a powerful hegemon, especially in light of the resentment against the United States in the Arab world and the great complexity of the forces and the issues involved there.

Lack of progress in resolving these problems, especially if violence persists, may jeopardize U.S. standing in the region and might even make it easier for radical and terrorist organizations to recruit people and resources against U.S. interests in the region and beyond. Yet, despite the opposition to U.S. policies in the region, it is only Washington that can play the decisive role in shaping the regional agenda. Thus far, no countervailing coalition has been able to form against U.S. hegemony in the absence of an external balancer. Even though the Europeans, Russians, and the United Nations play important roles in regional diplomacy and economic development (especially the European Union), they do not have the military, economic, and diplomatic resources required to balance U.S. hegemony in the region. Thus Arab states might appear willing to go on bandwagoning with the United States because of their high dependence on American military protection and economic assistance and its key role in brokering the Palestine issue. Yet Arab governments will try to hedge their bets and at most be very cautious in this bandwagoning because of the anti-U.S. sensibilities of their publics and because at this stage it is still unclear whether the United States will be able to resolve successfully the Iraqi and Palestinian issues.

Notes

1. In addition to competition and hegemony, there are two other major types of great-power regional engagement: cooperation and disengagement. See Benjamin Miller and Korina Kagan, "The Great Powers and Regional Conflicts: Eastern Europe and the Balkans from the Post-Napoleonic Era to the Post-Cold War Era," *International Studies Quarterly* 41 (March 1997): 51–85; Benjamin Miller, "Between War and Peace: Systemic Effects and Regional Transitions of the Middle

East from the Cold War to the Post-Cold War," *Security Studies* 11 (Autumn 2001): 1–52; and Benjamin Miller, *Regional War and Peace: States, Nations and the Great Powers*, University of Haifa (unpublished manuscript, 2003).

2. Kenneth Waltz, *Theory of International Politics* (Reading, Mass.: Addison-Wesley, 1979).

3. See Jack S. Levy's chapter, "What Do Great Powers Balance Against and When?" in this volume.

4. See Miller, "Between War and Peace" and *Regional War and Peace*.

5. Levy, this volume.

6. For a related point, see David A. Lake, "Regional Security Complexes: A Systems Approach," in David A. Lake and Patrick M. Morgan (eds.), *Regional Orders: Building Security in a New World* (University Park: Penn State University Press, 1997), 60–61.

7. This is based on the key distinction in the realist-systemic literature between balance of power and hegemonic theories. See Joseph Nye Jr., *Bound to Lead* (New York: Basic, 1990); Benjamin Miller, "Competing Realist Perspectives on Great Power Crisis Behavior," *Security Studies* 5 (Spring 1996): 309–57; and Levy, this volume.

8. Waltz, *Theory*, chap. 8.

9. See James J. Wirtz's chapter, "The Balance of Power Paradox" in this volume.

10. Miller and Kagan, "The Great Powers," 59.

11. For examples and citations, see ibid. See also, Michael I. Handel, "Does the Dog Wag the Tail or Vice Versa? Patron-Client Relations," *Jerusalem Journal of International Relations* 6 (1982): 24–35; and Robert O. Keohane, "The Big Influence of Small Allies," *Foreign Policy*, no. 2 (Spring 1971): 161–82.

12. See Nye, *Bound to Lead*, 37–48; Jack S. Levy, "Long Cycles, Hegemonic Transitions, and the Long Peace," in C. Kegley (ed.), *The Long Postwar Peace* (New York: HarperCollins, 1991), 147–76; Michael C. Webb and Stephen D. Krasner, "Hegemonic Stability Theory: An Empirical Assessment," *Review of International Studies* 15 (1989): 183–98. For an application to regional orders, see William I. Zartman, "Systems of World Order and Regional Conflict Reduction," in Zartman and Victor A. Kremenyuk (eds.), *Cooperative Security: Reducing Third World Wars* (Syracuse: Syracuse University Press, 1995), 4–8.

13. Benjamin Miller, "The Logic of U.S. Military Intervention in the Post-Cold War Era," *Contemporary Security Policy* 19 (December 1998): 72–109.

14. On balancing versus bandwagoning, see Stephen Walt, *The Origins of Alliances* (Ithaca: Cornell University Press, 1987); Paul W Schroeder, "Historical Reality vs. Neo-realist Theory," *International Security* 19 (Summer 1994): 108–48; and in the same issue, Randall Schweller, "Bandwagoning for Profit: Bringing the Revisionist State Back In," 72–107.

15. On the debate between defensive and offensive realism, see Michael E. Brown, Sean Lynn-Jones, and Steven Miller (eds.), *The Perils of Anarchy: Contem-*

porary Realism and International Security (Cambridge, Mass.: MIT Press, 1995);
Benjamin Frankel, "Restating the Realist Case: An Introduction," *Security Studies*
5 (Spring 1996), ix–xx; and Sean Lynn-Jones, "Realism and America's Rise: A
Review Essay," *International Security* 23 (Fall 1998): 157–82.

16. On U.S. hegemony in the post-Cold War era, see William C. Wohlforth,
"The Stability of a Unipolar World," *International Security* 24 (Summer 1999): 5–
41.

17. Walt, *The Origins of Alliances*, 22–26.

18. Carl L. Brown, *International Politics and the Middle East: Old Rules, Dangerous Game* (Princeton: Princeton University Press, 1984).

19. Fawaz Gerges, *The Superpowers and the Middle East: Regional and International Politics, 1955–1967* (Boulder, Colo.: Westview, 1994), 24–40.

20. On Soviet support of Syria in the context of its crisis with Turkey, see
Galia Golan, *Soviet Policies in the Middle East* (Cambridge: Cambridge University
Press, 1990), 140–42.

21. Walt, *Origins of Alliances,* examines in-depth the formation of alliances in
the postwar Middle East, and concludes that balancing rather than bandwagoning
was the dominant pattern. Thus, the acceleration of the peace process between
Egypt and Israel under American leadership in the 1970s led both to reinforcement of Soviet relations with Syria, Iraq, Libya, and South Yemen, to rapprochement between these states and even alignment between such rivals as Jordan and
Syria.

22. The only exceptions to U.S. non-leadership were U.S. President Ronald
Reagan's September 1, 1982, statement on peace in the Middle East, and Secretary
of State George P. Shultz's attempt to broker the ill-fated Israeli-Lebanese peace
treaty of May 17, 1983. On these attempts, see Steven L. Spiegel, *The Other Arab-Israeli Conflict: Making America's Middle East Policy, from Truman to Reagan*
(Chicago: University of Chicago Press, 1985), chap. 10; and Harold H. Saunders,
"Regulating Soviet-U.S. Competition and Cooperation in the Arab-Israeli Arena,
1967–86," in Alexander George, Philip Farley, and Alexander Dallin (eds.), *U.S.-Soviet Security Cooperation: Achievements, Failures, Lessons* (New York: Oxford
University Press, 1988), 570–74.

23. Notable examples include the rejection of the various peace initiatives
floated by U.S. Secretary of State William P. Rogers in 1969 and 1971, including
the first of them that emerged from the two-power talks (December 1969); Secretary of State Henry Kissinger's attempt to reach an interim agreement between
Jordan and Israel (1974), and his first effort (March 1975) to achieve a second
Israeli-Egyptian interim accord; and the Reagan peace plan of September 1, 1982.
On the first case, see William Quandt, *Decade of Decisions: American Policy Toward
the Arab-Israeli Conflict, 1967–1976* (Berkeley: University of California Press, 1977),
chaps. 3 and 5; Nadav Safran, *Israel—The Embattled Ally* (Cambridge: Belknap
Press of Harvard University Press, 1978), chaps. 22 and 23. On Kissinger, see
Quandt, *Decade of Decisions,* chaps. 7 and 8; Safran, *Israel—the Embattled Ally,*

chap. 26; and the joint U.S.-Soviet statement of 1977, in Spiegel, *The Other Arab-Israeli Conflict*, 337–40. On Reagan's plan, see Spiegel, *The Other Arab-Israeli Conflict*, chap. 10. For a list of pro-Israeli initiatives in Congress and a short discussion of U.S. domestic sources of Israel's influence, see Abraham Ben-Zvi, *The American Approach to Superpower Collaboration in the Middle East, 1973–1986* (Tel-Aviv: Jaffee Center for Strategic Studies, 1986), 71–75.

24. Another example was the success of Kuwait in extracting help from both superpowers to defend its tanker fleet during the Iran-Iraq War.

25. See Walt, *Origins of Alliances*, 206–12.

26. Avraham Sela, *The Decline of the Arab-Israeli Conflict: Middle East Politics and the Quest for Regional Order* (Albany: State University of New York Press, 1998).

27. P. J. Vatikiotis, "Inter-Arab Relations," in A. L. Udovitch (ed.), *The Middle East: Oil, Conflict and Hope* (Lexington, Mass.: Heath, 1976), cited in Gabriel Ben-Dor, *State and Conflict in the Middle East: Emergence of the Post-Colonial State* (New York: Praeger, 1983), 141.

28. Sela, *The Decline*, 15.

29. Elie Podeh, *The Quest For Hegemony in the Arab World: The Struggle over the Baghdad Pact* (Leiden: Brill, 1995).

30. Ben-Dor, *State and Conflict*, 144.

31. Podeh, *The Quest For Hegemony*, chap. 1.

32. Sela, *The Decline*, 17–19; Eli Podeh, "Leader, Hegemon or Primus Inter Pares: Egypt's Place in the Arab System in the Twentieth Century," unpublished manuscript, Hebrew University, 2002.

33. Avi Kober, "Arab Perceptions of Post-Cold War Israel: From Balance-of-Threats to Balance-of-Power Thinking," *Review of International Affairs* 1 (Summer 2002): 30.

34. Sela, The *Decline*, 37–41, 51–53; Ben-Dor, *State and Conflict*, 145.

35. For example, in 1988 the figures in dollars were $1.8 billion and $1.301 billion in military aid to Israel and Egypt respectively and $1.2 billion and $873 million in economic aid to the two countries. For a comparison, a large recipient of U.S. aid such as Turkey received in that year $493.5 million in military aid and $32.4 million in economic aid. Source: Agency for International Development, cited in the Congressional Quarterly, *The Middle East*, 7th ed. (Washington, D.C., 1991), 77.

36. See Steven Spiegel, "Eagle in the Middle East," in Robert J. Lieber (ed.), *Eagle Adrift: American Foreign Policy at the End of the Century* (New York: Longman, 1997), 302.

37. Itamar Rabinovich, "Syria in 1990," *Current History* 552 (1991): 30.

38. Daniel Pipes, "Is Damascus Ready for Peace," *Foreign Affairs* 70 (Fall 1991): 41–42.

39. Shlomo Gazit, "The Middle East: Main Strategic Trends," in Shlomo Gazit

(ed.), *The Middle East Military Balance, 1992–1993,* 3–25 (Tel-Aviv: Jaffee Center for Strategic Studies, 1993), 9.

40. Dalia D. Kaye, "Madrid's Forgotten Forum: The Middle East Multilaterals," *Washington Quarterly* 20 (Winter 1997): 169.

41. See Yair Evron, "Gulf Crisis and War: Regional Rules of the Game and Policy and Theoretical Implications," *Security Studies* 4 (Autumn 1994): 137. On the strong connection between the outcome of the Gulf War and the Arab-Israeli peace process, see Don Peretz, *Palestinians, Refugees and the Middle East Peace Process* (Washington, D.C.: U.S. Institute of Peace Press, 1993), 39.

42. Madiha Rashid Al-Madfai, *Jordan, the United States and the Middle East Peace Process, 1974–1991* (Cambridge: Cambridge University Press, 1993), 205–6.

43. Cheryl A. Rubenberg, "The Gulf War, the Palestinians, and the New World Order," in Tareq Y. Ismael and Jacqueline S. Ismael (eds.), *The Gulf War and the New World Order* (Gainesville: University Press of Florida, 1994), 325; Efraim Inbar, "Israeli Negotiations with Syria," *Israel Affairs* 1 (1995): 90; David J. Pervin, "Global Effects on Regional Relations: Differences Between Preventive and Promoting Action," paper presented at the annual meeting of the American Political Science Association, Boston, September 3–6, 1998, 20.

44. On the PLO in the post-Gulf War period, see David J. Pervin, "Building Order in Arab-Israeli Relations: From Balance to Concert?" in David A. Lake and Patrick M. Morgan (eds.), *Regional Orders* (University Park: Penn State University Press, 1997), 281–82.

45. Evron, "Gulf Crisis and War," 134–36.

46. William Quandt, *Peace Process: American Diplomacy and the Arab-Israeli Conflict Since 1967,* 2nd ed. (Berkeley: University of California Press, 2001), 235.

47. A. F. K Organski, *The $36 Billion Bargain: Strategy and Politics in U.S. Assistance to Israel* (New York: Columbia University Press, 1990), 142.

48. Quandt, "Peace Process," 235; see also Michael C. Hudson, "To Play the Hegemon: Fifty Years of U.S. Policy toward the Middle East," *Middle East Journal* 50 (Summer 1996): 335.

49. Moshe Arens, *Broken Covenant: American Foreign Policy and the Crisis Between the U.S. and Israel* (New York: Simon and Schuster, 1995), 246.

50. Pervin, "Building Order," 280; El Hassan Bin Talal, "Jordan and the Peace Process," *Middle East Policy* 3 (1994): 31–40.

51. Pervin, "Building Order," 282–83.

52. Denis J. Sullivan, "Introduction: Reinventing U.S. Foreign Assistance," *Middle East Policy* 4 (1996): 2.

53. The PA was established following initial implementation of the Oslo accords in 1994.

54. Peretz, *Palestinians, Refugees,* 84.

55. Sara Roy, "U.S. Economic Aid to the West Bank and Gaza Strip: The Politics of Peace," *Middle East Policy* 4 (October 1996): 69.

56. Stephen Zunes, "The Strategic Functions of U.S. Aid to Israel," *Middle East Policy* 4 (1996): 95.

57. Abraham Ben-Zvi, *The United States and Israel: The Limits of the Special Relationship* (New York: Columbia University Press, 1993), 200.

58. See Arens, *Broken Covenant*, 248. Moshe Arens was then Israel's defense minister. See also Ben-Zvi, *The United States and Israel*, 201.

59. Quandt, *Peace Process*, 310. For details regarding the U.S. pressure on Israel using loan guarantees, see Ben-Zvi, *The United States and Israel*, 203; and Robert J. Lieber, "The American Role in a Regional Security Regime," in Efraim Inbar (ed.), *Regional Security Regimes: Israel and Its Neighbors* (Albany: SUNY Press, 1995), 70.

60. Arens, *Broken Covenant*, 294, 298, 301.

61. For an excellent analysis of the changing balance of threat in the Middle East in the 1990s, see Kober, "Arab Perceptions," 27.

62. William B. Quandt, "Security Arrangements in the Persian Gulf," in Geoffrey Kemp and Janice Stein (eds.), *Powderkeg in the Middle East* (Washington, D.C.: American Association for the Advancement of Science, 1995), 323–24; Daniel Byman, "After the Storm: U.S. Policy Toward Iraq Since 1991," *Political Science Quarterly* 115 (Winter 2000–01): 493–516.

63. Shai Feldman, *The Future of U.S.-Israel Strategic Cooperation* (Washington, D.C.: Washington Institute for Near East Policy, 1996), 35.

64. See Miller, "The Logic of U.S. Military Interventions," 88–90.

65. Elaine Sciolino, "Palestinians Fight, but Iraq and Iran May Be the Winners," *New York Times*, November 5, 2000, section *Week in Review*, 3.

66. Itamar Rabinovich, *The Brink of Peace* (Princeton: Princeton University Press, 1998).

67. Miller, "The Logic of U.S. Military Intervention."

CHAPTER 10

Bipolarity and Balancing in East Asia

ROBERT S. ROSS

In the aftermath of the Cold War, the United States emerged as the world's sole superpower. Nonetheless, balance of power politics continues to play a dominant role in international politics. This chapter argues that balance of power politics has been especially pronounced in East Asia, where a bipolar balance of power system has succeeded the East Asian great-power triangle that emerged in the second half of the Cold War. It demonstrates that East Asian bipolarity is characterized by the expansionist tendencies of the region's superior power, the United States, and the traditional balancing behavior of its weaker pole, China.

This chapter argues that the bipolar balance of power system in East Asia is relatively stable. First, there are no candidate great powers in the region. Japan and Russia lack the attributes necessary to contend with China and the United States and achieve great-power status. Second, because of the combination of bipolarity and geography, great-power competition between China and the United States should experience minimal pressure for arms races, crises, and war. U.S.-China bipolarity will be far less costly and dangerous that the U.S.-Soviet Cold War rivalry. Third, well into the 21st century neither China nor the United States will be able challenge each other's dominance in their respective spheres of influence. The rise of China does not portend instability and the emergence of a new balance of power. This chapter concludes with a discussion of the prospect for restoring a global balance of power not through the rise of China but through Sino-Russian cooperation, just as Sino-Soviet cooperation balanced American power after World War II.

The Balance of Power in Post-Cold War East Asia

The United States is the world's only superpower. But the existence of a single superpower does not necessarily imply global hegemony. Regional structures can diverge from the dominant global pattern of international relations. The analytical distinction between a superpower and a regional power makes this clear. As William Fox defined the term over fifty-five years ago, a superpower is a traditional great power in regions outside its home region, while regional powers "enjoy . . . great-power status" but their "interests and influence are great in only a single theater of power conflict."[1] More recently, John Mearsheimer has observed that once a great power establishes dominance in its own region, it seeks influence in other regions to prevent competitors from emerging.[2] But rarely can it dominate the other regions populated by potential competitors. The reason for this is clear. As Kenneth Boulding explained, due to the "loss of strength gradient," a great power's capabilities are significantly eroded in distant regions, as supply and communications links become attenuated. Mearsheimer argues that the loss of strength gradient is particularly pronounced when large bodies of water separate regions. A superpower's global superiority is frequently reduced to parity in relative power in distant regions.[3] Thus a balance of power system can develop within various regions because at great distances a superpower may simply be one among other regional powers contending for security and resources.[4]

Regional balance of power systems have coexisted with a single superpower at various times in history. During the latter half of the 19th century England was the world's dominant power and perhaps its only superpower. It not only was a great power in Europe but participated as a great power affecting the balance of power in many distant regions, including China, South Asia, the Caribbean, Central Asia, and the Middle East. Nonetheless, England did not possess hegemony over Europe or over other more distant regions. In Northeast Asia, Japan and Russia also were great powers. Similarly, from the end of World War II until the 1956 Soviet arms transfer to Egypt, the United States was the world's only superpower but shared influence in Europe and Northeast Asia with the Soviet Union.

Since the end of the Cold War, a bipolar East Asian balance of power has coexisted with America's global role as the sole superpower. The United

States does not possess hegemony in East Asia, but shares with China great-power status in the regional balance of power. This statement should not be controversial. In the latter half of the Cold War, a "strategic triangle" in East Asia, composed of the United States, Russia, and China, coexisted with a global system comprised of two superpowers. This system first emerged in the early 1960s when China ceased playing a subordinate role in East Asia to the Soviet Union and independently challenged U.S. power in Indochina.[5] East Asian multipolarity became more apparent when the United States withdrew from Indochina in 1973 and ceded responsibility to China for balancing Soviet power on the mainland of East Asia.[6]

The collapse of Soviet power in 1991 did not usher in a period of U.S. regional hegemony, but rather an era of East Asian bipolarity composed of the remaining two great powers—China and the United States. The major strategic beneficiary in East Asia of the collapse of the Soviet Union was not the United States but China, which moved quickly to fill the vacuum left by the loss of Soviet influence. On the Korean Peninsula, Sino-Soviet competition in North Korea was followed by Chinese dominance of North Korea's economy and security. The Soviet withdrawal from Vietnam transformed Indochina into a Chinese sphere of influence. In contrast, the U.S. strategic presence in East Asia did not expand following the retrenchment of Soviet power. The end of the Cold War consolidated China's great-power status and led to a bipolar regional structure.

CHINA: THE MAINLAND GREAT POWER

The bipolar East Asian order reflects Chinese strategic dominance of mainland East Asia. In Northeast Asia, North Korea's location on the Chinese border and Pyongyang's self-imposed strategic and economic isolation has yielded China hegemony over North Korean security and economic activity. Along the full length of the Sino-Russian border, China enjoys conventional military superiority—due as much to Russian weakness as to Chinese force modernization. Moscow's inability to pay its soldiers, fund its weapons industries, and maintain its military infrastructure has weakened both the material capabilities and the morale of the Russian army.[7] The Russian military cannot manage its many domestic minority movements and its numerous smaller neighbors, much less contend with the better funded, disciplined, and trained Chinese army.[8] In Central Asia, the Chinese army not only enjoys similar military advantages vis-à-vis Russia regarding the new border states of Kazakhstan, Kyrgyzstan, and Tajikistan, but Beijing's growing economic presence in this region gives China additional advantages. The recent introduction of a U.S. military presence into Central Asia has not diminished China's status as a great power. China's strategic and economic assets in Central Asia continue to give it influence, as reflected in recent warnings from Beijing to Kazakhstan to avoid close military cooperation with the United States.[9]

China similarly dominates mainland Southeast Asia. Burma has been a de facto Chinese protectorate since the end of World War II, and as Sino-Burmese economic ties developed beginning in the late 1970s, Chinese influence has expanded. Thailand, once firmly allied with the United States, quickly shifted to strategic alignment with China following the final withdrawal of the American military presence from mainland Southeast Asia in 1975. Only China had the credibility and capabilities necessary to offset Soviet and Vietnamese threats to Thai security.[10] Then, after the Soviet withdrawal from Indochina, the Vietnamese government in Hanoi grudgingly accommodated itself to China's greater relative power by accepting China's terms for peace in Cambodia. Once Vietnam's forces withdrew from Cambodian territory, the Hun Sen leadership in Phnom Penh quickly developed close relations with China to balance Vietnamese power, so that Beijing was content to work with this erstwhile Vietnamese "puppet regime."[11]

Thus, by 1991 China had achieved dominance over mainland East Asia. The only exception to this dominance has been South Korea's alliance with the United States. But even here the strategic situation is ambiguous. Because Washington is Seoul's ally and possesses bases in South Korea, it continues to dominate South Korea's strategic calculus. But Seoul has been pursuing strategic hedging, developing strategic ties with China in preparation for either possible U.S. reconsideration of its commitment to South Korean security or for Korean reunification, when Seoul will face a common border with China. By the mid-1990s, Beijing and Seoul had developed close strategic ties and Chinese-South Korean military cooperation had improved. The two sides also share concerns about Japanese military potential. In addition, the trend in Sino–South Korean economic ties benefits China. In 2001, China became the largest target of South Korean direct foreign investment. By 2002, it had become South Korea's largest export market.[12]

THE UNITED STATES: THE MARITIME GREAT POWER

China dominates mainland East Asia, but the United States dominates maritime East Asia. American maritime hegemony reflects the combination of U.S. military access to naval facilities throughout East Asia and its advanced air and naval capabilities. Despite the fact that the United States no longer possesses any formal military bases in Southeast Asia—it lost its bases in Thailand in 1975 and withdrew from its bases in the Philippines in 1991—the U.S. Navy, asserting that it is interested in "places, not bases," takes advantage of the excellent air and naval facilities that exist throughout maritime Southeast Asia. Moreover, these bases are located in relatively stable countries. Washington now has agreements in place that give its navy access to facilities in Singapore, Malaysia, Indonesia, and Brunei. It has reached a visiting forces agreement with the Philippines, the first step toward having renewed access to facilities at Subic Bay, and has expanded its military presence there following the September 11, 2001, terrorist attacks in the United States. Such region-wide naval access means that U.S. aircraft carriers freely navigate Southeast Asian waters.[13] Because other powers do not have access to facilities in even one of these countries, do not have aircraft carriers, and do not have land-based aircraft that can project power into the maritime theater, the U.S. Navy dominates maritime Southeast Asia, including the critical shipping lanes connecting East Asia with the Middle East.

The balance of power in maritime Northeast Asia is vastly more complicated than in maritime Southeast Asia because Chinese, Russian, and Korean land-based aircraft are within range of important maritime theaters. Nonetheless, even in this region the combination of U.S. bases in Japan and superior U.S. carrier-based air capabilities allows the United States to dominate the Northeast Asian naval theater. Despite their deployment on the perimeters of Northeast Asia's maritime zones, Chinese aircraft cannot challenge American aircraft in any theater, including over mainland China. Whereas the United States continues to develop more advanced aircraft for 21st-century contingencies, Beijing will continue to rely on Russia's 1970s generation Su-27 and Su-30 aircraft as the backbone of its early 21st-century air force.[14] This technology gap underscores China's vulnerability to air combat with carrier-based and Japan-based U.S. aircraft in the East China Sea and the Sea of Japan, and ensures that U.S. air superiority in Northeast Asian waters will endure for the foreseeable future.[15]

Counting Powers: Two, But Why Not Three or Four?

China and the United States are East Asian great powers, but why is East Asia not bipolar or multipolar? Should Japan and Russia be considered great powers? Counting great powers is difficult. The standard measure of a great power's military strength is its ability to *contend in war* with (rather than *defeat*) any other country in the system. Establishing East Asia as multipolar requires an estimate of the relative war-fighting capabilities of the contenders for great-power status, but this calculation is difficult because the only true measure of military power is war itself.

Counting poles also can be done by examining whether a state possesses the political and strategic attributes of great-power status—spheres of influence and responsibility for the regional security order. If a great power has regional hegemony, then the entire region is its sphere of influence. The more great powers there are, the greater the number of regional divisions among them. Such divisions and spheres of influence reflect the behavior of non-great powers that seek either protection from an adversary by aligning with a another great power (that is, balancing), or cooperation with an adversary in response to its unchecked capabilities (that is, bandwagoning).[16] Evidence of great-power status also is reflected in a state's level of responsibility for maintaining regional order. Great powers have a "place at the table," a "voice" in regional affairs, because their interests must be considered if a negotiated solution is to be effective. This voice emanates from military power. The interests of allied lesser powers are advocated by their great-power representatives, the leaders of the spheres of influence.

JAPAN: ISLAND POWER, REGIONAL SUBORDINATE

In the late 19th century, Japan defeated China and coerced it to cede territory to Japan, including Taiwan. In 1905 it defeated the Russian navy and army and ended Russian expansionism in Northeast Asia. After World War I, Japan established dominance over Korea and much of China, and controlled the regional seas. It then occupied most of East Asia and fought the United States in a long and difficult war for control of the Pacific. For nearly a century Japan was a great power, but the strategic and domestic circumstances that enabled Tokyo to achieve and maintain that status no longer exist and are unlikely to be replicated, even well into the 21st century.

Japan's great-power success in the late 19th and early 20th centuries reflected opportunism in a regional power vacuum. China, the region's traditional hegemon, suffered from corruption, political and military divisions, and prolonged economic and military decline. The region's most dominant power, Great Britain, experienced relative decline as its European competitors launched navies that contended with British forces near their home waters. No longer capable of maintaining its two-power naval standard against Russian and French naval expansion while at the same time keeping up its dominant naval presence in East Asia, London signed the 1902 Anglo-Japanese alliance to encourage Japan to resist Russian inroads into Manchuria and Korea and to secure Japanese cooperation in defense of British interests in China.[17] Meanwhile, the United States had yet to mobilize its military potential to assume great-power responsibilities outside the Western Hemisphere. Thus, Japan's only obstacle to Northeast Asian primacy was Russia.

In the 1904 Russo-Japanese war, Tokyo took advantage of its superior power-projection capabilities in Northeast Asia and the cooperation of Britain to inflict a stunning defeat on overextended and isolated Russian forces. Tokyo's victory allowed it to achieve preeminence in both Korea and Manchuria, where it acquired Russian railways, bases, and treaty rights. Subsequently, Japan benefited from Russian domestic instability after the 1917 Bolshevik revolution, and then from Soviet preoccupation with German power in the 1930s. On the eve of World War II, Japan enjoyed a free hand in Northeast Asia and turned its sights toward expansion into Southeast Asia. Subsequent Japanese occupation of Indochina in 1941 was made easier by France's defeat during the war in Europe.[18]

Japanese expansion achieved impressive results. Nonetheless, even when Tokyo enjoyed the most opportune external circumstances for empire building, its leaders were unable to overcome internal obstacles to great-power competition. The most important of these obstacles were resource constraints and strategic liabilities imposed by geography. On the one hand, these constraints drove Japanese expansionism. In the 20th century, Japanese leaders were acutely aware that the islands' limited indigenous resources made Japan's economic future and military capabilities dependent on its great-power rivals. Thus a determining factor in Japan's drive for regional hegemony during the early part of the century was its search for economic autonomy. On the other hand, each new foray into a weakened and divided China, rather than stabilizing Japan's imperial resource base, led to an expanded front and, ironically, actually increased Japan's dependency on imported resources, eliciting additional expansion to meet the need for additional resources. As late as 1939, Tokyo imported over 91 percent of the military's commodities and equipment, most of which came from the United States. Japan was critically dependent on the United States for scrap iron, aluminum, nickel, and petroleum products.[19] This continued and deepening economic dependency led to incessant conquest, eventually culminating in Japanese expansion into Southeast Asia and to World War II in the Pacific.[20]

Japan's bid for great-power self-reliance failed not only when the international circumstances were most favorable, but also when its domestic system was uniquely oriented toward strategic expansion. During the height of Tokyo's empire building in the 1930s, the Japanese government exercised unparalleled peacetime control over the civilian economy. By the end of the decade, the government controlled allocation of both strategic resources and finished products.[21] Nonetheless, the Japanese military could not simultaneously carry out expansionism, achieve autarchy, and compete with the United States for regional dominance.[22]

Ultimately, Japan's bid for great-power status contributed to its demise. Imperial overexpansion in the 1930s taxed Tokyo's ability to compete with a better qualified great power—the United States—and directly contributed to its defeat in World War II. Could Japan once again make a bid for great-power stature, in the 21st century? In a word, no. To the extent that the Japanese empire almost succeeded in the 1930s, it was because of strategic and domestic conditions that will not be repeated. In the 1930s China was not capable of being a great power and the United States had not decided to become a great power. Domestically, Japan's economy is far more decentralized today than in the 1930s, so that a bid for greater military budgets and economic autonomy would be even more difficult to manage. Meanwhile, in the 21st century, Japan's trade surplus with the United States makes it hostage to continued access to the U.S. market as an aging and shrinking population places a greater strain on the Japanese economy and social fabric. Its dependency on imported energy resources, including petroleum from U.S. allies in the Middle East brought through U.S.-controlled shipping lanes, creates similar vulnerabilities.[23] In the 21st century, a Japanese bid to attain great-power military capabilities would lead to greater strategic dependency and, thus, increased vulnerability to heightened great-power conflict than was the case during the 1930s.

In the era of air power, Japan faces an additional geopolitical obstacle to achieving great-power status. For example, prior to the development of air power, the English Channel served as a formidable moat insulating British resources and industrial bases from attack so that they could serve British naval expansion.[24] But as World War II revealed, in the era of aircraft and missiles the English Channel can no longer provide a buffer for England's strategic resources. Japan faces a similar geo-strategic problem. Whereas Japan's insular geography gave it considerable security from attack for much of its history, in the era of air power its economy and infrastructure have become vulnerable to attack from the sea. Such threats came from American aircraft based on carriers and on Saipan, Guam, and Tinian, and ultimately Okinawa during World War II; from regional land-based aircraft, such as Soviet aircraft deployed in the Far East in the 1980s; from North Korean missiles beginning in the 1990s; and perhaps later in the 21st century from Chinese aircraft and missiles.[25]

Mahan's observation in 1900 that Japan's size and its proximity to other East Asian powers diminished its great-power potential for the early 20th century is especially relevant for the early 21st century.[26] Well into the 21st century, Tokyo will not be able to achieve autonomous security and compete with the United States for regional influence, much less contend with the United States in a war. It will have little choice but to remain within America's strategic orbit, dependent on U.S. military strength for security.

Japan's limited role in the East Asian balance of power is reflected in the regional strategic order. Unlike the United States, Japan has no allies and no spheres of influence. No state in the region depends on Japan for security. Rather, Japan, together with South Korea and Taiwan, depends on the United States for security against its more powerful neighbors, including countries with nuclear weapons and long-range missiles. Unlike China, Japan has not been able to compel its neighbors to accommodate its security concerns. Rather, because it operates within the U.S. alliance system, Japan is compelled to tolerate conflicts with its neighbors, including disputes with South Korea over territory and Japan's alleged responsibility to atone for its colonial history.

Japan's secondary regional role also is reflected in its marginal contribution to the maintenance of local order. Since World War II, Japan has tried to exercise leadership in regional disputes. When the United States has been slow to respond to conflict, Japan has tried to fill the void. But the sole instrument Japanese diplomacy has been able to wield is exhortation, and local powers often ignore Japan's efforts. Japanese initiatives to resolve the Malaysian-Indonesian conflict in the mid-1960s failed. Similarly, its mediation of the Cambodian civil war during the 1980s was largely irrelevant. Since the 1950s, Japan has been, at best, a marginal actor in the diplomacy of the Korean Peninsula. China and the United States have been the two great powers most responsible for keeping the peace on the Korean Peninsula and for constraining North Korea's effort to acquire nuclear weapons. Finally, the Taiwan problem is a U.S.-China issue; China warns Japan to stay out, whereas the United States seeks a greater Japanese commitment to defend Taiwan within the U.S.-Japan alliance.

RUSSIA: DISTANT NEIGHBOR, MARGINAL POWER

Russia was once an East Asian great power. During the second half of the 19th century, Russia expanded eastward, establishing control over Central Asia and mainland Northeast Asia, and wresting territory from the crumbling Chinese empire. With sovereign presence in Northeast Asia, Russia's great-power reach extended to northeast China, the Korean Peninsula, and the Pacific Ocean. Following World War II, the Soviet Union led one of the two alliance systems in East Asia and established naval bases on the Northeast Asian coastline. It contended for influence in Indochina first with the United States and then with China. But the circumstances that enabled the rise of Russia no longer exist. Russia may still be an East Asian country, but it is no longer an East Asian great power.

Even at the height of its regional influence, Russia was not able to establish a strong and reliable strategic presence in the Russian Far East and its status as a Northeast Asian great power was tenuous and intermittent. The reason is the inhospitable geography separating the Russian Far East from political centers in western Russia. Whereas western migration enabled the United States to consolidate its presence on its Pacific coast, Russians have never migrated east into Siberia in large numbers. Although the southeast sector of the Russian Far East can sustain agriculture, its isolation from Russia's population and industrial centers has obstructed development of the infrastructure necessary to support population and financial transfers to the region. Russia's ultimately fruitless effort to establish reliable rail links with the Russian Far East reflected the obstacles posed by the cold and harsh

Siberian expanses.[27] The result has been an enduring lack of the manpower and natural resources necessary to sustain a large Russian army and naval presence in the North Pacific, and to minimize dependency on foreign resources.

Russian expansion into the Russian Far East and Manchuria during the second half of the 19th century and early 20th century reflected the anomaly of Chinese weakness rather than a norm of Russian strength. Indeed, at times Russian forces were so overextended that, had China known of Russia's strategic situation, it could easily have reversed St. Petersburg's military advances. At other times, China's preoccupation with the threats posed by other powers compelled it to acquiesce to Russian incursions into Chinese territory.[28]

Russia's imperial ambitions did not enable it to place the Far East under direct administrative or political control. Southern Siberian borders, especially in the Amur region, were open to Chinese migration and the area's economy remained dependent on foreign suppliers. During the last quarter of the 19th century, 80 percent of the civilians in Vladivostok were Chinese or Korean. In 1877, the imperial Pacific Squadron, to avoid total dependence on foreign merchants in Vladivostok, began to purchase coal directly from suppliers in San Francisco and to use repair facilities in Japan. In 1885, it still depended on imported coal as well as winter anchorages in Nagasaki. That same year, St. Petersburg could deploy only 15,000 troops east of Lake Baikal. As late as 1912, Russians were only 58 percent of the Vladivostok population.[29] These resource and logistical difficulties offset the Russian advantage in the overall balance of capabilities between Japanese and Russian forces during the 1904–1905 Russo-Japanese War. St. Petersburg could not respond to Japan's naval blockade of Port Arthur by using overland routes to resupply its Pacific Fleet and Far Eastern ground forces, so that the Japanese army easily landed and defeated the Russian army, while the Japanese Navy took advantage of its readily available harbors, supply depots, and coal supplies to destroy the Russian Pacific and Baltic Sea fleets.[30]

Russia's strategic position in Northeast Asia began to erode during World War I and virtually collapsed following the 1917 revolution and the ensuing civil war. Meanwhile, economic integration of the Far East with the European regions remained elusive. As late as 1925, Chinese merchants controlled the retail trade in much of the Far East, while Japanese firms dominated the region's banking and shipping, and controlled 90 percent of the fisheries. In 1920, Japanese forces moved into northern Sakhalin and stayed until 1925, withdrawing only after the Soviet Union agreed to unfettered Japanese access to Sakhalin's natural resources.[31] Not until the late 1950s did Moscow begin to reestablish a strong presence in the Far East. In the 1970s it revived the Baikal-Amur Railway project, but it was never fully operative. Even at the height of its authority in the Far East, Moscow was unable to invest the resources necessary for the region's economic development.[32]

In the 1980s, the Soviet Union made a major effort to establish a strong military presence in the Far East. It used Vladivostok as the base for its expanding Pacific Fleet and deployed forty-five divisions in the Sino-Soviet border region. Nevertheless, just as at the turn of the century, the Pacific Fleet depended on a vulnerable railway system and on equally vulnerable sea and air routes for resupply, so it was the most exposed of the Soviet fleets. And the maritime geography of Northeast Asia continued to plague Soviet access to blue water: prompt offensive action by the U.S. Seventh Fleet could devastate Soviet naval forces before they could leave the Sea of Japan. Moreover, although the Soviet Pacific Fleet never came close to achieving the capabilities of the U.S. Seventh Fleet, and Moscow maintained only about half of its Far East divisions at full strength, the burden of maintaining the Pacific Fleet in Vladivostok as well as ground forces along the Sino-Soviet border in a barren and isolated region, was ultimately part of the imperial overexpansion that contributed to the demise of the Soviet empire.[33]

Today's Russian presence in the Far East is closer to the historical norm. The Far East economy is far poorer and less developed than the Russian economy west of the Urals. Moscow's political and military presence in the Far East is weak, so that regional political autonomy and policy independence is strong. Unable to patrol its perimeters, contemporary Russia has borders that can be as porous to Chinese migration and trade as were Russian borders for most of the 19th and 20th centuries. China's stronger economic presence in Northeast Asia creates economic ties between China and the Far East that further challenge the economic integration of the Far East with the rest of Russia.[34] In short, now that China is no longer weak and internally divided, Beijing enjoys the geopolitical advantages over Russia derived from its large population and industrial centers and its agriculture resources in mainland Northeast Asia, abutting the Russian Far East.

In the contemporary regional order, Russian security is dependent on Chinese forbearance. Chinese forces dominate the Sino-Russian border, and the political and military vacuum in the Russian Far East exposes Russia to the threat of Chinese military expansion. Whereas the United States provides for Japanese security against other great powers, China keeps Russia secure by its policy of cooperation. Russia is subordinate to Chinese power in the regional balance of power. In East Asia it cannot contend with China in a conventional war, much less with the United States.

Russia's insufficient conventional military power and its corresponding subordinate great-power status is reflected in its role in the regional order. Russia has no spheres of influence in East Asia. It withdrew its troops from Mongolia and ended its support for the Vietnamese occupation of Cambodia in the late 1980s, in return for China's agreement to a Sino-Soviet rapprochement, thus ceding to Beijing economic and military domination of these erstwhile Soviet spheres of influence. Similarly, it no longer competes with China for influence in North Korea. Moscow's remaining influence beyond its borders is in Central Asia, far from Northeast Asia. Yet even there, in a region much closer to Russia's industrial and population base, Moscow must share influence with China and acknowledge Beijing's dominance in the countries bordering China. It is no accident that the multilateral economic forum of China, Russia, and the Central Asian states is called the Shanghai Cooperation Organization.

Not only does Russia lack spheres of influence, but it also is denied a place at the table, a voice in regional affairs. Despite its common border with North Korea, and its obvious interest in both the course of the Korean conflict and the strategic implications of Korean unification, like Japan, Russia has been a peripheral player in the diplomacy of the Korean Peninsula. It has even less influence in great-power diplomacy over more distant issues, including the Taiwan conflict and territorial disputes in the South China Sea.

Bipolar Balancing: U.S. Power and China's Response

The bipolar balancing dynamics in East Asia reflect an unusual process. Over the last ten years the rising power also has been the superior power. The United States won the Cold War and is now superior to both its former adversaries and its coalition partners, including China. Since then, the United States has expanded its power relative to China. But while the

United States has been expanding its capabilities, China has been conforming to the expectations of balance of power theory. Rather than accommodating U.S. power, Beijing has been seeking security vis-à-vis the United States by mobilizing international and domestic resources to enhance China's relative power.

THE UNITED STATES: THE RISING SUPERIOR POWER

Since the end of the Cold War, rather than stand still or consolidate its existing East Asian presence, the United States has, in conformation with the expectations of offensive realism, steadily expanded its regional military capabilities.[35] Washington has strengthened the U.S.-Japan alliance and encouraged Tokyo to expand Japan's defense capabilities and its contribution to U.S.-Japan wartime military cooperation. It also has encouraged Australia to enhance its contribution to preparations for war in East Asia, particularly in a Taiwan contingency. And it has enhanced relations with India based on common U.S.-Indian interests in opposing Chinese power.

The United States is also improving security relations with Taiwan, bringing U.S. power to within ninety miles of the Chinese coast. By increasing its arms sales to Taiwan and training the Taiwan military to use advanced U.S. military technologies, the United States is both encouraging Taiwan to resist Beijing's pressure and enhancing its own influence on the island. By gradually improving ties between the U.S. and Taiwan militaries, including discussions of joint planning for war, interoperability, and real-time intelligence sharing from satellite downlinks, Washington is establishing a strategic presence and military operations center in Chinese coastal waters.[36] As small islands off the coasts of great powers, the geo-strategic similarities between Taiwan and Cuba are evident. The similarities between Soviet policy toward Cuba in the early 1960s and U.S. policy toward Taiwan since the late 1990s also are evident. By establishing a strategic presence on the Chinese perimeter, the United States is challenging the U.S.-China modus vivendi of the late Cold War period and expanding its relative power vis-à-vis China.

While enhancing its political relations with countries on China's periphery, the United States also has strengthened its forward military presence in the region by redeploying military forces from Europe to East Asia.[37] Even though the carrier *Kitty Hawk*, which is based in Japan, provides significant political symbolism and potent firepower, the U.S. defense budget for fiscal year 2003 allocates funding to increase the U.S. carrier presence in East Asian waters.[38] Because an enlarged maritime presence will require increased logistical support, the United States has sought greater access to other countries' naval facilities in the region. The opening in March 2001 of Singapore's Changi port facility, which can accommodate a U.S. carrier, is an important element in this process. With the *Kitty Hawk* already based in the region, Changi can facilitate extended deployment of a second U.S. aircraft carrier. In addition, the United States is gradually resuming close defense cooperation with the Philippines and is seeking permission to deploy a greater naval presence there.[39]

The United States also is enlarging its regional submarine presence. Between late 2002 and 2004, the U.S. deployed three *Los Angeles*-class nuclear-powered submarines at Guam.[40] As well as enhancing overall U.S. war-fighting capabilities, a strong U.S. submarine forward presence gives the United States the power to blockade mainland ports in the event of war, thus curtailing Chinese wartime trade and preventing mainland warships from ever leaving harbor.[41] The development and deployment of American nuclear-powered guided-missile submarines (SSGNs) in East Asia similarly increase U.S. war-fighting capabilities. These converted Trident ballistic-missile submarines will be able to launch as many as 154 precision-guided Tomahawk land-attack missiles each, thus offering a secure platform from which to hold important military targets in China at risk.[42]

The United States also is improving the forward presence of American air power in East Asia. In August 2002, the United States began stockpiling conventional air-launched cruise missiles (CALCMs) at Andersen Air Force base on Guam. This stockpile will allow U.S. bombers to reload in the theater rather than return to the United States for munitions. Ready access to the 600 mile-range CALCMs will permit U.S. aircraft to target China's surface fleet in the Western Pacific, thus undermining China's blockade and attack capabilities, and also target Chinese military and civilian assets while remaining out of range of China's air defenses.[43] The Pentagon is considering expanding its air-power presence at Andersen airbase as well.[44] The United States already deploys forty-eight F-15s at the Kadena Air Force base on Okinawa. Deployment of additional military aircraft on Guam would considerably augment U.S. power on China's periphery. Moreover, Andersen is a more reliable base than Kadena for U.S. operations, especially in a Taiwan-centered contingency. On the continental side of the balance, since October 2001 the United States has been developing an air- and ground-force presence in Tajikistan, one of China's neighbors in Central Asia.[45]

While expanding its military presence on China's periphery, the United States has mobilized its domestic resources to expand its global and regional power. In the early 1990s, U.S. defense spending was more than the next six or seven countries' defense budgets combined. Since then, U.S. defense spending has dramatically increased, so that the FY 2003 defense budget *was* greater than the sum of the next 35 defense budgets. The Pentagon's hardware acquisitions similarly reflect an expansionist impulse. The new aircraft carriers *Harry S Truman* and *Ronald Reagan* were put to sea since the late 1990s. The next generation of power-projection vessels is coming along, including new aircraft carriers and SSGNs that will possess enhanced information warfare capabilities and long-range missile capabilities. The Pentagon has ordered the next generation of aircraft, despite the fact that China's most advanced aircraft for the next twenty years will be the Soviet-built 1970s-era Su-27 and 1980s-era Su-30, which are inferior to the U.S. aircraft already in use. The Defense Department also has continued to modernize long-range, precision-guided missiles.[46]

While increasing its conventional capabilities on China's periphery, the United States also has strengthened its strategic nuclear superiority. Despite possessing an overwhelming advantage in both the numbers and quality of its nuclear warheads and delivery systems, the United States has gone farther by seeking to nullify the minimal deterrence capability of other states and achieve a nuclear first-strike capability. Such strategic superiority will bolster American resolve to use conventional capabilities against regional adversaries and will strengthen extended deterrent threats.[47] China is central to these trends in U.S. policy. Concern about China's nascent nuclear capability contributed to the 2002 Nuclear Posture Review, which emphasized U.S. acquisition of preemptive capabilities for use in limited war situations against states with limited nuclear stockpiles, including against China. U.S. interest in missile defense reflects similar concerns. An effective missile defense system would neutralize China's deterrent, thus enhancing U.S. resolve in regional conflicts involving Chinese security interests, such as the Taiwan issue.[48]

Rather than seek to maintain its high level of security, the United States has sought to enhance and extend its superiority. It may be motivated by the potential rise and long-term threat of Chinese power, but given both current U.S. security levels and the significant gap in U.S. and Chinese technological and military capabilities, the United States is expending considerable immediate resources to prepare for the possibility that a significant challenger might emerge by about the middle of the century.

CHINA: PROTRACTED BALANCING OF U.S. SUPREMACY

China has responded to growing U.S. power by increasing its defense budget and improving its capabilities. Beijing has sought the military hardware necessary for short-term maintenance of the status quo in the Taiwan Strait and to achieve the long-term goal of unification of Taiwan with the mainland. As the United States strengthens its preemptive capabilities, China is modernizing its strategic missile forces. At the same time, China must develop the advanced economic base necessary to compete with the United States in an era of advanced technology warfare. Adding another component to its balancing strategy, China also has been seeking international support to help it constrain U.S. power.

Since 1995, China has rapidly increased its defense spending. Whereas China's publicly declared defense budget stayed basically unchanged from the mid-1970s, in 1995 and again by 2000 it approximately doubled, and will likely double again by 2006. From 2001 to 2004, the Chinese defense budget grew at an average rate of 14 percent per year. Although much of the increased funding is for salaries and infrastructure renovation, the increases are widely understood to reflect greater Chinese concern about the likelihood of war in the Taiwan Strait, and the probability of U.S. military intervention in support of Taiwan. In addition, the costs of imported hardware from Russia are not fully reflected in the public defense budget.[49]

China's focus on the U.S. maritime challenge to Chinese coastal security and Chinese interests in the Taiwan Strait is reflected in both Beijing's military imports from Russia and domestic weapons production. China has purchased two Russian *Sovremenny*-class destroyers equipped with the advanced Moskit missile. Most recently, China agreed to purchase from Russia two ship-based S-300 air-defense missile systems, which can provide the *Sovremenny* destroyers with air defense capability. China's counter-maritime strategy also is reflected in its purchase of two Russian *Kilo*-class submarines. The submarines can play an access-denial role, interfering with U.S. wartime penetration of Chinese coastal waters, thus compelling the U.S. Navy to conduct operations further from the Taiwan military theater. Access denial was the Soviet Union's primary maritime strategy during the later stages of the Cold War. China also could use the submarines to complicate U.S. efforts to frustrate a Chinese blockade of Taiwan.[50]

China has been purchasing advanced Soviet-era aircraft, including the Su-27 and Su-30, from Moscow. These aircraft fulfill two roles for the Chinese military. First, they fit China's strategy to undermine Taiwan's effort to maintain air superiority over the Taiwan Strait, and Taipei's confidence that it can challenge Chinese interests without risk of war. They correspond to Taiwan's purchase of 150 U.S. F-16s and sixty French Mirage jets, and its domestically manufactured Ching-kuo fighter. While helping to deter Taiwan from declaring independence, these aircraft also contribute to Beijing's long-term effort to coerce Taiwan to unify formally with the mainland. Second, the imported Russian aircraft contribute to China's long-term objective to defend its extensive coastline. They represent Beijing's best and likely most feasible effort over the next fifteen to twenty years to offset the ability of U.S. aircraft, based on carriers and on Okinawa, to penetrate Chinese airspace and challenge the security of China's interior provinces.[51]

While acquiring Soviet ships, missiles, and aircraft, China has been developing its indigenous conventional missile capabilities. Since 1995 it has been deploying approximately 50 to 100 short-range DF-15 missiles per year in a Fujian province across from Taiwan. The accuracy of these missiles has steadily improved. Their immediate purpose is to deter Taiwan from formally declaring sovereign independence from the mainland, by posing an assured threat of retaliation against Taiwan's military facilities and civilian infrastructure. As the accuracy of these missiles improves, they may challenge the security of U.S. naval vessels operating around the straits. China also is working on cruise missile production facilities. Cruise missiles will simultaneously serve China's immediate interest in the Taiwan Strait and its long-term goal of enhancing Chinese security against U.S. military dominance in Chinese coastal waters.[52]

China is developing not only its conventional war-fighting capabilities, but also its strategic nuclear arsenal. There is considerable uncertainty whether Beijing possesses a survivable second-strike capability, considered necessary for dealing with the United States as a great power. Indeed, given the combination of the technology and basing mode of China's intercontinental ballistic missiles (ICBMs), advanced U.S. surveillance capabilities, and the accuracy of U.S. precision-guided conventional weapons and nuclear warheads, China may possess no survivable nuclear capability. In response to its vulnerability to a preemptive strike, China is developing a solid-fuel ICBM that will enable a quick launch-on-warning. When combined with missile mobility, China's next-generation ICBM arsenal might have a minimal second-strike capability, but China will probably not be able to deploy such a solid-fuel ICBM with the range to reach the continental United States for another five to ten years.[53]

It becomes apparent from this discussion that China is responding to U.S. supremacy by working to bolster its capabilities across the military spectrum. Equally important, Chinese leaders understand that the primary source of U.S. military power is its high-technology economy. The development of a market system and the pace of economic reform in China in part reflect the pressures of international politics. In an example of emulation of the most successful state, China is attempting to create the modern economic and social institutions needed to support a modern military. Chinese officials call this "Comprehensive National Power." Moreover, government leaders have developed programs to enhance the technological capacity of those industries at the nexus of China's civilian-military economy. Related is Beijing's effort to foster a high-technology research community in both the civilian sector and in the universities with ties with China's defense industries; Chinese leaders are trying to emulate America's strengths to enhance their own national security.[54]

China also is mobilizing international economic and political resources to balance American power. The most obvious trend in this regard is China's tolerance of growing U.S. military power in East Asia. China's ability to develop its military power is considerably dependent on its ability to exploit continued access to the international economy for markets, foreign investment capital, and new technology. The advanced industrial powers most able to provide China with markets, capital, and technology are located within the U.S. strategic orbit and within the U.S.-dominated global economic system. At the pinnacle of these powers stands China's largest trading partner, the United States itself. As long as China refrains from forcefully challenging the regional status quo, Washington will lack the will or the ability to compel China's most important economic partners to limit their economic ties with China. In addition, premature tension with the United

States would require China to allocate scarce financial resources away from long-term domestic infrastructure and technology development and toward immediate defense needs. To counter the U.S. threat, it would have to buy additional quantities of outdated and ineffective military equipment, undermining the prospect for its long-term modernization and its attainment of greater security vis-à-vis the United States.

Both Chinese security today and Beijing's long-term strategy to balance U.S. power in the future depend on China's willingness to cooperate with the United States, which explains the absence of active and overt diplomatic balancing in Chinese foreign policy and China's tolerance of U.S. expansion on its perimeter. Rather than contend with Washington over Taiwan, missile defense, U.S.-Japanese security cooperation, or the new U.S. military presence in Central Asia, Beijing has thus far sought a "peaceful international environment." As a prerequisite to the mobilization of international economic resources, the development of comprehensive national power and the ability to balance U.S. power, maintaining a peaceful international environment is at the forefront of China's security policy, and presents its best option for achieving unification of Taiwan with the mainland.[55]

But Beijing is not only seeking to mobilize the resources of the United States and its allies. It also is cooperating with Russia, Washington's primary strategic competitor in Eastern Europe and Central Asia. In addition to enhancing its defense capability by buying Russian military equipment, Beijing tries to use common Sino-Russian interests to constrain U.S. policy. Russia has joined China in opposition to U.S. development of a missile defense capability and a long-term U.S. strategic presence in Central Asia. China uses frequent summit meetings between the two countries to express mutual opposition to these U.S. policies, as well as to American "hegemony" and interference in the domestic affairs of other countries. Sino-Russian willingness to resolve border disputes and minimize security conflicts in Central Asia through the Shanghai Cooperation Organization reflects a similar effort to remove sources of tension so that each country can focus on the primary strategic challenge—the United States. The resolution of conflicts between Great Britain and the United States in the Caribbean, Britain and Japan in East Asia during the first decade of the 20th century, and Sino-American rapprochement in the 1970s, reflected similar strategies. These "loose" bilateral relationships did not entail extensive strategic cooperation, but they were part of the balance of power process.

Nonetheless, Sino-Russian cooperation will not make it easier for China or Russia to deal with their most pressing security issues. China cannot help Moscow limit North Atlantic Treaty Organization (NATO) expansion, and Russia cannot influence U.S. policy toward Taiwan. Moreover, neither can compensate the other for the loss of economic ties with the United States and its allies, ties that represent China's and Russia's primary long-term balancing strategies. Hence, neither prioritizes Sino-Russian cooperation over their respective bilateral relationships with the United States, and each is willing to negotiate agreements with the United States that sacrifice the interests of the other. This has been the case with regard to bilateral arms control agreements, which Russia has sought to finalize with the United States despite the fact that U.S. development of a missile defense capability will undermine Chinese security. But, as in past periods of great-power balancing, the absence of a tight alliance does not indicate an absence of balancing. In the 1970s, in the context of U.S.-China strategic cooperation, the United States reached agreements with the Soviet Union that harmed Chinese security. The current "loose" alignment between Russia and China, accompanied by a bilateral reduction in conflict, best serves their interests by enabling each to maximize the pace of balancing through mobilization of international and domestic resources.

Prospects for a Balance of Power in East Asia

A useful assessment of long-term trends in the East Asian balance of power must focus on two sets of issues. First, within the current bipolar order, what is the likelihood of arms races, crises, and war? Second, given China's efforts at balancing U.S. power, what is the prospect that Beijing will be able to challenge the status quo in East Asia and establish a new balance of power? Will China be able be able to "roll back" America's strategic presence in maritime East Asia?

BIPOLARITY, GEOGRAPHY, AND THE SECURITY DILEMMA

Structural realism predicts that the bipolarity of East Asian politics leads to two primary outcomes, one positive, one negative. The positive outcome is that the clarity of threat compels the great powers to mobilize the domestic resources necessary to maintain a regional balance of power without recourse to major war.[56] This prediction seems borne out by China's balancing behavior. Beijing is relying primarily on domestic resources to balance U.S. power. But structural realism also offers a negative prognosis that, because bipolarity exacerbates the security dilemma, balancing will be characterized by high threat perception and therefore unnecessarily high tension and costly foreign policies. In contrast to multipolarity, in a bipolar balance, clarity of threat leads to an intense concern for reputation and repeated "tests of will" over regional issues, no matter how peripheral to the balance of power. The Cold War U.S.-Soviet conflict seems to validate this argument, with its nuclear arm races, numerous crises, and repeated great-power interventions in the Third World.[57]

In the 21st century, will a bipolar East Asia be similarly plagued by high tension and contentious foreign policies? The East Asian balance of power is bipolar, but polarity is only one element contributing to the character of great-power relations. East Asia is not only bipolar, but it also is divided into distinct continental and maritime spheres of influence. The contrasting interests of maritime powers and continental powers, and the geography of East Asia, contribute to the prospect of 21st-century great-power conflict characterized by a relatively low level of tension. Different geographically determined interests can lead states to prefer different weapons systems. This can have a profound impact on the security dilemma. The combination of geography and weapons specialization can lead to a defensive bias that mitigates the security dilemma and thus the effect of bipolarity on the prevalence of crises and arms races; such an outcome might even reduce the role of nuclear weapons in preserving national security.[58]

In a confrontation between a land power and maritime power, each side's military strengths are at a disadvantage in the other's theater. Thus, China is inferior to the United States in maritime theaters and the United States is inferior to China in ground force activities on mainland East Asia. This dichotomy means that the defensive force enjoys an advantage in each theater. In these circumstances, neither side has to fear that the other side's provocative diplomacy or troop movements are a prelude to attack and thus immediate escalate to full military readiness. Crises can be slower to develop, allowing the protagonists to manage their reactions to avoid unnecessary escalation. In a mainland contingency, China's massive conventional retaliatory capability allows its leaders to observe U.S. behavior rather than prematurely prepare for war. Thus, in 1994 and 2003, when the United States prepared to attack North Korea's nuclear weapons production sites and risked a larger war on the Korean Peninsula, China did not put its forces on alert and it did not prepare for imminent war with the United States. Chinese superiority on the East Asian mainland encourages Beijing's confidence that it can defend its borders against the United States, even after an initial U.S. engagement and despite overwhelming overall U.S. superiority.[59]

Similarly, the U.S. ability to retaliate and rapidly destroy China's surface fleet allows Washington to wait for China to fire the first shot. This is the case in the Taiwan theater, despite the fact that the island is so close to the mainland and is situated within both the maritime and continental theaters. Each great power's distinct abilities can be brought to bear on the cross-strait balance. For this reason, the Taiwan issue has remained unresolved for over fifty years. Nonetheless, geography influences politics to diminish the likelihood of crises in the Taiwan Strait. Chinese capabilities, especially missile forces and aircraft, can threaten Taiwan, but they do not give China a decisive first-strike capability against U.S. naval forces. U.S. naval superiority ensures that even should China strike first, it would not be able to deny the United States the ability to devastate Chinese maritime forces and frustrate Beijing's ability to coerce Taiwan into unification. In these circumstances, Chinese posturing, military signaling, and political use of force do not lead to U.S. preparations for war and do not escalate into crises. Such was the case in 1996, when China conducted provocative military exercises in the Taiwan Strait and the United States responded by dispatching two aircraft carriers to the vicinity of the Taiwan theater. This was a mutual show of force, but the United States did not consider itself in a crisis and it did not prepare for war.[60]

These mainland-maritime dynamics also affect the prospect for arms races. Because each power has a defensive advantage in its own theater, both can resist an equivalent escalatory response to the other's military acquisitions. Each augmentation of China's land power capabilities does not create a corresponding diminution of U.S. security in maritime East Asia. Similarly, an enhanced U.S. maritime presence in the South China Sea does not bring an equivalent decrease in Chinese security on the mainland. Bipolar pressures for a spiraling arms race are thus minimized. Because China and the United States feel secure with the conventional balance within their respective theaters, neither is compelled to adopt a massive nuclear retaliation strategy, either to deter an attack on its own forces or to make credible an extended deterrence commitment. Thus, neither side greatly fears that the other would use nuclear weapons first during a crisis, and there is little likelihood of a nuclear arms race between them.

If these constructive dynamics exist within the U.S.-China relationship, why did they not characterize the bipolar U.S.-Soviet struggle, which was equally a contest between a land power and sea power? Again, the answer lies in geography. Whereas in East Asia geography mitigates the pressures of bipolarity, the openness of the Europe landscape reinforced bipolar pressures, aggravating the security dilemma. Because of geography, the United States could not rely on maritime containment of the Soviet Union to achieve its vital interests. It required a military presence on mainland Europe to deny the Soviet Union the combination of a secure continental base and access to strategic seas. Thus, the Cold War confrontation on the European continent brought together the army of a continental power and an army of a maritime power. Because of a widely perceived Soviet conventional force advantage, NATO believed that Moscow would benefit from an offensive attack.[61] Whereas in East Asia geography offsets 21st-century bipolar pressures to mitigate the security dilemma, European geography reinforced Cold War bipolarity to aggravate the security dilemma. This pressure resulted in the rapid escalation of the Cold War in the 1940s, and the various Berlin crises, in which the two powers stood literally face-to-face.

Soviet conventional offensive advantages also contributed to the nuclear arms race. U.S. leaders believed that they could not mobilize the resources to maintain sufficient ground forces in Europe to deny the Soviet Union the benefits of an offensive strategy and thus deter a Soviet attack on Western Europe. Their response was the Eisenhower administration's "New Look," whereby the United States would rely on nuclear forces and the threat of massive retaliation to offset Soviet conventional force superiority and to deter an invasion of Western Europe. This strategy required the Pentagon to increase its nuclear forces and contributed to the nuclear security dilemma.[62] The combination of Cold-War bipolarity and European geography resulted in the forty-year nuclear arms race. In East Asia, by contrast, geography and the resulting defensive advantage held by each great power in its respective sphere of influence diminish each power's reliance on nuclear weapons for deterrence and thus offset bipolar pressures for spiraling escalation of nuclear capabilities.

The geopolitics of 21st-century East Asia offsets the heightened great-power tensions inherent in bipolar situations, but it reinforces the impact of bipolarity on great-power management of international order. In contrast to great-power cooperation in a multipolar balance, the great powers in bipolar structures not only have a greater stake in international order, but their disproportionate share of capabilities gives them the ability to assume the burden of order and to accept the free-riding of smaller states. This is easier when allies' contributions to security and their ability to resist are negligible.[63] In East Asia, China towers over its smaller neighbors and the United States towers over its security partners. But geopolitics reinforces these dynamics. Because the Chinese and American spheres of influence are geographically distinct and separated by water, intervention by one power in its own sphere does not threaten the interests of the other power in its sphere. In these circumstances, intervention is less likely to elicit great-power tension.[64] Freed from the worry of great-power retaliation, each country has a relatively freer hand to impose order on its allies. Thus, in the late 1980s and early 1990s, China managed the conflict in Cambodia to achieve both regional order and its security interests in Indochina without eliciting U.S. concern and countermeasures. Similarly, U.S. domination of the international response to the collapse of political order and separatism in Indonesia in the late 1990s did not elicit Beijing's opposition. In contrast, Soviet military interventions in Eastern Europe during the 1950s and 1960s led to heightened NATO concern over Soviet intentions.

THE RISE OF CHINA AND A NEW BALANCE OF POWER?

For China to establish a new balance of power in East Asia, it will have to close the gap in capabilities between itself and the United States and establish a strong naval presence. Although China is developing its military capabilities, it has not been able to alter the U.S.-Chinese balance of power. On the contrary, U.S. consolidation of its strategic relationships in Asia, its increased regional deployments and its advances in modern weaponry have expanded U.S. military superiority over China. As Chinese leaders recognize, China must develop its economy and social institutions before it can challenge U.S. superiority. This will not be easy.

China's ability to establish economic parity with the United States is undermined by America's head start. Due to the large difference in the size of the two countries' economies, America's smaller growth rate still allows it to increase its absolute lead when it comes to the gap in size between the two economies. During the 1990s, the gap between the U.S. and Chinese gross domestic product grew even though China's annual growth rate was more than twice that of the United States. According to some studies, if the Chinese economy grows at an annual rate of 6 percent and that of the U.S. grows 3 percent annually, China will not catch up to the United States until 2043.[65] This economic reality places significant long-term constraints on China's ability to spend the resources necessary to close the gap between U.S. and Chinese military capabilities.

But China's ability to balance U.S. power and challenge U.S. maritime supremacy will require far more than economic growth and military spending. In the 19th century, converting wealth to power was relatively easy. Technologies for steel and iron production and the manufacturing of guns and railways were easily copied and could be readily developed with sufficient investment. By contrast, in the 21st century, money cannot purchase the intellectual and social infrastructure necessary for the development of an advanced economy. Nations can use foreign investment to manufacture domestically advanced technology goods, but great-power capability requires indigenous manufacturing capabilities. Thus, the manufacture of high-speed microprocessor computer chips in China by foreign corporations, for example, no more signifies a growing sophistication in China's high-technology manufacturing industries than does the People's Liberation Army's (PLA) use of imported Soviet military aircraft represent an advance by China's defense industries. Until China can build the factories that manufacture high-technology products, which will require development of first-class universities and research centers and the capacity to move basic research into the commercial sector, it will be dependent on the U.S.-dominated international economy for maintenance and repairs, spare parts, and next year's technology, and it will not be more able to contend in a war with the United States.

America's head start in financial resources, technology, and military capabilities, and the difficulties of copying the U.S. economic and social infrastructures, impose a significant barrier to China's ability to balance U.S. power. But China's multiple threat environment also will limit its balancing capabilities. Thirteen countries border China, and its long border with Russia will remain a significant security concern. As Chinese commentators frequently observe, although Russia today is economically, politically, and militarily weak, it retains the resources required to pose a formidable military threat someday to China. This is the case especially in Central Asia, a theater close to the Russian heartland but far from China's industrial and population centers, and separated by inhospitable desert climate and terrain. China's Central Asian frontier is Beijing's strategic vulnerability just as the Russian Far East is Moscow's strategic vulnerability. Thus, the prospect of Sino-Soviet competition for the allegiance of the Central Asian states, in a reenactment of the 19th century "great game" between Russia and Britain, cannot be dismissed. Moreover, not only does Moscow continue to deploy its forces in the Central Asian countries, but many Russians believe that China poses the greatest long-term threat to Russian security. Whereas U.S. naval forces and territory are protected from China by the Pacific Ocean, Russian territory is vulnerable to Chinese land forces.[66] The mere fact that Russia and China are neighbors means that Chinese leaders cannot be confident that China's borders will remain secure and prevents them from focusing on the development of China's maritime power.

China's border concerns are not limited to Russian power. In Central Asia there are small countries that border China with weak governments and whose territory could be used by larger powers to threaten China's territorial integrity. Moreover, China must pay attention to the long-term prospect for domestic instability in its western provinces, where religious and ethnic minorities identify with the majority populations of China's potentially hostile and unstable neighbors.[67] Southwest China is bordered by India, which seeks regional hegemony and may have great-power aspirations beyond South Asia. Southern China is bordered by Vietnam, which still yearns for a great-power ally to enable it to come out from under China's strategic shadow. In Northeast Asia, the Korean Peninsula can be used by a great power to threaten China's industrial heartland, as Japan and then the United States did in the first half of the 20th century.

China has to be confident in a stable strategic status quo on its land borders before it can devote budgetary resources for building naval power. A powerful navy is necessary for China to establish strategic influence off the East Asian mainland and to challenge America in its maritime sphere of influence so that it can become a "rising power" throughout East Asia. Mahan went so far as to argue that "history has conclusively demonstrated the inability of a state with even a single continental frontier to compete in naval development with one that is insular, although of smaller population and resources."[68] The challenge to the land power seeking maritime power is even greater in the 21st century, when the relative costs and technology requirements of maritime power projection include construction of the air-craft carrier and its specialized aircraft, as well as the associated support ves-sels and advanced technologies necessary to protect the carrier.

Given the technological and financial requirements of maritime power, by 2025 China could at best develop a "luxury fleet" similar to the one devel-oped by the Soviet Union in the latter stage of the Cold War. Such a second-order fleet, if supported by effective land-based aircraft, might be able to mount a credible coastal defense by using access denial to push the U.S. Navy further from the Chinese mainland, and to block unrestricted U.S. penetration of Chinese air space. It also might be able to disrupt U.S. naval activities further from shore. But such limited capabilities could not provide the foundation for a great-power military able to challenge U.S. supremacy in maritime East Asia.[69]

The Balance of Power in the 21st Century

China's ability to catch up with American economic and strategic power is very much in doubt. The combination of U.S. technology and military pol-icy is expanding America's comprehensive superiority over China. China is responding by modernizing its military and developing its economy. Despite each side's best effort to enhance its relative power, the balance of power in East Asia will remain stable well into the 21st century.

Growing U.S. superiority and military deployments in East Asia help to consolidate the existing strategic status quo rather than challenge it. Amer-ica's increasing presence in maritime East Asia reinforces U.S. power in its existing sphere of influence. Enhanced U.S. regional deployments do not bolster American war-fighting capability on mainland East Asia, and can-not provide the basis for a "roll back" strategy, whereby the United States would expand its power at the expense of China's sphere of influence. China's improving capabilities similarly reinforce the strategic status quo. China's military is developing the ability to project power into maritime

East Asia from forces deployed on the Chinese coast. The resulting power projection capability will likely enhance China's coastal security, but it still will not be able to challenge American domination of the East Asian littoral, where U.S. allies and naval and air force bases are located. Long-term U.S. naval and air superiority provide the United States with the ability to resist any Chinese attempt to develop maritime capabilities that can challenge U.S. power.

East Asia is bipolar, but there will remain only one superpower. China will not be able to challenge the status quo in East Asia, much less develop the superpower capabilities necessary to establish a global bipolar system. Nonetheless, that does not mean that U.S. global power will not be balanced. Rather, it suggests that a multipolar balance of power, characterized by a counter-American global alliance, is the likely entity to establish a global balance.

The post-Cold War system is very much like the post-World War II system. The United States has emerged from the most recent great-power competition looming over its former rivals and coalition partners, just as it did in 1945. The difference today is of degree, not kind—the United States is simply more powerful today than it was then. Hence, it will take longer for competitors to restore a global balance of power in the 21st century. And just as after World War II, a multipolar coalition will be required to contend with America's superpower, multiregional strategic heft. Only a Sino-Russian alliance will be able to balance U.S. power simultaneously in Europe and East Asia.

China and Russia have already laid the basis for a possible counter-American alliance. Neither country will have to become America's equal on its own for their combined power to enable challenges to U.S. global power. China certainly was not America's equal in the 1950s and 1960s when, in alliance with the Soviet Union, it challenged U.S. strategic ambitions on the Korean Peninsula, in Indochina, and on Taiwan. Rather, China and Russia each have to develop sufficient domestic stability and be able to devote sufficient resources to long-term military modernization so that they can draw confidence from each other's strengths and risk war with the United States. When this occurs, America's global reach will once again confront global challenges, undermining Washington's ability to focus its resources on one power in one region, thus restoring a global balance of power through the combination of a "partial rise" of China and Russia, and a corresponding "stretch" of U.S. resources over multiple theaters.

Russia will recover its great-power capabilities. Such has been the case following every Russian setback since the early 19th century. When it does recover, in the next decade or two, it will not likely be as an East Asian great power. Its recent turn as a great power in the east was an aberration, reflecting unique and non-replicable regional conditions. Moreover, during Russia's ongoing recovery, its ability to project power into East Asia will be the last to develop. But it will develop capabilities in Central Asia and Eastern Europe, based on its ground force orientation and these regions' proximity to Russia's economic and population centers. In these circumstances, Moscow will likely prioritize its strategic objectives rather than simultaneously contend with China and the United States, and it will likely emphasize its security vis-à-vis the United States rather than vis-à-vis China. Not only will the United States be more powerful than China, but it also will possess a strategic presence on Russia's most sensitive borders. Moscow will focus its resources on diminishing the U.S. strategic presence on its western border.

China similarly will have to prioritize its military modernization program and its strategic objectives. Given its own ground-force capability, it will likely be able to contend with the Russian military in Central Asia while holding the Russian Far East hostage to Moscow's cooperation in Central Asia. But China will remain concerned about the U.S. strategic presence on its coastal perimeter. Just as Russia will prioritize the "roll back" of the American presence in Eastern Europe, China will prioritize the roll back of the U.S. presence on Taiwan. Common interest in resisting U.S. power in their respective theaters drove the Sino-Soviet alliance in the 1950s, and will likely be the basis of enhanced Sino-Russian strategic cooperation in the 21st century.

In a global system comprising one superpower, multiple regional balances can be the basis of the global balance of power. In the 21st century, the United States will be the only superpower, but there will be two bipolar systems, one in Europe and one in East Asia. Together, based on Chinese and Russian balancing behavior, these regional systems will reestablish a global balance of power.

Notes

1. William T. R. Fox, *The Superpowers: The United States, Britain, and the Soviet Union—Their Responsibility for Peace* (New York: Harcourt Brace, 1944). For an implicit yet similar definition, see Colin S. Gray, *The Politics of Super Power* (Lexington: University Press of Kentucky, 1988), 45.

2. John Mearsheimer, *The Tragedy of Great Power Politics* (New York: Norton, 2001).

3. Kenneth E. Boulding, *Conflict and Defense: A General Theory* (New York: Harper & Row, 1963); Mearsheimer, *Tragedy.*

4. For considerations of the interplay between global and regional orders, see David A. Lake and Patrick M. Morgan (eds.), *Regional Orders: Building Security in a New World* (University Park: Penn State University Press, 1997); Barry Buzan, "A Framework for Regional Security Analysis," in Barry Buzan and Gowher Rizvi (eds.), *South Asian Insecurity and the Great Powers* (London: Macmillan, 1986).

5. See, for example, Glenn H. Snyder and Paul Diesing, *Conflict Among Nations: Bargaining, Decision Making, and System Structure in International Crises* (Princeton: Princeton University Press, 1977), 462–70; Joshua S. Goldstein and John R. Freeman, *Three-Way Street: Strategic Reciprocity in World Politics* (Chicago: University of Chicago Press, 1990); Robert S. Ross (ed.), *China, the United States, and the Soviet Union: Tripolarity and Policy Making in the Cold War* (Armonk, N.Y.: M.E. Sharpe, 1993); and Lowell Dittmer, "The Strategic Triangle: An Elementary Game-Theoretic Analysis," *World Politics* 31 (July 1981): 484–511. On the rise of China in a great-power role, see Gerald Segal, *The Great Power Triangle* (New York: St. Martin's, 1982).

6. On the sources of U.S.-China rapprochement, see Robert S. Ross, *Negotiating Cooperation: The United States and China, 1969–1989* (Stanford: Stanford University Press, 1995).

7. See, for example, Aleksey Georgiyevich Arbatov, "Military Reform," *Mirovaya Ekonomika i Mezhdunarodnyye Otnosheniya* 4 (July 17, 1997), in the Foreign Broadcast Information Service (FBIS), July 18, 1997 (UMA-97-136-S); *Sovetskaya Rossiya*, July 9, 1998, in FBIS, July 10, 1998 (SOV-98-190); *Interfax*, December 4, 1997, in FBIS, December 5, 1997 (UMA-97-338); NTV (Moscow), February 6, 1998, in FBIS, February 17, 1998 (UMA-98-44). Also see Stephen J. Blank, "Who's Minding the Store? The Failure of Russian Security Policy," *Problems of Post-Communism* 45 (March–April 1998).

8. On recent improvements in People's Liberation Army (PLA) training, see June Teufel Dryer, "The New Officer Corps: Implications for the Future," *China Quarterly* 146 (June 1996): 315–35; Dennis J. Blasko, Philip T. Klapkis, and John F. Corbett Jr., "Training Tomorrow's PLA: A Mixed Bag of Tricks," *China Quarterly* 146 (June 1996): 448–524.

9. See Almaty Kazakh Commercial TV, May 2, 2002, in FBIS, May 2, 2002 (Document ID: CEP20020502000119).

10. On the evolution of Thai security policy, see Sukhumbhand Paribatra, "Dictates of Security: Thailand's Relations with the PRC," in Joyce K. Kallgren, Noordin Sopiee, and Soedjati Djiwandono (eds.), *ASEAN and China: An Evolving Relationship* (Berkeley: Institute of East Asian Studies, University of California, 1988); Khien Theeravit, "The United States, Thailand, and the Indochinese Conflict," in Hans H. Indorf, *Thai-American Relations in Contemporary Affairs* (Singapore: Executive Publications, 1982).

11. On Vietnamese accommodation to Chinese power, see Michael Leifer, "Vietnam's Foreign Policy in the Post-Soviet Era: Coping with Vulnerability," in Robert S. Ross (ed.), *East Asia in Transition: Toward a New Regional Order* (Armonk, N.Y.: M.E. Sharpe, 1995). On China's victory in Indochina, see Robert S. Ross, "China and the Cambodian Peace Process: The Benefits of Coercive Diplomacy," *Asian Survey* 31 (December 1991).

12. "China Becomes South Korea's Number One Investment Target," *China Daily*, February 2, 2002, http://www1.chinadaily.com.cn/news/2002-02-05/55641.html. On the development of China-South Korean ties, see Victor D. Cha, "Engaging China: The View from Korea," in Alastair Iain Johnston and Robert S. Ross (eds.), *Engaging China: Management of a Rising Power* (London: Routledge, 1999).

13. For the Pentagon's explanation of its naval strategy, see United States Department of Defense, *East Asia Strategy Report* (Washington, D.C.: U.S. Department of Defense, 1995); United States Senate, Senate Armed Forces Committee, Testimony of Adm. Charles R. Larson, Commander in Chief, U.S. Pacific Command, U.S. Senate, 103rd Congress, second session, March 2, 1994; United States House of Representatives, House Committee on National Security, Statement of Adm. Joseph W. Prueher, U.S. House of Representatives, 105th Congress, second session, March 4, 1998. The agreement with the Philippines was announced in Manila by U.S. Secretary of Defense William Cohen on January 14, 1998.

14. On the Chinese Air Force, see for example, Kenneth W. Allen, "China and the Use of Force: The Role of the PLA Air Force," Center for Naval Analysis, forthcoming; Paul H. B. Godwin, "PLA Doctrine, Strategy, and Capabilities Toward 2000," in *China Quarterly* 146 (June 1996): 443–87.

15. David A. Schlapak, David T. Orletsky, and Barry A. Wilson, *Dire Strait?: Military Aspects of the China-Taiwan Confrontation and Options for U.S. Policy* (Santa Monica, Calif.: RAND, 2000), 38–45.

16. Stephen Walt, *The Origin of Alliances* (Ithaca: Cornell University Press, 1987).

17. Aaron L. Friedberg, *The Weary Titan: Britain and the Experience of Relative Decline, 1895–1905* (Princeton: Princeton University Press, 1988); Ian Nish, *The Anglo-Japanese Alliance: The Diplomacy of Two Island Empires, 1894–1907* (London: Athlone, 1966); John King Fairbank, Edwin O. Reischauer, Albert M.

Craig, *East Asia: Tradition and Transformation* (Boston: Houghton Mifflin, 1978), 555–56.

18. Ian Nish, *The Origins of the Russo-Japanese War* (New York: Longman, 1985); Fairbank, *East Asia: Tradition and Transformation*, 555–56, 692–93, 755–56; Michael A. Barnhart, *Japan Prepares for Total War: The Search for Economic Security, 1919–1941* (Ithaca: Cornell University Press, 1987).

19. Barnhart, *Japan Prepares*, 91–94, 156.

20. Ibid., 198–203; Akira Iriye, *Across the Pacific* (Imprint Publications, 1992), 207–08.

21. Barnhart, *Japan Prepares*, 67–75, 154.

22. See Robert Scalapino's cogent discussion of the strategic context of Japan's failure to achieve its great-power ambitions in James William Morley (ed.), *The Fateful Choice: Japan's Advance into Southeast Asia, 1939–1941* (New York: Columbia University Press, 1980), 121–23.

23. Also see Michael M. May, "Correspondence: Japan as a Superpower?" *International Security* 18 (Winter 1993–94). On Japan's energy vulnerability, see Michael M. May, *Energy and Security in East Asia* (Stanford: Institute for International Studies, Stanford University, 1998).

24. Halford J. Mackinder, *Democratic Ideals and Reality* (Westport, Conn.: Greenwood, 1981), 55–57.

25. On the importance of the navy in the U.S. bombing of Japan, see George W. Baer, *One Hundred Years of Sea Power: 1890–1990* (Stanford: Stanford University Press, 1993), 262–72.

26. Alfred T. Mahan, *The Problem of Asia* (Port Washington, N.Y.: Kennikat, 1970), 106–7.

27. For an enlightening discussion of Russian frustration at trying to overcome the geographic obstacles of expansion into the Far East, see Walter A. McDougall, *Let the Sea Make a Noise: A History of the North Pacific from Magellan to MacArthur* (New York: Basic, 1993).

28. See the excellent treatment of the Sino-Russian territorial conflict in S. C. M. Paine, *Imperial Rivals: China, Russia, and Their Disputed Frontier* (Armonk, N.Y.: M.E. Sharpe, 1997), 52–57, 87–88.

29. John J. Stephan, *The Russian Far East: A History* (Stanford: Stanford University Press, 1994), 57, 84–85; David Wolff, "Russia Finds Its Limits: Crossing Borders into Manchuria," in Stephen Kotkin and David Wolff (eds.), *Rediscovering Russia in Asia: Siberia and the Russian Far East* (Armonk, N.Y.: M.E. Sharpe, 1995), 42.

30. Donald W. Mitchell, *A History of Russian and Soviet Sea Power* (New York: Macmillan, 1974), 204–10 and 216–33; chaps. 11, 12.

31. Stephan, *The Russian Far East*, 163; Hara Teruyuki, "Japan Moves North: The Japanese Occupation of Northern Sakhalin (1920s)," in Kotkin and Wolff (eds.), *Rediscovering Russia in Asia*.

32. Stephan, *Russian Far East,* 266. In post-Soviet Russia, the Baikal-Amur Railway continues to be plagued with various problems. See *Delovy Mir,* July 25– July 29, 1997, in FBIS, August 18, 1997 (SOV-970157-S).

33. On Soviet naval facilities in the Far East, see Baer, *One Hundred Years of Sea Power.* On overall Soviet conventional deployments in the Far East, see Paul F. Langer, "Soviet Military Power in Asia," in Donald S. Zagoria (ed.), *Soviet Policy in Asia* (New Haven: Yale University Press, 1982); Robert A Scalapino, "Asia in a Global Context: Strategic Issues for the Soviet Union," and Harry Gelman, "The Soviet Far East Military Buildup: Motives and Prospects," in Richard H. Solomon and Masataka Kosaka (eds.), *The Soviet Far East Military Buildup: Nuclear Dilemmas and Asian Security* (Dover, Mass.: Auburn, 1986); Harry Gelman, *The Soviet Far East Buildup and Soviet Risk-Taking Against China* (Santa Monica, Calif.: RAND, 1982).

34. On contemporary Sino-Russian relations, see Elizabeth Wishnick, *Mending Fences: The Evolution of Moscow's China Policy from Brezhnev to Yeltsin* (Seattle: University of Washington Press, 2002); James Clay Moltz, "Regional Tensions in the Russo-Japanese Rapprochement," *Asian Survey* 35 (June 1995); Gilbert Rozman, "Northeast China: Waiting for Regionalism," *Problems of Post-Communism* 45 (July–August 1998): 3–13; Gilbert Rozman, "The Crisis of the Russian Far East: Who Is to Blame?" *Problems of Post-Communism* 44 (September–October 1997): 3–12.

35. On offensive realism, see Mearsheimer, *Tragedy.*

36. For a discussion of recent developments in the U.S.-Taiwan defense relationship, see *Washington Post,* April 30, 2002, 12; *China Times,* July 20, 2001. For a recent Chinese assessment of these trends, see *Shijie Zhishi* (*World Outlook*), April 1, 2002, in FBIS/China, April 11, 2002; "Where Lie the Mistakes of Bush's Policy Toward Taiwan," *Renmin Ribao* (English edition), April 26, 2002, at http://english.peopledaily.com.cn/200204/26/print/20020426_94735.html.

37. U.S. Department of Defense (DoD), *Quadrennial Defense Review* (QDR) (Washington, D.C.: U.S. Department of Defense, 2001). For an analysis of this report, see Michael McDevitt, "The QDR and East Asia," *Proceedings,* March 2002, 87–88. Also see United States Department of Defense, "Special DoD News Briefing—Conventional Forces Study," June 22, 2001. On regional deployments, see *Washington Post,* April 30, 2002, 12; Yang Lei, "U.S. Strategy Is Pointed Straight at Asia," *Renmin Ribao* (Guangzhou South China News Supplement), April 3, 2001, in FBIS/China, document number FBIS-CHI-2001-0403.

38. U.S. Department of Defense, *Annual Report to the President and the Congress, 2002,* chap. 5; available at http://www.defenselink.mil/execsec/adr2002/index.htm.

39. U.S. DoD, *QDR 2001*; U.S. House of Representatives, House International Relations Committee, Subcommittee on East Asia and the Pacific and Subcommittee on Middle East and South Asia, Statement of Adm. Dennis C. Blair, Commander in Chief U.S. Pacific Command, to the Subcommittees, February 27,

2002; Thomas E. Ricks and Walter Pincus, "Pentagon Plans Major Changes in U.S. Strategy," *Washington Post*, May 7, 2001, 1; and James Dao, "Army to Move Some Weapons Out of Europe," *New York Times*, August 31, 2001, 16; *Straits Times*, June 4, 2002.

40. U.S. DoD, *Annual Report 2002*, chap. 5; James Brook, "U.S. Makes Guam a Hub of Asia Strategy," International Herald Tribune, April 8, 2004, 2.

41. For Chinese attention to these trends, see, for example, Cai Wei, "Mei Haijun Zhunbei Jinnian Xiaji jiang Sansou Luoshanji ji He Jianting Bushu dao Guandao" [U.S. Navy This Year in the Summer Will Deploy Three *Los Angeles*-Class Nuclear Submarines to Guam], *Huanqiu Shibao*, May 9, 2002, 17; Lei, "U.S. Strategy Is Pointed Straight at Asia"; Wu Qingli, "At Whom Is the U.S. Asia-Pacific Strategic Spearhead Pointed," and Han Xudong and Wei Konghu, "United States Overhauls Military Strategy, Shifts Focus from Europe to Asia," *Liaowang*, May 21, 2001, in FBIS, Document Number FBIS-CHI-2001-0530; *Renmin Wang*, March 29, 2002, in FBIS, Document Number FBIS-CHI-2002-0331. For a Chinese discussion of U.S. rapid deployment capabilities, see Zhai, *Lengzhanhou de Meiguo Junshi Zhanlue*, 93–94.

42. Owen R. Cote Jr., *The Future of the Trident Force: Enabling Access in Access-Constrained Environments* (Cambridge: Security Studies Program, Massachusetts Institute of Technology, 2002); U.S. DoD, *QDR 2001*; Robert Aronson, "SSGN: A 'Second Career' for the Boomer Force," *Undersea Warfare* 2 (Winter 1999), available at http://www.chinfo.navy.mil/navpalib/cno/n87/usw/issue_6/ssgn.html. For a Chinese discussion of the vulnerability of China's coast to U.S. strikes, see "Kongjun Zhihui Xueyuan Zhuanjia Tan—21 Shiji de Fangkong Geming" [Air Force Command College Experts Discuss—The 21st Century Revolution in Air Defense], *Jiefang Junbao*, May 16, 2001, 9; Yu Kaitang and Cao Shuxin (eds.), *Tezhong Kongxi Mubiao yu Dui Kang Lilun Yanjiu* [Theoretical Research on Special Air-attack Targets and Counterattack] (Beijing: Guofang Daxue Chubanshe, 2000); Wang and Zhang, *Zhanyi Xue*, chap. 12; Wang and Chen, *Daying Gao Jishu Jubu Zhanzheng*.

43. Jim Mannion, "Pentagon Moves Cruise Missiles to Guam," *Space Daily*, available at http://www.spacedaily.com/news/missiles-00d.html.

44. Adam J. Hebert, "Footholds on the Asian Rim," *Air Force* 85 (November 2002), available at http://www.afa.org/magazine/Nov2002/1102rim.asp.

45. For an early Chinese response to the U.S. presence, see Gao Qifu, "U.S. Wishful Thinking on Its Military Presence in Central Asia and Its Real Purpose," *Liaowang*, April 29, 2002, in FBIS/China, May 6, 2002.

46. For a discussion of the U.S. war in Afghanistan, see Michael E. O'Hanlon, "A Flawed Masterpiece," *Foreign Affairs* 81 (May/June 2002), and *New York Times*, April 9, 2002, A14. Defense budget figures are from the International Institute of Strategic Studies, *Military Balance 2003–2004*, at http://www.iiss.org/membersarea.php.

47. For U.S. emphasis on the strategic role of precision-guided conventional

weaponry, see the excerpts from the DoD, *2002 Nuclear Policy Review*, available at
http://www.globalsecurity.org/wmd/library/policy/dod/npr.htm; also see Michael
R. Gordon, "U.S. Nuclear Plan Sees New Targets and New Weapons," *New York
Times*, March 10, 2002, 1; *Boston Globe*, May 14, 2002.

48. See, for example, Keith B. Payne, *The Fallacies of Cold War Deterrence and
a New Direction* (Lexington: University Press of Kentucky, 2001), chap. 6; Peter
W. Rodman, *Shield Embattled: Missile Defense as a Foreign Policy Problem* (Wash-
ington, D.C.: Nixon Center, 2002), 43–55; Richard D. Fisher, "China Increasing
Its Missile Forces While Opposing U.S. Missile Defense," Heritage Foundation,
Backgrounder, no. 1268 (April 7, 1999).

49. On the recent increases, see John Pomfret, "China Raises Defense Budget
Again: Push to Increase Regional Influence Hampered by Army's Struggle to
Modernize," *Washington Post*, March 5, 2002, A10; Ching Ching Ni, "China to
Boost Defense Spending by 12 Percent," *Los Angeles Times*, March 7, 2000, 4.

50. On trends in the Chinese Navy, see Bernard D. Cole, *The Great Wall at
Sea: China's Navy Enters the Twenty-First Century* (Annapolis, Md.: Naval Institute
Press, 2001).

51. On China's Air Force, see Allen, "PLA Air Force Operations and Modernization;" Allen, "China and the Use of Force."

52. U.S. Department of Defense, *Annual Report on the Military Power of the
People's Republic of China* (Washington, D.C.: Department of Defense, 2003),
47–48; National Intelligence Council (NIC), *Foreign Missile Developments and
the Ballistic Missile Threat Through 2015* (Washington, D.C.: National Intelligence
Council, 2001), 8–9; Mark Stokes, "Weapons of Precise Destruction: PLA Space
and Theater Missile Development," in NIC, *China and Weapons of Mass Destruction: Implications for the United States* (Washington, D.C.: United States National
Intelligence Council, 2000).

53. U.S. Department of Defense, *Annual Report on the Military Power of the
People's Republic of China*, 31; NIC, *Foreign Missile Developments*, 8–9; Bates Gill
and James Mulvenon, "The Chinese Strategic Rocket Forces: Transition to Credi-
ble Deterrence," in NIC, *China and Weapons of Mass Destruction*, 34–40; "NRDC
Nuclear Notebook: Chinese Nuclear Forces, 2001," in *Bulletin of the Atomic Scien-
tists*, 57 (September/October, 2001), 71–72; also see John Wilson Lewis and Hua
Di, "China's Ballistic Missile Programs: Technologies, Strategies, and Goals,"
International Security 17 (Fall 1992): 5–40.

54. On China's high-technology development strategy, see Evan A. Feigen-
baum, *China's Techno-Warriors: National Security and Strategic Competition from
the Nuclear to the Information Age* (Stanford: Stanford University Press, 2003).

55. See, for example, Zhang Wannian, *Dangdai Shijie Junshi yu Zhongguo
Guofang* [Contemporary World Military Affairs and Chinese National Defense]
(Zhonggong Zhongyang Dangxiao Chubanshe, 2000), 76–77; Chu Shulong,
"Zhongguo de Guojia Liyi, Guojia Liliang he Guojia Zhanlue" [China's National
Interest, National Strength, and National Strategy], *Zhanlue yu Guanli*, no. 4

(1999): 16–17; Shi Yinhong, "Guanyu Taiwan Wenti de Jixiang Bixu Zhengshi de Da Zhanlue Wenti [Several Great Strategic Issues Regarding the Taiwan Issue that Must Be Squarely Faced], *Zhanlue yu Guanli*, no. 2 (2000), 31; Wang Yizhou, "Mianxiang 21 Shiji de Zhongguo Waijiao: San Xuqiu de Xunqiu ji qi Pingheng" [Chinese Diplomacy Facing the 21st Century: The Search for the Three Musts and their Balance], *Zhanlue yu Guanli*, no. 6 (1999), 21.

56. Kenneth N. Waltz, *Theory of International Politics* (Reading, Mass.: Addison-Wesley, 1979), chap. 8; Glenn H. Snyder, *Alliance Politics* (Ithaca: Cornell University Press, 1998), 346–49.

57. See Robert Jervis, *Systems Affects: Complexity in Political and Social Life* (Princeton: Princeton University Press, 1997), 118–22, for a discussion of why bipolarity produces heightened great-power tension, including intervention in the Third World. See Waltz, *Theory of International Politics*, chap. 8, for the application of bipolar arguments to the Cold War.

58. On the impact of weapons systems on the security dilemma, see Robert Jervis, "Cooperation Under the Security Dilemma," *World Politics* 30 (January 1978): 167–214; see Waltz, *Theory of International Politics*, 93, 118, on the assumption of emulation.

59. Interviews with Chinese military officers and civilian analysts, Beijing, 2003.

60. Robert S. Ross, "The 1995–96 Taiwan Strait Confrontation: Coercion, Credibility, and the Use of Force," *International Security* 25 (Fall 2000): 87–123. Also see the memoir literature. Ashton B. Carter and William J. Perry, *Preventive Defense: A New Security Strategy for America* (Washington, D.C.: Brookings Institution, 1999), 92–93; Warren Christopher, *In the Stream of History: Shaping Foreign Policy for a New Era* (Stanford: Stanford University Press, 1998), 425–27.

61. Scholars have debated whether the Soviet Union really did enjoy the advantage of the offensive. For a careful consideration of how difficult it would be for NATO to resist a Soviet attack, even if it had two weeks to mobilize, see Richard K. Betts, *Surprise Attack: Lessons for Defense Planning* (Washington, D.C.: Brookings Institution, 1982), chap. 6. In contrast, see John Mearsheimer, "Why the Soviets Can't Win Quickly in Central Europe," *International Security* 7 (Summer 1982): 3–39. But as Jack Snyder shows, perception is more important than the reality in affecting security dilemma dynamics. See Snyder, *The Ideology of the Offensive* (Ithaca: Cornell University Press, 1984), 214–16.

62. See John Lewis Gaddis, *Strategies of Containment: A Critical Reappraisal of Postwar American National Security Policy* (New York: Oxford University Press, 1982), 167–68; Warner R. Schilling, et al., *American Arms and a Changing Europe: Dilemmas of Deterrence and Disarmament* (New York: Columbia University Press, 1973), 4–15; Jerome H. Kahan, *Security in the Nuclear Age: Developing U.S. Strategic Arms Policy* (Washington, D.C.: Brookings Institution, 1975), 12–13. On the dynamics of the arms race, see Robert Jervis, *Perception and Misperception in International Politics* (Princeton: Princeton University Press, 1976), chap. 3; Robert

Jervis, "Was the Cold War a Security Dilemma?," *Journal of Cold War Studies* 3 (Winter 2001), 55–58.

63. For a discussion of the advantages of bipolarity versus multipolarity in developing a security order premised on great-power cooperation, including management of spheres of influence, see Waltz, *Theory of International Politics*, 195–99, 204–9.

64. On the impact of geography and polarity on bandwagoning fears, see Robert Jervis, "Domino Beliefs and Strategic Behavior," in Robert Jervis and Jack Snyder, eds., *Dominoes and Bandwagoning: Strategic Beliefs and Great Power Competition in the Eurasian Rimland* (New York: Oxford University Press, 1991).

65. Chu, "Zhongguo de Guojia Liyi," 15-16.

66. On Sino-Russian security dynamics, see Jennifer Anderson, *The Limits of Sino-Russian Strategic Partnership*, Adelphi Paper no. 315 (London: International Institute for Strategic Studies, 1997).

67. On China's relations with the Central Asian States, see Ross H. Munro, "Central Asia and China," in Michael M. Mandelbaum (ed.), *Central Asia and the World: Kazakhstan, Uzbekistan, Tajikistan, Kyrgyzstan, and Turkmenistan* (New York: Council on Foreign Relations: 1994); Martha Brill Olcott, *Central Asia's New States: Independence, Foreign Policy, and Regional Security* (Washington, D.C.: United States Institute of Peace, 1996), 35, 82, 108–10. On China's recent problems with religious minorities and separatist activities, see, for example, ITAR-TASS, January 27, 1998, FBIS, January 29, 1998 (SOV-98-27); *Novoye Pokoleniye*, January 22, 1998, in FBIS, January 27, 1998 (SOV-98-25); *Delovaya Nedelya*, January 16, 1998, in FBIS, January 23, 1998 (SOV-98-21).

68. Alfred Thayer Mahan, *Retrospect and Prospect: Studies in International Relations* (London: Sampson, Low, Marston, 1902), quoted in Colin S. Gray, *The Navy in the Post-Cold War World: The Uses and Value of Strategic Air Power* (University Park: Penn State University Press, 1994), 89.

69. On the future of the Chinese Navy, see Cole, *The Great Wall at Sea*. For the concept of a "luxury fleet" and the limitations to a land power's maritime capabilities, see Gray, *The Politics of Super Power*, 49, 92–93.

CHAPTER 11

The South Asian Security Balance
in a Western Dominant World

RAJU G. C. THOMAS

Underlying theories and concepts of balance of power politics among states
are drawn primarily from the European and Western experience.[1] These theories are not representative of the experience elsewhere in the world, especially in South Asia, except indirectly through its linkages with the Western
world. During the colonial era, India was an appendage of imperial Britain's
global power politics in a European-dominated multipolar world that produced hard balancing. During the bipolar world of the Cold War, the military balance between India and Pakistan—two states unequal in size, population, and resources—was sustained by the two superpowers through both
hard and soft balancing. Historically, balance of power politics in South
Asia needs to be viewed mainly as appendages or corollaries of Western
great-power politics, first during the prewar European imperial era, and then
during the Cold War era.

The Indo-Pakistani nuclear and conventional relationship now operates
in a largely unipolar, American-dominated world, with China remaining a
third factor in the equation.[2] This contemporary trilateral power relationship
among India, Pakistan, and China is not unlike that which prevailed among
the United States, the Soviet Union, and China during the Cold War.
However, the nuclear and conventional balance between India and Pakistan
at the beginning of the 21st century suggests qualitative differences and outcomes when compared to the Cold War competition between the superpowers. In today's U.S.-Russian military relationship, for example, there is
virtually no threat of conflict even though a relative nuclear balance between
these states is accompanied by a conventional military imbalance. Similarly,
on the subcontinent, an Indo-Pakistani nuclear balance based on mutual
second-strike capabilities now prevails, accompanied by a conventional mil-

itary imbalance. But, unlike the asymmetric American-Russian conventional relationship, which works to America's military disadvantage, Indian conventional superiority works to Pakistan's military advantage. Thus, unilateral American conventional military actions in the former Yugoslavia, and Afghanistan, or potentially against North Korea do not risk a Russian conventional or nuclear military response. On the other hand, India's threat to take advantage of its conventional military superiority against Pakistan over its involvement in Kashmir risks a Pakistani nuclear response.

To explore how these competing pressures play out in South Asia, the chapter first describes the South Asian regional setting.

The South Asian Interstate System

The Western strategic concept of interstate relations based on countervailing power was not unknown in India even before it became a popular concept in European politics. In his 4th century BCE treatise *Arthashastra* (*The Science of Polity*), the Indian strategist Kautilya had advised his emperor on how to identify enemies and potential allies to create a system of countervailing power. Little of his strategic advice, however, was put into practice by subsequent Indian princes and emperors over the next 2,400 years. Two factors made it difficult to put Kautilya's ideas and the Western logic of balance of power politics into practice in South Asia.

First, 3,500 years of history and politics *within* South Asia have been largely chronological, incremental, and cumulative. Unlike Europe, South Asia never developed a multistate system based on separate languages and national cultures. Instead, politics in South Asia were driven by the simultaneous growth of, and often competitive interaction among, different languages, religions, and cultures. Three cultures in particular succeeded one another to play dominant roles in the history of the region: (1) the Hindu era lasted from about 1500 BCE to 1150 CE (including the intervening Buddhist period from circa 350–50 BCE); (2) Muslim rule followed between 1150 CE and 1550 CE; and (3) British colonialism subsumed the first two from about 1550 CE to 1947, when India and Pakistan were created out of British India. Policies or patterns of military balancing within South Asia were not apparent during any of these periods, although the British conquest of India made the region a pawn on the European balance of power chessboard.

Second, while balance of power politics in Europe and its manifestation overseas occurred mainly among *nation-states*, political relations in South Asia occurred mainly among multi-linguistic and multireligious *kingdoms* and *empires*—not nation-states, despite the regional linguistic and religious parallels between the European continent and the Indian subcontinent. Unlike Europe, "nation-states" have rarely existed in South Asia. Instead, great multiethnic empires arose and disintegrated. They were replaced by lesser empires and minor kingdoms that were either multiethnic or dominated by an ethnic, religious, or cultural group; even these nations, however, rarely encompassed all members of a particular ethnic group within their boundaries. Thus, empires such as those of the Mauryans, Guptas, Moghuls, Marattas, and Sikhs involved the subjugation of several ethnic groups by a dominant conquering group, while kingdoms such as those of Jaipur, Holkar, Hyderabad, Kashmir, and Mysore were either ethnically hybrid, or they left a significant percentage of the majority ethnic group's members outside their borders. These differences help explain why the regional Indian kingdoms and empires did not give in to the natural inclination to forge a system of countervailing powers to maintain their independence and territorial sovereignty.

The ease with which foreign powers invaded India, and the rise of grand empires within India, can at least in part be attributed to this disinclination toward balancing against greater internal or external threats by the subcontinent's competing political units. There is no record of a coalition of forces being forged to contain any of these greater threats. There were tendencies toward bandwagoning among the kingdoms and principalities, however, especially when the invading force or rising power was perceived to be benevolent. Thus, the enlightened and tolerant Moghul emperor Akbar was able to expand his empire without much resistance. By contrast, the cruel and intolerant Moghul emperor Aurangzeb was resisted fiercely by Hindu and Sikh kingdoms, but these efforts failed because the rulers never forged common alliances to stem the Moghul incursion. Similarly, the advance of the British empire beginning in the 17th century met with bandwagoning rather than balancing by regional rulers. Following the British defeat of the French in 1751, the British East India Company was able to recruit local Indian soldiers with monetary inducements and by exploiting inter-ethnic rivalry. Later the British simply coopted local Indian rulers into giving up their sovereignty with the argument that local troops could not stop their advancing forces. When about half of India had fallen to the British in a series of Anglo-Maratha and Anglo-Sikh wars, the rest of the Indian maharajahs and nawabs signed treaties of peace with the British that guaranteed them a certain degree of autonomy within their kingdoms in exchange for their acceptance of overall British control.

THE BALANCE OF EMPIRES AND THE IMPERIAL BUFFER SYSTEM

Balance of power politics went from being mainly a European-driven phenomenon to one that dominated world politics during the five centuries of empire building and maintenance by the European powers, from the beginning of the 16th to the mid-20th century. The European game was reflected in Asia by the British Indian empire at the center; the Ottoman empire of the Middle East on British India's western side; the Russian Czarist empire, including Central Asia, to the northwest; the weak Chinese imperial kingdom (subject to European extraterritorial rights) to the north; the empire of French Indochina to the east, and the Dutch East Indian empire to the southeast. These empires were separated by buffer states: Persia (now Iran) between the British and the Ottoman empires; Afghanistan between the British and the Czarist empires; Tibet between the British empire and the Chinese imperial kingdom; and Siam (now Thailand) between the British and the French Indochinese empires. The Bay of Bengal separated the British Indian and Dutch East Indies empires.

There was a plan and a method to these European arrangements among their far-flung empires. Just as the British played "the great balancer" in the European state system, the European imperial system in Asia was likewise largely managed and manipulated by the British. Buffer states were crucial to this extended Asian balance of power, as illustrated by Afghanistan and—less successfully—Tibet, because the threat to the British Indian empire was perceived to come mainly from Czarist Russia, and to a lesser extent from the potential resurgence of China. Both Afghanistan and Tibet were ideal British prototypes of buffer states in the "Great Game" of balance of power politics.

The strategic importance of Afghanistan for the defense of the British Indian empire was derived from British leaders' reading of Indian history. Until the invasions of the European powers in the 16th century by sea, and the later threat of a Japanese invasion through Burma during World War II, the major invasions of India had been launched by Aryan, Greek, Persian,

Arab, Turkish, Afghan, and Mongol advances through Afghanistan. Thus the British defense of India's northwest frontier—considered the most vulnerable point of entry into the subcontinent—called first for the maintenance of Afghanistan as a buffer against Russian encroachment, and second, for some control of the territory's internal events.

The British concept of a buffer state was probably best enunciated by Sir Arthur Balfour in 1903, when he noted the "non-conducting qualities" of Afghanistan. According to Balfour, "so long as it [Afghanistan] possesses few roads, and no railways, it will be impossible for Russia to make effective use of her great numerical superiority at any point immediately vital to the Empire."[3] Crucial to British defense of its Indian empire was a conceptual boundary called the Kabul-Kandahar Line. To the northwest of this line, mountains protected Kabul, and further southwest, desert protected Kandahar. If the non-conducting qualities of 19th-century Afghanistan were maintained (in other words, if the country were left undeveloped and its infrastructure primitive), Russia would fight at a disadvantage if it attempted to force its way across the Kabul-Kandahar Line because of the vast, barren, and difficult terrain that lay beyond. Conversely, Britain would be at a similar disadvantage in any attempt to push beyond Herat and the Oxus River into Russian-controlled Central Asia.

THE MAKING OF THE DURAND AND MACMAHON LINES

The defense policy of the British Indian empire (that included Burma) led to the drawing of the Durand Line in 1892 separating British India from Afghanistan and the Czarist empire beyond, and the McMahon Line in 1914 separating British India from Tibet and the Chinese imperial kingdom. The Durand Line was dictated by Sir Henry Mortimer Durand to the Amir of Afghanistan, Abdur Rahman Khan, on the instructions of the Viceroy of India, Lord Lansdowne. Lansdowne had directed his emissary to draw the boundary beyond the Khyber Pass, thus dividing the Pashtun tribes on either side of the border and flying in the face of the Pashtun Amirs of Afghanistan, who had always sought a "Greater Pashtunistan" that would unite all Pashtuns on either side of the Khyber Pass.[4] In this way, the Durand Line laid the seeds of perpetual conflict between Afghanistan and Pakistan. Indeed, Afghanistan was the only state to vote against the admission of the newly created Pakistan to the United Nations in 1947.

The history of the MacMahon Line is more involved. In the early 1900s, the British government estimated that the Manchu dynasty's intentions toward Tibet were about to become aggressive. Indeed, this was a major policy change for the Chinese, who had generally had a nonbelligerent attitude toward their western neighbor. During the previous 200 years, Chinese imperial forces had occupied Lhasa only twice.[5] According to historian Neville Maxwell, the British believed that "China [had] embarked on her own kind of forward policy towards her Central Asian marches, meaning to turn them from loosely controlled protectorates into full provinces of the Empire."[6] By 1910, China had achieved a position of power in Tibet, making the threat to the British from that direction more ominous than any threat from Russia through Afghanistan. "China, in a word, has come to the gates of India, and the fact has to be reckoned with," noted an editorial in a London newspaper in 1910.[7] The Nationalist revolution led by Sun Yatsen in 1911 produced immediate chaos in China and loss of control over Tibet. But this situation further impressed the British of the need to conduct their own forward policy and make a formal demarcation of the boundaries between Nationalist China and British India.

In order to draw the boundary between British India and China, and to maintain Tibet as a buffer state, the British organized a conference at Simla in 1914. The British declared at the conference that there would be a tripartite meeting involving the plenipotentiaries of China, British India, and Tibet. The Tibetan delegate was to be treated as an equal representative of a sovereign state. China objected to this tacit recognition of Tibet's independent status, but to no avail. The British negotiator was Sir Henry MacMahon, who as a young officer had accompanied Sir Henry Durand twenty-nine years earlier to demarcate the boundary with Afghanistan. The delineation of the MacMahon Line finalized at the Simla conference was equally controversial and laid the ground for conflict between independent India and communist China more than forty years later.[8]

Similar controversies and ambiguities arose in the drawing of the boundaries between Tibet and Kashmir, especially since Kashmir was a princely state ruled by a Dogra Hindu maharajah. But since on external matters the British could dictate policy to the Indian princely states, imperial interests trumped regional concerns. The British had proposed at least three alternatives on the demarcation of boundaries between the ethnically Tibetan

Ladakh province of Kashmir and Tibet, which left the status of the disputed Aksai Chin plateau unresolved until the present day.[9]

By the late 20th century, following the demise of the great European empires, the utility of buffer states in great-power politics was in decline, in favor of access and alliances. The Cold War launched a competition between the Soviet Union and the United States to assist in the development of Afghanistan's infrastructure. By 1979, Afghanistan's efforts at modernization with Soviet assistance had mitigated its "non-conducting" qualities so as to bring the Soviet and Pakistan borders closer together, within twenty hours by road. With the reconstruction of Afghanistan following massive American bombing over four months in 2001, Central and South Asia have become neighbors. Sir Arthur Balfour's 1903 concept of the buffer state has been erased. Meanwhile, China's control of Tibet is now irreversible. China and India are neighbors.

INDIA AND MILITARY BALANCES IN THE NEHRU-GANDHI ERA

The differences between India and Pakistan are central to understanding South Asia's security relationships during the Cold War, but the Indo-Pakistan rivalry was not unique in the region. Secondary disputes involved India and China, and Pakistan and Afghanistan. The leaders of Bangladesh, Nepal, Bhutan, and Sri Lanka had their own security concerns, particularly worries about domination by either India or China. Apart from conflicting interests, economic and military capabilities between the antagonistic states in the region—India and Pakistan, India and China, and Pakistan and Afghanistan— were highly uneven. When crises arose in the region, states made efforts to compensate for these unequal relationships by forming alliances.

Pakistani efforts to correct the Indo-Pakistani imbalance prompted a search for military assistance and support among the United States, China, France, and some of the Muslim states of the Middle East. Pakistan enjoyed its greatest success when it received relatively high quality arms after joining the U.S.-sponsored South-East Asian Treaty Organization (SEATO) in 1954, and the 1955 Central Treaty Organization (CENTO). Pakistan also received considerable military assistance and diplomatic support from China. Indian efforts to correct the Sino-Indian military imbalance included the quest for military sales and diplomatic support from the United States, the Soviet

Union, and Western Europe. India received much aid from the Soviet Union, which sold India arms for soft currency. The Soviets also coproduced the Mig-21 aircraft in India, eventually transferring the technology to India. New Delhi signed similar arms sales and coproduction arrangements for aircraft and tanks with Britain and France on commercial terms that led to no alliance commitments.

At the outset of the Cold War, India rejected calls by the United States to join its alliance systems to counter threats from the communist world. Like President Woodrow Wilson, who considered balance of power politics the underlying cause of World War I, Indian Prime Minister Jawaharlal Nehru believed that alliances and counteralliances were the underlying causes of wars. He adopted a policy of nonalignment between East and West, but leaned heavily toward the Soviet Union for military support against an American-armed Pakistan. In a speech to the Indian Council of World Affairs in 1949, Nehru argued that India should remain aloof from a global system of military balances: "If war comes, it comes. It has to be faced. The prevention of war may include providing for our own defense and you can understand that, but that should not include challenges, counter-challenges, mutual cursing, threats, etc. These certainly will not prevent war, but only make it come nearer."[10] Not only did he believe that military nonalignment would reduce the prospect of war and the need for larger defense budgets, but also that military weakness did not necessarily imply a reduction in Indian political influence in the world: "The fact of the matter is that in spite of our weakness in a military sense—because obviously we are not a great military power, we are not an industrially advanced power—India even counts in world affairs."[11]

Following severe criticism in the Indian parliament for having signed away Tibet's independence to China in the Nehru-Chou Enlai Sino-Indian Treaty on Tibet in 1954, Nehru responded: "Several Honourable Members have referred to the 'melancholy chapter of Tibet.' I really do not understand. I have given the most earnest thought to this matter. What did any Honourable Member of this House expect us to do in regard to Tibet at any time? Did we fail, or did we do a wrong thing? The fact is, and it is a major fact of the middle of the 20th century, that China has become a great power, united and strong."[12] According to Nehru, the realities of relative power had to be respected, reminiscent of the Athenian advice to the Melians that "the strong do what they have to do, and the weak accept what they must."

What Nehru's government had not foreseen was the indirect, and perhaps inadvertent, threat that would arise from the American-Pakistani alliances under SEATO and CENTO. The military risk to India had escalated not as a result of hostile behavior by the Soviet Union and China, but as a result of the U.S. decision to arm Pakistan. Escalating Sino-Indian tensions, which culminated in war in 1962, raised further doubts about Nehru's nonalignment policy. In particular, the Jan Sangh Party, which later became the Bharatiya Janata Party, voiced its dissent toward the policy, now an official platform of Nehru's Congress Party. In its 1967 election manifesto—following the 1962 Sino-Indian war and the 1965 Indo-Pakistani war—the Jan Sangh Party claimed that "the policy of nonalignment was formulated against the background of the Cold War between two power blocs. . . . Today when we are aggressed, we must have allies."[13]

Four years later, during the East Pakistan civil war and shifting alignments in the Washington-Moscow-Beijing strategic triangle, India moved toward a quasi-alliance relationship with the Soviet Union. The revelation of Secretary of State Henry Kissinger's secret visit to Beijing in July 1971, and the evolving Sino-American rapprochement, called for a response from India to reduce the prospect of Chinese or American military intervention in New Delhi's plans to resolve the East Pakistan civil war by military force. Although the signing of the Indo-Soviet Treaty of Peace and Friendship on August 9, 1971, was explained as a natural evolution of relations between the two countries and not a departure from India's nonalignment policy, the treaty had military implications for both sides.[14]

By the mid-1970s, the linkages between regional and global strategic conditions reflected classic conventional balance of power relationships, notwithstanding the fact that the United States, the Soviet Union, and China were nuclear weapons states. They followed the Kautilyan and balance of power principle: "an enemy of my enemy is my friend." (See Table 11.1.)

After the December 1971 Indo-Pakistani war, there was growing recognition among India's leaders that the Indo-Soviet Treaty of Peace and Friendship that Prime Minister Indira Gandhi forged in August 1971 was probably insufficient to deter Chinese or U.S. intervention in the wars of South Asia. Hence, India maintained its nuclear weapons option, which Indira Gandhi chose to demonstrate in a "peaceful nuclear explosion" in May 1974. India did not exploit its new nuclear capability following Western condemnations of the test, but willingness to exercise the nuclear option remained intrinsic to Indian security planning thereafter. In late 1988, Congress Prime Minister

TABLE II.I

Cold War Conflict Postures and State Alignments

Regional Conflicts	Global Conflicts
India–Pakistan	United States–USSR
India–China	United States–China (before 1971)
Pakistan–Afghanistan	China–USSR (after 1963)

Interrelated Conflicts		Alignment Tendencies
Pakistan v. India, India v. China	←	Pakistan and China
India v. China, China v. USSR	←	India and USSR
Afghan. v. Pakistan, Pak. v. India	←	Afghanistan and India
China v. USSR, USSR v. US	←	China and United States

Group One Alignment	Group Two Alignment
Pakistan, China, United States	India, USSR, Afghanistan

Rajiv Gandhi reportedly considered ending India's self-imposed nonnuclear weapons status amid fears that Pakistan was proceeding covertly toward a nuclear weapons capability. Similarly, Congress Prime Minister Narasimha Rao was set to conduct a series of nuclear tests in 1995 when the United States discovered the plans and threatened severe economic and political consequences if India went ahead. Both Congress prime ministers eventually pulled back from the brink, perhaps because of the severe economic sanctions that would follow. Almost ten years after the Cold War ended, India finally entered the ranks of the nuclear weapons states under a Bharatiya Janata Party–led coalition government, when it conducted five nuclear tests in May 1998 intended, according to comments made at the time by Defense Minister George Fernandes, as a warning against possible Chinese adventurism.

Balance of Power in the Age of Globalization

Ambiguity and uncertainty characterized world politics in the aftermath of the collapse of the Soviet Union in 1990. NATO's attack on Serbia in 1999, and al-Qaeda's terrorist attack on the United States on September 11, 2001, produced sudden and dramatic shifts in strategic conditions and political compulsions toward balancing and bandwagoning among global and regional powers. The primary force that now drives relations among the global and regional powers in the early 21st century, however, is economics, and the American economy is perceived to be the engine that drives the world economy. Globalization, therefore, encourages states to bandwagon with the dominant economic power, the United States. Despite U.S.-led attacks against Serbia, Afghanistan, and Iraq over less than a dozen years, globalization subdues pressures to engage in military balancing by other major states.

ABSENCE OF COUNTERVAILING POWER AND ITS CONSEQUENCES

The Indian decision to go nuclear in 1998 needs to be considered in the context of the new global order. K. Subrahmanyam, a long-time advocate of a nuclear India, presented the renewed and urgent case for a strong nuclear force posture:

> When in May 1998, India conducted the nuclear tests and justified them on the grounds that the security environment had deteriorated, many in the world and in India raised the question as to what precisely had happened to arrive at that conclusion. Now it must be clear to everyone that the present international security environment is the worst since the end of World War II. . . . The UN has been rendered redundant since there is no balance of power in the world and the entire industrial world, barring a ramshackle Russia, is under U.S. overlordship. It is not accidental that the only countries voicing strong protests against the bombing in Yugoslavia happen to be Russia, China and India, all nuclear weapon powers.[15]

Subrahmanyam was responding to a conundrum that became apparent by the end of the Cold War: nuclear deterrence cannot deter a conventional great-power attack against third-party states, especially where there is no balance of conventional military strength between the United States, Russia, and China. Balance of power theory suggests that only a system of countervailing power may ensure the sovereignty and independence of large and small states.[16] A dominant-state system cannot ensure such security for middle and small powers. While American leaders and observers argue that

world peace and justice have a better chance without a prevailing global balance of military power, there is ambiguity at the regional level where it is
dependent on American foreign policy goals, for example, South Asia and
the Middle East.[17] Israeli military preponderance continues to be advanced
against antagonistic Arab states, while a balance was advanced for Pakistan
against India during the Cold War as essential for regional stability. A preponderant India is now perceived as more stable for South Asia, but such
regional imbalances in the Middle East and South Asia are subject to the
American goal of maintaining preponderance between the West and the rest
as best for global stability.

However, as balance of power theorists have argued, such a preponderance of power cannot guarantee the independence and sovereignty of other
states. U.S. military dominance, backed by its ability to control economic
rewards for those who oppose or support American policies, has changed the
character of the United Nations. During the Yugoslav crisis in the 1990s, the
UN system was reduced to an obedient appendage of the United States and
the West, a return to the early years of the organization, when its membership did not include the emerging independent Afro-Asian bloc of states.
With the collapse of the Soviet Union and the Warsaw Pact alliance, voting
in the Security Council was then almost always in favor of U.S. policies.[18]
During the Iraqi crisis, there was overwhelming political opposition to
Anglo-American threats to use force, reflected in voting patterns at the UN.
The United States overcame this problem by bypassing the UN Security
Council. Subsequently, all states were once again on board the American
bandwagon for fear of U.S. economic retribution, or of being left out of the
economic spoils in Iraq arising from American military victory. The unusual
phenomena of what Stephen Walt named "bandwagoning" with the dominant power—instead of balancing—has become commonplace.[19] States with
veto powers, Russia, China, and France, have rarely ventured to veto U.S.
sponsored or supported UN resolutions. France threatened to veto an
Anglo-American sponsored Security Council resolution authorizing the use
of force in Iraq in March 2003. The Bush administration declared the United
Nations redundant. An anti-France, and indeed, an anti-everything French,
campaign was launched by several members of the U.S. Congress. Most
states do not dare or care to challenge the United States, for military and
especially economic reasons.

THE CASE FOR HEGEMONIC STABILITY

There is some merit in the concept of hegemonic stability as reflected in the post-Cold War era. In contrast to most balance of power theories, hegemonic stability theory posits that global peace and prosperity may be more likely in a world dominated by a benevolent state. A study of the European balance of power system over several centuries by A. F. K. Organski concluded that balance of power politics was likely to generate instability and wars, while a preponderance of power was more likely to produce peace and stability.[20] According to Organski, under conditions of military preponderance, the weaker state dare not attack, while the stronger state need not attack, and therefore peace endures. Especially when the dominant state or group of states is considered to be benevolent, just, and without territorial ambitions, a preponderance of military power may be the most desirable condition for world peace.[21] Today, some believe that peace, security, and justice for all will prevail under the new Pax Americana.

A similar case may be made for establishing stability in South Asia under Indian hegemony. Perhaps it was India's military preponderance after the 1971 Indo-Pakistani war and the breakup of Pakistan that deterred Islamabad from engaging in another war with India over Kashmir, especially during the outbreak of the violent secessionist movement there in 1989. But the right of humanitarian intervention invoked by the United States and demonstrated in the assault against Serbia over its Albanian Muslim majority population in Kosovo has added a new dimension to the debate about the benign nature of military preponderance. A nuclear weapons state possessing an assured retaliatory capability may be able to deter an attack on itself, but it cannot deter attacks on its allies and friends. Russia's inability to prevent an attack by NATO on Serbia, which Moscow perceived as its protectorate, illustrates the problem of defending allies and friends under nuclear balances and conventional imbalances. Russia may be able to deter U.S. military intervention in its suppression of the secessionist movement in Chechnya, but it cannot provide India with credible extended deterrence against Western military intervention. States that feel severely threatened by existing nuclear powers must be able to deter aggression or defend themselves on their own if an attack were to take place. Only an independent nuclear capability can guarantee the viability of a nuclear deterrent if and when it is needed. One of the basic problems with Organski's preponderance theory is that the preponderant power is not supposed to initiate a war against a weaker state. NATO's assault on Serbia bypassing the UN Security Council demonstrated the weakness of the "preponderance-equals-peace" theory, and the strength of the arguments underlying the need to maintain a balance of power among states to preserve the territorial integrity and sovereignty of states. This problem was demonstrated again in 2003 when the United States and Britain attacked Iraq, bypassing the United Nations and against the protests of veto-holding members Russia, China, and France, as well as much of the rest of the world.

INDIA'S RESPONSE TO THE NEW WORLD SECURITY ORDER

Although Western humanitarian enthusiasts have declared the end of a world based on military balances and the sanctity of the Westphalian state, India continues to insist on its territorial integrity and sovereignty, especially in terms of its internal security management. Many Indian officials believe that undermining the sovereignty of states beyond voluntary multilateral economic and military agreements (such as the World Trade Organization, the Non-Proliferation Treaty, the Biological Weapons Convention, and the Chemical Weapons Convention) could lead to more "Yugoslavias." International intervention in ethnic conflicts might only prompt more humanitarian crises as ethnic groups resort to insurgency and terrorism to secede from existing multiethnic states.

In addressing today's lack of countervailing power, India has sought both to balance the dominance of the United States and its NATO allies and seek to advance economic ties with the West, especially the United States. The fact is that Russia, China, and India depend on the United States and the West for their markets and investments. There are economic constraints on forging a formal trilateral counteralliance to NATO, which might have occurred under similar conditions in the 19th century but cannot in the 21st. Attempts to do so may quickly be averted through Western economic incentives and disincentives. Additionally, the probability of a Sino-Indian strategic partnership would seem small given India's earlier declaration that its nuclear weapons tests were directed against China. China's close military ties with Pakistan following the 1962 Sino-Indian and 1965 Indo-Pakistani wars remain a further obstacle to establishing a Sino-Indian strategic partnership.

Despite these historical obstacles to cooperation, however, NATO's use of force against Serbia without sanction from the UN Security Council prompted several short-term countermoves from Russia, China, India, and Indonesia.

RUSSIA AND CHINA

In July 2001, Russia and China signed a "treaty of friendship and coopera-tion," the first such treaty since the era of Stalin and Mao. It committed the two former communist giants for the next twenty years "to oppose jointly much of the framework for international security that the United States is seeking to erect after the Cold War."[22] The first part "obligated both to refrain from assisting opposition movements of ethnic minorities. This is tacit acceptance by Beijing of Moscow's ongoing battle in Chechnya and by Russia of China's suppression of unrest in Tibet and Xinjiang. Enhancing stability in Inner Asia is the first element of the new Chinese-Russian secu-rity alliance.[23] A second part of the treaty recognizes a Chinese sphere of influence encompassing Mongolia and much of Eurasia. A third part acknowledges Russian interests in the Caucasus and Chinese maritime inter-ests along the eastern coast of the Asian mainland. Both parties affirm the territorial integrity of each other's boundaries, accepting that Chechnya is a part of Russia and Taiwan is a part of China. Furthermore, the Chinese-Russian treaty is a nonaggression pact, whereby both parties agree to main-tain a peaceful border so that they can divert security resources elsewhere. The treaty obligates both parties to refrain from using force or economic pressure in their relations, and eventually to reduce the forces stationed on their common border.[24]

Presidents Vladimir Putin of Russia and Jiang Zemin of China went to considerable lengths to explain that the treaty had no military relevance but was merely an agreement between neighbors to establish stability conducive to Asian economic growth and development. As it stands, the security con-notations of the treaty are diluted by the fact that China had a trade volume with the United States of $115 billion in 2000, compared with less than $10 billion with Russia.[25] Subsequent to the Sino-Russian treaty, Putin vocifer-ously opposed NATO expansion. In an interview with the Italian newspaper *Corriere della Sera*, Putin stated: "In the West, everyone says, 'We don't want new divisions in Europe, we don't want new Berlin Walls.' Good. We com-pletely agree. . . . But when NATO enlarges, division doesn't disappear, it simply moves toward our borders. . . . The divisions will continue until there is a single security area in Europe."[26]

INDIA AND CHINA

On June 14, 1999, a week after the hostilities ended in the Balkans, India and China established a "Security Dialogue," which was described by their foreign ministers as a response to NATO's actions.[27] China also moved toward a more neutral stance between India and Pakistan by distancing itself from Pakistani activities in the Kargil sector of Kashmir. This position was reiterated by Chinese Foreign Ministry spokesperson Zhang Qiyue, when she met with an Indian delegation in November 2000. According to Qiyue, Chinese officials did not perceive India as a rival or threat but as a partner in maintaining global stability and peace.[28] In January 2001, Indian Prime Minister Atal Behari Vajpayee and Chinese Premier Li Peng agreed to finalize the definition of the Line of Actual Control along their adjoining frontier "as soon as possible."[29] They declared that both sides were satisfied with the 1993 and 1996 agreements on maintaining peace and tranquility along the border. Vajpayee stated that "As two great civilizations and neighbors, India and China are engaged in the process of resolving, and putting behind us, past differences and forging a new and dynamic relationship for the 21st century for the benefit of our two countries and the world." These statements reflect a return to Nehru's and Chinese Foreign Minister Chou Enlai's joint declarations of peaceful coexistence embodied in the 1954 Sino-Indian Treaty.

A sharp deterioration in Sino-American relations in the aftermath of the bombing of the Chinese embassy in Belgrade in May 1999, allegations of Chinese nuclear spying in the United States in 2000, and the prolonged detention in China of an American reconnaissance plane disabled in a collision with a Chinese fighter aircraft, no doubt raised Washington's interest in forging closer Indo-American security ties. Observing this shift, Jim Hoagland of the *Washington Post* suggested in July 2001 "that the chances of serious conflict between India and China may now outrank the more obvious antagonisms between China and Taiwan as a threat to global stability. The balance of power across the Himalayas could be more tenuous than the confrontation across the Taiwan Strait."[30] With the prospect of a resolution of the Sino-Indian border dispute within reach, however, there are no major disputes left between India and China to trigger serious conflict. The excuse provided in May 1998 by Indian Defense Minister George Fernandes, that

India's nuclear tests were in response to the growing Chinese threat, has not been heard since.

INDIA AND RUSSIA

In spring 1999, there was similar Indian interest in the call by then Russian prime minister Yevgeny Primakov to forge a counteralliance against NATO among Russia, China, and India. Following NATO's air assault on Serbia in 1999 to stop Serbia's brutal efforts to suppress the Albanian Muslim secessionist movement in the province of Kosovo, a China-India-Russia "anti-NATO axis" had started to coalesce by fall 1999, to check the unbridled use of American military power.[31] Russian-Indian cooperation took more concrete shape during Putin's visit to India in October 2000, when the two governments entered into a limited strategic partnership. Vajpayee declared that the two countries shared common concerns and interests, and that "the history of the last five decades demonstrates that close Indo-Russian understanding is essential to peace and stability in Asia and the world. This is what makes India and Russia strategic partners. Our friendship is not based on short-term calculations, but transcends the twists and turns of history and politics."[32] Putin claimed that a multipolar world was a safer world and that the new Indo-Russian strategic partnership would contribute to global stability.

The central feature of the partnership was an immediate $3 billion defense deal, with a further $2.5 billion earmarked for India's purchase of sophisticated Russian weapons.[33] In June 2001, a protocol was signed between the two countries whereby Russia would supply $10 billion worth of weaponry and other military hardware over the coming decade.[34]

INDIA AND INDONESIA

The threat of Western dominance and the right of humanitarian intervention also drew Indonesia and India closer together. During an exchange of visits by Vajpayee and Indonesian President Abdurrahman Wahid in January 2001, both Wahid and Indonesian Defense Minister Mohamad Mahfud Mahmudin proposed a quadrilateral alliance of Russia, China, India, and Indonesia.[35] At a joint press conference on January 11 in Jakarta, Wahid referred to the recent proposal put forward by Mahfud for a defense pact among the four nations, and said that while the proposal did not come up in his talks with Vajpayee, it would be discussed at the ministerial level later.

Subsequently, Indian Foreign Minister Jaswant Singh claimed that India did not believe in alliances. Notably, however, Wahid supported Vajpayee's stand on Kashmir. Five Indo-Indonesian agreements were eventually signed in Jakarta, including the formation of a joint commission for defense cooperation. Indonesia's desire for such an alliance is understandable. It had just suffered the loss of East Timor, a province annexed in 1974 by Indonesia when the Portuguese relinquished their colony, that had been home to a growing independence movement ever since. Western diplomats and the United Nations had intervened for humanitarian reasons to halt the slaughter of East Timorese pro-independence protestors by army-backed militias, and in the process forced Jakarta to free the province. Indonesia's annexation of the island, however, was no different from India's forcible annexation of Portuguese Goa in 1961 against the protests of Portugal. Referring to what appeared to be a new appreciation of each other's bilateral concerns, Vajpayee declared that "as multi- ethnic, multi-religious and diverse societies, both our countries support each other's unity and territorial integrity."[36]

If nothing else, a propensity existed at the turn of the century to forge a diluted, quadrilateral quasi-alliance relationship among India, Russia, China, and Indonesia as a balance to NATO. This counterbalance was limited in its formal commitments, unity, and effectiveness, however, by low perceptions in India, Russia, and China of potential American military intervention in their internal wars of secession in Kashmir, Chechnya, and Xinjiang. They are, after all, large states with nuclear weapons capabilities. Economic dependence of these countries on the NATO members, especially the United States, generates incentives to bandwagon with the dominant state rather than balance it, thereby discouraging the earlier momentum among these three powers toward formalizing a military counteralliance to NATO.

Bandwagoning with the United States After September 11

Political and strategic conditions changed in the aftermath of the terrorist group al-Qaeda's attack on the United States on September 11, 2001. The United States and India—and indeed much of the rest of the world including Russia and China—found common cause in the war against terrorism. India, itself a target of al-Qaeda's terrorist operations in Kashmir, was among the first countries to rush to the American side with offers of military bases and logistical support to fight terrorist groups in Afghanistan. The United States, however, preferred to make use of better-located facilities in Pakistan, while attempting simultaneously to soothe India's fears that a return to the old Pakistani-American military alliance was imminent. American policy-makers stepped up diplomatic efforts to encourage rapprochement between India and Pakistan over Kashmir, to facilitate the international campaign against transnational terrorism.

THE END OF HARD BALANCING?

After the September 11 attack, momentum for a Russia-China-India quasi-alliance abruptly died. During U.S. President George W. Bush's visit to Shanghai in October 2001, Jiang Zemin declared his government's support in the war against terrorism. Indeed, the visit of Jiang Zemin to the United States in October 2002 appeared to herald a new Sino-American friendship. Likewise, during the visit of the Indian prime minister to Moscow in November 2001, Putin and Vajpayee proclaimed a common cause against transnational Islamic terrorism in Chechnya and Kashmir, and common cause with the United States in combating global terrorism. Russia is already a Partnership for Peace member of NATO, and might even attempt to become a full-fledged member, perhaps expanding the organization into a Russia-North Atlantic Council. Almost all states appear to have jumped on the American antiterrorism bandwagon with various degrees of conviction and support. The dreaded unipolar world was getting more unipolar under United States control and domination.

The lingering remnants of East-West confrontational politics diminished further when Bush and Putin agreed on November 13, 2001, to reduce their numbers of nuclear warheads on strategic delivery systems to between 1,700 and 2,200 over the next ten years. This agreement overrides the START-II agreement, which required both the United States and Russia to reduce their strategic nuclear warheads to 3,500 by 2003. Progress is being made by the two major nuclear weapons powers toward comprehensive nuclear disarma-ment as required by Article 6 of the Nuclear Non-Proliferation Treaty (NPT). India's attempt to achieve global nuclear deterrence with its pro-jected long-range missile program now appears less justifiable amid the new nuclear arms reductions agreed to by the United States and Russia, and its common global cause with the United States against worldwide networks of terrorism.

As Indian analysts pointed out in 1999, weaker states may perceive the deployment of nuclear weapons as a means to deter Western military intervention, notwithstanding the new wave of global unity and amity among states to combat global terrorism. Realists and balance of power theorists would argue that, lacking a system of global countervailing conventional power, nuclear deterrence would remain a more acceptable long-term strategy (assuming that the strategy of terrorism is not a viable option for states) against the threat of military intervention, no matter how remote this prospect may seem at present. Conditions in Chechnya, Kashmir, and Xinjiang are not fundamentally different from the situation that prompted NATO intervention in Kosovo. They are all Muslim majority provinces of a larger sovereign state seeking independence through violent means. Only the degree of state violence invoked to defeat the violent separatist movements has varied. What makes Western military intervention unthinkable in these cases is that Russia, India, and China have large military establishments equipped with nuclear weapons.

The Conventional-Nuclear Balance in South Asia

During the Cold War, the United States and the Soviet Union intervened in the civil wars of Vietnam and Afghanistan and were defeated. The explanation for this phenomenon, where major nuclear superpowers were humbled after ten years of war by minor and even backward states, may be extrapolated from Glen Snyder's "stability-instability paradox." Snyder's paradox suggests that when mutual nuclear deterrence prevails between two great powers, they become inclined to fight one another indirectly at lower levels of conventional or unconventional warfare. For example, the United States and the Soviet Union were compelled to fight each other's armed proxies in Vietnam and Afghanistan. Without the support of the other—noncombatant—superpower, however, neither North Vietnam nor Afghanistan could have emerged victorious in their wars of attrition. A similar pattern has prevailed in Kashmir since 1989. In light of India's and Pakistan's latent nuclear status from the mid-1980s onward, India has been compelled to fight

Pakistan's proxies, the well-armed and well-trained Kashmiri and non-Kashmiri mujahideen. The resort to terrorism by Kashmiri separatists from sanctuaries across the border in Pakistan renders India's conventional weapons capabilities ineffective. The India-Pakistan military balance under these circumstances is not easily defined.

The stability-instability paradox was tested during the 1999 crisis over Kargil, when India conducted a limited ground war against Pakistani irregular and regular forces. Unlike Vietnam and Afghanistan, victory has thus far eluded the Kashmiri separatists and their Pakistani sponsors. The difference may be found in Indian motivation, logistical convenience, and the willingness to suffer casualties to keep Kashmir. India also was prevented from expanding the war across the international frontier into Pakistan's districts of Punjab and Sindh for fear of nuclear escalation. It always has been difficult for India to defend Kashmir against a Pakistani assault from its side of the Line of Control despite a quantitative military advantage over Pakistan of approximately two to one in armed forces and weapons systems. However, the qualitative military balance needs to be defined by the terrain on which wars are fought in South Asia, the technology of weapons systems, and the time factor. India is at a disadvantage in ground defense against Pakistan in Kashmir and China along the Himalayan footholds. Pakistan possessed the technological advantage with its U.S. supplied weapons systems during the 1965 war, an advantage that has shifted to India overwhelmingly. The short duration wars of two to three weeks as in 1965 and 1971 render India's military superiority ineffective. To neutralize the disadvantages of terrain in the earlier wars of 1965 and 1971, India expanded conflicts across the international frontier by driving its forces toward Lahore and Karachi, threatening to seize the two main cities of Pakistan. Despite the armed Indian buildup along the Pakistan border, India's military options are now limited because Pakistan has threatened that it will escalate an Indian-initiated conventional war to a full-scale nuclear war. The nuclearization of South Asia initiated by India in May 1998 has worked to New Delhi's disadvantage.

Unable to match India's conventional superiority, Pakistan has found the balance at a higher level of military capability, that is, a deterrent posture based on nuclear weapons and missile delivery systems. At the nuclear level, a quantitative balance is irrelevant. Now that it has a retaliatory strike capability, Pakistan is able to deter India from launching even conventional wars for fear of escalation to nuclear war. A nuclear security guarantee from the United States could not have provided Pakistan with this level of deterrence capability.

The deployment of nuclear weapons by India appears irrelevant for deterring cross-border and transnational terrorism conducted by non-state actors. Nuclear deterrence may be effective only toward another state and not against irrational or irresponsible individuals or groups willing to commit suicide for their cause. Irresponsible or irrational non-state actors carry greater credibility when they threaten to use nuclear weapons.[37] If such weapons are acquired by these actors, nuclear deterrence will fail. If the more extreme Kashmiri separatist groups should acquire nuclear weapons, they could compel India to capitulate in future confrontations over Kashmir. This danger has compromised India's ability to maintain its territorial integrity and political unity at the beginning of the new century. Against such a threat, the Indian deployment of nuclear weapons may be an exercise in strategic futility. The prevalence of insurgency and terrorism alongside the deployment of conventional and nuclear weapons make the India-Pakistan balance of power difficult to determine or define.

Non-State Actors, Terrorism, and the Balance of Power

Balance of power politics face an uncertain future at the onset of the 21st century. The operations of the old conventional military balance were supplanted by the mixed nuclear-conventional military balance and then further supplanted by economic and cultural globalization. The most crucial transformation complicating much of the earlier types of balances has been the rise of non-state actors who use terrorism to achieve their objectives. If the advent of nuclear weapons had eclipsed the defense function of war, leading to a reliance on deterrence, the rise of transnational terrorism as a form of military coercion has in turn eclipsed both conventional and nuclear military capabilities. If terrorism in theory may be defined as the willingness of individuals and groups to risk their lives to attack anything, anywhere, at anytime, then there would appear to be no conventional or nuclear defense or deterrence against transnational, non-state-sponsored terrorism. The war against terrorism seems unlikely to be won on the battlefield since the killing or bombing of suspected terrorists individually or collectively draws more adherents to the cause as illustrated especially in the cases of Israeli military actions in the Middle East, Russia in Chechnya, and India in Kashmir. Since the enemy is faceless, and there is not an identifiable "X" number of terrorists that can be targeted, eliminating this threat by state security forces remains complex and difficult. Thus the advent of transnational terrorism has changed the rules of the game for both the South Asian and global conventional and nuclear security balances.

AN EVOLVING INDIA-U.S.-ISRAEL SOFT ALLIANCE?

Complicating these trends after September 11 is India's growing military cooperation with the United States and Israel. A series of Indo-American joint military exercises utilizing land, air, and naval forces took place during 2001–2002, augmenting earlier sporadic joint exercises.[38] India and Israel have established a joint working group on counterterrorism, and Israel has made major sales of military equipment to India that include Barak anti-missile systems, Phalcon early warning command and control systems, Heron unmanned aerial vehicles, armor piercing shells, and ground sensors.[39]

The growing irrelevance of conventional and nuclear balances may be illustrated by the futility of the evolving soft alliance of India, the United States, and Israel. The resort to overwhelming military force by Israel against suspected Palestinian terrorists has not proven successful, and victory remains elusive for U.S. forces fighting against al-Qaeda in Afghanistan. Because transnational terrorism by non-state actors cannot be dealt with by conventional and nuclear military forces, the United States has chosen instead to bomb states with clearly defined boundaries governed by unsavory regimes. Such actions tend to aggravate the problem of terrorism.

As long as the United States and Israel continue to believe in the use of overwhelming counterforce against terrorism, linking up with them may only aggravate India's security problems, although India has not resorted to overwhelming military force to deal with terrorism in Kashmir. The threat of regional and global terrorism at the beginning of the 21st century is based on a network of fringe Islamic extremists who transcend national boundaries. If India, the United States, and Israel pursue individual state policies that apply military solutions to the problem of terrorism, they might generate common cause against all three allied states by radical Muslim groups. An American attack on Iraq may escalate terrorist violence in India and

Israel, and the violent suppression of terrorism in India and Israel may escalate terrorist attacks on the United States. Just as the value of alliances in the nuclear age based on credible extended deterrence appears dubious, the value and credibility of alliances to counter transnational terrorism are equally uncertain. So far, at least, India's new military ties with the United States and Israel have not produced a backlash against India in the Muslim world. New Delhi maintains close ties with Iran, Iraq, and Israel, three mutually antagonistic states, but this ecumenism may not be long lived.

The Muslim minority populations in the three countries, from whence terrorism might emerge, are fundamentally different in nature. There are less than 2 million practicing Muslims in the United States out of a total population of 280 million (0.7 percent). There are 1 million Arab Muslims in Israel out of a total population of 6 million (17 percent). There are 150 million Muslims in India out of a population of 1.1 billion (14 percent). In the United States and Israel, the Muslim minority populations are usually distinct and distinguishable from the majority population. On the Indian subcontinent—more so in India itself—Hindus and Muslims are ethnically the same people. A parallel does exist between Israel and India, in that terrorism is conducted mainly by infiltrators who originate outside their national boundaries, in the Palestinian territories and Pakistan.

Israeli-Indian military cooperation would link the Palestinian and Kashmiri problems in the eyes of much of the Muslim world. Indian political support for overwhelming military responses by the United States or Israel against Muslim states or populations might alienate 150 million Muslims in India. That would generate an internal security problem that could quickly become unmanageable in such a large and diversified country. If only 0.001 percent of disgruntled Indian Muslims (1,500) were to conduct provocative terrorist attacks against Hindus, and only 0.001 percent of Hindus (8,000) were to engage in overwhelming revenge attacks against Muslims, India's internal security and economic stability would collapse. The strategy of terrorism would appear to have rendered alliances obsolete.

Conclusion

Traditional theory postulated that for a balance of power system to operate in an anarchic society, three basic conditions must be fulfilled: (1) the main actors must be of relatively equal powers; (2) there must be a willingness to counter the dominant or rising power individually or through alliances; and (3) all states in the system must desire to maintain their independence, sovereignty, and territorial integrity. These three conditions are not fulfilled at the beginning of the 21st century. The United States is dominant without parallel in history. No other state or combination of states can match the technology of U.S. military capabilities. States are unable or unwilling to confront American military unilateralism as demonstrated in Yugoslavia in 1999, Afghanistan in 2001–2002, and Iraq in 2003. Economic dependency on the United States and the West has further compelled other states to avoid alienating the sole superpower. Globalization has made traditional state objectives such as sovereignty, territorial integrity, and independence in foreign policy, less relevant.

However, since the old world consisting of states possessing conventional and nuclear weapons continues to exist, balance of power politics remains relevant, even if it is demonstrated by the absence of such a system. After all, balance of power theory teaches that only power can deter power, and that the antidote to nuclear weapons is an opposing array of nuclear weapons and the threat of unacceptable damage in a nuclear exchange. Thus, facing no risk or restraint, U.S. policies have become increasingly aggressive, while its military capabilities continue to grow to meet its far-flung global role. These policies include the potential use of nuclear weapons against the "axis of evil"—Iraq, Iran, and North Korea—and also against Russia, China, Libya, and Syria. There are plans to use nuclear weapons to retaliate against chemical and biological weapons attacks as well as against "surprising military developments" that are not yet defined. New weapons will include bunker-busting mini-nukes and nuclear weapons that minimize collateral damage.[40]

If such rising U.S. military capabilities are perceived as threats to other states, there will be compulsions to offset them by conventional and nuclear arms buildups through overt or covert means to deter an attack or raise the costs of military intervention. Globalization and economic dependency on the United States, on the other hand, are likely to reduce or eliminate the compulsions toward military balancing. Thus, India's nuclear weapon and missile capabilities that include short-range, intermediate-range, and intercontinental ballistic missiles appear to serve as an immediate regional deterrent against Pakistan and China, and as a long-term global deterrent against the other major nuclear-weapon states, especially the United States and

Britain, should circumstances change in the distant future.[41] Conversely, Indian economic dependency on the United States reduces the compulsions for global military balancing and instead toward bandwagoning with the United States.

Notes

1. For various aspects of the theory and practice of balance of power politics, see Hans Morgenthau, *Politics Among Nations: The Struggle for Power and Peace*, 5th ed. (New York: Knopf, 1978), 171–228; Kenneth N. Waltz, *Theory of International Politics* (Reading, Mass.: Addison-Wesley, 1979), 79–106; Inis Claude, *Power and International Relations* (New York: Random House, 1962), 12–23; and Joseph S. Nye Jr., *Understanding International Conflicts* (Reading, Mass.: Addison-Wesley, Longman, 2000), 54–146.

2. For a contemporary study of regional power politics in South Asia, see chapters by Michael Krepon, Marvin G. Weinbaum, Jasjit Singh, Najam Rafique, Christian Koch, and Eric Arnett in *The Balance of Power in South Asia* (Abu Dhabi, UAE: Emirates Center for Strategic Studies and Research, 2000).

3. Memorandum by the Secretary of State, A. J. Balfour, April 30, 1903, Committee on Imperial Defence, Public Record Office, No. CAB 6, 1. Document on microfilm at the University Research Library, University of California, Los Angeles. Also, Raju G. C. Thomas, "The Afghanistan Crisis and South Asian Security," *The Journal of Strategic Studies* 4 (December 1981): 415–34.

4. From Sultan Mohammed Khan (ed.), *The Life of Abdur Rahman Khan, Amir of Afghanistan*, vol. 2 (London: John Murray, 1900), 158.

5. For a comprehensive study of the problem, see Rajesh Kadian, *Tibet, India and China: Critical Choices, Uncertain Future* (New Delhi: Vision, 1999).

6. Neville Maxwell, *India's China War* (London: Jonathan Cape, 1970), 41. Also see Alastair Lamb, *The China-India Border: The Origins of the Disputed Boundaries* (London: Oxford University Press, 1964); *The McMahon Line*, 2 volumes (London: Routledge and Kegan Paul, 1966); *Asian Frontiers* (London: Pall Mall, 1968); *The Sino-Indian Border in Ladakh* (Columbia: University of South Carolina Press, 1973); *Tibet, China and India, 1914–1950: A History of Imperial Diplomacy* (Hertingfordbury, Hertfordshire: Roxford, 1989).

7. Cited by Maxwell, *India's China War*, 42.

8. Ibid., 48.

9. See Steven A. Hoffmann, *India and the China Crisis* (Berkeley: University of California Press, 1990), 3–30.

10. Jawaharlal Nehru, *India's Foreign Policy: Selected Speeches, September 1946– April 1961* (New Delhi: Publications Division, Government of India, 1961), 46.

11. Ibid., 47.

12. Ibid., 304.

13. From the 1967 election manifesto of the Jan Sangh, in K. Raman Pillai, *India's Foreign Policy: Basic Issues and Attitudes* (Meerut: Meenakshi Prakashan, 1969), 232.

14. Articles 8, 9, and 10 of the Indo-Soviet treaty were essentially alliance clauses. See *Current Digest of the Soviet Press*, August 23, 1971.

15. K. Subrahmanyam, "Clear and Present Danger: U.S. Path to Unipolar Hegemony," *Times of India*, May 3, 1999.

16. One of the more persuasive arguments for balance of power conditions was made in Claude, *Power*, 41–66, 88–93.

17. Fred Hiatt, "Whose New World Order? Russia Is Wondering Who Left the U.S. in Charge of Everyone Else," *Washington Post: National Weekly Edition*, November 14–20, 1994.

18. The need for a power balance in the manipulations at the United Nations is provided by Inis L. Claude Jr., "The Management of Power in the Changing United Nations," in Richard A. Falk, Samuel S. Kim, and Saul H. Mendlovitz (eds.), *The United Nations and a Just World Order* (Boulder, Colo.: Westview, 1991), 143–152.

19. Stephen Walt, "Alliances: Balancing and Bandwagoning," in Robert Art and Robert Jervis (eds.), *International Politics* (New York: Addison-Wesley Longman, 2000), 110–117. See also chapters in the same book by Kenneth N. Waltz, "Peace, Stability and Nuclear Weapons," 461–75, and Robert J. Art, "The Dangers of NBC Spread," 476–81.

20. See A. F. K. Organski, *World Politics* (New York: Knopf, 1958); and A. F. K. Organski and Jacek Kugler, *The War Ledger* (Chicago: University of Chicago Press, 1980).

21. James H. Schampel, "Parity or Preponderance: One More Look," *International Studies Notes* 19 (Fall 1994): 1–6.

22. See Patrick E. Tyler, "Russia and China Sign 'Friendship' Pact," *New York Times*, July 17, 2001.

23. This quote and assessment are from Bruce A. Elleman and Sarah C. M. Paine, "Security Pact with Russia Bolsters China's Power," Op-ed in the *International Herald Tribune*, August 6, 2001.

24. Ibid.

25. Figures are from Tyler, "Russia and China."

26. Ibid.

27. See Seema Guha, "China, India to Set Up Security Dialogue," *Times of India*, June 15, 1999.

28. "India's Development Not a Threat: China," *The Hindu*, December 1, 2000.

29. See "India, China Decide to Stop Fencing Over Boundary," *Times of India*, January 16, 2001.

30. See Jim Hoagland, "Rethinking Asia in India's Favor," *Washington Post*, July 1, 2001.

31. Tyler Marshall, "Anti-NATO Axis Poses Threat, Experts Say," *Los Angeles Times*, September 27, 1999. According to Marshall, U.S. analysts were warily eyeing the evolving post-Kosovo China-India-Russia coalition intended to check American military power.

32. Quoted from Press Trust of India report of October 4, 2000, in the *India Network News Digest*, vol. 12, issue 170 (October 4, 2000).

33. Under this deal, India would purchase and then produce under license 310 T-90 tanks, acquire the aircraft carrier *Admiral Gorshkov*, obtain the transfer of technology and licensed production of 140 Sukhoi-30 MKI multi-role fighters, and help establish a bilateral commission on military technical cooperation. In addition, the two sides agreed on the lease by India of four Tu-22 Backfire Bombers, a maritime reconnaissance and strike aircraft fitted with 300-km range air-to-ground missiles and capable of flying at three times the speed of sound, and five more Kamov-31 airborne early warning helicopters for its navy. See Dinesh Kumar, "India, Russia Ink $3bn Defence Deals," *Times of India*, October 5, 2000. See also Vladimir Radyuhin, "Secrecy on Defence, Nuclear Deals," *Hindu*, October 6, 2000.

34. See "Russia and India Consolidate Military Ties," and "The Indo-Pakistan Military Balance," *BBC World/South Asia*, February 13, and July 4, 2001.

35. Amit Baruah, "Wahid Supports Vajpayee Position on Kashmir," *India Network News Digest*, vol. 13, issue 8 (January 12, 2001).

36. Ibid.

37. Graham Allison pointed out that attempts to steal nuclear weapons or weapons-usable material have been a recurring fact, especially in Russia and some of the former Soviet republics. With some forty pounds of highly enriched uranium, or less than half that weight in plutonium, a terrorist organization could, with materials otherwise available off the shelf, produce a nuclear device in less than a year. Allison concluded that terrorists would not find it difficult to sneak such a nuclear device into the United States. The nuclear material required is actually smaller than a football. Even a fully assembled device, such as a suitcase nuclear weapon, could be shipped in a container, in the hull of a ship or in a trunk carried by an aircraft. The Ummah Tameer-e-Nau (UTN) is a private Pakistani group that may have sought to develop such nuclear bombs for al-Qaeda operations worldwide—including against India. Founded by a Pakistani nuclear scientist, the UTN claimed to be a relief organization helping deprived civilians in Afghanistan. UTN was, however, put on Washington's list of suspected terrorist groups. See John F. Burns, "Uneasy Ally in Terror War Suddenly Feels More U.S. Pressure," *New York Times*, December 21, 2001.

38. See "U.S. Air Force Contingent Arrives in New Delhi for Joint Exercises," *Hindu*, October 18, 2002; "IAF, USAF Joint Exercises at Agra, *Press Trust of India*, October 17, 2002; "Indo-U.S. Joint Army Exercises Begin at Alaska," *United News of India*, September 29, 2002; "Indo-American Naval Exercises Begin," *Press Trust*

of India, September 30, 2002; "Indo-U.S. Ties Getting Stronger," *Press Trust of India*, September 27, 2002.

39. Shishir Gupta, "Indo-Israel Ties: Force Multiplier," *India Today*, July 29, 2002.

40. According to a Los Angeles Times report, much of this information is contained in a still classified document called the Nuclear Posture Review, delivered to some members of Congress in January 2002. See William M. Arkin, "Nuclear Warfare: Secret Plan Outlines the Unthinkable," *Los Angeles Times*, March 10, 2002.

41. See Raju G. C. Thomas, "India's Nuclear and Missile Programs: Strategy, Intentions, Capabilities," in Raju G. C. Thomas and Amit Gupta (eds.), *India's Nuclear Security* (Boulder, Colo.: Lynne Rienner, 2000), 87–122. See also chapters by K. Subrahmanyam, "India and the International Nuclear Order," and Bharat Karnad, "India's Force Planning Imperative: The Thermo-Nuclear Option," in Damodar Sardesai and Raju G. C. Thomas (eds.), *Nuclear India in the Twenty-First Century* (New York: Palgrave-Macmillan, 2002), 63–84, 105–138.

CHAPTER 12

Regime Type and Regional Security in Latin America: Toward a "Balance of Identity" Theory

MICHAEL BARLETTA AND HAROLD TRINKUNAS

Many analyses of Latin American international relations fall within the realist tradition.[1] David Mares, for instance, has recently confirmed realist expectations regarding the crucial role of power in determining the international behavior of states in Latin America, although with an important caveat: state leaders in the region must pay close attention to the preferences of domestic constituencies when making decisions about war and peace.[2] It is difficult, however, to find evidence of balance of power behavior in Latin America in the post-Cold War period. This is not an anomaly, but rather a product of the evolution toward a regional security system in which patterns of conflict and cooperation are driven by regime type, not power. In our analysis of two historical case studies, we observe surprising behavioral anomalies that appear inexplicable or directly contradictory to balance of power axioms. While power-balancing behavior was evident in South America in the 19th century,[3] its prevalence in the 20th century and now is less clear. Through inductive analysis we seek to develop instead the basis for what we term a "balance of identity" theory, in which the human struggle for security centers not on the relative distribution of military capabilities among states, but on the distribution of political actors' identities with respect to their control over states. The recurrent conflicts we observe among states are not primarily to shape their relative power, but rather to determine their regime type.

In this chapter, we examine the predominant roles of identity and ideology in shaping the international relations of Latin America. We contrast the tenets of balance of identity directly with balance of power. The political actors we examine include states, subnational factions—those groups or parties seeking to gain control of states—and the transnational ideological movements manifest in these organizational forms. It is important to understand that domestic as well as foreign actors can pose extreme security threats that drive political actors' behavior. Actors routinely identify other actors as allies or enemies depending not on their territorial location or nationality, but rather on their ideology, political projects, and preferred type of political regime.

At least in Latin America, the competition for power among states is less pervasive, less important, and typically less lethal than the competition among internal factions within states. As they compete for power, these factions make alliances and enemies abroad as well as at home. Democrats and autocrats are inherent enemies who fight to the death to gain and maintain control over *all* states in a geographic subregion. They do so in pursuit of security at home and in their regional neighborhood, and regardless of the consequences for the relative distribution of military power among states. For the democrats, a weak neighboring state dominated by an authoritarian regime is far more dangerous than a strong one governed by fellow democrats. Dictators tend to see the world in exactly the same way, except of course finding their friends among like-minded autocrats and their foes among democratic reformers of whatever nationality.

The balance of identity theory we present draws on the work of Steven David and John Owen. The remainder of this chapter is presented in three parts. First, we present the theoretical basis for explaining actors' "identity balancing" behavior, define key terms, and outline causal pathways by which shared ideas about identity shape political behavior. Second, we present two case studies that illustrate the trend toward identity as a predominant factor in regional politics: the Contadora peace process in Central America and the Southern Cone of South America, both in the 1980s. We conclude by reviewing evidence of similar phenomena in the 1990s, and analyzing their implications for balance of power theories.

Theory

In this volume's introduction, T. V. Paul succinctly captures the central assumptions and concerns of balance of power approaches to explaining state behavior in security affairs, emphasizing that under anarchy states must struggle to preserve their security and independence, and that great powers' efforts to arm themselves and to ally with others against common adversaries are fundamental to the prospects for international peace.

Stephen Walt's "balance of threat" theory offers a nuanced understanding of how states assess external dangers. Walt identifies four attributes of a state that determine how threatening it is perceived by others: aggregate power, offensive military capabilities, physical proximity to the perceiver, and past and present demonstrations of offensive intent.[4] Walt improves on earlier balance of power theories by emphasizing that it is not power alone, but power coupled with offensive intentions, that constitutes the threats against which states balance or bandwagon.[5] Because all states are not created equally, differences in regime type and levels of economic and institutional development can also influence the setting of security priorities.

Stephen David's conception of "omnibalancing" helps identify the security priorities of various types of regimes because it captures distinctive features of the security environment confronting leaders in the developing world.[6] Noting the uncertain legitimacy of regimes in "artificial" Third World states led by narrow authoritarian factions in countries split by ethnic, regional, and other divisions, David observes that military coups greatly outnumber foreign invasions. Facing serious domestic threats, which are often more deadly than the menace posed by external armies, Third World leaders frequently accommodate foreign adversaries in order to focus resources on confronting their enemies at home. Simultaneously threatened by internal and external enemies, such leaders must balance in all directions at once. The domestic environment thus replicates the anarchy—that is, lack of a legitimate authority to adjudicate conflicts—of the international realm. David further notes that, given the limited conventional capabilities of most Third World states, internal threats can provide better opportunities for outside actors to wield inexpensive and effective influence over the policies of their unstable neighbors than outright aggression.[7]

David's view of the way leaders of extremely weak states perceive threats generally describes the situation facing Latin American states, though many of these states are older and their borders generally more stable than most countries in the developing world. His main point—direct threats faced by leaders of weak states are typically posed by domestic foes rather than foreign challengers—applies to the Latin American cases considered here. In balance of identity theory, we incorporate David's insights to explain consistent patterns in interest identification and threat perception, and to direct attention to parallel and potentially reinforcing transnational or multinational cleavages. By taking into account the identity of the actors who govern and those who contest control of the state, we can anticipate which actors will ally with each other regardless of national borders, and which actors are likely to end up in conflict even if this means that they will end up fighting their fellow citizens. Furthermore, our case studies illuminate how regime export and intervention can be more effective and economical policy instruments than resorting to war for reshaping a regional security environment.

John Owen has recently noted that efforts at regime export are actually quite common in world politics. His work suggests that states have frequently expended scarce resources to impose their own institutions of governance on foreign societies.[8] He demonstrates that by using "rhetoric, subversion, economic inducements such as aid or sanctions, and the threat and direct use of force," states regularly have imposed their domestic institutions on others throughout the last several centuries.[9] According to Owen:

> "Transnational ideological struggles cause ideologues across states to favor close relations with great powers ruled by their chosen ideology. A country that needs to increase its power—such as one involved in a hot or cold war—may pull lesser states into its sphere of influence by promoting in those states the institutions called for by the ideology; such institutions make it more likely that the ideologues supporting them will rule."[10]

We propose two modifications to Owen's concept of regime export. First, we think it useful to conceptualize the political actors engaged in regime promotion in terms of their identities.[11] We use the term *identity* to refer to political collectives (states, factions, movements, etc.). Thus an actor's identity is their sense of who they are and who they are not; what they stand for and what they are against.[12] Social and political identities can be defined primarily in terms of nationality, but in Latin America as in other historical and geographic contexts, ideological distinctions or alternative political projects also can serve to define the collective identities of political actors.[13]

Actors' identities are of causal significance because they orient actors' understandings of themselves, others, and the world. These understandings enable actors to identify their interests, so that they can take action to pursue their objectives.[14] Actors identify other actors as adversaries or allies in terms of others' perceived identities, that is, in terms of what is perceived to be their "inherent" character, nature, or ideology. In terms of Walt's analysis

TABLE 12.1.

Regime Export Strategies

	Overt/Direct	*Covert/Indirect*
Military Force	Imposition	Subversion
No Military Force	Engagement	Isolation

of the components of threats, actors' identities serve as fundamental criteria-shaping assessments of offensive (or benign) intent.

Second, actors use several alternative strategies to shape the nature of a potential opponent's regime. Facing external security threats, great powers employ such strategies as internal and external balancing and bandwagoning, as well as the "conservation of enemies."[15] Lesser powers, and especially states in the Third World, likewise employ these strategies, though often in the context of "omnibalancing" against both foreign and domestic threats. In short, this range of strategies involves efforts to defend against or to limit security threats posed by current enemies or potential adversaries.

But the most and least powerful states—as well as subnational and transnational actors—can adopt another range of strategies to end the enmities or adversarial relationships that create threats in the first place. Employing Owen's terminology, these can be called "regime export" strategies: efforts to change the type of regime governing a given state. Such strategies include both overt and direct means (for example, military force through conventional war), and covert and indirect measures (for example, funding, training, or organizing insurgents) to bring about or encourage change in the type of foreign—or domestic—government. Although in practice actors often bundle these strategies to maximize their impact and increase their prospects for success, it is possible to identify four broad strategies of regime export: *imposition* and *subversion* involve the direct or indirect exercise of force or other means to undermine adversaries; while *engagement* and *isolation* rely on nonmilitary steps to bring about regime change. Table 12.1 presents these four options in abstract terms.

The following two case studies illustrate three of these four regime promotion strategies.

The Contadora Peace Process: Promoting Democracy in Central America During the 1980s

If there is any region of the world where theories of hegemony should provide the most salient explanation for the structure of international politics, it is in Central America and the Caribbean. This is a logical assumption given strong U.S. interests in the region dating back to the 1850s, and repeated forcible U.S. intervention to protect those interests after the Spanish American War (1898). The states of the region remain so weak that no credible counterbalancing alliance to the United States can form. Their most reasonable response therefore would be to bandwagon with the hegemon.[16] Under these circumstances, structural theories would predict that state concerns for relative gains should be low because local capabilities are weak and the hegemon is very powerful, and has a strong and often demonstrated interest in maintaining regional stability on terms favorable to itself. Positive responses by regional states, particularly those in Central America, to recent U.S. led efforts to develop a free trade area of the Americas confirm that bandwagoning and a concern for absolute rather than relative gains are the dominant strategy, at least in the economic realm.

Interstate behavior in the Central America region during the 1980s, however, challenges realist expectations. The success of the Sandinista revolutionary movement in Nicaragua and the threatened victory of Marxist insurgents in El Salvador led to intense U.S. involvement in the region during the 1980s, ranging from military training and assistance and vigorous diplomacy, to direct subversion of governments and movements perceived as hostile. Given the demise of détente between the United States and the Soviet Union at the end of the Carter administration and increased bipolar friction during the early years of the Reagan administration, most states in Central and South America could have been expected to bandwagon with the hegemon and capitulate to its policies toward the developing regional conflict. A group of Central and South American states (Mexico, Venezuela, Colombia, and Panama, later joined by a larger support group of South American states that included Argentina, Brazil, and Uruguay) nevertheless rejected this approach. These states, known collectively as the Contadora Group, led consistent efforts in favor of peace and democracy that went against U.S. foreign policy in Central America, contrary to what traditional realist expectations of interstate behavior would predict.[17]

The Contadora Group could not counterbalance the United States in terms of a conventional assessment of power. So why did they choose to oppose, often subtly but sometimes openly, U.S. policy toward Central America? Two ideological camps in the region differed notably in their assessment of threats to Central America, U.S. foreign policy, and potential strategies to deal with both. The interactive effects between the strategic options pursued by these two contending camps significantly constrained U.S. policy in the region, and may have prevented interstate war.

The 1979 Nicaraguan revolution and the prolonged leftist insurgencies experienced by El Salvador and Guatemala during the decade that followed were assumed by many in the United States and the region to have been promoted by the Soviet Union and Cuba, making the region another arena for Cold War confrontation. U.S. support in the form of funds, training, and weapons for its regional allies in El Salvador and Honduras was intended to counter Soviet and Cuban support for Nicaragua and its Marxist allies among the FMLN insurgents in El Salvador. Supporters of this perspective included not only members of the Reagan White House, but also the U.S. Defense Department, Republican members of Congress, conservative think tanks, the military elites in El Salvador, Honduras, Nicaragua, and Guatemala, and civilian and military members of the Nicaraguan Resistance (commonly called Contras, short for counterrevolutionaries). Although there were some ideological differences among the members of this coalition, the basis of their shared identity was a conservative anticommunism, reinforced by common Cold War experiences, that led them to fear the negative impact of the revolutionary movement in Nicaragua on U.S. regional interests, far out of proportion with the actual shift in the balance of power.[18]

The leaders of the so-called Contadora Group of states were on the whole convinced anticommunists and well aware of U.S. security interests in the region. They believed, however, there were alternatives to U.S. military intervention that would promote democracy and development, goals that war would inevitably undermine. From this perspective, U.S. and Soviet efforts to back regional allies would only exacerbate the security dilemma faced by Central American states, aggravate armed conflict, and stifle incipient democratization in the region. Beginning with a meeting on the Panamanian island of Contadora in 1983, the leaders of these states jump-started a peace process designed to minimize the security dilemma facing states in the region by limiting arms and promoting democracy.[19] This approach found a responsive audience among liberal members of the U.S. Congress and within the NGO (nongovernmental organization) community that worked on Central American issues. Many of the U.S. members of this coalition shared a common background of opposition to the Vietnam War, and this experience led them to value democratization, human rights, and nonintervention. The shared identity developed through antiwar activism during the 1960s translated into a 1980s preference for minimizing U.S. military intervention in Central America and maximizing democratization and the protection of human rights.[20]

REGIONAL THREAT ASSESSMENT DURING THE 1980S

From the Reagan administration's perspective, the revolutionary movements in Nicaragua, El Salvador, and Guatemala were externally directed manifestations of Soviet policy in Central America. As Jeremy Slater points out, the 1984 Kissinger Commission Report neatly summarized the administration's hard-line analysis:

> The Soviet-Cuban thrust to make Central America part of their geostrategic challenge is what has turned the struggle in Central America into a security and political problem for the United States. Nicaragua is . . . a base for Soviet and Cuban efforts to penetrate the rest of the Central American isthmus, with El Salvador the target of first opportunity.

Slater also suggested that Nicaragua was seen by the Reagan administration as the first in a series of dominos that could potentially fall in Central America, echoing the language used to describe the perceived communist threat to Southeast Asia in the 1960s and 1970s.[21] From this perspective, the Central American situation was an immediate and vital threat to U.S. national interests, and Nicaraguan behavior was only explainable in the context of the overall U.S.-Soviet global confrontation. The threat assessments made by regional militaries were similarly uncompromising in their view of the Marxist threat to their states. Moreover, because they understood the threat in military rather than political terms, they were especially hostile to political solutions to local strife, such as land reform, that they perceived to be sponsored by their ideological adversaries.[22] The shared assessment of the security threat by hard-liners among U.S. policymakers and regional military commanders naturally influenced their strategic choices in the direction of subversion.

The shared identity of the Contadora Group was a more complex phenomenon, drawing on both Mexico's historic opposition to U.S. intervention and Venezuela's traditional support for the expansion of democracy in Latin America. Overlapping ideologies and beliefs, rather than a shared identity built through a common historical experience, drew these disparate actors together. From the perspective of the group's members, the threat to Central American stability originated in poverty, inequality, and praetorianism, rather than externally sponsored communist subversion. War would only impede any possibility of economic development, the necessary solution to poverty. They also believed that the U.S. imposition of an East-West framework on the regional conflict reinforced the tendency toward war and encouraged authoritarian elements within the region, particularly within its all-too-powerful and autonomous militaries. Moreover, the Reagan administration's policy of overt military support for El Salvador and Honduras and semi-covert support for the Contras recalled the armed interventionism that Latin American states had worked to contain.[23] Democrats in the U.S. Congress sympathized with this analysis of the region's problems, since they favored democratization and were opposed to any further militarization of the conflict, a view echoed by numerous civil society organizations that sprang up during the Central American conflict.[24] The remedy the Contadora Group developed, first codified in the 1983 Document of Objectives, included the removal of extra-regional military support and forces, regional arms control, and the promotion of free elections and democracy.[25]

STRATEGIC CHOICES

The preferences and the threat assessments of both coalitions inevitably led them to choose regime export as their solution to the Central American conflict. Hard-liners in the Reagan administration perceived a threat to vital U.S. national interests in Central America. From their perspective, revolutionary Nicaragua was the thin edge of the wedge, and no agreement signed by the Sandinista government could be trusted. The only truly acceptable solution was a new government in Nicaragua, and the preservation of the anticommunist regime in El Salvador.[26] Of political and economic reforms, Reagan stated, "You do not try to fight a civil war and institute reforms at the same time. Get rid of the war. Then go forward with the reforms."[27] For their part, the Contadora Group of states saw the Central American conflict tending inevitably toward open war, which would be a catastrophe for the region. Even though not all the states in this group were democratic themselves (Venezuela had the most credible credentials of all of them), they all saw democracy as a first step toward defusing regional tensions. They believed that democratic governments would be less likely to go to war, and they saw peace as a precondition for economic development in the region. This led them to include support for democratization in the Contadora peace proposals.[28]

U.S. policy toward Central America during the first six years of the Reagan administration focused primarily on finding military solutions to the region's problems. In the Nicaraguan case, hard-liners in the Reagan administration pushed for a (not so) covert war of subversion against the Sandinista regime, carried out by the U.S.-supplied Contras beginning in 1981. Although William Casey, director of the U.S. Central Intelligence Agency, initially described Contra operations to Congress as an effort to interdict Sandinista supplies to Salvadoran Farabundo Marti de Liberacion Nacional (FMLN) insurgents, privately they were always seen by administration hard-liners as part of an effort to pressure and hopefully overthrow the Nicaraguan government. More overt U.S. efforts included a number of highly publicized military exercises in the region (such as Big Pine II in 1983) and the mining of Nicaraguan harbors.[29] Interestingly, U.S. efforts to subvert Nicaragua began long before its revolutionary government built up enough weapons and troop strength to alter the balance of power.[30] In El Salvador, the Reagan administration also sought to impose a military solution, providing hundreds of millions of dollars in security assistance to the Salvadoran armed forces every year along with military training.[31] Although hard-liners in the Reagan administration were adept at winning the policy battle within the executive branch, they faced considerable opposition from Congress, where Democrats controlled the lower chamber, and from a U.S. public that did not support armed intervention in the region.[32] This dissension naturally led to an emphasis on covert U.S. operations, and a considerable effort by the United States to clean up the public image of its regional allies and restrain their instincts toward more repressive and brutal solutions for their ideological adversaries.

Given the inadequacy of their power capabilities to constrain U.S. policies in Central America, the Contadora Group chose a strategy of engagement. Beginning in 1983, Contadora states organized a series of regional diplomatic encounters designed to produce a peace process, which led to the formation of working groups and a secretariat. The process eventually resulted in a treaty that all of the regional states, including Nicaragua, would sign, known as the Revised Act of 1984. Although U.S. officials publicly supported these efforts, they opposed it in practice because it impeded the efforts of U.S. hard-liners to achieve regime change in Nicaragua.[33] Behind the scenes, the United States worked through the Tegucigalpa Group (composed of Costa Rica, Honduras, and El Salvador) to modify the content of the Revised Act in an effort to provoke rejection by Nicaragua. During 1985 and 1986, the Contadora Group struggled diplomatically to shape an agreement that would meet U.S. objections and be acceptable to Nicaragua.

Although Nicaragua eventually acquiesced to a revised treaty in 1986, the Reagan administration and Congress disagreed vehemently over whether the United States should follow suit. In the face of eventual U.S. rejection, the Contadora Group was unable to achieve a negotiated solution, and it receded from the scene.[34] The Central American states then took the lead, under the leadership of Costa Rican President Oscar Arias, and concluded a regional peace treaty known as the Esquipulas II agreement in 1987. They benefited considerably from the political cover provided by U.S. Speaker of the House Jim Wright (D-TX), who was able successfully to oppose the hard-line policies of the Reagan administration, already weakened because of the Iran-Contra scandal.[35] Although concluded by different actors from the group that started it, the Central American peace process was able to constrain U.S. policy, thereby preventing the outbreak of regional war and preparing the ground for a regional democratization process.[36]

EXPLAINING THE RESOLUTION
OF THE CENTRAL AMERICAN CONFLICT

There are two reasons why a balance of identity approach provides a better explanation of events in Central America during the 1980s than traditional balance of power theories. First, the U.S. threat assessment and policy response to the Central American crisis were out of proportion to the actual impact on its national interests, as Slater has argued. The policy objective the Reagan administration chose, regime export, can be explained only in ideological terms.[37] According to U.S. policymakers, their preference for a strategy of subversion against Sandinista Nicaragua had more to do with hiding their activities from the U.S. Congress than from fear of their foreign opponents. In this same vein, administration efforts to restrain the human rights abuses of its allies in the Salvadoran military were intended at least as much for the audience on Capitol Hill as for the benefit of the Salvadoran people. The primacy of the battle for public opinion in U.S. policymaking suggests that identity and ideology predominated over calculations of international power during this conflict.

Second, the efforts of the Contadora Group to oppose U.S. policy, even within the limits imposed by U.S. hegemony, argue against a power-based explanation of the behavior of these Latin American states. It would have made more sense, from a power perspective, for the Contadora states to acquiesce to U.S. policy. Rather, they chose to pursue diametrically opposed policies that sought to place diplomatic constraints on U.S. behavior. The Contadora states' choice of a strategy of engagement is consonant with their shared identity as states with a preference for peace, democracy, and nonintervention. Any rational assessment of their relative power vis-à-vis the United States could as easily have led them to choose a strategy of isolating the parties in conflict, or even bandwagoning with the U.S. strategy of subversion, the path followed by El Salvador and Honduras.

Democratic Security in the Southern Cone in the 1980s

At the same time that the Contadora Group was working to restrain the regional hegemon, Argentina and Brazil engaged in behaviors directly contradicting the expectations of balance of power theory. These longtime rivals for preeminence in South America turned away from the ultimate instrument of military balancing—nuclear weapons—in order to reduce regional tensions, consolidate democratic governance, and address the most dangerous security threats facing both states: military coups at home and authoritarian dictators abroad.

REGIONAL ACTORS AND SECURITY THREATS

In Argentina, President Raúl Alfonsín's Unión Cívica Radical (UCR) party championed the transformation of regional relations. On taking power in December 1983, UCR leaders found Argentina surrounded by military governments in Chile, Brazil, Uruguay, and Paraguay. By 1985, transitions to civilian rule in Uruguay and Brazil permitted democracy advocates in the three states to create a subregional community of democratic states that sought to employ foreign policy as an instrument for consolidating democratic governance.[38]

The regional security environment confronting Argentine and Brazilian policymakers in the early 1980s was predisposed for military balancing. The 1982 Malvinas/Falklands War sparked a sudden and unexpected rise in the salience of interstate war in the region, and the military potential of nuclear energy. Great Britain, a nuclear-weapons state determined to retain control over its colonial possession, defeated territorially dissatisfied Argentina in a bloody war off the Argentine coast. Britain employed a nuclear-powered submarine to inflict the worst blow of the war, sinking the cruiser *General Belgrano* and killing hundreds of sailors and officers of the Argentine Navy; five submarines also were used to blockade the entire Argentine fleet in port. This was the first time that a nuclear-propelled attack submarine had been employed to destroy an enemy ship in war. In Buenos Aires, rumors circulated that Britain had made nuclear threats against Argentina, and British news reports "confirmed" these threats after the conflict. London was widely seen as having violated the Treaty of Tlatelolco, that aims to make Latin America a nuclear-weapons-free zone. South American policymakers viewed U.S. support for British reconquest of the islands as an abrogation of the inter-American defensive alliance, voiding the U.S. security guarantee to Latin American states against extra-regional incursions. These circumstances presented an ominous scenario: Argentina was primed to turn its latent nuclear technological capability into military power and go for the bomb.

Brazilian officials were acutely aware of this potential turn in Argentine policy. Argentina's emerging nuclear capability had been an important motivation behind Brazilian nuclear efforts in the 1970s. The eruption of the 1982 war surprised Brazil, and postwar military analyses of the conflict identified Argentina's unpredictability, conventional capabilities, and postwar rearmament program as grounds for serious concern.[39] In November

1983, Argentine officials revealed a clandestine uranium enrichment facility, alarming international observers who feared the plant would enable nuclear weapons production. Early in 1984, a Brazilian Army Ministry official publicly urged development of an "Autonomous Strategic Nuclear Force." Given the war's outcome and Argentina's enrichment capability, he argued that Brazil had to expect that its neighbor would develop "peaceful nuclear explosives"—technically equivalent to atomic weapons—as well as nuclear-powered submarines.[40]

The stage was set for a nuclear arms race in South America, yet nuclear-balancing behavior never materialized. On the contrary, following the transition to civilian democratic rule in Brazil in 1985, the two countries abjured balance of power politics to embark instead on a rapid process of nuclear cooperation, political collaboration, and economic integration. Within four years, democratizers in Argentina and Brazil successfully used engagement strategies—and isolation and "subversion" strategies against military governments—to reshape the regional security context.

IDENTIFYING FRIENDS AND FOES

UCR officials presumed that democratic neighbors would bolster Argentine security, while military regimes would inevitably threaten it. They believed that both foreign and domestic armed forces were threats to peace and security; that foreign peoples were natural allies; and that foreign states were enemies or allies depending on whether they were ruled by military officials or by democratizing civilian leaders. In the words of Argentine Foreign Minister Dante Caputo, "Authoritarian regimes, because they are supported by either a dominant minority or through alignment with a foreign power, are oriented to consider international relations—just like those within their own societies—in terms of domination."[41]

Oriented by this conceptual framework, the Alfonsín government understood nuclear and bilateral affairs, and economic interchange, as questions of democratic security. They saw nuclear confidence building and cooperation as a means to reduce regional tensions, and thereby undercut the threat posed by their armed forces. Such a "diversionary peace"[42] would eliminate a key rationale for military autonomy and claims on state resources, and thereby contribute to democratic consolidation at home and abroad. Argentine foreign policymakers presumed their civilian counterparts in Brazil shared this understanding.[43] They used public discourse, private negotiations, symbolic actions, and bilateral and regional institutions to diffuse their understanding of the relationships between democracy and security to their Brazilian counterparts. As a leading authority on bilateral relations noted, these appeals helped create "on the part of both governments the vision that this rapprochement can constitute an instrument to reciprocally fortify their respective processes of democratic transition."[44] Common economic and political experiences fostered a sense of identification between the civilian governments of Brazil and Argentina, which led to unprecedented affinity in bilateral relations and initiation of a program of cooperation and bilateral integration.[45] Alfonsín's counterpart in Brazil, José Sarney, likewise came to see geopolitically oriented foreign policy as a "stimulus to military interference in politics."[46]

Alfonsín government officials framed regional security affairs in this way because of their sense of identity, their ideology, and the agenda they confronted on assuming office. First, Alfonsín and other UCR Party leaders were human rights activists and advocates of constitutional democratic rule. Second, UCR thinking on international relations had been strongly influenced by Kantian idealist thought for a century,[47] and party doctrine was "confirmed," in a negative sense, by the excruciating experience of military rule. Brutal repression at home and a futile diversionary war abroad corroborated UCR officials' ideological predisposition to reject realpolitik as not only immoral but also disastrous. Third, UCR officials were acutely aware that recent Argentine history had been punctuated by military coups that perennially terminated fleeting civilian governments. Hence, they defined the consolidation of democracy as their primary political objective and a driving national imperative. In Caputo's words, their "nearly-obsessive objective was the establishment of democratic processes," and toward this end they made foreign policy an instrument of domestic policy.[48]

DEMOCRATIC SECURITY STRATEGIES: TRANSNATIONAL
COALITIONS, INTEGRATION, AND CONFIDENCE BUILDING

To reshape regional relations in the service of democratic consolidation, the Alfonsín government employed political, economic, and security measures. These measures included covert political intervention to encourage democratic transitions in Chile and Paraguay, and a reciprocal support network among new democratic governments in Brazil, Uruguay, and Southern Europe. The Argentine government sought to create enduring foundations for peace by promoting economic integration among neighboring states, and to use compelling symbolic actions to encourage key constituencies and the public to accept the transformation of regional relations. They fostered pacific relations abroad to undercut the influence of domestic rivals that could profit from foreign conflict.

Promoting a democratic transition from the military rule of General Augusto Pinochet in Chile was, in the words of Foreign Minister Caputo, "always considered a transcendent political objective for the consolidation of our own democratic system."[49] Hence, the UCR government identified resolution of the Argentine-Chilean dispute over the Beagle Channel as its first foreign policy priority. UCR officials feared that the Chilean armed forces might provoke conflict with Argentina in an attempt to bolster domestic support and block political liberalization—as their Argentine counterparts had attempted in their "diversionary war" occupation of the Malvinas/Falklands[50]—and that this would catalyze the revival of the Argentine military in national politics. Following a national plebiscite in Argentina supporting peaceful resolution of the dispute, UCR officials engaged in surreptitious efforts to advance a transition to democracy within Chile, while publicly shunning Pinochet. Moreover, Alfonsín made any major initiative toward economic integration between Argentina and Chile contingent on the latter's democratization.[51]

In addition, UCR officials employed innovative diplomacy to bolster international support for democratic rule where it existed and to promote transitions to democracy where the military remained in power. The 1986 Argentine-Brazilian integration accords included a declaration that the process would be opened eventually to all Latin American states that were democratically governed. Argentina signed economic cooperation accords with Italy in 1987 and Spain in 1988; both included clauses voiding the agreement in the event of a military coup, thus making cooperation contingent on the perpetuation of democratic governance.[52] The Alfonsín administration promoted, albeit without success during its tenure, revision of the Organization of American States charter to include a binding commitment by member states to promote democratic rule and to punish deviations from this pledge.[53] UCR officials believed that such international linkages provided support for democracy in moments of crisis, notably during the *cara-*

pintada military uprisings in Argentina, by making clear that a coup would provoke international sanctions.[54]

Likewise, the transformation of Brazilian policy extended beyond relations with democratic Argentina and Uruguay. Although the Pinochet government had been a close ally of Brazil during military rule, the Sarney government suspended arms sales and sought to isolate Chile. Later, after rejecting Paraguayan participation in negotiations leading to the formation of the Mercosur trade group on the grounds that it was not a democracy, Brazil and Argentina immediately extended formal recognition when a democratic government took power.[55] Working together, democratic leaders constructed a mutual support network to aid their efforts to consolidate democratic rule. Oriented by their shared understanding of democratic security, in 1986 the two civilian governments launched an ambitious program of economic integration to create societal interest favoring pacific relations.

Brazil and Argentina reached economic integration pacts in 1986 and 1988. UCR officials viewed these as "instrumental to delegitimize the predominance of geopolitical, and, by extension, authoritarian thinking in foreign and domestic policy."[56] In designing the bilateral integration project, Argentine and Brazilian negotiators focused on capital goods to create common interests in a leading industrial sector, and nuclear confidence building to dispel suspicions and promote common interests in a second strategic sector. Their promotion of regional integration to foster democratic consolidation was informed by their understanding of the European Community's formation, in which democracy and integration were seen as intrinsically linked.[57] The two governments sought to increase bilateral economic interdependence and to build coalitions of societal allies committed to close and peaceful relations. Despite the fact that the concrete gains of the integration effort were modest during this period, officials persevered in encouraging integration.[58]

At this same time, Brazilian and Argentine civilian officials rejected nuclear weapons as an instrument of military balancing. Instead, they employed nuclear confidence building to bolster their democratic regimes. Through collaborative efforts and dramatic actions, they sought to eliminate the possibility that nuclear development could pose a reciprocal security threat.

Symbolic acts in nuclear matters provided the most compelling demonstration of common values, especially the reciprocal presidential visits to the countries' formerly clandestine uranium enrichment facilities. Most striking was Alfonsín's co-inauguration with Sarney of Brazil's ultracentrifuge enrichment plant at Iperó in April 1988. In a previously unthinkable public act, the president of Argentina co-inaugurated the Brazilian Navy facility designed to enable development of nuclear-powered submarines. From a balance of power perspective, the plant could provide Brazil the type of maritime power that had checked the Argentine fleet in 1982, or worse, produce weapons-grade fissile material.

As risky as these steps appear from a conventional security perspective, these potent symbolic actions worked; they undercut the plausibility of a power-politics interpretation of nuclear development. The possibility that either country could acquire nuclear weapons had perpetuated suspicions and military scenarios identifying the other state as a threat to national security. Bilateral nuclear cooperation served to exorcise these "dangerous spirits."[59] In particular, it helped isolate sectors in the Brazilian military—notably in the Air Force—that advocated development of nuclear arms under the guise of a "peaceful nuclear explosive" program. By 1988, soldiers and civilians in both countries ceased viewing the other as a security threat.[60] As a direct result of nuclear transparency, military planners in both countries revised war plans in light of diminished reciprocal threats.[61]

Failure to Balance in the Post-Cold War Era

Balance of power behavior has been absent in Latin American relations since the end of the Cold War, despite the fact that preconditions and catalysts that should have sparked internal and external balancing exist. Enduring territorial disputes, subregional political rivalries, and fixation on symbols of military power among armed forces not always constrained by effective civilian oversight all exist in Latin America. Catalysts of conflict include Brazil's acquisition of A-4 aircraft and a second aircraft carrier and resumption of its nuclear-powered attack submarine program in 2000, all of which failed to provoke countervailing responses in South America. Likewise, repeated incursions by guerillas of the Fuerzas Armadas Revolucionarias de Colombia (FARC) into Panamanian territory did not prompt Panama to restore its armed forces, which it abolished in 1991 (as Costa Rica had done in 1949).

Balance of power theory cannot adequately account for Latin American behavior even in the two developments since 1989 most apt to spur regional balancing: a bloody war between Peru and Ecuador and Chile's acquisition of advanced fighter aircraft. Instead, the increasing institutionalization of a democratic identity among states in the Western Hemisphere has led to long-term outcomes that do not conform with realist expectations.

The Ecuador-Peru border clashes of 1995 were the most significant interstate armed conflict in Latin America since the Malvinas/Falklands War in 1982. Roots of the conflict date to 1941, when Ecuador lost a third of its territory to Peru. Since then, it has sought to regain access to the Amazon Basin. As balance of power theories would predict, Ecuador significantly improved its military capabilities in pursuit of its territorial goal. In 1995, Ecuador challenged Peruvian control over the Cenepa region by infiltrating forces into this densely forested and poorly demarcated area of their mutual border. Caught off guard, Peru escalated the conflict but achieved little military success, as geography favored a defensive standoff. Ecuador won the diplomatic battle by forcing Peru into negotiations under the guarantor nations of the 1941 Rio Protocol—Argentina, Brazil, Chile, and the United States. In 1998, the guarantors worked out a settlement that both sides accepted.

Although geography and the correlation of military forces shaped the outcome of the conflict, balance of power theory cannot explain why the conflict erupted in 1995, why it concluded with an Ecuadorian victory, and why power-balancing behavior has not followed in its wake. Additionally, neither Peru nor Ecuador has engaged in self-help behavior since the conflict. Instead, military budgets and force levels have stabilized or dropped dramatically.[62] Nor has Peru sought regional alliances to compensate for its declining power relative to Ecuador, which has not engaged in comparable military downsizing or restructuring. Peru's decisions to reduce its armed forces and military capabilities were driven by democratically elected civilian leaders who aimed to degrade the autonomy and power of the Peruvian armed forces in domestic politics, regardless of the impact on the balance of power with Ecuador.[63]

In the second case, Chile's acquisition of advanced fighter aircraft provoked widespread concern but still no visible balancing behavior. Regional states became increasingly alarmed for two reasons: the United States overturned a twenty-five–year ban on such sales to the region in 1997; and Chile took advantage of the opportunity to purchase F-16 fighters from the United

States in 2002. All of Chile's neighbors, and critics in the United States, denounced Santiago's decision to modernize its air force, emphasizing the risk of a regional arms race.[64] Prospects for an arms race were heightened by the U.S. decision to sell such weapons to other Latin American customers, and greater efforts by Lockheed Martin and other firms to market potent weapons in the region.

But when the decision to sell the aircraft to Chile was finalized, only Brazil reacted in a power-balancing fashion, announcing a competition to upgrade its aging air force equipment. The size of the contract, $700 million, mirrored the scale of the Chilean acquisition.[65] The new administration of Luis Ignacio da Silva overturned its predecessor's decision to acquire U.S. F-16s, however, announcing in 2003 that Brazil was deferring the acquisition of advanced aircraft to increase spending on combating hunger. Meanwhile, other Latin American countries reacted to Chile's increasing capabilities diplomatically, calling for agreed regional limitations on defense spending, and confidence-building measures such as common standards for defense budgeting. The Andean Charter for Peace, comprising Bolivia, Colombia, Ecuador, Peru, and Venezuela, is one example of these efforts, and it cites a shared commitment to democracy in the region to support peace and diminish the need for defense spending.[66] The charter conspicuously appeals to Latin America's shared democratic identity to establish an "Andean Zone of Peace." In brief, rather than balancing through alliances or arms racing, Chile's neighbors relied on shared identity to negotiate collaborative efforts to reduce defense spending, ban the use of land mines, and limit acquisition of air-to-air missiles. Far from provoking a regional arms race, the U.S. and Chilean catalysts appear to be motivating only greater interest in the Inter-American Convention on Transparency in Conventional Weapons Acquisitions. This manifests a shared consensus, as expressed in the Santiago Declaration of the Fifth Defense Ministerial of the Americas, in November 2002, that "democracy and its institutions constitute essential elements for hemispheric security."[67]

Conclusion

As recently as the early 1980s, democracy was widely considered an endangered species in Latin America. Authoritarian regimes controlled states throughout the region, and most observers feared that the few civilian democracies that existed inevitably would revert to authoritarian rule. Fortunately, this widespread pessimism proved unfounded.[68] Likewise, the bellicose nationalist rhetoric, geopolitical discourse fixated on relative gains, diminishing intra-regional trade, and failure of the inter-American defense alliance that plagued South American relations in the 1970s and early 1980s failed to ignite regional wars and arms races.[69]

As of 2003, the democrats are clearly winning, and the hemisphere is increasingly secure from the threat of interstate war. The "Resolution on Representative Democracy" adopted by the General Assembly of the Organization of American States (OAS) in Santiago in 1991, and the "Inter-American Democratic Charter" concluded in Lima in 2001, were milestones in regional relations. Differences in national interests and frustrations in implementation notwithstanding, the democratic member states of the OAS have established a hemispheric support network to deter coups and buttress democratic rule. Cuba stands isolated and alone outside the political and legal consensus dominating the Western Hemisphere: the shared belief that constitutional democracy is the only legitimate form of governance, and that its interruption endangers the well-being not only of a state's citizens but also the security of peoples and governments in neighboring states. Methods of democratic regime export have become more institutionalized and effective over the decades. From a rag-tag transnational movement to topple dictators in the Caribbean, through ad hoc efforts to build reciprocal support for consolidating democracy in the Southern Cone, democratic regime export strategies of engagement, "subversion," and isolation are now enshrined in the international law of the Americas.

Notes

1. Jack Child, *Geopolitics and Conflict in South America: Quarrels among Neighbors* (New York: Praeger, 1985).

2. David R. Mares, *Violent Peace* (New York: Columbia University Press, 2001).

3. Robert Burr, *By Reason or Force: Chile and the Balance of Power in South America, 1830–1905* (Englewood Cliffs, N.J.: Prentice Hall, 1967).

4. Stephen M. Walt, *The Origins of Alliances* (Ithaca: Cornell University Press, 1987), 21–28.

5. Distinctions between hard, soft, and asymmetric balancing (see chapter by Paul in this volume) offer little insight into the historical experiences examined in this study, and hence are not employed here.

6. Steven R. David, "Explaining Third World Alignment," *World Politics* 43 (January 1991): 233–56. See also Steven R. David, "The Primacy of Internal War," in Stephanie G. Neuman (ed.), *International Relations Theory and the Third World* (New York: St. Martin's, 1998).

7. David, "Explaining Third World Alignment," 241.

8. John M. Owen IV, "The Foreign Imposition of Domestic Institutions," *International Organization* 56 (Spring 2002): 375–409.

9. The overt use of force to impose domestic institutions, however, has been concentrated in three historical waves: 1600–1650, 1790–1850, and 1917–2000. Owen, "The Foreign Imposition," 379, 376.

10. Ibid., 377.

11. In other work, Owen engages this issue. John M. Owen IV, "Transnational Liberalism and U.S. Primacy," *International Security* 26 (Winter 2001/02): 117–52. In this study, he considers identity as it relates to ideology and the identification of enemies. See Owen, "Transnational Liberalism," 122–23.

12. On how state identities shape national security behaviors, see Ronald L. Jepperson, Alexander Wendt, and Peter J. Katzenstein, "Norms, Identity, and Culture in National Security," and Paul Kowert and Jeffrey Legro, "Norms, Identity and Their Limits: A Theoretical Reprise," in Peter J. Katzenstein (ed.), *The Culture of National Security: Norms and Identity in World Politics* (New York: Columbia University Press, 1996), 33–73, 451–97.

13. Latin American history is marked by the region's disassociation of war and nationalism. Miguel Angel Centeno, *Blood and Debt: War and the Nation-State in Latin America* (University Park: Penn State University Press, 2002).

14. See Martha Finnemore, *National Interests in International Society* (Ithaca: Cornell University Press, 1996). Finnemore writes, however, in terms of shared ideas and social norms rather than "identity" in analyzing processes by which states define national interests.

15. Frederick H. Hartmann, *The Conservation of Enemies: A Study in Enmity* (Westport, Conn.: Greenwood, 1982).

16. The only successful case of balancing involved the revolutionary regime in Cuba seeking an alliance with an extra-regional power, the Soviet Union, in the 1960s.

17. Jack Child (ed.), *Conflict in Central America* (New York: St. Martin's, 1986), 144–48.

18. Kenneth Roberts, "Bullying and Bargaining: The United States, Nicaragua and Conflict Resolution in Central America," *International Security* 15 (Autumn 1990): 74–76; William M. Leogrande, *Our Own Backyard: The United States in Central America, 1977–1992* (Chapel Hill: University of North Carolina Press, 1998), 53–56, 86–90.

19. José Alberto Zambrano Velasco, *Centroamerica y Contadora: Enfrentamiento Ideólogico y Político* (Caracas: Editorial Ex Libris, 1989), 113–19. The Document of Objectives, which all the chief executives of the Contadora states subscribed to in September 1983, spells out twenty-one goals of the Contadora Group of states, which include peace, respect for human rights and international law, and democratization as the top four objectives. For an English translation of this document, see app. A, Child, *Conflict in Central America*, 159–63.

20. Bruce M. Bagley, "Contadora: The Failure of Diplomacy," *Journal of Interamerican Studies and World Affairs* 28 (Autumn 1986): 1–3. Roberts, "Bullying and Bargaining," 81–83. Interestingly, the U.S. State Department and the civilian leadership of the front-line states (El Salvador, Honduras, Costa Rica) wavered in their alignment. Civilian leaders in the region often concurred with the threat assessment of the Contadora states, yet were subject to heavy pressure from the United States and their own militaries to support military action. Some key players in the U.S. State Department sympathized with the strategies of the Contadora Group but were constrained by their allegiance to the Reagan administration in pursuing this inclination. Leogrande, *Our Own Backyard*, ix–xii, 7.

21. Jeremy Slater, "Dominos in Central America: Will They Fall? Does It Matter?" *International Security* 12 (Autumn 1987): 105–8.

22. William Stanley, *The Protection Racket State: Elite Politics, Military Extortion and Civil War in El Salvador* (Philadelphia: Temple University Press, 1996), 218–31. Leogrande, *Our Own Backyard*, 116–18, 297–99.

23. Roberts, "Bullying and Bargaining," 83.

24. Leogrande, *Our Own Backyard*, 5–10, 433–34.

25. Bagley, "Contadora," 3–7.

26. Ibid., 9.

27. Leogrande, *Our Own Backyard*, 90.

28. Roberts, "Bullying and Bargaining," 90–94.

29. Leogrande, *Our Own Backyard*, 285–91, 316–40.

30. Slater, "Dominos in Central America," 110–11.

31. Stanley, *The Protection Racket*, 226–31.

32. Leogrande, *Our Own Backyard*, 216–18, 288, 337–38.

33. Child, *Conflict in Central America*, 146–47.

34. Bagley, "Contadora," 11–21.

35. Leogrande, *Our Own Backyard*, 514–25.

36. Roberts, "Bullying and Bargaining," 100–101.

37. Slater, "Dominos in Central America," 103–4.

38. This case study is drawn from Michael Barletta, "Ambiguity, Autonomy, and the Atom: Emergence of the Argentine-Brazilian Nuclear Regime," PhD dissertation (Madison: University of Wisconsin-Madison, 2000); excerpt published as "Democratic Security and Diversionary Peace: Nuclear Confidence-Building in Argentina and Brazil," *National Security Studies Quarterly* 5 (Summer 1999): 19–38.

39. Barletta interviews with Roberto Godoy (defense correspondent, *Correio Popular*), Campinas, March 24, 1995; and with Maximiliano Eduardo da Silva Fonseca (Minister of the Navy, 1979–84), September 25, 1995; Stanley Hilton, "The Brazilian Military: Changing Strategic Perceptions and the Question of Mission," *Armed Forces and Society* 13 (1987): 337.

40. Marco Antonio Felício da Silva "Necessidade de Nuclearização das Forças Armadas Brasileiras," *A Defesa Nacional* (March–April 1984): 124, 120.

41. Dante Caputo, "Línea Conceptual y Hechos Fundamentales de la Política Exterior del Radicalismo 1983–1989" (Buenos Aires: manuscript, 1990): 17.

42. Scott Sagan suggested this term.

43. This analysis is based primarily on interviews by Michael Barletta with officials in or intimately familiar with the Alfonsín administration, including Raúl Alconada Sempé (vice-chancellor, 1984–87), Buenos Aires, July 20, 1994; Dante Caputo (Minister of Foreign Relations, 1983–88), Buenos Aires, July 19, 1994; Carlos Chérniak (UCR advisor in House of Deputies, 1985–89), Buenos Aires, July 13, 1994; Jorge F. Sábato (vice-chancellor for nuclear affairs, 1984–87), Buenos Aires, March 10, 1994; Mario Toer (member, "Esmeralda" advisory group to Alfonsín), Córdoba, November 5, 1993.

44. Mónica Hirst and Roberto Russell, "Democracia y Política Exterior: Los Casos de Argentina y Brasil," *Documentos e Informes de Investigación* 55 (Buenos Aires: Facultad Latinoamericana de Ciencias Sociales, 1987), 160; Mônica Hirst (ed.), *Argentina-Brasil: El Largo Camino de la Integración* (Buenos Aires: Editorial Legasa, 1988), 191–96.

45. Mónica Hirst, "Las Iniciativas Latinoamericanas de Concertación: Su Influencia sobre las Condiciones de Paz en la Región," in *Desarme y Desarrollo: Condiciones Internacionales y Perspectivas* (Buenos Aires: Grupo Editor Latinoamericano/ Fundación Arturo Illia, 1990), 3; Barletta interviews with Félix Peña (undersecretary for Mercosur and Interamerican economic relations), Buenos Aires, June 22 and 27, 1994.

46. David J. Meyers (ed.), *Regional Hegemons: Threat Perceptions and Strategic Responses* (Boulder, Colo.: Westview, 1991), 239.

47. Dominique Fournier, "Democratic Consolidation and Foreign Policy: The Cases of Post-Authoritarian Argentina and Chile, 1983–1993," PhD dissertation (Oxford: St. Anthony's College, Oxford University, 1996); Raúl Alfonsín, *Qué es el radicalismo?* (Buenos Aires: Editorial Sudamericana, 1983).

48. Barletta interview with Caputo, 1995.

49. Caputo, "Línea Conceptual y Hechos Fundamentales," 19.

50. Jack S. Levy and Lili Vakili, "Diversionary Action by Authoritarian Regimes: Argentina in the Falklands/Malvinas Case," in Manus I. Midlarsky (ed.), *Internationalization of Communal Strife* (London: Routledge, 1992), 118–46.

51. Barletta interviews with Alconada Sempé and Caputo; Oscar Camilión, "Tres años de política exterior argentina," *América Latina/Internacional* 4 (1987): 107; Fournier, "Democratic Consolidation and Foreign Policy," 97–98, 116, 112;

358   BARLETTA AND TRINKUNAS

Roberto Russell (ed.), *Política Exterior y Toma de Decisiones en América Latina* (Buenos Aires: Grupo Editor Latinoamericano, 1990), 55–56.

52. Carlos J. Moneta, "El Acercamiento Argentina-Brasil: de la Tensión y el Conflicto a la Competencia Cooperativa," *Anuario Estratégico de América Latina, 1986* (Ciudad de México: CLEE/Instituto Venezolano de Estudios Sociales y Políticos, 1987), 32; Roberto Russell, "Sistemas de creencias y Política Exterior Argentina: 1976–1989," Edición Facultad Latinoamericana de Ciencias Sociales. Serie de Documentos e Informes de Investigación, July 1996, 51; Roberto Russell, "Type of Regime, Changes of Governments and Foreign Policy: The Case of Argentina, 1976–1991," *Documentos e Informes de Investigación* 127 (Buenos Aires: Facultad Latinoamericana de Ciencias Sociales, 1992), 25, note 33.

53. Fournier, "Democratic Consolidation and Foreign Policy," 79.

54. Dante Caputo, "Entrevista," *América Latina/Internacional* 6 (1989): 261.

55. Dávila-Villers, "Competition and Co-operation," 269, 271; Hirst and Russell, "Democracia y Política Exterior," 39.

56. Fournier, "Democratic Consolidation and Foreign Policy," 97.

57. Bruno, "Algunas reflexiones," 12; Mónica Hirst, "Reflexiones para un Análisis Político del MERCOSUR," in *Documentos e Informes de Investigación* 120 (Buenos Aires: Facultad Latinoamericana de Ciencias Sociales, 1991), 4; Roberto Lavagna, "Argentina-Brasil: una política de cambio estratégico," *Instituto de Economia Aplicada y Sociedad* 11/12 (1987): 8.

58. Mario Rapoport and Andrés Musacchio (eds.), *La Comunidad Europea y el Mercosur: Una Evaluación Comparada* (Buenos Aires: Fundación de Investigaciones Históricas, Económicas y Sociales/Fundación Konrad Adenauer, 1993), 133; Luigi Manzetti, "Argentine-Brazilian Economic Integration: An Early Appraisal," *Latin American Research Review* 25 (1990): 128–29; Mónica Hirst and María Regina Soares de Lima, "Crisis y toma de decisión en la política exterior brasileña," in Roberto Russell (ed.), *Política Exterior y Toma de Decisiones en América Latina* (Buenos Aires: Grupo Editor Latinoamericano, 1990), 83.

59. Oscar Camilión, "La Evaluación Argentina," in Mónica Hirst (ed.), *Argentina-Brasil: El Largo Camino de la Integración* (Buenos Aires: Editorial Legasa, 1988), 162.

60. Camilión, "La Evaluación Argentina," 157.

61. Barletta interviews with Antonio Federico Moreno (Director of Planning, Argentine Joint Chiefs of Staff, 1980s-90s), Buenos Aires, June 29, 1994; and Manoel Augusto Teixeira (Director of Planning, Brazilian Army Ministry, 1984–87), Sao Paulo, November 13, 1994.

62. Trinkunas interview with U.S. officer in the Peru Military Assistance Group of the U.S. embassy in Lima, Peru, November 2002.

63. Trinkunas interview with Enrique Obando, president of the Instituto de Estudios Politicos y Estratégicos, Lima, Peru, November 2002. IDEPE is one of the only civilian defense think tanks in Peru.

64. Anthony Faiola, "Chile Near Deal on U.S. Warplanes, Arms Sale Would

Be Most Significant to Continent in Two Decades," *Washington Post*, November 17, 2001, A23.

65. Larry Rohter, "Brazil Steps on U.S. Toes with a Plan for Fighter Jets," *New York Times*, August 5, 2001.

66. General Secretariat, Permanent Council of the Organization of American States, "Comparative Outline of Subregional Security Models in the Americas," OEA/Ser.G/CP/CSH-509/02, November 7, 2002.

67. Ministers of Defense of the Americas and Heads of Participating Delegations in the Fifth Conference of Ministers of Defense of the Americas, "Declaration of Santiago, Chile," November 19–22, 2002, 2.

68. Tom Farer (ed.), *Beyond Sovereignty: Collectively Defending Democracy in the Americas* (Baltimore: Johns Hopkins University Press, 1996), 1–2.

69. Andrew Hurrell, "An Emerging Security Community in South America?" in Emanuel Adler and Michael Barnett (eds.), *Security Communities* (Cambridge: Cambridge University Press, 1998), 234, 231.

Conclusions: Balance of Power
at the Turn of the New Century

MICHEL FORTMANN, T. V. PAUL, AND JAMES J. WIRTZ

This volume assessed the presence and relevance of balance of power dynamics in post-Cold War international politics. Our contributors presented a critical survey of the theoretical debate surrounding the concept of balance of power, explored the relevance of balance of power behavior in world politics, and assessed the theory's validity in key regions of the world. Recent writings suggested that the waning of the Cold War would be accompanied by a decline in the attention paid to balance of power theory and realism, the larger theoretical framework in which balance of power is embedded.[1]

Our first objective was to assess the overall usefulness of the concept of balance of power in explaining current international politics. We asked our contributors to ponder several questions:

— Has the post-Cold War debate about balance of power succeeded in clarifying the key issues and ambiguities that have plagued the theory up to now?
— Does balance of power theory pass the "post-Cold War test" by demonstrating its continued relevance as a useful explanation of world politics? Can we contribute to the debate between defenders and opponents of realism?
— Do theorists offer anything new to classical balance of power theory and the long-lasting debate surrounding the concept? Or, as John Vasquez has expressed it, is this aspect of the realist research paradigm slowly degenerating without producing any new facts and ideas?[2]

Our second objective was to assess the relevance of balance of power theory by examining how well it can account for contemporary events. In other words, our contributors explored whether balance of power remains useful as a guide (or an explanatory tool) in understanding international relations. In general terms, we wanted to identify global developments or trends favoring or hindering a return to balance of power politics among major power actors. In so doing we also assessed the durability and stability of the "unipolar moment," and the responses of various states to U.S. hegemony. One of the key questions we raised: How long will the status of the United States as the only superpower remain unchallenged? We thus took a close look at the meaning of catastrophic terrorism and other so-called asymmetric challenges, and their impact on the current international order and balance of power. We asked our contributors to assess whether or not terrorism should be perceived as a new kind of balancing involving subnational actors.

A third component of this project has been to estimate the role that balance of power considerations and politics play in several regions of the world. Even if there seems to be hardly any balancing behavior at the systemic level, specific regions of the world may provide examples of balance of power dynamics, especially where traditional rivalries and conflicts persist. The regions of the Middle East, Africa, and South, Central, and East Asia today are rife with interstate tensions, even as the United States, the remaining superpower, seems willing to exercise its power across the globe. Countries like China, Russia, India, Israel, and Iran, faced with the twin risks of conflict in their backyard and American intervention, have been increasingly sensitive to power relations both in their immediate neighborhoods and at the global level. We thus have attempted to test a number of propositions inherent in balance of power theory by examining whether or not states in different regions of the world follow its axioms. We also have asked our contributors to determine what takes the place of balancing if it is not the dominant national security strategy of states. Do states bandwagon; free ride; buck-pass; embrace nonalignment, regionalism, or multilateralism; resort to international or regional organizations; or pursue some other noncoercive strategy?

Balance of Power Today

At the outset it is to be affirmed—based on our contributors' analyses—that at the global level very little traditional hard balancing takes place today. International politics since 1990 does not correspond to the realist world of hard balancing obtained through alliances and arms races. Eligible states— Russia, China, and the European Union (especially France, the United Kingdom, and Germany)—have exhibited little propensity for hard balancing, despite the pronouncements made by leaders and analysts in several countries about the need to balance increasing American power.

In fact, the challenge to balance of power theory at the systemic level began with the collapse of the Soviet Union. It remains a puzzle to realist theory as to why the Soviet Union would abandon its vast empire and the balancing coalition it built around Eastern Europe and several developing states, all without defeat in a major war, a condition that led to dramatic changes in the distribution of power and alteration of the global balance of power in the past. Thus the collapse of history's most significant balancing effort without a proper catalyst generates difficulties for realist theory.[3] Since its collapse, Russian power has weakened and its limited efforts to strike balancing coalitions with China and India have gone nowhere. The latter two states, although uneasy with the U.S. power, still have more economic and political ties with Washington than with Moscow. The United States offers them more in trade and investment than does any other single state. This economic interaction, coupled with the continuous U.S. engagement with these actors, makes the need for hard balancing less urgent for them.

The absence of hard balancing does not mean states blindly bandwagon with the United States. In 2003, much of the world failed to cooperate with the United States in its war with Iraq, despite forceful efforts by the Bush administration to punish those who opposed and reward those who supported its prosecution of the war. Bandwagoning with the United States occurred only among a few minor states, as none of the great powers or major economic powers actively supported the U.S. invasion of Iraq. The increasing power of the United States and the unilateralist policies of the Bush administration, however, have been met with opposition by some eligible states, especially France, Russia, and Germany. They exhibited this opposition through diplomatic balancing in international institutions, akin to the soft balancing strategies presented in the introduction of this volume. Although they did not succeed in preventing or delaying the U.S. offensive, Washington failed to receive broad international legitimacy in the military action through a UN approval and as a result faced much difficulty in gaining support of states to help the postwar reconstruction of Iraq.

Historically, when confronted with the rising and threatening power of a hegemon, eligible states often would form balancing coalitions to countervail, deter, and decrease the power and threatening behavior of that state. However, the absence of hard balancing vis-à-vis the United States is striking. The U.S. conventional capability is increasing manyfold as a result of its investments in new Revolution in Military Affairs (RMA) weaponry, especially precision guided munitions. In 2003, the United States accounted for nearly half of the world's total military spending. Why do eligible states not pursue matching arms build up vis-à-vis the United States? It may partially be due to their possession of nuclear weapons that give them confidence that the United States will not directly attack them. Why then did they perceive otherwise and spend so much more on nuclear and conventional weaponry during the Cold War era? Moreover, if proposed missile defense systems are successfully developed and deployed, it could undercut the value of the nuclear deterrent of the second-ranking nuclear states. What might then account for their lack of hard balancing against the United States? A variety of factors seem to be pertinent here, some of which are discussed in various chapters. First, the power disparity between the United States and other eligible states is so great that an overt challenge will provoke aggressive response by the hegemon and the challenger is likely to fail in a military competition. Most of the eligible great powers are heavily dependent on the United States for trade and investment. The eligible states, especially, Russia, China, and India, have embarked on economic liberalization policies whose success relies on direct and indirect investment by U.S.-based multinational corporations. The increasing insertion of these states into the globalized economic order means low-key reactions to military activities by the hegemon in the periphery, especially if such activities do not affect their security directly.

Second, transnational terrorism has emerged as a common challenge to all great powers. The United States is in the vanguard of the struggle against this common enemy, and hence, the great powers see a larger common threat to defeat, which is for now more important than attempting to constrain U.S. power and unilateralist behavior. Although this menace was more pronouncedly felt since September 2001, it does partially account for great-power behavior vis-à-vis the United States since then.

Realists would counter with the argument that it is too early to predict if hard balancing will occur against the United States. It is not unrealistic to expect that this balancing would emerge within a decade, a realistic period for a new trend to become discernable in international politics. One of the difficulties about timing the arrival of balance of power is that there is no way to know exactly when a hegemon becomes a major threat or when it will decline; all that is known is that it will decline. The Roman empire and several other empires in different regions of the world lasted over 300–500 years. In the modern international system imperial powers such as Britain survived over 200 years with its hegemony waxing and waning over time. Further, multipolarity since the 18th century and bipolarity since 1945 did not last long, suggesting that the optimum balancing that realists talk about has never been a permanent state of affairs. World history is marked by the nonrecurrence of balancing and balance of power politics, and this insight is illustrated by many of our chapters. We agree with realists that the timing issue needs to be addressed, but it is in the hypothetical realm at this point in history to predict when the next balancing coalition will emerge.

A decade of international politics (since the end of the Cold War) provides sufficient material to assess the value of the theory, especially because significant events can occur within short decades (for example, the 1980s and the 1940s). Even though there is merit in the argument that the ultimate test of balance of power theory cannot be developed until appropriate conditions in the international system reappear, we believe that one of the most important scope conditions for balancing is present today—that is, the military power of the hegemon is increasing at a fast pace (and threatening to some)—but no coalition is in sight to countervail that power in the short or medium terms. The U.S. lead in RMA weapons and technology eventually may make others respond to this capability gap by undertaking countervailing actions. But, despite the dramatic widening of the gap between the United States and major states in their conventional and nuclear capabilities, none of the great powers—including China and Russia—are attempting to catch up rapidly. The more they wait, the wider the gap will become. It seems they have abandoned hard balancing for the moment. It may be possible that more Iraq-type interventions by the United States will force them to consider hard balancing, but it will be contingent on the threat posed by U.S. behavior to their security, not a response to a general increase in U.S. capabilities.

At the regional subsystemic level too, balancing does not appear to be the dominant pattern of the security behavior of states. Only in the Middle East, East Asia, and South Asia is some semblance of hard balancing visible. In Europe, even a realist such as Robert Art cannot see hard balancing occurring. Similarly in Eastern Europe, William Wohlforth, another realist, sees neither Russia vis-à-vis the United States nor the smaller states in the region vis-à-vis Russia engaging in hard balancing. In Latin America, based on the analysis of Michael Barletta and Harold Trinkunas, states do not seem to consider traditional balancing but have devised other strategies to achieve security. But the realist world may well be active in East Asia, South Asia, and the Middle East, largely due to the intense rivalries that persist in these regions. Even in these theaters, hard balancing is restrained and influenced by the active involvement of the United States in regional affairs. Further, conflict patterns in these regions have been stabilized with most states not fearing substantial challenges to their physical survival.[4]

Traditional hard balancing thus seems to occur only when (1) states face an intense military challenge to their security, (2) states face extinction due to increasing power of a rising state, and (3) states are engaged in intense enduring rivalries. If the international environment is benign and its physical security is not challenged, an eligible state may not worry about the rising power of the hegemon. Similarly, in regions where states do not engage in intense military competition and rivalry, their concerns of relative power may get muted. The European era from the 18th to late 20th century was very much akin to the realist world; states feared physical extinction if a rising or threatening power was not balanced. This condition has dramatically changed in the 21st century; barring a few regional challengers and enduring rivals, hard balancing as a security strategy for many of the nation-states today does not offer much value. Under such conditions, states would opt for low-cost alternatives.

Other Findings

The chapters in this volume generate several other findings.

First, balancing under near-unipolarity is a more complex undertaking than under bipolarity or multipolarity. This is equally true at the global/systemic and at the regional or subsystemic level. The source of this complexity lies in the paradoxical nature of the present international order. In the globalized context prevailing at the turn of the 21st century, states may at the same time fear and perceive the need for the support of each other. China's economic survival, for example, depends on U.S. cooperation. But Beijing's security also is threatened by Washington's actions in the region. Russia and India may worry about increasing U.S. power, but they need U.S. support in the economic realm and, in recent years, to combat terrorism in their own countries. The United States can be perceived by European, Middle Eastern, and Asian leaders both as an overbearing superpower and an essential component of the international economic system.

In security matters too, the U.S. presence in the regions offers certain guarantees of stability that are vital to the economic prosperity of concerned states. Thus European states, despite worries of increasing American power, may find it helpful when it comes to maintaining stability in Eastern and Central Europe. Similarly, China does seem to understand the value of American presence in East Asia, in terms of preventing the rise of Japan as a military power. This duality of American power is the reason for the type of mixed strategies that many regional powers pursue as well. Soft balancing seems particularly well suited to describe the behavior of many states today because it involves a mixture of cooperative and balancing behavior. To ascertain that a behavior constitutes soft balancing, however, one has to uncover the motives behind the action. Soft balancing thus puts perceptions and decision making back at the center of balance of power analysis. Future research could examine more carefully the conditions in which soft-balancing strategies emerge, succeed, or fail and the differences between soft balancing and regular diplomatic bargaining.

Second, the successful outcome of balancing efforts (both hard and soft) by states is not automatic. The dictum, "great powers will rise" does not mean that they will automatically succeed in toppling an existing hegemon. Moreover, as with any strategy, balancing may result in defeat due to lack of resources, poor planning, and faulty execution. Even if history tells us that empires did not last too long, this does not mean that balancing was always the primary cause of their downfall.

Third, balances of power do not appear or reproduce in a mechanical fashion. More often than not human agency is needed to initiate balancing. Decision makers intervene in several ways in the working of the balance of power mechanics. They perceive (or not) a growing power differential, they define it (or not) as a threat, and they chose to act on it (or abstain from doing so). There lies a problem with the neorealist understanding of balance of power. Neorealists assume balancing will be automatic in the face of a rising hegemon, whereas intentional balancing requires active preparations by states to deter or defeat a rising hegemon.[5] The editors of this volume are inclined to adopt the latter position.

Fourth, states need not always balance even when they face intense competition. In fact, they have at their disposal a whole array of methods to address a rising power. They may buck-pass, free ride, bandwagon, hide, unite, and transcend to obtain security. Weaker actors also could attempt to compensate for their inferiority and balance stronger powers by using asymmetric strategies. Paul Schroeder has described the multiple strategies that European states adopted in the face of hegemonic threats throughout modern history. While confronting Napoleon Bonaparte, for instance, regional powers initially accepted French hegemony and adopted strategies such as transcending and grouping in place of balancing. Napoleon's overthrow occurred only when he failed to accommodate those states in a reasonable fashion.[6] The historical and contemporary analyses presented in several chapters of this volume support Schroeder's earlier findings.

Fifth, in view of the diversity of balancing behavior, the main flaw in the neorealist argument on balancing is that it cannot predict when or how states will act. The choice of tactics and timing depends on many factors, such as the level of perceived threat and economic or military capacity of the balancing states. Taking into account the state's security environment and the presence or absence of alternative security mechanisms, however, may allow an observer to explain these choices more clearly.

AN ELUSIVE CONCEPT

The balance of power concept has always been controversial, both as an explanation and as a guide to foreign policy. The analyses in most of the chapters in this volume suggest that this assessment of balance of power theory has not changed significantly. Our effort has not been to reinvent balance of power theory, but to examine some of its commonly held principles in a broad array of settings, while offering new ways to look at state security strategies in the contemporary world. In their chapters, the contributors reflect the diversity in balance of power logic, although there is general agreement on some of its core axioms, that is, states seek to survive, power preponderance of one actor or a single coalition of actors is unstable, and states will form countervailing coalitions to balance powerful or threatening states.

Why does the concept of balance of power remain vague and nebulous?[7]

Other than definitional problems surrounding the notions of balance, power, equilibrium, or stability,[8] should balance of power be defined simply as a state strategy? Or does it describe a "system" of relations between states? Is balance of power a prescriptive or descriptive theory? Is it about strategies or outcomes? What type of behavior does it describe? As noted humorously in a recent study: "No helpful handbook on 'how to implement a balance of power policy' ever appeared."[9] Chapters in this volume reflect the persistent disagreements that characterize the ongoing debate about balance of power and its meaning. In most cases, however, the contributors treat "balancing" as a policy or strategy and "balance of power" as an outcome, although these two dimensions are intimately interlinked.

Another problem that has traditionally plagued balance of power theory, and finds an echo in many of the chapters in this volume, stems from the fact that "there is no single balance of power theory, but instead a multiplicity of theories."[10] It may well be that every single school of realism, from neorealism to classical and neoclassical realism, from defensive to offensive realism, has provided us with its own version of balance of power theory. As Jack Levy argues in his chapter, we have thus an abundance of theoretical sketches, a plethora of competing assumptions and hypotheses, but relatively few empirical studies that would help resolve some of the longstanding debates about the empirical validity of balance of power theories. The recent debate about balancing, however, leaves most of the traditional issues raised by the theory unresolved.

Does this lack of rigor mean that balance of power theory should be discarded as a dying branch of realism, condemned to rehash old theoretical and conceptual issues without generating any new facts? Some of our more critical participants would certainly agree with that statement. In their view, the balance of power metaphor belongs to another era of international relations when *Bismarkeian* or *Clausewitzian* perceptions and attitudes held sway. From this perspective, which is best exemplified by Jack Levy's chapter, the notion of balance of power has applied most aptly in the European context of great-power competition from the 16th to the 19th century. In his chapter, Edward Rhodes also states that today, nuclear weapons render the notion of a balance or imbalance of military power increasingly meaningless. Rhodes suggests that with the end of the strategic competition between the United States and Russia, liberal institutional values have replaced the norms of realpolitik. By contrast, other contributors would respond that, even as a controversial theory, balance of power is indispensable to understanding contemporary international relations. It also has important implications for international relations theory and practice. As Michael Sheehan puts it: "For all its inconsistencies and ambiguities, the balance of power concept has been intellectually and politically significant in the development of the current international system and precisely because of that it remains significant and worthy of study."[11] The majority of our contributors do not advocate a total rejection of balance of power theory, although many are skeptical of its operations in the current international order.

Thus, the core objective of the volume has been to bring fresh ideas to the theoretical discussion about balance of power and its empirical validity. In that process, we believe we offer theoretical diversity and clarity to many of the axioms inherent in balance of power. First, the notion of *soft balancing* as presented in the introductory chapter by T. V. Paul appears to be essential to understanding states' reactions to U.S. hegemony. With this in mind, traditional *hard balancing* should not necessarily be perceived as an automatic response of states to hegemony or unipolarity. This is not to say that hard balancing against U.S. predominance will not occur, although the timing remains a matter of conjecture. As Kenneth Waltz states: "[Balance of Power] Theory enables one to say that a new balance of power will form but not to say how long it will take. National and international conditions determine that."[12]

In previous eras, the global or regional distribution of power in immediate postwar periods facilitated the rapid establishment of a new general equilibrium, but in the current context of preponderant U.S. power, no state has been able to challenge Washington for long, either at the global or the subsystemic level. The constraints are daunting for any actor to bring an end to unipolarity by translating aggregate economic potential into concrete capabilities including "a defense industry and power projection capabilities that can play in the same league as those of the United States."[13] This implies that today, most great powers will perceive hard balancing as costly, dangerous and condemned to failure. For want of the necessary resources to take up the challenge, they will bide their time, perhaps bandwagon opportunistically for a while, or pursue a mix of policies involving—concurrently or successively—cooperative gestures and discrete or covert balancing (especially of the internal kind because it is less visible). They might use international institutions as a way to bind the hegemon, or form temporary coalitions to bargain and reduce the unilateral exercise of power by the United States. The weak do not accept their lot passively, even if the Athenians were correct in their pronouncement to the much weaker Melians: The strong do what they can, and the weak suffer what they must. *Soft* balancing provides a way to solve one of the central puzzles in international relations theory after the Cold War, that is, the apparent absence of intense *hard* balancing at the global level.

Soft balancing is often temporary and issue-specific, however, and its transformation into hard balancing is not occurring as rapidly as realists might expect. If classical balance of power theory is inadequate to explain state behavior at the turn of the century, should we use the toolbox provided by other approaches that have looked at balancing and related behaviors from different theoretical perspectives? Perhaps the answer lies in the expansion of the concept of balance of power beyond its traditional use to explain the formation of military alliances or decisions to use force in world politics. We may well need to broaden our understanding of balance of power by looking at alternative or nontraditional approaches to balancing, including institutional and economic means.[14] Thus, under conditions of near-unipolarity, soft balancing makes a lot of sense for weaker states that are upset by American unilateralism and increasing militarism, if they want to avoid direct confrontation with the hegemon. Both coalition building and arms buildups, the twin routes of traditional balancing, are extremely difficult today and could immediately result in economic and military retaliation by the hegemon. This does not mean that soft balancing strategies will stay in a challenger's diplomatic arsenal forever, or that they necessarily will succeed. Indeed, soft-balancing strategies are ad hoc and can become hard balancing only if and when the hegemon's behavior becomes intolerable to the weaker powers, which then succeed in striking a balancing coalition.

Further, it is extremely difficult to calculate what constitutes optimum power balances, which again suggests that it is time to look for ways to broaden the concept of "balancing." Taking into account the fact that balance of power is a matter of perception, even constructivism can illuminate certain aspects of the phenomenon of balancing as it manifests today. In his chapter, for example, Rhodes looks at the transformation of war and its meaning for balance of power as an applied concept. Balance of power is relevant in a world where states fear that their sovereignty and independence will be fundamentally altered, especially if a hegemonic power emerges with the desire to change the sovereign state system into an empire. Balancing also was the way states behaved from the mid-17th to the mid-20th century, when trinitarian notions of warfare—based on nation-states, mass armies, and popular support—held sway. In the contemporary world, democracy, liberal ideas, ongoing advances in technology, and the availability of weapons of mass destruction all have made the trinitarian conception of war obsolete, and the concept of balance of power itself anachronistic.

International political economy is another promising theoretical avenue explored in this volume. Mark Brawley, for example, offers a discussion of the economic components of balance of power and its associated theories, such as external balancing, internal balancing, bandwagoning, buck-passing, and appeasement. The key objective of these strategies is to bid for time with the hope of accruing wealth that can be translated into power. Such calculations may explain the absence of balancing against the United States. Eligible and potential powers such as the European Union, Russia, China, Japan, and India are constrained by the dearth of allies and their own desire to maximize wealth. The economic theme of balancing is picked up by Robert Art in his chapter on the European Union. The EU, according to Art, is attempting to balance both economically and through institutions. The rate at which a state actually can transform wealth to power is critical in determining whether it will attempt balancing or not. For major powers, if powerful allies are not available and the rate of transformation of wealth is slow, bandwagoning and appeasement could become viable strategies.

China is a significant future candidate for balancing the United States, but in the short and medium terms, according to Robert Ross, it is constrained by lack of allies and a need to concentrate on strengthening its economy. Similarly, Russia, due to its relative economic weakness, is likely to bandwagon with the United States, while Japan and the EU would be expected to buck-pass. India's future balancing behavior will depend on who emerges as the major threat to its security, the United States or China. This does not mean that the major powers will keep quiet in the face of objectionable U.S. policies, but they will fail to resort to force or economic sanction to challenge Washington frontally. Economic factors are increasingly important in state calculations about the desirability of engaging in balance of power politics, although not many of our contributors say this openly; the U.S. position as the engine of economic globalization constrains other major states from resorting to traditional balancing strategies.

Summing Up

The most significant finding in the preceding chapters is that state behavior in the contemporary era does not correspond to traditional hard balancing as depicted in realist theories. Balancing is not as common an occurrence as realists expect, although in some regions states pursue balancing strategies more often than in others. These regions are the ones with intense enduring rivalries and military competitions. Hard balancing is one strategy, among many others, that states pursue in international politics to avoid domination and obtain security, while a balance of power is an outcome that may or may not occur as a result of those strategies.

If a state is not confronting an intense rivalry, it may lower its strategic goals and pursue other means, including liberal institutionalist and regime export strategies, to obtain security in an increasingly complex international system. Realist theories of balancing seem to work well when states are in an environment of intense competition and rivalry, but when the environment becomes less threatening, states minimize their balancing efforts. Relative gains concerns that dominate the competitive world depicted in realism may no longer be felt acutely. Thus the relative gains enjoyed by the United States today do not seem to worry eligible states as much as they would under a system dominated by acute great or regional-power rivalry. Moreover, faced with the twin forces of economic globalization and American hegemonic power, most states have adopted buck-passing, bandwagoning, or hedging strategies, despite their desire to see U.S. power balanced. In some circumstances, they have assumed limited balancing strategies, such as ad hoc groupings and institutional bargaining, similar to the soft-balancing strategies presented in the introduction to this volume. But in the overwhelming majority of cases, no active balancing has occurred in the international arena since the end of the Cold War.

This does not mean, however, that the present state of affairs will continue indefinitely. We have no way to predict the exact timing by which rising great powers will resort to hard balancing, but it is most likely to appear when one or more major powers gains sufficient capabilities to challenge the U.S. power, or when unilateral interventions by the United States become so intolerable to other great powers that they create balancing coalitions to challenge the power of the hegemon. As long as the United States does not threaten the physical survival and security of potential great-power challengers and as long as it can offer considerable economic and security benefits to various states, it is unlikely that a balancing coalition will emerge anytime soon. States will use institutional mechanisms to constrain American power whenever it looks menacing, and this tactic may prove to be a low-cost alternative to hard-balancing strategies. But if America changes its grand strategy to pursue an empire, it may well provoke eligible states to resort to hard balancing. For, empires, especially led by great powers, tend to challenge the security and physical existence of other independent political entities.

Notes

1. For arguments in this vein, see John A. Vasquez and Colin Elman (eds.), *Realism and the Balancing of Power: A New Debate* (Upper Saddle River, N.J.: Prentice Hall, 2003); G. John Ikenberry (ed.), *America Unbound: The Future of Balance of Power* (Ithaca: Cornell University Press, 2003).

2. John Vasquez, "The Realist Paradigm and Degenerative versus Progressive Research Programs: An Appraisal of Neotraditional Research on Waltz's Balancing Proposition," *American Political Science Review* 91 (December 1997): 899–912.

3. We owe this point to one of our reviewers.

4. On Asia, see Muthiah Alagappa (ed.), *Asian Security Order: Instrumental and Normative Features* (Stanford: Stanford University Press, 2003).

5. For the distinction between automatic and manual balancing, see Colin Elman, "Introduction: Appraising Balance of Power Theory," in Vasquez and Elman (eds.), *Realism and the Balancing of Power*, 10–11. Neorealism's excessive focus on holistic understanding of international politics may partially account for its weakness in this area. See Patrick James, "Systemism and International Relations: Toward a Reassessment of Realism," in Michael Brecher and Frank P. Harvey (eds.), *Realism and Institutionalism in International Studies* (Ann Arbor: University of Michigan Press, 2002), 118–32.

6. Paul W. Schroeder, "Why Realism Does Not Work Well for International History," in Vasquez and Elman (eds.), *Realism and the Balancing of Power*, 114–27; Schroeder, "Historical Reality Versus Neorealist Theory," *International Security* 19 (Summer 1994): 108–48.

7. Michael Sheehan, *Balance of Power: History and Theory* (New York: Routledge, 1996), xi.

8. Jack S. Levy, "The Causes of War: A Review of Theories and Evidence," in Philip E. Tetlock et al., (eds.), *Behavior, Society, and Nuclear War* (New York: Oxford University Press, 1989), 228–29.

9. Sheehan, *Balance of Power*, 75.

10. Levy, "The Causes," 228–29.

11. Sheehan, *The Balance*, 196.

12. Kenneth N. Waltz, "Structural Realism After the Cold War," *International Security* 25 (Summer 2000): 30.

13. William C. Wohlforth, "The Stability of a Unipolar World," *International Security* 24 (Summer 1999): 30.

14. William Hogg, *Report to the International Security Outreach Program* (ISROP), Montreal, June 2002, 3.

Index